Visual J++
Java
Programming

Jim Flynn
Bill Clarke

Contributing Authors

Jeff Marin
Tom San Pietro

New Riders Publishing, Indianapolis, Indiana

Visual J++ Java Programming

By Jim Flynn and Bill Clarke

Published by:
New Riders Publishing
201 West 103rd Street
Indianapolis, IN 46290 USA

Copyright © 1996 by New Riders Publishing

Printed in the United States of America 1 2 3 4 5 6 7 8 9 0

Library of Congress Cataloging-in-Publication Data

CIP data available upon request

Warning and Disclaimer

This book is designed to provide information about the Java computer program. Every effort has been made to make this book as complete and as accurate as possible, but no warranty or fitness is implied.

The information is provided on an "as is" basis. The authors and New Riders Publishing shall have neither liability nor responsibility to any person or entity with respect to any loss or damages arising from the information contained in this book or from the use of the disks or programs that may accompany it.

Publisher	Don Fowley
Publishing Manager	Julie Fairweather
Marketing Manager	Mary Foote
Managing Editor	Carla Hall

Product Development Specialist
Sean Angus

Software Specialist
Steve Flatt

Senior Editor
Sarah Kearns

Development Editor
Robert Mullen, Christopher Cleveland

Project Editor
Gina Brown

Copy Editors
Dan Axelrod, Sydney Jones, Carrie Peterson, Cliff Shubs, Molly Warnes

Technical Editor
Greg Guntle

Acquisitions Coordinator
Tracy Turgeson

Administrative Coordinator
Karen Opal

Cover Designer
Karen Ruggles

Cover Illustrator
Jerry Blank

Cover Production
Aren Howell

Book Designer
Sandra Schroeder

Production Manager
Kelly Dobbs

Production Team Supervisor
Laurie Casey

Graphics Image Specialists
Dan Harris
Wil Cruz

Production Analysts
Jason Hand
Erich Richter

Production Team
Kim Cofer, Janelle Herber, Mindy Kuhn, Christopher Morris, Elizabeth SanMiguel

Indexer
Christopher Cleveland

About the Authors

Jim Flynn *(General Manager, @Work Technologies)* has over 13 years of computer industry experience. Jim began his career developing mainframe and Unix-based engineering applications for AT&T. He also held positions at AT&T as a project leader, computer systems engineer, and account executive. Jim is a well-known author and commentator on Internet technology. He has written numerous articles on Java, ActiveX, and other technical topics for *Datamation, Java Report, Computer Technology Review, VAR Business, Document Imaging Service Bureau News,* and *Butterworths Journal of International Banking and Financial Law.* Jim has a bachelor of science degree from Manhattan College and a masters of business administration degree from New York University.

Bill Clarke *(Chief Technologist, @Work Technologies)* is rapidly becoming known in the Internet community as one of the leading experts on the Java programming language. He has over 13 years of system design and programming experience. Bill has been creating mission-critical object-oriented applications for the last 5 years. In addition to Java, Bill has a great deal of experience developing commercially successful client/server applications in Visual C++ for Windows 3.1 and for Windows NT. Bill received a bachelor of science degree from Stevens Institute of Technology.

Contributing Authors

Jeff Marin has over 11 years of computer industry experience. He has developed applications for the brokerage, trading, document management, and manufacturing industries. Jeff is an expert on object-oriented programming in Visual C++ and Java. His areas of expertise include the Unix, Windows 95, and Windows NT environments.

Tom San Pietro has over 11 years of computer industry experience. He has developed mission-critical trading applications for the banking industry. Tom's particular strengths are object-oriented theory and design, Sun, and Sybase environments.

Trademark Acknowledgments

All terms mentioned in this book that are known to be trademarks or service marks have been appropriately capitalized. New Riders Publishing cannot attest to the accuracy of this information. Use of a term in this book should not be regarded as affecting the validity of any trademark or service mark. Visual J++ is a registered trademark of Microsoft. Java is a registered trademark of Sun Microsystems.

Dedications

From Jim Flynn:

To my parents, Ann and Jim. Thanks for loving me no matter what.

To my sister Kathy. Words can't describe how important it's been to have you to look up to.

To my brother Chris. Your sensitivity and strength of character are qualities that I'll always admire, but never achieve.

To my brother Eddie. You're the best bubba.

To Tim. Thanks for letting me mooch off you for all those conferences.

To Stuart, John, Paul, and Jose. I owe you guys so much for being my friends.

To Jean, the love of my life. You gave me your strength when I was about to falter, advice when I desperately needed it, and criticism when I had it coming. But most of all, you always gave me your love. God only knows where I'd be without you. Thank you my sweetheart.

To all of the above. I love you.

From Bill Clarke:

To my parents Charles and Audrey. Thank you for a lifetime of love and for believing in me.

To my brother Raymond. Thanks for always being there.

To my sister Laverne. You are always willing to listen to me ramble on about my work.

To my friends Lester and Rakesh. Your encouragement means a lot to me.

To Lim and Ying SooHoo. Thank you for the potions that heal the body and soothe the soul.

To my wife Maryanne, the center of my universe. You give me the confidence and strength to accomplish anything. Thank you for your love and companionship through life's adventures. I love you.

Acknowledgments

We'd like to thank our editors at New Riders: Gina Brown, Sydney Jones, Cliff Shubs, and Chris Cleveland. They all deserve high praise for their patience, skill, and effort. We'd especially like to thank our acquisitions editor, Sean Angus, for having faith in us and for his constant encouragement. Bob Mullen was vital to our writing effort. His wisdom and experience helped us to create a much better book. We owe an enormous debt to our technical editor, Greg Guntle, for his diligent testing and expert advice. We'd like to mention that Hyer Bercaw, Microsoft's excellent Visual J++ product manager, was always responsive to our questions and requests. Finally, we'd like to thank our dear friends, Kathy Das Gupta and Ulf Svensson, for their encouragement, support, and advice.

Contents at a Glance

Table of Contents

13 Working with UI Components in Visual J++   393

14 Advanced Multithreading and Exception Handling   435

Introduction

Attack! Charge! Kill! Kill! Kill!

The preceding title is a fairly accurate assessment of Sun Microsystems' attitude these days. One of the main reasons for this bravado can be summed up rather succinctly—Java!

Java is an exciting new programming language developed by Sun's JavaSoft division. It is specifically designed to run over wide area networks, such as the public Internet. Web pages that were previously static come alive in Java with animation, behavior, and intelligence.

The usefulness of Java, however, does not end with pretty animations. Because of its unique capabilities, Java makes it possible to deliver distributed object-oriented applications to millions of web users. By shifting the emphasis from the desktop to the network, Java has ushered in the era of *network-centric* computing.

Java, more than any other development language, is uniquely suited for distributing executable content over the Internet. Java programs download dynamically from web servers and can execute as applets within a Java-enabled web browser, or as stand-alone applications.

Why this Book?

If you're reading this, you probably have some experience in other development languages. If so, you're probably saying to yourself, "Wait a minute! Why do I have to learn another programming language? What's so special about Java?" Well, do you want to learn why network-centric computing is having a profound impact on your profession? Do you want to learn how to develop these types of applications? If the answer to either of these questions is yes, then you should learn Java.

This Book Focuses on Microsoft's Visual J++

This book is unique because it not only provides a comprehensive discussion of the Java language, but it also presents an indepth tutorial on how to use Microsoft's world-class Visual J++ Java development environment. The tools provided by Visual J++ represent the shortest path to productivity in Java for almost any developer.

Visual J++ From a Professional Developer's Point of View

The authors of this book have many years of experience in developing commercially successful software packages. They were able to focus on the aspects of the language that are most important to people who want to create industrial-strength business applications in Java. Specifically, this book shows the reader how to:

➤ Understand the basics of the Java language and environment

➤ Use the Visual J++ Applet Wizard to quickly develop starter code for Java projects

➤ Quickly locate and eliminate programming bugs by using the powerful Visual J++ Debugger

➤ Use the Visual J++ Resource Editor and Wizard to visually design and implement user interfaces

➤ Take advantage of Java's advanced features, such as networking, multithreading, and exception handling, to build world-class Java software

➤ Use ActiveX technologies, such as Authenticode security, COM integration, and ActiveX scripting, to create killer Java programs that solve real-business problems

So if you want to gain a comprehensive understanding of the Java language while turbo-charging your productivity with Visual J++, then this book is for you!

First Let Us Demolish Some Myths

Never before has a development environment attracted so much positive, and some negative, commentary. Java has been the subject of a great deal of hype, however, some of Java's critics have attempted to dismiss it without having the vaguest understanding of what Java is.

To begin our discussion, it helps to get a few things straight.

Java is not

➤ A cross between Visual Basic and C

➤ A high-level scripting language

➤ Something that you need a web browser to run

Java is

➤ A new language that is based on C++, with all the most problematic features left out

➤ Robust and object-oriented

➤ Platform independent

➤ Designed for secure distributed processing

What Can I Develop with Java?

This question is easy to answer—just about anything! Many detractors have suggested that Java can only be used to develop tiny applets that must run within a web browser. This is yet another myth. Java can be used to develop stand-alone applications and web page applets. In fact, the language is robust enough that it can be used to develop just about any application that could be written in C or C++.

This book will teach you how to develop both Java applications and applets by using Visual J++.

Overview of this Book

Visual J++ Java Programming is divided into four parts.

Part I: Introduction to Visual J++

This part of the book provides an overview of Java and explains the unique features of the language. Instructions are given on how to install, set up, and use Visual J++.

Part I includes the following chapters

➤ Chapter 1: Overview of Visual J++ and Java

➤ Chapter 2: Getting Started

Part II: The Java Language

This part of the book discusses the fundamentals of the Java language. First, the reader learns the basic syntax. Next, an in-depth discussion is presented on how classes are defined and used in Java. The last part of this section introduces two Java-specific topics—interfaces and packages. Interfaces define additional characteristics for Java objects and packages that are used to organize classes.

Part II includes the following chapters

➤ Chapter 3: Basic Java Syntax

➤ Chapter 4: Java Classes and Objects

➤ Chapter 5: Java Interfaces and Packages

Part III: Building Java Programs

Part III focuses on all of the topics that you need to understand to become a highly productive Java programmer. The topics are presented in a logical order with examples that frequently build on one another. In the shortest possible time, you'll be using Visual J++ to build advanced software that can solve any business problem.

Part III includes the following chapters

➤ Chapter 6: Java Programming Architecture

➤ Chapter 7: Building Your First Java Applet By Using Visual J++

➤ Chapter 8: The Visual J++ Debugger

➤ Chapter 9: Working with Graphics, Fonts, and Colors

➤ Chapter 10: Handling Events

➤ Chapter 11: Building a User Interface

➤ Chapter 12: More AWT Containers

➤ Chapter 13: Working with UI Components in Visual J++

➤ Chapter 14: Advanced Multithreading and Exception Handling

➤ Chapter 15: Working with IO Streams and Sockets

➤ Chapter 16: Fun with Sound and Animation

➤ Chapter 17: Java and the ActiveX Platform

The grand finale of Part III also discusses how Java fits into Microsoft's ActiveX platform. Specifically, you learn how to use ActiveX technology to make your Java programs more functional, more customized, and more secure.

Throughout the book, you'll learn how to program in the standard Java language, but you'll also find out how to put the Visual J++ tools to use so that you can build programs better and faster. After you learn how to use Java's *Abstract Windowing Toolkit (AWT)* classes to build a user interface, for example, you'll find out how to use the Visual J++ Resource Editor and Java Resource Wizard to instantly generate AWT-based source code.

Part IV: Appendices

The final section of the book is the appendices. These contain Java and Visual J++ related reference material.

➤ Appendix A: API Hierarchical Charts

➤ Appendix B: Glossary

Conventions Used in this Book

To assist the user in working through this book, a number of special sections are visually separated from the rest of the text. These sections appear throughout the book and are denoted as follows:

New Term—any new term or concept should be clearly defined before going into specifics.

Note—information that is used to complement the concepts presented in the main text.

Tips—special hints, techniques, and insights. In most cases these tidbits were discovered through many, sometimes painful, hours of working with early versions of the Java language and Visual J++.

Warning—things that we wish somebody told us about as we were learning a particular feature of Java. If you don't pay attention to these sections, you may get into trouble.

Code Walkthrough—these sections are sometimes included to explain some of the sample code included in the text. These narratives are meant to help the user analyze and understand the logic and functionality of the code.

The Accompanying CD

This book includes a CD that contains the following software at no additional charge:

➤ The Microsoft Internet Explorer/3.0 Java-enabled web browser, with free upgrade access

➤ All Java source code for the examples and listings used in this book

➤ New Riders Internet Security Professional Reference in HTML Format

➤ A Vast Supply of NT Utilities for your use

The authors will post additional information regarding this book, as well as updates and upgrades to the software contained on the CD, on their web site at `http://www.worktechs.com`.

New Riders Publishing

The staff of New Riders Publishing is committed to bringing you the very best in computer reference material. Each New Riders book is the result of months of work by authors and staff who research and refine the information contained within its covers.

As part of this commitment to you, New Riders invites your input. Please let us know if you enjoy this book, if you have trouble with the information and examples presented, or if you have a suggestion for the next edition.

Please note, though: New Riders staff cannot serve as a technical resource for Visual J++, Java, or for questions about software- or hardware-related problems. Please refer to the documentation that accompanies Visual J++, Java or to the application's Help systems.

If you have a question or comment about any New Riders book, there are several ways to contact New Riders Publishing. We will respond to as many readers as we can. Your name, address, or phone number will never become part of a mailing list or be used for any purpose other than to help us continue to bring you the best books possible. You can write us at the following address:

New Riders Publishing
Attn: Publisher
201 W. 103rd Street
Indianapolis, IN 46290

If you prefer, you can fax New Riders Publishing at 317-817-7448.

You can also send electronic mail to New Riders at the following Internet address:

sangus@newriders.mcp.com

New Riders Publishing is an imprint of Macmillan Computer Publishing. To obtain a catalog or information, or to purchase any Macmillan Computer Publishing book, call 800-428-5331 or visit our web site at `http://www.mcp.com`.

Thank you for selecting *Visual J++ Java Programming*!

Part I

Introduction to Visual J++

Chapter 1

Overview of Visual J++ and Java

This chapter discusses why Java is a great development language and how it relates to Microsoft's ActiveX platform. The following topics are covered in this chapter:

➤ The thin client computing model

➤ Why Java is an ideal thin client programming language

➤ An overview of Microsoft's ActiveX platform

➤ Java as an ActiveX technology

So, you want to be a Java programmer. Do you know why? Well, if you don't, you're about to find out.

When you're finished with this chapter, you'll be ready to start learning how to create great Java programs with a powerful tool—Microsoft's Visual J++.

Java: The Breakthrough Development Language

Even before the first production release of Java was made available in the beginning of 1996, it had become apparent that Java was destined to be the most popular development language for distributed, Internet-based applications. The reason for this is because Java is a great language for developing programs that can be dynamically delivered over a network. Furthermore, because of Java's inherent ease-of-use, stability, and robust features, it has a good chance of becoming the general purpose object-oriented development language of choice.

The Thin Client Computing Model

Have you ever tried to install an application and find that you can't use the software because one of your computer's dynamic link libraries (DLLs) is out of date? Have you ever attempted to change a workstation's configuration, but then messed things up so badly that you had to re-install everything? The consensus, even in the contentious computer industry, is almost unanimous—PCs and PC applications are complicated, hard to maintain, and easy to mess up. Under these circumstances, it's easy to understand how a backlash has occurred.

As a result of the problems related to traditional desktop computing, a new computing model, called the thin client, is rapidly gaining acceptance from the entire computer industry. At its most basic level, the thin client model only has two requirements:

➤ A workstation with a web browser able to display standard Hypertext Markup Language (HTML) pages

➤ A network connection

That's it! By using nothing but a thin client, users can unlock the unlimited information resources of the public Internet. In addition, organizations are finding that the same technologies that make the Internet popular can also be applied to their own internal information sharing and collaborative computing needs.

Hypertext Markup Language (HTML), is a text-based standard for defining the layout and content of documents on the web. HTML supports hotlinks between pages, which provide an extremely simple mechanism for navigating among web sites.

The advantages of the thin client over traditional client/server software can be summed up as follows:

➤ Web browsers are cheap or free.

➤ Faulty client configurations are virtually eliminated.

➤ No intrusive software needs to be installed for each application.

➤ Browsers provide a universal user interface that is extremely easy to master.

➤ Web technology is based on platform-independent standards, such as TCP/IP and HTML.

Because of the advantages of the thin client model, you can get information to your end-users, anytime, anywhere. Moreover, you can implement inexpensive web-based applications quickly.

The Drawbacks of the Thin Client

Although the benefits of the thin client are quite compelling, it does have some disadvantages. Consider the following examples:

➤ **Local processing power is underutilized.** With a strictly thin client, you have to make requests to the server for even the simplest operation. In doing so, you're limited by the speed of the network and the capacity of the server.

➤ **No drag-and-drop.** You can't drag-and-drop objects in a traditional HTML page the same way you can in most high-end desktop applications.

➤ **No multiple document interface.** In a traditional HTML page, you cannot open several documents and tile or cascade them within a single application. Some argue that you can use HTML frames, but in frames you don't get the same level of functionality.

➤ **Other basic functions are not supported.** The thin client does not provide the same high-end user interface capabilities of desktop applications. When you want to mark-up a document, for example, or zoom-in and zoom-out of a document, the user interface limitations of the strictly thin client quickly become apparent.

Java and the Thin Client

The drawbacks of the make it difficult to provide the kind of functionality, response time, and user interface features that can compete with desktop-centric applications. That's where Java comes on the scene! With Java you can create sophisticated software that maintains almost all the advantages of the thin client.

Java software does not need to be pre-installed. You access a web page containing a small application or applet, and it's delivered to you dynamically. These applets offer virtually all the functionality of traditional desktop applications. When you're finished with an applet, however, your workstation is left in essentially the same condition as it was before you started.

Java versus the Plug-In

One way software vendors attempt to enhance the thin client is by creating programs that can plug-in to a web browser. This approach, is not problem free. What happens, for example, when you access ten different web pages that require you to install ten different plug-ins? Presto! Your thin client turns into a fat client, along with having the same old problems (provided you were able to muster the patience to install all ten plug-ins).

Plug-ins are not all bad though; many good plug-ins are available that serve useful purposes. The problem is that these are special-purpose binary executables that must be explicitly installed on the desktop, and are not, therefore, much better than traditional fat desktop applications.

Java: C++ Without the Fangs

The Java language can trace its roots back to C++. The creators of Java have added some features that are not present in C++, but perhaps more importantly, they left out all the C++ features that caused the most problems. In doing so, the creators of Java proved the wisdom of the maxim—sometimes less is more.

The main attributes of Java that make it a great programming language include:

➤ **Automatic garbage collection.** Java automatically releases resources taken up by objects when these objects are no longer needed by a program.

➤ **No pointers.** Java does not enable you to access an address in physical memory.

➤ **No multiple inheritance.** You cannot define a class in Java that inherits characteristics from more than one parent.

➤ **Platform-independence.** You can run Java programs on any machine that supports a standard Java environment.

➤ **A high level of security.** Java programs can be prevented from performing potentially dangerous functions, such as accessing a local hard drive.

➤ **Dynamic software distribution.** New versions of programs are delivered to end users at runtime.

Automatic Garbage Collection

Java's automatic garbage collection capability enables developers to write programs without having to worry about including code to clean up unused variables and objects. To understand how automatic garbage collection works, consider the following pseudo code:

```
x = new Object1
x = new Object2
x = new Object3
```

As shown in the preceding code, variable x is set equal to the value of three new objects, one after another. Doing this in a language like C++ causes a potentially serious problem—the dreaded memory leak. At the end of the last operation, x is equal to *Object3*. *Object1* and *Object2*, however, have been created and are still taking up resources. If the program does this enough times, it eventually runs out of memory! In Java, however, this is not a problem because of automatic garbage collection. If a Java program performed an operation as shown in the preceding pseudo code, the automatic garbage collection process detects that no other object is referencing *Object1* and *Object2*. Consequently, the objects are deleted, and the resources they're using are released.

A *memory leak* is a condition that frequently occurs in programs written in languages such as C++ when code is not included to deallocate or dispose of variables and objects after they are no longer required by the program.

It is difficult to overemphasize the importance of Java's automatic garbage collection feature. It eliminates one of the main sources of programming bugs and frees the developer from wasting time dealing with memory management issues. In fact, even if you take away all Java's other strengths, garbage collection still makes it a better programming language than most.

No Pointers

The creators of Java left out the capability to use pointers to access physical memory addresses. This was done for three main reasons.

➤ Pointers cause a security risk because they can be used by sinister developers to access the memory space of other programs.

➤ Pointers cause programming bugs when misused by less competent developers.

➤ Pointers can make programs too complicated.

The creators of Java have provided functionality in the language that in most cases, make pointers unnecessary. What are pointers typically used for anyway? For handling arrays? Well, Java enables you to declare just about anything as an array, and to use it like an object in your program. Consequently, when you program in Java, you find that you really don't need pointers.

No Multiple Inheritance

Java does not enable you to declare an object that has more than one parent. This eliminates the complex class hierarchies that result when multiple inheritance is poorly utilized. Just as you can get along without pointers in Java, in most cases, Java's single inheritance provides all the functionality you need to define your classes.

If you happen to be a fan of Dr. Moreau, you might be disappointed that you can't define an object that inherits characteristics from a chicken, an octopus, and a human. (How would a thing like this walk anyway?). At the same time, however, other developers will be happier not to have to maintain your code!

Platform-Independence

When you develop a Java program under Windows, the target platform is the Java Virtual Machine (JVM). The target platform on Unix, the Macintosh, and even an AS/400 are all the same—the JVM! Consequently, as long as the target computer has a standard JVM, any Java program will be able to run on it.

The *Java Virtual Machine (JVM)* provides a standard Java execution environment, regardless of the underlying platform. This makes it possible to run any standard Java program on any computer platform that supports a JVM.

In contrast to most other development languages, when you compile a Java program, you don't create binary executables. Instead, you create something known as bytecode.

Bytecode refers to the Java programs that can be executed by any JVM. Whereas Java source files have a .java extension, bytecode files have a .class extension.

A bytecode program can be thought of as a predigested executable—it is as close as possible to machine instructions without being specific to any particular platform. The platform-specific translation is performed at runtime by the JVM of the computer, on which the Java program happens to be executing.

For any platform to be Java compatible, it must provide the basic functionality that any standard Java bytecode program may require to execute. This functionality is provided by the JVM.

A High Level of Security

When you download a binary program over a network from an unknown source, you have no way of knowing that the program is not going to corrupt, destroy, or steal the data that you already have stored on your workstation. This is due to the fact that by their very nature, binary executables have direct access to your hardware (see figure 1.1).

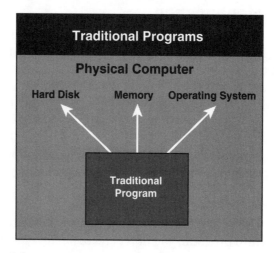

Figure 1.1:
Traditional executables have direct access to a host computer.

Java applets that are downloaded over a network are prevented from performing potentially dangerous functions, such as reading from or writing to the local hard drive. This greatly reduces the security risk that you take when you execute a program written by an individual or organization of dubious character and motives. The Java security model, also known as the Java *sandbox* (see figure 1.2) limits what applets can and cannot do.

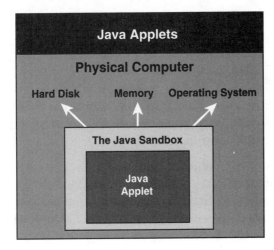

Figure 1.2:
The sandbox prevents applets from directly accessing the host computer.

In addition to Java's sandbox security, the *bytecode loader* automatically checks Java executables for suspicious code at runtime.

Dynamic Software Distribution

When you access a web page that contains a Java applet, you automatically download the latest version of the software. This download happens faster because Java bytecode is much more lightweight than traditional executables. It is more lightweight because most of the functionality required by the applet is already present in the target machine's JVM. When a Java applet utilizes one of the standard Java classes, for example, it is dynamically bound to the applet at runtime.

Microsoft's ActiveX Platform

At first it seemed as though Java and the Internet revolution took Microsoft by surprise. Then in early 1996, Microsoft announced its ActiveX platform. ActiveX is a term that describes a collection of technologies, rather than any one product.

The main parts of the ActiveX platform can be summarized as follows:

➤ **ActiveX controls.** Small, self-contained executables that can be integrated with desktop applications, or delivered over a network.

➤ **ActiveX scripting.** Programs that can be used to customize and add functionality to HTML pages, Java applets, and ActiveX controls.

➤ **Document objects.** Compound documents that derive their behavior and functionality from one or more software objects. An Excel document, for example, can be made to play inline—inside of the Internet Explorer (IE) web browser.

➤ **Database access.** The Microsoft tools and interfaces that make it possible to distribute database information to both desktop and network-based applications.

ActiveX Controls: Making the OCX Network-Centric

ActiveX controls are the progeny of the OCX, or OLE control. Both are small software objects that can be linked with other software objects to build more specialized applications. Although the OCX is desktop-centric, Microsoft has made the ActiveX control more suitable for the Internet. In doing so, the company had to tackle the following problems:

➤ OCXs are traditionally binary executables. Therefore, they have direct access to the physical computer. This can cause a grave security risk, especially on the anonymous Internet.

➤ OCXs are usually too large to download dynamically over a low-speed modem link.

➤ OCXs connect to resources, such as files, synchronously. This can be highly inefficient when a resource is accessed over a high latency network, such as the Internet.

➤ Traditionally, OCX support only exists in Windows.

To address the shortcomings of the OCX with regard to network-centric computing, Microsoft has introduced several enhancements in the ActiveX platform. The next few sections discuss how Microsoft has transformed the desktop-centric OCX into a network-centric ActiveX control.

Authenticode Security

When you go into your local software retailer, you feel pretty confident that the software you purchase is going to be safe to install on your computer. In the unlikely event that something does happen, you can always hold the store, if not the software manufacturer, liable for any damages.

Whereas Java users are protected from malevolent programs by the sandbox, there is virtually no way to protect your computer against a binary executable, and most ActiveX controls are binary executables. To reduce the security risk inherent in ActiveX controls, Microsoft first implemented *Authenticode* security technology in the IE web browser version 3.0. Authenticode involves putting a digital signature on executables.

A valid digital signature proves two things about the executable:

➤ The identity of the signer

➤ That the file hasn't been altered since it was signed

A *digital signature* (see fig. 1.3) is a verifiable, almost incontrovertible, fingerprint that proves the signer's identity and that the file has not been altered since it was signed.

Figure 1.3:
A digital signature can be embedded into an executable file.

When IE accesses a web page containing an ActiveX control, it checks to determine whether the control has been digitally signed. Depending on how the user configured IE's security options, any ActiveX control that does not contain a valid signature from a trusted source can be prevented from executing.

Because Authenticode technology can be used to verify the origin and integrity of a binary executable downloaded over a network, it makes Internet-based ActiveX controls as secure as the software that you purchase from a retail software vendor.

Authenticode technology can be used to sign Java applets as well as ActiveX controls. When running in IE, signed applets can be trusted, and therefore, can be enabled to execute outside of the Java sandbox—they can, for example, access the hard drive. How to use Authenticode to sign Java applets is covered in Chapter 17, "Java and the ActiveX Platform."

Reducing Control Size

With ActiveX, developers can reduce the size of OCXs by up to 75 percent (see fig. 1.4). Consequently, when you need to deliver a control over a network, you can reduce download time by eliminating some of the features that came standard with the OCX. At the same time, you can still create high-octane ActiveX controls for use in desktop applications.

Traditional OCXs must implement certain interfaces defined by Microsoft. Although explaining all the functions of these interfaces is beyond the scope of this book, it should suffice to say that with ActiveX, the number of interfaces that a control is required to implement is reduced. Consequently, the size of the resulting ActiveX control is smaller than it would have been required to be if it had been implemented as a traditional OCX.

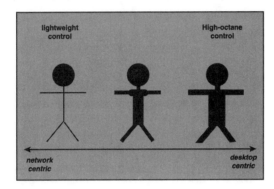

Figure 1.4:
An ActiveX control can be more lightweight than a traditional OCX.

Asynchronous Monikers

A moniker is a named resource, such as a file. Traditional OCXs access resources synchronously. Consequently, if an OCX accesses a file, it pauses until the entire input/output operation is complete.

This is fine for local resources, but it doesn't work very well for accessing a resource across the busy Internet. That's why ActiveX controls support asynchronous monikers. This enables an ActiveX control to perform input/output operations without causing a delay in other processing tasks.

When an program operation is performed *asynchronously*, it doesn't cause the entire program to wait until the operation completes before performing any other operation. When a resource is accessed by using an asynchronous moniker, the program can perform other tasks while it is waiting for the resource.

ActiveX On Non-Windows Platforms

To prove that they're serious about making ActiveX cross-platform, Microsoft has pledged to provide support for ActiveX controls on the Mac as well as the most popular variants of the Unix operating system. This represents a serious challenge, even for a company with Microsoft's resources.

Even when ActiveX is ported to other operating systems, ActiveX controls are still binary executables (unless written in Java). Therefore, at a minimum, they have to be recompiled before being run on other platforms.

ActiveX or Java?

After hearing all about what ActiveX controls are, you might start to think that Java and ActiveX controls sound quite similar. So which technology should you use? The answer to this question depends on the requirements and demands of the situation.

In general, developing ActiveX controls in a language such as C++ is probably more appropriate when:

➤ You have existing OCX controls

➤ Your development staff is not yet trained in Java

➤ All target users are on the Windows platform

➤ All target users have Authenticode-enabled web browsers, such as IE

On the other hand, Java fits best when:

➤ You need to support many platforms, such as Windows, Mac, and Unix

➤ You have skilled Java programmers on staff, or you are willing to make the worthwhile investment in training

➤ You are undertaking a new development effort, and you want to use a more stable, simple, and powerful object-oriented programming language

➤ Your target users don't have Authenticode-enabled browsers, or are unwilling to take the risk of running ActiveX controls outside of the sandbox

Java as an ActiveX Technology

At the time that Microsoft announced the ActiveX platform, the company also announced that they were licensing Java from Sun and building Java capability into Developer Studio (Visual J++) as well as all forthcoming versions of Internet Explorer. Soon after, Microsoft announced that they would build a JVM into all the Windows platforms, even Windows 3.1. Moreover, as part of the agreement with Sun, Microsoft is to provide the reference implementation of the JVM for the Windows environment.

By definition, the *reference implementation* of the JVM is available (in source code form) to all Java licensees.

Perhaps the most clever part of Microsoft's Java strategy is that in maintaining the reference implementation for Windows, the company has been able to build support for ActiveX controls into the JVM. This support enables developers to integrate existing ActiveX controls with their Java programs.

Java and the Component Object Model

Microsoft provides support for Java and ActiveX control integration through a standard interface known as the *Component*

Object Model (COM). Indeed, COM serves as the underlying foundation for integrating almost all the various ActiveX technologies (see fig. 1.5).

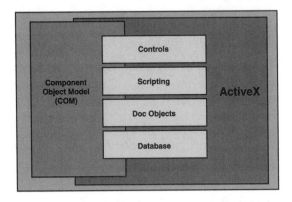

Figure 1.5:
ActiveX is built on the Component Object Model.

Through COM, an object can expose its functionality. These functions are invoked by other objects. With NT 4.0, Microsoft has introduced Distributed COM, or DCOM. Now, not only can COM objects interact on a desktop, but they can also interact across a network!

The battle between DCOM and another distributed object standard called CORBA (Common Object Request Broker Architecture), is far from decided. Most experts, however, feel that while CORBA will dominate the Unix market, DCOM will be the strongest on Windows NT.

Another neat thing about COM is that it is language-independent. Until recently, COM objects were developed in C/C++. Today you can develop COM objects in almost any language, such as C++, Visual Basic, and even Java.

Pay attention to news about a new standard from JavaSoft called *JavaBeans*. This distributed object architecture for Java promises to enable you to integrate your Java programs with both DCOM and CORBA.

The Visual J++ Advantage

When it comes to COM and ActiveX, a great thing about Visual J++ is that it provides tools that enable you to integrate your Java programs with ActiveX controls. This means that you can develop new programs in Java without discarding your existing investment in Windows-based controls.

If you integrate your Java programs with binary ActiveX controls, you are likely to loose the benefits of Java's platform-independence. Although this may not be a problem for you, it is important that you consider the possibility of lost platform-independence when designing your programs.

So why should you learn Java? Quite simply, because it is a powerful, cross-platform, development language that is designed for a distributed network-centric environment. At the same time, all the problematic features of C++ have been left out. And finally, because of its compelling advantages, Java is likely to establish itself as the general purpose object-oriented development language of choice.

Now that you know why Java is so great, you might want to know why you should use Visual J++. Again, the answer is fairly simple—Visual J++ is a world-class Java development environment, produced by the world's leading software vendor. Furthermore, by adding the hooks into COM, Microsoft has made it easier to create Java programs that can take advantage of the functionality available in thousands of existing ActiveX controls.

Summary

The explosive growth of the Internet and the World Wide Web have helped make the thin client computing model popular. A thin client requires a network connection and a web browser that can receive and display Hypertext Markup Language (HTML). Applications based on the thin client model use the web browser as a universal interface. Although thin client applications have many advantages, some disadvantages do arise when it is compared to more robust desktop-centric applications.

Java is an ideal programming language that can be used to create more robust thin client applications. By using Java, you can add sophisticated functionality and intelligence to thin clients without the burden of having to install fat desktop applications.

Java's main advantages over traditional programming languages, such as C++, are automatic garbage collection, enhanced security, simplicity, platform-independence, and dynamic software distribution.

Microsoft's ActiveX platform provides technologies that enable developers to add network-centric capabilities to OCXs, turning them into ActiveX controls that can be securely and dynamically distributed over a network, such as the Internet. ActiveX controls can be integrated with Java programs through Microsoft's Component Object Model (COM). Visual J++ provides the tools that enable developers to implement this integration.

Questions

1. What are the main advantages of the thin client computing model?

2. What are the main disadvantages of the thin client computing model?

3. Are web browser plug-ins inherently bad?

4. Why are memory leaks not a problem in Java?

5. Why was multiple inheritance left out of Java?

6. When you develop a Java program, what is the target platform?

7. What are the main parts of Microsoft's ActiveX platform?

8. How did Microsoft make ActiveX controls network-centric?

9. Through what standard interface can you integrate ActiveX controls and Java programs?

Answers

1. The main advantages of the thin client computing model are:

   ➤ Web browsers are cheap or free.

   ➤ No faulty client configurations.

   ➤ No intrusive software must be installed on the desktop.

   ➤ Browsers provide a universal interface.

   ➤ Web technology is based on platform-independent standards.

2. The main disadvantages of the thin client model are:

   ➤ Local processing power is underutilized.

   ➤ Strictly thin clients do not provide very good support for high-end features such as drag-and-drop, multiple document interfaces, and other user interface capabilities that make an application more intuitive and productive.

3. No. Plug-ins are not inherently bad. Many plug-ins are extremely useful and thus add a great deal of value for the end-user. On the other hand, because plug-ins are typically binary executables that must be explicitly installed on the user's workstation, they have many of the disadvantages of traditional desktop-centric, or fat, applications.

4. Java's automatic garbage collection feature eliminates memory leaks. In addition, it eliminates the need for programmers to waste time on memory management issues.

5. Multiple inheritance was left out of Java to eliminate the complex class hierarchies that typically result in C++ when multiple inheritance is poorly utilized.

6. The target platform of any Java program is always the Java Virtual Machine (JVM). In this way Java programs can be developed and compiled once, and then run on any machine that supports a standard JVM.

7. The main parts of Microsoft's ActiveX platform are:

    ➤ ActiveX controls

    ➤ ActiveX scripting

    ➤ Document objects

    ➤ Database access

8. Microsoft enables developers to create network-centric ActiveX controls by providing the following:

    ➤ Authenticode technology makes binary ActiveX controls as secure as software purchased from a retail store.

    ➤ ActiveX controls can be made smaller than traditional OCXs by leaving out some of the features that came standard with the OCXs.

    ➤ Asynchronous monikers enable ActiveX controls to access network-based resources without delaying the processing of other tasks.

    ➤ Microsoft is working hard to bring all the ActiveX technologies to the Macintosh and Unix environments.

9. ActiveX controls and Java programs can be integrated through the Component Object Model (COM) interface.

Chapter 2

Getting Started

The objective of this chapter is to get you started by using Visual J++ as your Java development environment. To achieve this objective, the following topics are covered:

➤ The Microsoft Developer Studio family of products

➤ How to install Visual J++

➤ A whirlwind tour of Visual J++ features

➤ Getting a feel for the Visual J++ user interface

When you're finished reading this chapter, you should have Visual J++ installed, and you should have a good understanding of the environment's most important features. Because the purpose of this chapter is to introduce you to Visual J++, this chapter discusses all the main capabilities of the application, but does not provide detailed instructions on how to use any particular tool. The topics introduced here are explained in detail where appropriate throughout this book.

If you've already worked with Developer Studio or some other integrated development environment (IDE), most of the concepts discussed in this chapter should be fairly easy to understand. If you're unfamiliar with IDEs in general, don't let this chapter intimidate you. You don't need to be an expert on all the capabilities provided by Visual J++ to start developing Java programs and have a lot of fun in the process!

The Developer Studio Advantage

Visual J++ is part of Microsoft's Developer Studio IDE. This is an important advantage because it enables Microsoft to provide Java programmers with almost all the same functionality and add-on applications that are available to Visual C++ programmers.

Developer Studio is Microsoft's flagship software development environment. Because Visual J++ is integrated with Developer Studio, it is more than just a Java IDE—Visual J++ is part of an integrated suite of powerful tools that are targeted at professional developers. Microsoft has invested a great deal of effort (and money) to give these tools the functionality required by both individual programmers and development teams. In addition to Visual J++, the following software packages are integrated with Developer Studio.

➤ *Visual C++*—An integrated development environment that enables programmers to rapidly code, test, and debug C++ programs. The functionality and user interface provided by Visual C++ is almost exactly the same as Visual J++.

➤ *Fortran PowerStation*—A Fortran development environment that provides the same features and user interface as Visual C++ and Visual J++.

➤ *Visual Test*—A tool that automates software testing. This product was originally developed by Microsoft; however, it is now owned by a company called Rational Software. Rational has pledged to maintain compatibility with Developer Studio.

➤ *Visual SourceSafe*—A source code control system that can be used with Developer Studio projects. This application's features include source code archiving and version control.

Developer Studio is capable of supporting multiple programming languages. Now you can develop in C++, Fortran, and Java in the same IDE.

Because Developer Studio is already integrated with so many industrial-strength packages, Visual J++ can satisfy the demanding requirements of even the most ambitious Java development efforts. Moreover, although most Visual C++ developers should find Java's syntax and structure fairly easy to master, learning a new IDE can be a significant chore. Not only is Visual J++ a world-class Java development environment, but because of its similarities to Visual C++, it will undoubtedly shorten the learning curve for just about any Visual C++ programmer migrating to Java.

Visual C++ release 4.0 or higher is compatible with Visual J++. The version of Developer Studio installed with Visual C++ Standard Edition, however, is not compatible with Visual J++. If you want to run both Visual J++ and Visual C++ Standard Edition, install the applications in separate directories.

Installing Visual J++

Visual J++ is easy to set up, but before you get started, take some time to read the following sections, which discuss the workstation requirements and the Visual J++ installation procedures. This will make the process of installing Visual J++ a lot smoother.

Workstation Requirements

Visual J++ is a very sophisticated application. Therefore, it has some rather demanding hardware requirements. The following list shows the hardware and system software requirements specified by Microsoft.

➤ Personal computer with an Intel 486 or higher processor (a Pentium 100 is recommended).

➤ Microsoft Windows 95 or Windows NT Workstation operating system version 4.0 or higher.

➤ In Windows 95, Visual J++ requires at least 8 megabytes of memory (12 megabytes is recommended). If you run Visual J++ on Windows NT Workstation, 16 megabytes of memory is required (20 megabytes is recommended).

➤ 20 megabytes of hard disk space is required for a typical installation. The minimum installation requires 14 megabytes.

➤ CD-ROM drive.

➤ VGA or higher monitor (Super VGA recommended).

➤ Microsoft Mouse or compatible pointing device.

The Visual J++ CD

Because Visual J++, Professional Edition is distributed on a CD, you need access to a locally attached or network-attached CD-ROM drive. In addition to Visual J++, this CD contains the following software:

➤ *Microsoft's Java-enabled Internet Explorer Web browser—* Visual J++ uses Internet Explorer for testing Java applets.

➤ *Sample Java code from Microsoft and Sun—*These sample Java programs demonstrate the capabilities of the standard Java language as well as the ActiveX/COM enhancements to the Java Virtual Machine (JVM) that were implemented by Microsoft.

➤ *The Cabinet File Developer's kit—*This kit provides utilities that enable you to store your Java program files and data in compressed archive files.

➤ *The Code Signing Developer's kit—*This kit provides utilities that enable you to put a digital signature on your executable files.

➤ *Third-party sample programs*—These are sample Java programs that were created by using third-party tools, such as Liquid Motion, a 2D Java animation package from a company called DimensionX.

The Msdev directory on the Visual J++ CD should contain a Microsoft Write format file named vjread.wri. Microsoft puts late-breaking news (compatibility issues, bugs, changes, and so on) about Visual J++ in this file. It is a good idea to review the contents of this file before you install Visual J++.

Running the Install Program

To start the installation, insert the Visual J++ CD on a computer that is already running Windows 95 or Windows NT with the aforementioned requirements. The autoplay CD feature of these operating systems automatically runs the setup program on the Visual J++ CD. The rest of the installation steps are outlined as follows:

1. When the setup program on the Visual J++ CD starts, you will see a screen similar to figure 2.1.

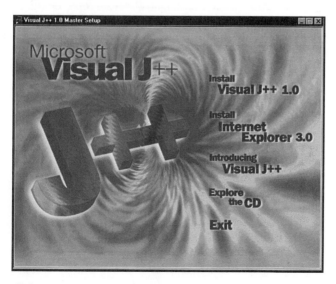

Figure 2.1:

The Visual J++ install screen.

2. Choose "Install Visual J++ 1.0." You should see the Welcome to Microsoft Visual J++ screen (see fig. 2.2).

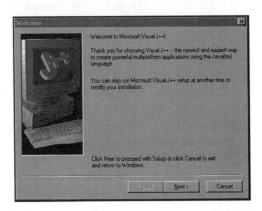

Figure 2.2:

The Welcome to Visual J++ screen.

3. Choose the Next button. You should see the license agreement. Choose Yes (choosing No cancels the installation). You should, of course, also read the End User License Agreement.

4. You should see the Registration screen (see fig. 2.3). Verify your User name and Organization for which this copy of Visual J++ is licensed. Enter the CD key that came with the Visual J++ CD.

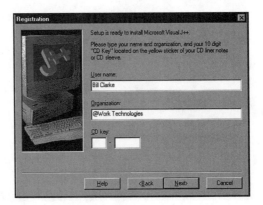

Figure 2.3:

The Registration screen.

5. You should see the choices for the type of installation (see fig. 2.4). Unless you are short on disk space, you should choose the Typical installation option. This option takes the most disk space. Other choices are a Minimum installation, CD-ROM installation, and a Custom installation. These choices are typical of most Microsoft products.

If you choose a custom installation, you can install the source code for all the standard Java classes developed by JavaSoft by choosing the Java Class Library Source Code option. When you install the source code for these classes, you'll be able to see how your program interacts with the standard Java classes when you run the Visual J++ debugger.

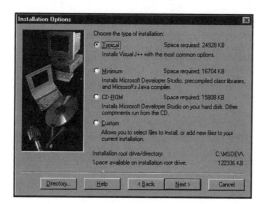

Figure 2.4:

Installation options.

After you choose the type of installation, choose the Next> button.

6. You should see the screen in figure 2.5 informing you of the changes that Visual J++ will make. Choose the Next> button.

7. You should see a message that Visual J++ requires the installation of Internet Explorer 3.0 with Java support (see fig. 2.6). Choose the Install button to install Internet Explorer.

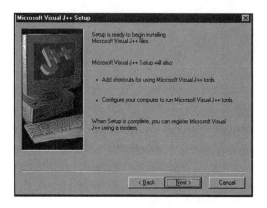

Figure 2.5:

Microsoft Visual J++ Setup.

Figure 2.6:

Installing Internet Explorer.

8. You should see a status indicator while the Internet Explorer files are copied. If you see a message asking if you want to replace a newer file with an older file, always keep the newer file.

At the end of the copy, you should see the Register Visual J++ screen to perform online registration (see fig. 2.7). To be able to register online, you must have a modem that has been properly configured.

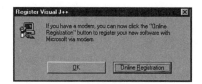

Figure 2.7:

Register Visual J++.

9. After the registration option, you should see the screen in figure 2.8 informing you that the setup has been completed. You will have to restart your computer before you use Visual J++. When your computer restarts, the Internet Explorer launches automatically and displays a Welcome screen.

Figure 2.8:

The Visual J++ setup complete message.

When you install the Java-enabled Internet Explorer browser, you get Microsoft's Java Virtual Machine (JVM) for Windows 95 and NT 4.0. In addition to supporting all the standard functionality of the JVM provided by Sun, Microsoft JVM supports the integration of Java programs and ActiveX controls. Through ActiveX integration, developers can write Java programs that utilize existing C, C++, and Visual Basic routines.

A Whirlwind Tour of Visual J++

Like any good IDE, Visual J++ comes equipped with a number of tools provided by Microsoft that will help you to create better Java applets in a shorter amount of time. The most important tools included in Visual J++ are:

➤ *Text editor*—An editor for source code and other text files.

➤ *Compiler*—Turns Java source code files into standard bytecode executables.

➤ *Debugger*—Enables you to quickly locate and fix problems in a Java program.

➤ *Graphic Development Tools*—A series of tools provided by Visual J++, such as the Java Resource Wizard, that make it easier for you to develop and work with Java programs.

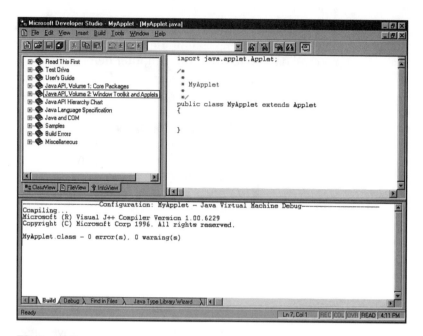

Figure 2.9:

Visual J++ provides a text editor, a compiler, and an assortment of graphical development tools.

Text Editor

Microsoft has modified the Developer Studio text editor so that it understands Java syntax. The editor color-codes Java statements, making it easier for developers to identify typos as they enter in commands. Java reserved words, for example, such as *true, false,* and *null* are shown in blue, whereas the surrounding text is shown in black. Single and multiline comments are color-coded in green. In addition, the text editor can create and edit HyperText Markup Language (HTML) files. The text editor highlights the standard Java-related HTML tags such as <applet> or <param>, as well as tag attributes, such as height, width, and so on.

Working with HTML in Visual J++ is covered in Chapter 7, "Building Your First Java Applet By Using Visual J++."

The Visual J++ text editor provides a context-sensitive pop-up command menu accessed by right-clicking. The text editor is integrated with the other tools, such as the Visual J++ compiler, debugger, and Project Workspace window. When a compiler error occurs, for example, the user can find the errant line of code in the text editor by double-clicking on the error message in the Visual J++ output window.

Compiler

Even though JavaSoft provides a Java compiler (javac.exe) with the Windows version of its Java Developer's Kit (JDK), Microsoft decided to write their own compiler (jvc.exe) from scratch. A Java compiler translates Java source code into a format known as bytecode. Because bytecode is close to machine code, but still platform-independent, it can be efficiently translated into the native instructions of any Java-enabled platform at runtime.

Java bytecode is described in Chapter 1, "Overview of Visual J++ and Java."

The Microsoft compiler can be run from the command line and is totally integrated with Visual J++. The compiler has two modes—release and debug. When run in debug, the compiler creates all the appropriate bytecode so that the program can be run in the Visual J++ debugger. After you compile a Java program, you can execute it in the Internet Explorer browser or from the command line by using the Java interpreter (jview.exe) that comes with Microsoft's JVM for Windows.

Debugger

The Visual J++ debugger provides almost all the capabilities provided by the Visual C++ debugger. In fact, the same dialog boxes, debug toolbar, and shortcut keys are used in the Visual J++ debugger.

The Visual J++ debugger supports location breakpoints (breakpoints on a specific line of code) as well as conditional location breakpoints that only pause the debugger when a specific condition is met. Breakpoints can be set in the text editor by using the pop-up command menu from the Project Toolbar or by using the Breakpoints dialog box, which can be accessed from the Edit pull-down menu.

One of the strongest features of Visual J++ is its integration with the Internet Explorer browser. By using the Internet Explorer, applets can be debugged in their natural habitat. In other words, if an applet interacts with its environment, which may include other applets, scripts, and ActiveX controls, it is extremely useful for the developer to be able to debug the applet as it executes within that environment.

Integrating Java applets with ActiveX controls and scripts is covered in Chapter 17, "Java and the ActiveX Platform."

The Visual J++ debugger supports a series of commands that enable the developer to step through a project's code. As each line executes, the developer can view information about the project in a series of dynamically updating debug windows. These windows include:

➤ *Variable*—This window displays the value of variables that are important to the current context of the program, such as the current line, current method, and so on.

➤ *Watch*—This window enables developers to specify the variables and expressions that they want to inspect while debugging a program. Developers can also change variable values by using this window.

➤ *Disassembly*—This window displays the bytecode of the project. The context-sensitive pop-up menu can be used to switch between a line of compiled bytecode and the source code line in the text editor.

In addition to the debug windows, Visual J++ also has a Quickwatch dialog box. This dialog box provides much of the same functionality as the Watch window; however, the Quickwatch dialog box might be more convenient because a variable can be added to this dialog box by highlighting the corresponding code in the text editor.

The Visual J++ debugger is covered in greater detail in Chapter 8, "The Visual J++ Debugger."

Graphical Development Tools

In addition to the standard IDE features, Visual J++ provides a number of graphical development tools, the most important of which include:

➤ *Project Workspace window*—Displays the Books Online table of contents and a graphical view of the classes, methods, variables, and files in a Visual J++ project.

➤ *Java Applet Wizard*—Steps you through the process of creating starter code for a project.

➤ *Java Resource Wizard*—Generates standard Java code for a user interface from a Windows resource file.

➤ *Java Type Library Wizard*—Generates Java code that enables you to integrate Java programs and ActiveX controls.

The Project Workspace Window

As with most IDEs, Visual J++ creates projects as a series of files that are typically organized in a directory. A Visual J++ project includes Java source code, bytecode, HTML, and image files. In addition, Visual J++ automatically generates a main project file in the project's directory (Visual J++ project files have an .mdp extension). When a project file is opened in Visual J++, all the important information about the project is displayed in the Project Workspace window.

Creating Visual J++ projects is covered in Chapter 4, "Java Classes and Objects."

The Project Workspace window includes the following panes:

➤ *ClassView*—This pane provides a highly graphical view of the classes, methods, and variables included in a project. Icons indicate the type of entity. Icons used to identify methods, for example, are distinct from icons used to identify variables. In addition, ClassView icons indicate access protections, such as private, public, and so on. Double-clicking on a class or method in the Project Workspace window's ClassView pane displays the corresponding code in the text editor.

➤ *FileView*—This pane displays the Java, HTML, and resource files included in the project. You can control the text editor from the FileView pane just as you can from the ClassView pane. Double-clicking on an HTML file, for example, causes the text editor to display the contents of the file.

➤ *InfoView*—This pane navigates the Visual J++ Books Online help files, which include a User's Guide, a Java application programming interface (API) Reference, and information regarding Java-COM integration. When you right-click, a context-sensitive command menu displays, which can be used to search for a particular topic.

The Visual J++ Applet Wizard

The Visual J++ Applet Wizard walks the developer through a series of dialog boxes used to instantly create starter code for a Java project. The Applet Wizard creates projects that can run as web page-based applets, stand-alone applications, or both. Based on user input, Visual J++ automatically creates the appropriate Java and HTML code. The user has the option to generate code that runs on multiple execution threads and includes a sample animation.

The Applet Wizard is covered in greater detail in Chapter 7, "Building Your First Java Applet By Using Visual J++."

The Java Resource Wizard

Developer Studio has a Resource Editor (see fig. 2.10) that can be used to create resource template files (denoted with an .rct extension). Resource templates define the layout of user interface controls, such as buttons and text fields, within a Windows application. By using the Visual J++ Java Resource Wizard, these same resource files can be automatically converted into Java code that uses the standard Java classes. One of the biggest time savers is that the Java Resource Wizard automatically creates a source code for a layout manager class developed by Microsoft called DialogLayout. Layout managers define how user interface components are sized and positioned on a display. The Visual J++-generated layout manager addresses one of the most aggravating shortcomings of the standard Java layout managers by supporting the fixed placement and sizing of user interface components within a display area. In short, DialogLayout saves developers a lot of time.

Layout managers are covered in Chapter 11, "Building a User Interface." The Resource Editor and Java Resource Wizard are covered in Chapter 13, "Working with UI Components in Visual J++."

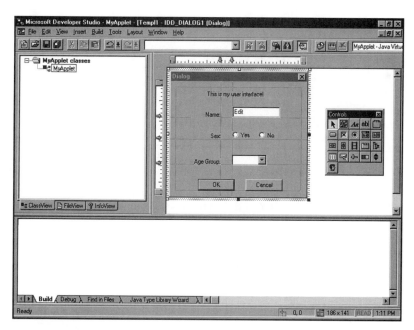

Figure 2.10:

The Resource Editor and Resource Wizard enable developers to visually create a user interface.

The Java Type Library Wizard

As mentioned previously, Microsoft JVM supports the integration of Java with ActiveX controls. Java programs can access ActiveX controls via the Component Object Model (COM) interface. To use a COM object in a Java program, a corresponding Java class must be defined. By using the Visual J++ Java Type Library Wizard, developers can create Java classes that serve as an abstraction layer for COM objects. A type library is essentially a description including parameters, functions, return types, and so on of an ActiveX object.

Integrating Java programs and ActiveX controls is covered in Chapter 17, "Java and the ActiveX Platform."

Familiarizing Yourself with the Visual J++ User Interface

If you've worked with Developer Studio before, you've probably realized that you will learn Java much faster because you already know a lot about the Visual J++ user interface. If you're new to Developer Studio, you might find the IDE a bit overwhelming at first. Do not despair! After you get used to the Visual J++ paradigm, you'll find that the user interface is actually very efficient and intuitive. The remainder of this chapter provides a few tips and insights that will help you get a good feel for working with Visual J++.

Dockable Windows and Toolbars

Visual J++ displays information in a number of windows, many of which can be configured to float or to be docked to a particular side of the application. All the Visual J++ toolbars can be docked or made to float. Figure 2.11 shows how the Visual J++ Standard toolbar, Project Workspace window, and Output window appear when they are made to float.

Figure 2.12 shows the same windows and toolbar shown in figure 2.11, but in a docked state.

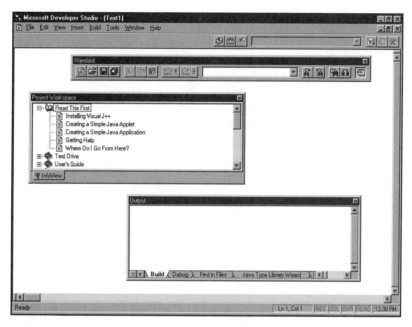

Figure 2.11:

Floating windows and toolbar.

Figure 2.12:

Docked windows and toolbar.

To dock or undock a dockable window or toolbar, you can do one of the following:

➤ Use your mouse to point at a spot in toolbar's free space (area between buttons) or on a window's frame. Press the left mouse button and drag the toolbar or window to the area of the application where you want to redock or float the window or toolbar.

➤ Double-click on a toolbar's free space or on a window's frame. This causes the dock state of the window or toolbar to toggle between docked and floating.

The dockable windows and toolbars provided by Visual J++ can sometimes require a bit of getting used to. The nice thing about these features is that they give users the flexibility to customize the development environment to suit personal preferences. At the same time, the default dock states of the Visual J++ toolbars and windows should be sufficient for users that are just starting to learn the IDE. As you become more proficient and comfortable with Visual J++, you should experiment with the customization capabilities. By building in a great deal of flexibility into Visual J++, Microsoft has created a sophisticated environment that you get started in quickly and continue to become more productive in as you progress.

 You can view many Visual J++ windows in full-screen mode. Choose Full Screen from the View pull-down menu when the appropriate window has the focus. To go back to normal view, click on the Normal View icon or press Esc.

Customizing Toolbars

Visual J++ has a series of toolbars that provide convenient and quick access to commands. When you use the toolbars, you don't have to invoke commands by choosing items from a pull-down menu and you don't have to remember shortcut keys.

You can configure the toolbars that Visual J++ displays by choosing the Toolbars option from the View pull-down menu. This displays the Toolbars dialog box shown in figure 2.13.

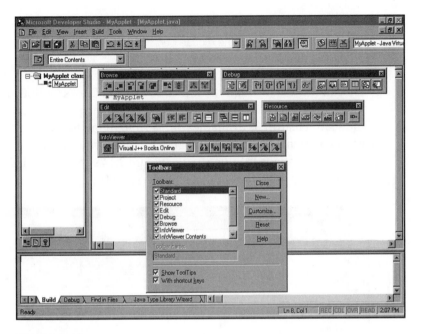

Figure 2.13:

The Toolbars dialog box.

In additional to the Toolbars dialog box, figure 2.13 shows the various toolbars available in Visual J++. These toolbars cover a wide range of functions. Each toolbar is discussed where appropriate in this book.

You can easily add a button to any toolbar or create a custom toolbar. Choose Customize from the Tools pull-down menu. Choose the Toolbars tab. Drag any button or command onto the toolbar. If you drag the button outside an existing toolbar, a custom toolbar is automatically created.

Getting Help

Developer Studio's Books Online feature provides a great deal of information that is available at any time as you are working in Visual J++. You can access Books Online by choosing the InfoView pane of the Project Workspace window or by pressing F1.

You can get Books Online help for any Java reserved word or standard Java class by positioning the mouse cursor on the word in the Visual J++ text editor and pressing the F1 key.

You can browse through the topics covered in Books Online, or search for a particular topic by using the search/query feature. The search feature is available from a Help menu that displays when you right-click inside the Books Online window or the Project Workspace InfoView pane. Figure 2.14 shows how the Books Online information displays in Visual J++.

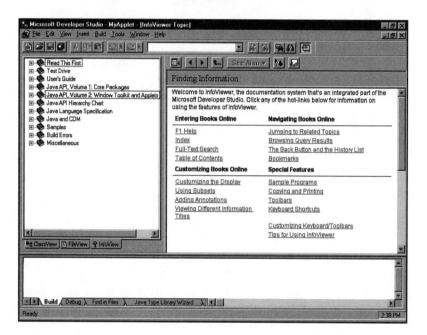

Figure 2.14:

Books Online information can be accessed at any time in Visual J++.

Even though this book provides a comprehensive discussion of all the most important topics related to both Visual J++ and the Java language, there will be times when you want to look up specific topics or find additional information. Books Online is a great place to start.

When you use Books Online, you can use a bookmark to mark your place. Choose Bookmark or InfoViewer Bookmark from the Edit pull-down menu and then type the name of the bookmark. You can return to the bookmark by pressing Ctrl+G and entering the name of the bookmark.

Summary

Visual J++ is a world-class Java development environment that is integrated with Microsoft's Developer Studio. Because several applications are integrated with Developer Studio, such as Visual Source Safe and Visual Test, Visual J++ can take advantage of the integrated functionality offered by these packages. Developers that have experience with Visual C++ and Fortran PowerStation should find the Visual J++ user interface familiar.

Visual J++ requires Windows 95 or Windows NT 4.0. Because Visual J++ is demanding on the hardware that it runs on, you should be careful to review the hardware and software requirements before you attempt to run the install program. The Visual J++ installation process is very straightforward and starts automatically when you put the Visual J++ CD in your workstation. You must also install Microsoft's Java-enabled Internet Explorer web browser even if you have another Java-enabled browser installed. This is because Visual J++ uses the Internet Explorer to test and debug applets.

Visual J++ provides a number of development tools found in any good integrated development environment such as a text editor, a compiler, and a debugger.

In addition to the typical development environment features, Visual J++ provides a number of additional tools. By using the Resource Editor, you can create resource templates that can be used to generate user interfaces for both Java and Windows-based programs. When you run the Java Resource Wizard, it creates standard Java user interface code. The Java Template Wizard creates Java code that can integrate Java programs with ActiveX controls. All the tools provided by Visual J++ are covered in detail in the appropriate chapters of this book.

The Visual J++ environment is highly sophisticated. Sometimes it takes a little time for developers to become familiar with all the features provided by the environment. Because the user interface is so flexible, individual programmers can maximize their productivity by customizing their personal development environment. A great deal of information on both Visual J++ and the Java language is provided in the Developer Studio's Books Online feature. Because Books Online is so well integrated with Visual J++, it should be the first place that developers look for additional information.

Questions

1. How does Visual J++ offer Visual C++ developers the fastest route to productivity in Java?

2. What is Visual SourceSafe?

3. What types of tools are typically provided in any good integrated development environment?

4. Why is Microsoft's Java-enabled Internet Explorer web browser installed when you install Visual J++?

5. How can you use Windows resource templates to generate a user interface for a Java program?

6. Is it a good idea to use the Visual J++ text editor to create HTML files?

7. What is one way that you can change the dock state of a dockable window in Visual J++?

8. If you need additional information on Visual J++, where is the best place to look? (After you look in this book, of course!)

Answers

1. Both Visual J++ and Visual C++ are add-ons to Microsoft's Developer Studio. Consequently, the two development environments have almost identical user interfaces. This

gives Visual C++ developers a big head start in learning Java because they don't have to learn whole new development environment.

2. Visual SourceSafe is a source code control system that can be used with Developer Studio projects. Its features include source code archiving and version control.

3. Any good integrated development environment typically provides at least a text editor, compiler, and debugger. The best environments, such as Visual J++, also provide graphical development tools.

4. The Internet Explorer web browser is installed when you install Visual J++ because Visual J++ uses the Internet Explorer to test and debug applets.

5. The Visual J++ Java Resource Wizard can be used to generate standard Java user interface code from Windows resource files (.rct files).

6. Yes, you should use the Visual J++ text editor to create and change your HTML files. The Visual J++ text editor understands HTML syntax and will color-code HTML accordingly.

7. An easy way to toggle the dock state of a dockable window in Visual J++ is to double-click on the window's frame.

8. Developer Studio's Books Online feature contains a great deal of information about both Visual J++ and the Java language. Because this information is integrated with Visual J++, it is always available while you work in the application.

Part II

The Java Language

Chapter 3

Basic Java Syntax

Part I of this book describes how the Java language is uniquely suited for building network-centric software and how the Visual J++ development environment can be used to simplify the tasks associated with Java software development. At this point, you should have installed Visual J++ and you should be ready to begin learning the basics of the Java language.

In this chapter, you will learn the syntax and statements required to build Java programs. Because Java is based on C++, this chapter discusses the similarities and differences between the two languages. So if you're familiar with C++, the concepts covered in this chapter may feel like a review. It is important, however, that you pay close attention to the differences between the two languages. This chapter emphasizes those differences.

This chapter covers the following basic concepts of the Java language:

➤ Reserved words

➤ Comments

➤ Variables

➤ Literals

➤ Operators

➤ Control flow

The Java Statement

In Java, as in C++, a statement ends in a semicolon. In fact, one look at a Java program will reveal to anyone familiar with C++ that Java statements are almost identical to C++ statements.

Reserved Words

Both the C++ and Java programming languages reserve certain words for special purposes. In Java, the word *long*, for example, is a reserved word that is used to declare a numeric variable of the long data type. Consequently, you cannot declare a class, method, or variable with the name *long*. If you did, a compiler error would be generated.

Some Java reserved words have not been implemented in the language yet—they are reserved for future use. You should not use these words in your programs, even though they have no implementation in the Java language.

Remember that Java's reserved words are case-sensitive. For example, *boolean*, *true*, *false*, and *null* are proper keywords in Java. A very common mistake that C++ programmers usually make when first working in Java is to use BOOL, TRUE, FALSE, and NULL, none of which are valid in Java.

The following is a list of Java reserved words

abstract #	*boolean #*
break	*byte*
byvalue *	*case*
catch	*char*

class	*const*
continue	*default*
do	*double*
else	*extends #*
false #	*final #*
finally #	*float*
for	*future ***
*generic ***	*goto ***
if	*implements #*
import #	*inner ***
instanceof #	*int*
interface #	*long*
native #	*new*
null #	*operator ***
*outer ***	*package #*
private	*protected*
public	*rest ***
return	*short*
static	*super #*
switch	*synchronized #*
this	*threadsafe #*
throw	*throws #*
*transient ***	*true #*
try	*var ***
void	*volatile ***
while	

* Reserved in Java for future use
# Not a reserved word in C++

The Visual J++ text editor detects and color-codes reserved words as illustrated in figure 3.1.

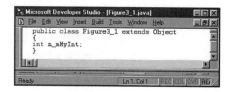

Figure 3.1:
Reserved words are indicated by the Visual J++ text editor.

By default, the reserved words shown in figure 3.1 (*public, class, extends,* and *int*) are automatically displayed in blue by the Visual J++ text editor.

At the time of this writing, the Visual J++ text editor did not always detect the words that are reserved for future use. It is important, however, to be careful not to use these words in your Java programs because they might cause problems when future releases of the Java language are introduced.

Comments

Java supports three types of comments: single-line, multiline, and program documentation. Single-line and multiline comments have identical implementations in C++.

Single-Line Comments

Just as in C++, when a double-slash (//) appears in a line of code, all the text to the right is treated as a comment. The following line of code contains a single-line comment.

```
int     nValue1; // This text is an important comment about
➥Value1
```

Multiline Comments

The comment delimiters slash-asterisk (/*) and asterisk-slash (*/) can also be used in Java. All text between /* and */ is treated as a comment by the compiler. The beginning and end of the comment can be on the same line or can span multiple lines as shown in the following example.

```
/* Class Name  : Class1
   Author      : Programmer #1
   Version     : 1.1
*/

public class Class1
...
```

Nested comments are not supported in Java. When the Java compiler encounters the beginning of a comment (/*), it will search the code for the next end comment delimiter (*/). You should, therefore, be careful when you use multiline comments. Fortunately, the Visual J++ text editor will detect and color-code comments, making them relatively easy to identify.

Figure 3.2 shows how single-line and multiline comments are displayed by the Visual J++ text editor.

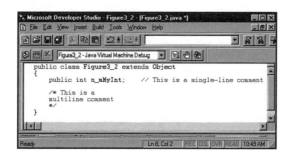

Figure 3.2:
Single and multiline comments in the Visual J++ text editor.

Program Documentation Comments

In addition to single-line and multiline comments, the Java language provides a type of comment that can be used to generate program documentation. A slash-double asterisk (/**) followed by an asterisk-slash (*/) delimits text to be included in the generated documentation. A program documentation comment can only be used immediately before a declaration and the comment will serve as a description of the declared entity. The documentation is generated by the javadoc utility that is included in the Java Developer's Kit (JDK).

If you want to use the *javadoc utility*, you will have to obtain a copy of the JDK from JavaSoft. An easy way to do this is to download the JDK directly from the JavaSoft web site at `http://www.javasoft.com`.

The following code shows how a program documentation comment might be added to a Java source file.

```
/**Class Name  : Class1
   Author      : Jane Doe
   Version     : 1.1
A description of the class functionality goes here...
*/
public class Class1
...
```

The javadoc utility will recognize the /** and */ comment delimiters and will know how to extract the information.

The javadoc utility must be executed from the command line. When you run javadoc against a Java source code file, the utility generates program documentation in the form of a hypertext markup language (HMTL) file.

If no input file is specified and you run the javadoc utility from the command line, the javadoc utility will indicate that it needs a Java class file as input. This is misleading because the input file must be a Java source code file, not a compiled Java bytecode class file.

Variables

A variable in Java can be one of eight fundamental data types, an object, or an array.

Variable names can begin with a letter, an underscore (_), or a dollar sign ($), but they cannot start with a number. Java is case-sensitive. A variable called Bolt, for example, is not the same as bolt.

Global variables do not exist in Java because the language is strictly object-oriented. Consequently, all variables must be members of a class.

No *typedef* exists in Java; therefore, the creation of new data types can only be achieved by creating a class to represent the new data type.

Fundamental Data Types

The fundamental data types built into the Java language are not objects. Data types can be categorized as an integer, a floating-point, a character, and a Boolean. Java data types are listed in table 3.1.

Table 3.1   Java Fundamental Data Types

Category	Data Type
Integer	*byte*
	short
	int
	long
Floating-point	*float*
	double
Character	*char*
Boolean	*boolean*

Because Java was designed to be platform independent, all data types have a fixed size regardless of the underlying hardware and operating system of the machine on which a program executes. That's why variables declared as *int* and *float* are always 32-bit variables, regardless of the platform.

Objects

In Java a variable can be an object. An object in Java is defined by its class. Objects are discussed in Chapter 4, "Java Classes and Objects."

String Objects

One type of object variable that merits mentioning at this point is the String object. In C++, strings are implemented as arrays of characters. In Java, string variables are implemented as instances of the String class provided by the Java language.

Note that the Java String class cannot be modified or subclassed. In other words, you cannot create a new class that inherits its characteristics from String.

The following code shows how a typical String variable can be declared and set in Java.

```
String myString = new String;
myString = "This is a String";
```

Because strings are objects, they provide a variety of methods that can be used to set, manipulate, and test the values that they contain.

Arrays

In Java, you can declare any fundamental data type or object as an array. In fact, Java treats all arrays as objects, even though no specific Array class exists in Java. This can be quite useful when working with arrays. All arrays have a *length* data member, for example, which holds the value of the number of elements in the array.

The following code declares an array of integers called *intArray[]* and an array of String values called *strArray[]*.

```
int nIntArray[];
String strArray[];
```

As you can see in the preceding examples, square brackets ([]) are used to declare an array. The array declaration must contain the name of the array and a variable data type.

The square brackets may be placed before the variable name, such as:

```
int [] nIntArray;
String [] strArray;
```

Arrays are instantiated by using the *new* operator or by a direct (or static) initialization of the array's elements. The following code creates an array of integers called *intArray* and an array of string values called *strArray[]*, both of which are created by using the new operator. An additional array of string values called *names* is directly initialized.

```
int [] nIntArray = new int[ 10 ];
String strArray[] = new String[ 10 ];
String [] names = { "Bill", "Joe", "Chris", "Andy" };
```

It is important to remember that in Java you cannot specify an array's dimension(s) on the left side of an initialization statement.

Accessing Arrays

Accessing the elements of an array is accomplished through array subscripting. Array subscripts begin with 0. The Java environment performs a bounds check with each subscript operation. If a subscript is invalid, an *ArrayIndexOutOfBoundsException* will be thrown. Exception handling will be covered in Chapter 14, "Advanced Multithreading and Exception Handling." Java does not enable access to illegal memory via array subscripting. This access limitation eliminates memory corruption issues, which commonly plague C and C++ programs.

The following code shows the various legal and illegal techniques for accessing and manipulating arrays.

```
String [] names = { "Bill", "Joe", "Chris", "Andy" };
String myName = names[ 3 ];   // myName assigned the
➥value "Andy"
String myName = names[ 4 ];   //
➥ArrayIndexOutOfBoundsException
names[ 3 ] = myName;          // The string myName is
➥assigned to names[3]
names[ 4 ] = myName;          //
➥ArrayIndexOutOfBoundsException
```

The Java environment implements an array of a fundamental data type, such as *int*, as an array of values. Space is allocated in the array for the actual data values. An array of objects is implemented as an array of references to the objects. Although Java does not provide pointers, such as C++, pointer arithmetic is provided via arrays of object references.

Multidimensional Arrays

Multidimensional arrays in Java are not like they are in C++. In C++, the program must allocate a large block of memory for a multidimensional array. In Java, a multidimensional array is implemented as an array of arrays. All memory allocation and garbage collection is handled automatically by the Java environment.

The following code declares a multidimensional array called *matrix* and sets the value of two of the array's elements.

```
int nMatrix[][] = new int [10][10];
nMatrix[0][0] = 1;
nMatrix[9][9] = 100;
```

Literals

In Java, literals refer to specific values, such as the integer 10 or the string *"@Work Technologies"*. The Java literal types are effectively the same as in C++; however, some differences are the following:

➤ Java supports a *Boolean* literal, which is represented by the reserved words *true* and *false*.

➤ Literal strings are treated as String objects and not as an array of characters.

➤ A character literal can be any character in the Unicode character set.

➤ The storage size of a Java literal is the same on all platforms. The size of a C++ literal varies depending on machine architecture.

Unicode is a character set that includes ASCII characters as well as thousands of characters that are used in many languages.

The following sections discuss the various literal types that can be used by Java programs: integers, floating-point, character, character string, and boolean.

Integers

Integer literals can be expressed in decimal, octal (base 8), and hexadecimal (base 16) formats. As in C++, a sequence of digits starting with a 0 is an octal number, and a sequence of digits starting with 0X or 0x is a hexadecimal number. The hexadecimal digits include a–f and A–F. If the letter l or L is appended to an integer literal, then that literal is held as a long data type.

Integers represent the data types that are listed in table 3.2. Remember that these data types have a fixed size regardless of the platform.

Table 3.2 Integer Data Types	
Data Type	**Size**
byte	8 bits
short	16 bits
int	32 bits
long	64 bits

Floating-Point

Floating-point literals consist of a base 10 integer part, a decimal point, and a fractional part. The storage for a floating-point literal can be a 32-bit *float* (single precision) or a 64-bit *double* (double precision). A suffix of f or F for float, and d or D for double, will force the type. You can use exponents with the letter e or E, followed by the exponent, and they may be negative.

The following line of code declares a float variable called *amt*.

```
float    amt = 3.25E-6f // use of negative exponent
                        // and forced type
```

Floating-point numbers represent any of the data types that are listed in table 3.3. These data types have a fixed size regardless of the platform.

Table 3.3 Floating-Point Data Types	
Data Type	**Size**
float	32 bits
double	64 bits

Character

A character literal is represented by a single character, or an escape sequence, enclosed in single quotation marks (''). The character may be any character from the Unicode character set and is stored as a 16-bit unsigned integer.

An *escape sequence* defines a nonprintable character, such as a line feed. In Java, escape sequences are preceded by a backslash (\).

Table 3.4 lists escape sequences that are valid Java character literals.

Table 3.4	Character Escape Sequences
Description	**Escape Sequence**
new-line	\n
horizontal tab	\t
backspace	\b
carriage return	\r
form feed	\f
backslash	\\
single quote	\'
double quote	\"
octal number	\0ddd
hexadecimal number	\0xddd
Unicode character	\udddd

Character String

A sequence of characters enclosed in double quotation marks represents a Java string literal. In Java, a string literal is implemented as a String object, not as an array of characters as in C and C++. An occurrence of a string literal causes an instance of a String object to be created.

Boolean

Java provides a *boolean* literal that consists of the keywords *true* and *false*. The boolean is a true literal and not a representation of an integer as it is in C and C++.

Operators

The operators provided in Java are listed in table 3.5. Notice that Java provides two right shift operators, >> and >>>. The >> operator is an arithmetic right shift operator, and >>> is a logical (pads with zeros on the left) right shift operator.

Table 3.5 List of Java Operators

Operator	Meaning
-	Unary negation
~	Bitwise complement
++	Increment
−−	Decrement
+	Addition
-	Subtraction
*	Multiplication
/	Division
%	Modulus
<	Less than
>	Greater than
<=	Less than or equal to
>=	Greater than or equal to
==	Equal to
!=	Not equal to
&&	Logical AND
||	Logical OR

Operator	Meaning
+=	Addition and assignment
-=	Subtraction and assignment
*=	Multiply and assignment
/=	Divide and assignment
%=	Modulus and assignment
!	Logical NOT
&	Bitwise AND
|	Bitwise OR
&=	Bitwise AND and assignment
|=	Bitwise OR and assignment
^	Bitwise XOR
<<	Left shift
>>	Right shift
>>>	Zero-fill right shift
<<=	Left shift and assignment
>>=	Right shift and assignment
>>>=	Zero-fill right shift and assignment
?:	Conditional operator
instanceof	Determines whether this class is an instance of the named class

Java does not support operator overloading. This capability was left out of the language because it can make code complex and confusing.

Order of Precedence

Table 3.6 lists the order of precedence of the operators, which differs from C++ in the addition of the >>>, >>>=, and *instanceof* operators. The Java environment will perform the calculations for the operators shown at the top of table 3.6 first and then work its way down the table. The order of precedence for operators that are at the same level in the table is from left to right.

Table 3.6 Operator Order of Precedence

First	Second	Third	Fourth	Fifth
.	[]	()		
++	--	!	~	instanceof
*	/	%		
+	-			
<<	>>	>>>		
<	>	<=	>=	
==	!=			
&				
^				
&&				
||				
?:				
=	op= (any operator assign)			

As many C++ and C programmers know, it is probably a good idea to define the order of precedence in Java programs by using parentheses.

Casting

Java provides the capability to cast objects and fundamental data types. The following syntax is the same as it is in C++.

```
int i  = 5;
char c = (int) i;
```

The preceding code performs a safe cast because in Java, *char* and *int* data types are both stored in 16 bits. As with C++, you need to avoid casting a variable to a type that is stored in fewer bytes. Casting a 64-bit *long* to a 32-bit *int*, for example, is not a good idea unless you can guarantee that the value stored in the *long* does not require more than 32 bits.

In contrast to C and C++, Java does not always enable implicit casting. The following code shows an example of a legal implicit cast and an illegal implicit cast.

```
int    nSource = 5;
long   lDestination1 = nSource;     // legal implicit cast
char   cDestination2 = nSource;     // Compile time error,
➥explicit
                                    // cast needed to
➥convert char to int
```

Table 3.7 lists the legal implicit casts that can be performed in Java.

Table 3.7   The Legal Implicit Casting That Can Be Performed in Java

Source Data Type	Destination Data Type
byte	short
	int
	long
	float
	double
short	int
	long
	float
	double
int	long
float	
double	
long	float
	double
float	double

The rules for casting objects are covered in Chapter 4.

Control Flow

Java control flow is almost identical to C and C++. Remember, however, that the *boolean* type can only equal *true* or *false*, not 0 or 1. A C or C++ programmer, for example, would write a control statement as follows:

```
while(1)
{
    statement;
}
```

or alternatively

```
while( nMyInteger )
{
    statement;
}
```

None of this sample code will compile in Java because the literal 1 and the variable *nMyInteger* are integers and not *boolean* values. The correct syntax in Java follows:

```
while(true)
{
    statement;
}
```

or alternatively

```
while( nMyInteger == 0 ) // the result of nMyInteger == 0
➥is a boolean
{
    statement;
}
```

The following is a list of statements that impact the flow of control in Java programs. Code blocks are delimited by curly brackets {} in Java. Optional statements are shown enclosed in square brackets [].

```
if( boolean )
{
    statement;
}
else
{
    statement;
}

switch( expression )
{
    case expression: statement;
              break;
    default: statement;
}

break [ label ];

continue [ label ];

return expression;

[ label: ] for( [expression]; [expression], [expression])
{
    statement;
}

[ label: ] while( boolean )
{
    statement;
}

[ label: ] do
{
    statement;
}while( boolean );
```

In Java, processing loops created by the *for, while,* or *do* statements can include an optional label. If a label is specified, the loop becomes a labeled loop.

Using Break and Continue Statements

In Java, the break and continue statements can be used with a label to perform a function similar to the goto statement in C and C++. A labeled break causes the program flow to break out of any number of enclosing loops and resume execution at the first line of code outside of the labeled loop (the loop specified in the break command.) A labeled continue causes the program flow to resume at the beginning of the specified labeled loop, which may be within the same loop or an enclosing loop. The following example contains a labeled break and a labeled continue.

```java
int i = 0;
int loop = 0;

System.out.println( "Start of Program" );
 // System.out.println is the equivalent of
 // a cout() or printf()

outerLoopLabel: while( loop < 5 )
{
     loop++;
     System.out.println("Start of loop #"+loop);

     innerLoopLabel: for( i=1; i < 3; i++ )
     {
         if( loop == 2 )
         {
             System.out.println( "→(continue
➥outLoopLabel)");
             continue outerLoopLabel;
         }
         if( loop == 3 )
         {
             System.out.println( "→(break
```

```
➥outerLoopLabel)");
                break outerLoopLabel;
            }

        System.out.println( "→(inner loop i
➥="+i+")");
      }

    System.out.println("End of loop #"+loop);
}

System.out.println( "End of program");
```

The preceding code produces the following output:

```
Start of Program
Start of loop #1
→(inner loop i =1)
→(inner loop i =2)
End of loop #1
Start of loop #2
→(continue outLoopLabel)
Start of loop #3
→(break outerLoopLabel)
End of program
```

You can see from the output that the labeled `continue` causes the program flow to leave the inner *for* loop and resume execution at the beginning of the outer *while* loop labeled *outerLoopLabel*. The labeled `break` causes the program flow to leave the inner *for* loop and resume execution after the outer *while* loop labeled *outerLoopLabel*.

If you use a `break` statement without a label, it will behave the same way in Java as it does in C++. A `break` statement will cause the program flow to break out of the current loop. A `continue` statement without a label will cause the program flow to resume at the top of the current loop.

Summary

The syntax of Java is based on C and C++. C++ programmers should have no trouble reading Java operators and statements. Java is similar to C++ in regard to syntax, precedence, and control flow.

Java and C++ reserve certain words for specific purposes. Programmers should not use words that are reserved for future use.

Because Java is platform independent, the size of the basic data types is always guaranteed to be the same on all platforms. A character is a 16-bit character from the Unicode character set. The Unicode character set is an international standard, which is a superset of ASCII.

Character arrays are instances of the String class. In Java, you can define arrays of any fundamental data type or object. Objects are easier to work with in Java because Java treats all arrays as objects.

Java provides a *boolean* type, with *true* and *false* being the valid values—you cannot use 0 for *false* and 1 for *true* as you might be accustomed to doing in C++. This rule applies for conditional statements that test a boolean value.

Java supports type casting but does not support implicit casting.

Java does not support operator overloading. Operator overloading was left out of Java because it is easy to abuse, as many C++ programmers do, and it results in highly confusing code.

Questions

1. What are the three formats for defining comments in Java?

2. Besides objects and the eight fundamental data types, what else can be a variable in Java?

3. Does Java support global variables?

4. What two Java data types are stored in 64 bits?

5. How are string literals different in Java than they are in C++?

6. What escape sequence is used for an octal number in Java?

7. What should you watch out for when casting a *long* to an *int* data type?

8. What Java statements would you use to perform the same task that you might use a `goto` statement for in C++?

9. Are TRUE, FALSE, and NULL valid keywords in Java?

Answers

1. The three types of comments supported by Java are single-line, multiline (or delimited), and program documentation.

   ➤ *Single-line* comments are denoted by //. Any text to the right of a single-line comment will be ignored by the Java compiler.

   ➤ *Multiline* comments can be created by placing comment text between the /* (begin comment) and */ (end comment) delimiters.

   ➤ *Program documentation* comments are placed between the /** and / delimiters. This type of comment is used by the javadoc utility, from the Sun Java Developer's Kit, to generate program documentation.

2. An array can be used as a variable. It should be noted that an array is actually an object in Java; however, it is a peculiar object because no class definition is available for an array and it cannot be extended.

3. No. Unlike C++, Java does not support global variables. All variables must be defined within a class.

4. Java stores *long* and *float* data types in 64 bits.

5. In Java, a *string* literal is implemented by using the *String* class. In C++, a *string* literal is implemented as an array of characters.

6. In Java, an octal number escape sequence literal is represented by \ddd.

7. When casting a *long* to an *int*, you must be sure that the value that you are casting can fit into an *int*. This is because a *long* data type in Java is always stored in 64 bits and an *int* is always stored in 32 bits. Consequently, a *long* variable can have a larger value than an *int* variable.

8. No statement in Java exists that performs the exact same function as a `goto` in C++, however, a `break` statement with a label can be used to exit a loop (*while, do while,* and *for*).

9. No. The lowercase *true, false,* and *null* are valid keywords in Java.

Chapter 4

Java Classes and Objects

In addition to being similar to C++ in syntax, Java supports most of the same object-oriented features. All Java programs must be organized into classes, which are used to create and manage objects. This chapter focuses on the concepts that are related to classes in Java.

The following topics are discussed in this chapter:

➤ Declaring classes

➤ Working with class variables and methods

➤ Constructing objects

➤ Scope and access control of class variables

➤ Inheritance

➤ Using the *this* and *super* variables

➤ Working with the Class class

➤ Creating classes, methods, and variables in Visual J++

The goal of this chapter is to provide you with the information that you need to grasp the class/object structure of Java. This chapter discusses the tools provided by the Visual J++ development environment for working with Java classes. If you are familiar with C++, you will find that Java classes are quite similar. You should, however, take note of the differences between the two languages. Some new concepts are introduced by Java and some C++ features have been altered or left out. This chapter explains how and why the creators of Java made the language different from C++, with regard to classes and objects.

Overview of Java Classes

Java classes are similar to C++ classes. Classes are used to create objects in Java and in C++. Classes are not objects, but function like blueprints that define the attributes and behaviors that objects have after they have been created or instantiated.

When a program creates an object, it creates an *instance* of the object's class. Therefore, the word *instantiate* is used interchangeably with the word *create* with regard to objects.

The following list describes some of the qualities of Java classes that are similar to C++ classes.

➤ Java classes have constructors, data members, methods, inheritance, static data, and static methods.

➤ Java methods can be overloaded.

➤ Java supports the concept of abstract or base classes.

➤ You can control access to data members and methods by declaring them to be public, private, or protected. For the most part, these access modifiers have the same meanings in Java and C++.

Java has some significant differences that impact the way you work with classes and the objects instantiated from them. The differences are the following:

➤ All Java classes are descendants of the Java Object class. If you declare a class without a base class, then the compiler makes the Object class its base class by default.

➤ Java does not have any pointers, all objects are created on the heap. When you create an object in Java, memory is allocated dynamically.

➤ Java does not have operator overloading capabilities. This feature was left out by Java's creators to keep the language simple.

➤ All Java methods are virtual by default. Java methods can be overridden, unless otherwise specified.

➤ In Java, when fundamental data types are passed to methods as parameters, they are passed by value. Objects are passed by reference. The value of the object's reference is passed, which is essentially the same as passing the object by reference.

➤ Java has runtime type checking.

➤ Multiple inheritance does not exist in Java. It is possible to define a class so that it implements a specified set of methods or interface. Interfaces are covered in detail in Chapter 5, "Java Interfaces and Packages."

➤ C++ programs can include procedural code, but the Java programming language is strictly object-oriented.

➤ The organization of classes differs between C++ and Java. Specifically:

> ➤ In Java, each class's source code is located in one file. The file names must be prefixed by the class name and the .java extension must be used. Java does not recognize separate header files and source files. All code is placed between the left and right braces that delimit the class declaration.

> ➤ In C++, classes are organized in class libraries. In Java, classes are organized in packages.

A Java *package* is a collection of related classes. The topic of packages is covered in detail in Chapter 5, "Java Interfaces and Packages."

Declaring Classes

The declaration of a class in Java is the same as in C++. The full syntax for class declarations, however, is quite different. The following code describes the full syntax for the declaration of a Java class.

```
[modifiers] class identifier [extends
➥SuperClass][implements Interface{,Interface}]
{
    class body
}
```

In the preceding code, you may notice two unfamiliar terms—*extends* and *implements*. These terms are discussed later in this chapter.

Basic Class Definition

Consider the following basic class declaration:

```
class Shape
{
    body of the class
}
```

In C++, you could use a declaration similar to the Java class declaration shown in the preceding code. The two classes would, however, have some important differences. In C++, this class would have no base class and could be used by any program or object. In Java, this class is derived from the Object class, the default super class. As a Java class, this class can only be used by other classes in the same package. For this class to be used by Java classes that are not in the same package, it would have to be explicitly declared as a public class.

A *super class*, also called a *parent class*, is the class from which another class is derived. A class inherits its basic attributes and behaviors from its super class.

The public Modifier and the extends Clause

The following code illustrates the use of the public modifier and the extends clause.

```
public class Shape extends Object
{
    body of the class
}
```

The super class name follows the extends clause in a class declaration. The following code shows the equivalent C++ declaration:

```
class Shape : public Object
{
    ...
};
```

Abstract Classes

When a class is declared as *abstract*, it cannot be directly instantiated. To use an abstract class, you must derive a new class from it. Only an abstract class can have abstract methods, which are methods that are declared, but not implemented.

The C++ equivalent of an abstract class is a class that contains a *pure virtual* method.

The following code declares the Shape class as an abstract base class that contains an *abstract( )* method.

```
public abstract class Shape
{
    public abstract String type();
}
```

The final Clause

C++ does not have an equivalent to the final clause. When a class is declared with a *final* modifier, you cannot derive a new class from it. Consequently, when you declare a class as final, be sure that the class contains all the necessary data members and methods. This is important because you cannot modify or enhance a final class by creating a subclass.

The abstract and final modifiers are mutually exclusive; however, each can be mixed with other modifiers, such as public.

Instance Variables

Instance variables apply to the individual objects that are instantiated from a class. Instance variables are declared within a class definition, but outside the body of any methods. An instance variable can be of any type and can be initialized in its declaration. The following code declares the m_Type and m_nLength instance variables:

```
class public Square extends Shape
{
    private String m_Type = "Square";
    protected int m_nLength;

    public void method1() {}
}
```

If not explicitly initialized, instance variables are assigned default initial values—zero for number types, false for booleans, and null for objects.

An instance variable can be made constant by starting its declaration with the keyword final. Final variables must be initialized. The following code declares the m_Type and m_nLength variables as final:

```
class public Square extends Shape
{
```

```
    private final String m_Type = "Square";   // OK
    protected final int m_nLength;            // error,
➥final variables
                                              // must be
➥initialized

    public void method1() {}
}
```

As indicated by the comments in the preceding code, the length variable's declaration generates a compiler error because all variables that are declared as final must be initialized.

If you are going to be programming in C++ and Java, remember to initialize variables that you declare in either language. This is good programming practice and it helps to ensure that you don't forget to initialize your C++ variables. Because C++ does not initialize variables for you, the habit of explicitly initializing variables can save you a lot of debugging time.

Class Variables

Class variables are similar to instance variables, except that they apply to all of the objects instantiated from a class. Only one value for each class variable can exist, regardless of how many objects have been created. Class variables exist even if no instances of a class exist; they are the equivalent of static members in C++. Not surprisingly, class variables are declared using the static modifier.

```
class public Square extends Shape
{
    private static String m_Type = "Square";
    protected int m_nLength;

    public void method1() {}
}
```

A static variable can be accessed via its class name, as shown in the following line of code:

```
Square.m_Type == "Square";
```

Methods

All class methods, except for constructors, must have a return type, which can be of any fundamental data type or object. Methods that don't return anything must be declared with a return type of void. The following code describes the syntax for the declaration of a Java method:

```
return_type method_name( type arg1, type arg2, ... )
{
    body of the method;
}
```

Java class methods can have an optional parameter list, which is a list of type and name pairs separated by commas. All parameter passing in Java is done by value (see listing 4.1).

When objects are passed to a method, a value representing the object's reference is passed. This process makes it possible for the target method to modify the contents of the object. It is very important, however, to remember that you cannot change the value of a fundamental data type, such as int or float, in the target method.

Listing 4.1   Java Parameter Passing

```
class public Square extends Shape
{
    private static final String m_Type = "Square";
    protected int m_nLength;
    public String type() { return m_Type; }
    public int length() { return m_nLength; }
    public void length( int nLen ) { m_nLength = nLen; }
}
public class DemonstrateShapes
{
```

```
    public void doubleSize( int nLen, Square s )
    {
      if (nLen == 0)
        nLen = 1;
      else nLen = nLen * 2;
      s.length( nLen );
    }
    public static void main( String args[] )
    {
      int nLen = 5;
      Square s = new Square();
      s.length( nLen );
      System.out.println( "len = " + nLen );
      System.out.println( "The Squares length is " + s.length()
➥);
      DemonstrateShapes ds = new DemonstrateShapes();
      ds.doubleSize( nLen, s );
      System.out.println( "len = " + nLen );
      System.out.println( "The Squares length is " + s.length()
➥);
    }
}
```

The *len* variable inside the *main( )* method remains unchanged even though it was passed to the *doubleSize( )* method. Because *len* is an *int*, which is a fundamental data type, *len* is passed by value. The *doubleSize( )* method uses this copy of the *len* variable to increase the length of the Square. Because Square is an object, its reference is passed by value to the *doubleSize( )* method. The Square whose length is set to 10, by the *doubleSize( )* method, is the same Square that was originally created by the *main( )* method.

The output of the preceding code is as follows:

```
len = 5

The Squares length is 5

len = 5

The Squares length is 10
```

Inheritance

Java supports inheritance, which is the capability of a class to inherit attributes and behaviors from its parent or super class. The extends keyword is used to establish an inheritance relationship between a subclass (derived class) and a super class.

Listing 4.2 declares the Shape super class and a number of subclasses that are derived from Shape.

Listing 4.2   Shape Classes

```
public abstract class Shape
{
   public abstract String type();
   public abstract void    draw();
}

class public Square extends Shape
{
   private static final String m_Type = "Square";
   protected int m_nLength;

   public String type() { return m_Type; }

   public int getLength() { return m_nLength; }
   public void setLength( int nLen ) { m_nLength = nLen; }
   public void draw() { System.out.println(
                        "All my sides are equal length"
➥); }
}

class public Rectangle extends Square
{
   private static final String m_Type = "Rectangle";
   protected int  m_nWidth;

   public String type() { return m_Type; }
   public int  getWidth() { return m_nWidth; }
   public void setWidth( int nWidth ) { m_nWidth = nWidth; }
```

```
    public void draw() { System.out.println(
       "I'm like a square but my height != to my width" ); }
}

class public Circle extends Shape
{
    private static final String m_Type = "Circle";
    protected int m_nDiameter;

    public String type() { return m_Type; }
    public int getDiameter() { return m_nDiameter; }
    public void setDiameter( int nDiam ) { m_nDiameter = nDiam;
}
    public void draw() { System.out.println(
       "All my points are equal distance from my center" ); }
}

class public Oval extends Circle
{
    private static final String m_Type = "Oval";
    protected int  m_nWidth;

    public String type() { return m_Type; }
    public int getWidth() { return m_nWidth; }
    public void setWidth( int nWidth ) { m_nWidth = nWidth; }
    public void draw() { System.out.println(
                "I'm a Circle that's been stretched \\
                in one direction" ); }
}
```

Listing 4.2 generates the classes included in the *Shape* inheritance hierarchy. Figure 4.1 illustrates the relationships between classes in the *Shape* inheritance hierarchy.

The Square and Circle classes inherit from the Shape class. Shape is an abstract base class that ensures that all of its descending classes have a method named *type()* and *draw()*. The *type()* method takes no parameters and returns a String value. The *draw()* method takes no parameters and does not return anything.

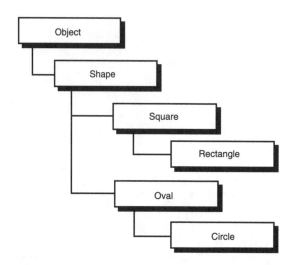

Figure 4.1:

Shape inheritance hierarchy.

The Rectangle class extends the Square class. It adds a width data member, but inherits its length from the Square class. Similarly, the Oval class extends the Circle class, adding a width data member, but inheriting Circle's diameter. Because each class has a unique shape, they must also have their own implementation of the *draw( )* method.

Overloading Methods

In C++ and Java, multiple methods can be defined with the same name, but the methods must have different parameter lists. This is known as method overloading.

In Java, methods can be overloaded by the type or number of their parameters. Overloading on return type only is not supported. When a method is invoked, Java tries to match the method name and parameter list used in the call with the appropriate predefined version of the method. Listing 4.3 demonstrates how methods can be overloaded.

Listing 4.3   Method Overloading

```
public class DemonstrateShapes
{
   public void draw( Square s )
   {
     System.out.println( "Drawing a Square of length " +

                                               s.length() );
   }
   public void draw( int x, int y, Square s )
   {
     System.out.println( "Drawing a Square of length " +
         s.length() + "at coordinate (" + x + "," + y + ")"
➡);
   }
   public void draw( Circle c )
   {
     System.out.println( "Drawing a Circle with \\
         a diameter of " + c.diameter() );
   }

   public static void main( String args[] )
   {
     Square s = new Square();
     s.length( 10.0F );

     Circle c = new Circle();
     c.diameter( 10.0F );

     DemonstrateShapes ds = new DemonstrateShapes();

     ds.draw( s );
     ds.draw( s, 20, 30 );
     ds.draw( c );
   }
}
```

In the DemonstrateShapes class, the *draw()* method is over-loaded because a different version of the method is declared for each object derived from Shape. The version of the *draw()* method that ultimately executes depends on the parameters passed to the method when it is invoked.

CODE WALKTHROUGH

The output of the preceding code shows that the appropriate *draw()* method was called based on the object type or the number of parameters passed to it. The following is the output of the preceding code example:

```
Drawing a Square of length 10

Drawing a Square of length 10 at coordinate (20,30)

Drawing a Circle with a diameter of 10
```

Overriding Methods

Java provides the capability for a subclass to override a method in its super class. In C++, methods cannot be overridden unless they are declared as virtual methods. In Java, however, every method can be overridden unless it is declared as *final*. A method in a subclass with the same signature (name and parameter list) as a method in its super class automatically overrides the super class' method.

In the Shape hierarchy, each class derived from Shape overrides the *draw()* method. Listing 4.4 creates various Shape objects and calls the *draw()* method of each.

Listing 4.4   Overriding Methods

```
public class DemonstrateShapes
{
    public static void main( String args[] )
    {
        Square s = new Square();
        Rectangle r = new Rectangle();
        Circle c = new Circle();
        Oval o = new Oval();

        drawShape( s );
        drawShape( r );
        drawShape( c );
        drawShape( o );
```

```
    }

    public void drawShape( Shape s )
    {
        s.draw();
    }
}
```

The following is the output of the preceding program code. A
different *draw()* method is called for each object type:

```
All my sides are equal length

I'm like a square but my height != to my width

All my points are equal distance from my center

I'm a Circle that's been stretched in one direction
```

Local Variables

Local variables are variables that are declared within the body of a
method. It is illegal to give a method's parameter the same name
as one of the method's local variables. Before a local variable can
be used, it must be initialized. A compiler error occurs whenever
a local variable is not initialized.

Class Methods and Code Blocks

You can associate methods and code blocks with a class, as
opposed to an instance of a class. Class variables use the static
modifier when declaring class methods and blocks of code.

Static code blocks can be used to implement code that is executed once for an entire class. A static variable might be initialized using a static code block. Static code blocks are useful when
initializing static arrays because it enables you to use a for loop to

initialize large arrays. In C++, the only way you can initialize an array is to provide a list of all the initializing values between a pair of curly brackets {}. This is not practical for very large arrays.

Listing 4.5 shows the initialization of a static variable *m_nIntArray[]* within a static code block. The *print( )* method is also declared as static.

Listing 4.5   Static Methods and Code Blocks

```java
public class foo
{
   static final int m_nArraySize = 10;
   static int m_IntArray[] = new int[ m_nArraySize ];

   static
   {
      for( int i = 0; i < m_nArraySize; i++ )
      {
         m_IntArray[ i ] = i;
      }
   }

   foo(){}

   public static void print()
   {
      for( int i; i < m_nArraySize; i++ )
      {
         System.out.println( "intArray[ " + i + " ] = " +
                             m_IntArray[i] );
      }
   }
}
```

Static methods can only access static variables and static methods. Static methods can be accessed via the class name or through a class instance. The static *print( )* method of the *foo* class can be called by using either of the following forms:

```
foo.print();
```

or

```
foo f = new foo();
f.print();
```

Variable Scope

All data members of a class, and all data members of any class'
super classes, are visible to the class. Remember that a data
member can be visible without being accessible. For example,
consider the following code:

```
public class Square extends Shape
{
    private int m_nLength = 10;
}

public class Rectangle extends Square
{
    private int m_nWidth = 5;

    public int m_nArea()
    {
        return m_nLength * m_nWidth;
    }
}
```

The code that defines the Rectangle class, shown in the preceding
code, generates a compiler error. Although the Rectangle subclass
can see the *m_nLength* variable declared in its super class
(Square), it has no direct access to it because the variable is
declared with the private access modifier.

When a Java program accesses a variable, the compiler searches
for it in the following order:

1. The local scope is searched, starting with the current code block. If the current code block is nested, then each successive code block within the method is searched.

2. The current class is searched for a data member that matches the variable name.

3. Each successive super class is searched, stopping with the *Object* class.

Failure to find a match causes a compiler error, indicating that the variable declaration was not found.

this and super Variables

When you code in an object-oriented language, such as Java, you may need to create an object that refers to itself. When an object needs to pass itself to another object, for example, the object must pass itself as a parameter. In C++, this process is accomplished using the *this* pointer. Java does not have pointers, but provides a *this* variable so that an object can refer to itself.

In the following Java code, the someObject object passes itself as a parameter to the *foo( )* method of the someOtherObject object. Although the syntax looks familiar, remember that in Java, *this* is not a pointer.

```
class someObject
{
    void someMemberFunction()
    {
        ...
        someOtherObject.foo( this );
        ...
    }
}
```

It is possible for an object to refer to one of its data members through the *this* variable. The following code shows why you might need to use the *this* variable to refer to a data member.

```
class someObject
{
   int nSomeValue = 0;

   void someMemberFunction( int nSomeValue)
   {
      this.nSomeValue = nSomeValue;
   }
}
```

The following line of Java code:

```
this.nSomeValue = nSomeValue;
```

is the equivalent to the following line of C++ code:

```
this->nSomeValue = nSomeValue;
```

In the preceding lines of code, the *this* variable is used to differentiate the class variable called *nSomeValue* from the local variable of the same name.

Java provides a *super* variable that enables an object to refer to its immediate super class. Returning to the Shape hierarchy discussed earlier, what if you need to call the Rectangle's *draw()* method from the Square's *draw()* method?

In C++, you would statically invoke the Square's *draw()* method as shown in the following code:

```
class Rectangle
{
   ...
   public void draw()
   {
      Square::draw();
      System.out.println(
        "I'm like a square but my height != to my width"
);
   }
   ...
}
```

In Java, you would reference the Square's *draw( )* method through the super variable, as shown in the following code:

```
class public Rectangle extends Square
{
   ...
   public void draw()
   {
      super.draw();
      System.out.println(
         "I'm like a square but my height != to my width"
);
   }
   ...
}
```

Constructors

When you declare a class in Java, you can declare constructors for that class. Constructors are methods that perform the required initializations for each new instance of a class.

Java constructor methods are similar in form and function to their C++ counterparts. In Java, constructors have the same name as the class they belong to; they don't return anything. They can take zero or more parameters, and they can be overloaded.

Constructors are used to ensure that all new objects are created in a valid initial state. Because Java objects are always created from the heap, object constructors are only called in conjunction with the new keyword. In fact, it is illegal to call a constructor at any time other than when creating an object with the new keyword.

For example, the following code shows a legal constructor call and an illegal constructor call.

```
Square s;  // declares s as a reference to a Square
           // no object created and no constructor called
```

```
    s = new Square();    // Square's default constructor is
    ➥called
    s.Square();          // Illegal constructor call
```

All Java classes have constructors. If you do not declare a constructor, the compiler automatically generates a default constructor for you. Unlike C++, when an object is created Java guarantees that all data members are initialized, and that all uninitialized data members are assigned default values. Numeric types are initialized to zero; boolean variables are set to false, and object references are to set to null.

Constructors can call other constructors in the same class, or constructors in its super class. Calls to other constructors must be the first statement in a constructor. If no other constructor of the super class is invoked, the default constructor of a super class is called automatically.

For example, the following code shows the definitions for the classes in the Shape hierarchy with constructors added.

Listing 4.6   Shape Classes with Constructors

```java
public abstract class Shape
{
    public Shape()
    {
        System.out.println( "I'm ready to draw a Shape" );
    }

    public abstract String type();
    public abstract void    draw();
}

class public Square extends Shape
{
    static final String m_Type = "Square";
    protected int m_nLength = 10;

    public Square()
```

continues

Listing 4.6 Continued

```
  {
    System.out.println(
      "I'm ready to draw a Square of length " + m_nLength);
  }

  public Square( int nLen )
  {
    m_nLength = nLen;
    System.out.println(
      "I'm ready to draw a Square of length " + m_nLength );
  }

  public String type() { return m_Type; }
  public int getLength() { return m_nLength; }
  public void setLength( int nLen ) { m_nLength = nLen; }

  public void draw()
  {
    System.out.println(
    "All my sides are equal length" );
  }
}

class public Rectangle extends Square
{
  static final String m_Type = "Rectangle";
  protected int  m_nWidth = 5;

  public Rectangle()
  {
    System.out.println(
      "I'm ready to draw a Square of length " + m_nLength +
      " and width " + m_nWidth );
  }

  public Rectangle( int nLen, int nWidth )
  {
    super( nLen );
    m_nWidth = nWidth;
```

```java
         System.out.println(
           "I'm ready to draw a Square of length " + m_nLength +
           " and width " + m_nWidth );
     }

  public String type() { return m_Type; }
  public int  getWidth() { return m_nWidth; }
  public void setWidth( int nWidth ) { m_nWidth = nWidth; }

  public void draw()
  {
     System.out.println(
       "I'm like a square but my height != to my width" );
  }
}

class public Circle extends Shape
{
  static final String m_Type = "Circle";
  protected int m_nDiameter = 10;


  public Circle()
  {
     System.out.println(
       "I'm ready to draw a Circle of diameter " + m_nDiameter
➡);
  }

  public Circle( int nDiam )
  {
     m_nDiameter = nDiam;
     System.out.println(
       "I'm ready to draw a Square of diameter " + m_nDiameter
➡);
  }

  public String type() { return m_Type; }
  public int getDiameter() { return m_nDiameter; }
  public void setDiameter( int nDiam ) { m_nDiameter = nDiam;
}
```

continues

Listing 4.6   Continued

```java
   public void draw()
   {
      System.out.println(
       "All my points are equal distance from my center" ); }
}

class public Oval extends Circle
{
   static final String m_Type = "Oval";
   protected int m_nWidth = 5F;

   public Oval()
   {
      System.out.println(
       "I'm ready to draw an Oval of diameter " + m_nDiameter
➡+
       " and width " + m_nWidth );
   }

   public Oval( int nDiam, int nWidth )
   {
      super( nDiam );
      width = nWidth;
      System.out.println(
       "I'm ready to draw an Oval of diameter " + m_nDiameter
➡+
       " and width " + m_nWidth );
   }

   public String type() { return m_Type; }
   public int getWidth() { return m_nWidth; }
   public void setWidth( int nWidth ) { m_nWidth = nWidth; }
   public void draw()
   {
      System.out.println(
       "I'm a Circle that's been stretched in one direction"
➡);
   }
}
```

The following code creates an object of each shape, which causes the constructors added in listing 4.6 to generate output. The output of the constructors enables you to determine which constructors are being called.

```java
public class DemonstrateShapes
{
   public static void main( String args[] )
   {
      Square s = new Square();
      Rectangle r = new Rectangle( 7, 15 );
      Circle c = new Circle( 7);
      Oval o = new Oval();
   }
}
```

The output from DemonstrateShapes class is shown here. The lines have been numbered to enable you to follow the explanation of the constructor calling order:

```
 1. I'm ready to draw a Shape

 2. I'm ready to draw a Square of length 10

 3. I'm ready to draw a Shape

 4. I'm ready to draw a Square of length 7

 5. I'm ready to draw a Rectangle of length 7 and width 15

 6. I'm ready to draw a Shape

 7. I'm ready to draw a Circle of diameter 7

 8. I'm ready to draw a Shape

 9. I'm ready to draw a Circle of diameter 10

10. I'm ready to draw an Oval of diameter 10 and width 5
```

The first object created is a Square, which is initialized by its default constructor. Lines 1 and 2 are output that occurs during the creation of the Square. Line 1 is printed from the default constructor of Shape, which is automatically called whenever a subclass doesn't invoke a super class constructor. Line 2 shows that the Square's length is 10, the default initialization value for the m_nLength data member.

Lines 3, 4, and 5 are output that occurs when the Rectangle object is constructed with the constructor being passed two arguments of type int; the length and width of the Rectangle. Line 3 is written by the default constructor of Shape. Line 4 is produced by the constructor of Square that takes one int as an argument. It is explicitly called in the first statement of the Rectangle's constructor.

A Circle object is created next, which produces output lines 6 and 7. Line 6 is output from Shape's default constructor, which is automatically called from Circle's constructor. Line 7 shows the Circle's diameter to be 7, which is the value passed as an argument to the constructor.

Lines 8, 9, and 10 are output that occurs when the Oval object is constructed by its default constructor. Line 8 is written by the default constructor of Shape. Line 9 is produced by the default constructor of Circle. Line 9 shows the Circle's diameter to be 10, the default initialization value for the diameter data member. Line 10 shows that the Oval's diameter is 10 and that its width is 5. The Oval's width is the default initialization value for an Oval's width. The diameter is the default initialization value of the m_nDiameter defined in the Circle class, which is inherited by Oval.

Constructor's cannot only call a super class constructor, but constructors can also call other constructors in the same class by using the this keyword. You can modify the default constructor for the Square class to set the value of m_nLength by calling the Square's constructor that takes one int as an argument, as demonstrated by the following code:

```
public Square()
{
    this( 10 );
```

```
    System.out.println(
        "I'm ready to draw a Square of length " +
   ➡m_nLength );
    }
```

As with any method, you must declare constructors as public if they are to be accessible from outside of an object's package.

Creating and Destroying Objects

You can create an object in Java by placing the new keyword in front of a call to the object's class constructor. This operation allocates memory for the object, calls the constructor that follows the new keyword, and returns a reference to a newly created and initialized object.

Java objects do not have destructors like C++ objects do; this is handled by Java's garbage collection. The Java environment keeps track of all memory allocations and automatically frees memory when a resource is no longer referenced. You never need to delete an object's memory as you do with the delete operator in C++. To free up non-memory resources, such as closing files or sockets, Java objects can override the *finalize( )* method. This method is called before the Java memory manager frees the objects memory. Remember that you have no control over when the *finalize( )* method is called. If you need to guarantee that a non-memory resource is freed as soon as you are finished with it, you have to invoke code to free up the resource.

Comparing Objects

Java provides two operators for comparing objects: equality (==) and inequality (!=). These operators test whether two object references refer to the same object. Because Java does not have an operator overloading feature, you cannot change the behavior of the equality operators as you can in C++.

If you want to compare the contents of two objects, you have to write a method to perform this function. The Java Object class provides an *equals()* method that can be overridden. The Object class's *equals()* method compares two object references, like the equality operator. The *equals()* method accepts a reference to an Object and compares the contents of the passed object (the parameter) to that of the current object.

The Java String class overrides the *equals( )* method. To determine if two String objects contain the same text, use the *equals( )* method. Using the == operator only tells whether the two *String* variables are referencing the same object.

Before creating an *equals()* method, it is important to decide what you want equals to mean. If two Squares objects are equal, for example, when their lengths are equal, then an *equals()* method could be coded as follows:

```
public boolean equals( Object o )
{
  if( o != null && o instanceof Square )
  {
    Square s = (Square) o;
    if( m_nLength == s.m_nLength ) return true;
  }
  return false;
}
```

As shown in the preceding code, the new version of the *equals()* method in the Square class overrides the *equals()* method in the Object class. Both classes have an *equals()* method that takes a reference to an Object and returns a boolean value. Because the object passed to the method is of type Object, you should first check to make sure that the *equals()* was actually passed as a reference to a Square. You accomplish this by using the instanceof operator.

The instanceof operator takes two operands. As shown in the previous code example, the object being checked (o) is placed to the right of the instanceof operator. The name of a class (Square) is placed to the right of the instanceof operator. If the object is an instance of the class, the statement returns a boolean true value. If the object is not an instance of the class, the statement returns a boolean false.

After the program determines that the variable o is an instance of a Square, it compare o's length to this Square's length. To access the m_nLength data member of the Object parameter, it must first be cast to a Square. Finally, the program checks the lengths of o and returns a true boolean value if they are equal, or a value of false is returned if they are not equal.

Casting in Java is similar to casting in C++. An object or primitive type is *cast* when it is converted to a new type or object. Casting of objects is covered in detail later in this chapter. Casting of primitive types is covered in Chapter 3, "Basic Java Syntax."

Copying Objects

The Java Object class provides a *clone( )* method that can be used to create copies of objects. The default implementation of this method creates a clone by performing a bitwise copy of the original object. This bitwise copy may or may not be the appropriate thing to do for any given class.

When a *bitwise* copy is made of an object, a new copy of the object is allocated and copied bit by bit. Although a completely new object is created, the original object is copied, including its references to other objects.

Cloning objects that contain only pure data types is simple. You must be careful, however, when cloning objects that reference other objects. The default *clone( )* method does not make copies of the referenced objects. The cloned object references the same objects that are referenced by the original object. To make an object cloneable, the object must implement the Cloneable interface, interfaces are covered in detail in Chapter 5, "Java Interfaces and Packages." To make an object's *clone( )* method available to other objects, the method must be declared as a public method.

Copying a Square Using the *clone()* Method

The Square class must be modified in order to enable it to get the default *clone()* method's behavior and make this method accessible to classes that are not part of the Shape hierarchy.

First, the declaration of the Square class must be modified so that Square implements the Cloneable interface. The Cloneable interface has no methods—you don't have to do anything with it, other than to declare that you've implemented it. For now you only need to know the fact that if you don't make this declaration, your Java program will get a CloneNotSupportedException when it tries to call Square's *clone()* method.

The declaration of the Square class should be modified as follows:

```
public class Square extends Object implements Cloneable
```

Next, a public clone method must be defined for Square. This method does the work of copying the object. The following code shows the starting point of a *clone()* method.

```
public Object clone()
{
   try
   {
      Square s = (Square) super.clone();

      // Any code to override the bitwise copy would
      // go here.

      return s;
   }
   catch( CloneNotSupportedException e )
   {
      // This shouldn't happen since we are cloneable
      throw new InternalError();
   }
}
```

After Square is declared to implement the Cloneable interface, the CloneNotSupportedException will not occur.

Because Object's *clone( )* method can throw a
CloneNotSupportedException, you need to include a catch
statement for it.

A Java program can indicate that an error condition has occurred
by *throwing* an exception. Exception handling in Java is similar to
exception handling in C++. Java exception handling is covered in
Chapter 14, "Advanced Multithreading and Exception Handling."

Copying a Square Using a *copy()* Method

If using the *clone( )* method seems like too much trouble just to
get a copy of an object, you can always write your own *copy( )*
method. You could, for example, copy a Square object by using
the following code:

```
class public Rectangle extends Square
{
   ...
   public void copy( Square s )
   {
      m_nLength = s.m_nLength;
   }
   ...
}
```

The *copy( )* method shown in the preceding code enables a Java
program to create a copy of a Square, as shown in the following
example:

```
Square s = new Square();
s1.copy( s );
```

You can emulate a C++ copy constructor by defining a constructor that takes a Square as a parameter.

```
public Square( Square s )
{
   super();
   m_nLength = s.m_nLength;
}
```

Access Control

Java provides three access modifiers that you should be familiar with from C++: public, protected, and private. In C++, the access level is defined for entire sections of declarations; however, in Java you can specify the access level as a part of each individual declaration. Methods and data members can be given access modifiers in Java.

Making a method or variable public makes it accessible from any object. A private data member can only be accessed from within the class in which it is defined. A subtle difference exists between Java and C++ in the issue of protected access. A Java class' protected members are accessible from the class in which they are defined, any subclass of that class, as well as any other class in the same package (a package in Java can be thought of as a collection of related classes). Packages are covered in Chapter 5, "Java Interfaces and Packages."

If you want to implement an access level that's the same as protected access in C++, you must use Java's private protected access modifiers. By using these modifiers you guarantee that a data member will only be accessible from within the class that it is declared in, or subclasses of that class.

The following code shows how various access modifiers can be used when declaring a method in Java:

```
public class APublicClass
{
   public int aPublicMethod() {
       ... // Accessible from any class
   }

   protected int aProtectedMethod(){
       ... // Accessible from this class, all subclasses,
   }         // and any other class in the same package

   private protected int aPrivateProtectedMethod(){
       ... // Accessible from this class and any of
   }      // any of its subclasses
```

```
    private   int aPrivateInt; // Accessible from this
➥class only
}
```

Classes, methods, and variables that are declared without an
access modifier are assigned the default modifier. The Java
language does not include a name or keyword for this level of
access; however, the term package level access is used to describe
this access level. When a class method or variable is declared
without an access modifier, it is accessible from all other classes
within the same package, thus the term package level access. A
similar access modifier in C++ would specify that a method can
only be called from classes that are in the same class library.

If you are a C++ programmer, you should pay extra attention to the
access control levels of the Java classes and methods you create. The
default access control in C++ is private. In contrast, declaring Java
classes and/or methods without access modifiers results in package level
access control, which may not be what you want to implement.

Casting Objects

As mentioned previously in this chapter, Java supports casting
between objects and uses a syntax that is similar to C++. The rule
for casting objects is that you can only cast up or down an inheritance chain. Therefore, what constitutes a valid cast depends on
the type of object that is being referenced.

The basic syntax for a cast in Java is as follows:

```
(typename) value
```

The typename specifies the object or data type to which the value
is to be converted. The value specifies the expression that results
in the value that is to be converted.

The following code demonstrates the various legal and illegal
techniques for casting a Rectangle object within the Shape
hierarchy:

```
Shape _s = new Rectangle();
Rectangle r = (Rectangle) _s;   // legal, _s is
➥referencing a
                                // Rectangle
Square s = (Square) _s;// legal, Square is a
                                // subclass of Rectangle
Circle c = (Circle) _s;         // Compiler Error
```

When working with objects from the Shape hierarchy, if a Java program is holding a reference to a Shape object, it is actually holding a reference to either a Square, Rectangle, Circle, or an Oval. This must be true because Shape is an abstract super class.

The following code demonstrates the various legal and illegal techniques for casting a Rectangle object within the Shape hierarchy:

```
Shape _s = new Square();

Rectangle r = (Rectangle) _s; // illegal, if you try to
➥use
                              // r you will get a run
➥time
                              // ClassCastException

Square s = (Square) _s;       // still legal

Circle c = (Circle) _s;       // still a Compiler Error
```

You should avoid casting objects, but if you must cast, use the instanceof operator prior to casting to avoid runtime errors associated with invalid casting.

Working with the Class Class

The Class class can be useful when creating sophisticated Java programs. The Class class cannot only be used to obtain information about a particular object, such as its class name, but the Class class can even be used to dynamically create new objects at runtime. For a detailed description of the methods provided by the Class class, consult the Java reference documentation. The following paragraphs discuss some of the more useful and interesting characteristics of the Class class.

Getting a Class Object

The Java environment maintains runtime information for all existing objects. This information includes the name of the object's class and a reference to the object's super class. When you want to get this information, you must use the *getClass()* method provided by the Object class. The *getClass()* method returns an object of the type Class, which encapsulates the runtime information of the object that it references.

Retrieving an Object's Class Name

All the classes in the Shape hierarchy maintain type information and provide a *type()* method that returns the class name as a String. The Class class makes this unnecessary. If you call the *getClass()* method provided by the Object class, a Class object is returned. You can then call the *getName()* method of the Class object, which returns a String value containing the class name.

The following code shows how the class name of a Square object can be retrieved using the Class class:

```
Square s = new Square();
System.out.println( "s is a " + s.getClass().getName() );
```

This preceding code prints out the following:

```
s is a Square
```

Creating a Class Object for a Class Name

The Class class provides a static *forName()* method, which returns an instance of a Class object for the indicated class name, The following code, for example, declares a variable called *c* and uses the *forName()* method to initialize *c* to an instance of the Class object for the Square class.

```
Class c = Class.forName( "Square" );
```

After you have created a Class object for the specified class name, you can use the Class object to instantiate an instance of the class indicated by the specified class name.

Using Class to Dynamically Create New Objects

The Class class provides a *newInstance()* method. This method returns an instance of the class represented by the Class object. The new object is initialized by its default constructor.

By using the *forName()* and *newInstance()* methods of the Class class, you can create an instance of a class that did not exist when your program was written. To demonstrate this point, consider the following declaration:

```
Shape s = (Shape)new Square();
```

You could get the same results using the *forName()* and *newInstance()* methods as follows:

```
Class c = Class.forName( "Square" );

Shape s = (Shape) c.newInstance();
```

To dynamically create a class, you could pass a *String* variable containing any class name to the *forName()* method, which creates a Class object for the specified class. The Class object's *newInstance()* method can then be used to create a new object for the class represented by the Class object.

The capability to dynamically instantiate new object types in Java is one of the most exciting features of the language. Suppose, for example, that you were to develop a graphics painting program. By using the Java Class class, you could give your program the capability to dynamically add new shapes (new object types) to its palette. The key point is that new objects can be added to an executing Java program dynamically. All Java needs is the class name of the object. This information can be provided by a user, via a prompt, or in an input file. Alternatively, a program could query a network-based repository to determine which objects are available and which ones it needs.

By using this approach, a program could create and incorporate new object types without requiring a recompile! The classes used to create these objects may not have existed when the program was written.

This capability to incorporate new objects is one of the reasons why Java is a superb language for building network-centric software. Clever developers can create Java programs that have the capability to become smarter dynamically whenever necessary.

Creating Classes, Methods, and Variables in Visual J++

The Visual J++ development environment provides a great deal of functionality that assists you in creating and organizing your Java classes.

Creating a Java Project

To start creating classes in Visual J++, the first thing you need to do is to create a Java project. As in Visual C++, when you create a project in Visual J++, a new directory is created to store the various files associated with the project.

To create a new project, you must choose the New option from the File pull-down menu in Visual J++. After doing so, the New dialog box, shown in figure 4.2, is displayed.

As shown in figure 4.2, the user is presented with the option of creating a text file, such as a Java source or HTML file, a project, a resource template—resource templates are covered in Chapter 11, "Building a User Interface," or a bitmap file. When the user chooses Project Workspace and clicks OK, the New Project Workspace dialog box displays, as shown in figure 4.3.

Figure 4.2:

Creating a new project in Visual J++.

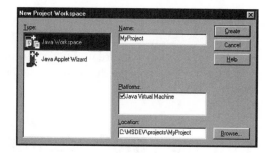

Figure 4.3:

The New Project Workspace dialog box.

The New Project Workspace dialog box presents the user with the options that appear in table 4.1.

Table 4.1   New Project Workspace Dialog Options

Option Name	Option Description
Type	The user can choose to create an empty project workspace—one with no classes or HTML files—or the user may choose the Java Applet Wizard to create the basic HTML and Java source files—the Java Applet Wizard is covered in Chapter 7, "Building Your First Java Applet By Using Visual J++."
Name	The user must enter the desired name of the project in this edit field. In figure 4.3, the name MyProject has already been entered.
Platform	The only platform available in Java is the Java Virtual Machine (JVM).
Location	This is the directory location of your project.

When the user clicks the Create button in the New Project Workspace dialog box, a new project is created. Figure 4.4 shows how the project is displayed in the Visual J++ Project Workspace window.

Figure 4.4:
The ClassView Pane of the Project Workspace window.

If you look in the lower-left corner of figure 4.4, you will notice that the Project Workspace window is composed of the three panes discussed in table 4.2.

Table 4.2 Project Workspace Window Panes

Pane Name	Pane Description
ClassView	Shows information regarding the classes, methods, and variables in the project
FileView	Shows the Java source files, files with a .java extension, of the project
InfoView	Shows the books online information that is available in Visual J++

Creating Classes

After you have created a project, creating a Java class is very straightforward. First you must click the project in the Project Workspace window with the right mouse button. This causes the pop-up menu shown in figure 4.5 to display.

When the user chooses Create New Class from the pop-up menu, the Create New Class dialog box displays, as shown in figure 4.6.

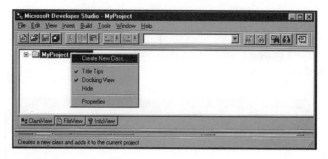

Figure 4.5:

Pop-up menu for creating a new class.

Figure 4.6:

The Create New Class dialog box.

The Create New Class dialog box provides the user with the options that are listed in table 4.3.

Table 4.3 Options for Creating a New Class

Option Name	Option Description
Name	The name of the class. Java requires that the name of the class matches the name of the file that contains the class. The standard naming convention is to capitalize the first letter of the class name, as well as any subsequent words in the name (for example, MyClass).
Extends	The user should enter the name of the parent class in this field. Remember Java does not have multiple inheritance capabilities. Consequently, only one class name can be entered in the Extends field.

Option Name	Option Description
Package	The collection of classes to which the new class will belong. Packages are covered in detail in Chapter 5, "Java Interfaces and Packages."
Modifiers	Class modifiers can be specified by choosing one or two of these check box options. Remember, a class cannot be both abstract and final.

In figure 4.6, a new public class called MyClass is created when the user clicks OK. MyClass is defined as a subclass of the Applet class.

Classes in the ClassView Pane and Text Editor

When you create a class in Visual J++, as is shown in figures 4.2 through 4.6, a class source file is automatically generated according the options chosen. Figure 4.7 shows how Visual J++ displays the new MyClass class in both the ClassView pane and the Visual J++ Text Editor.

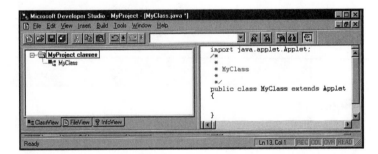

Figure 4.7:
The MyClass class.

The classes associated with a project may not always be displayed in the ClassView pane immediately after being created. When this happens, click the plus sign (+) next to the project name in the ClassView pane and the classes associated with the project will display.

As shown in figure 4.7, Visual J++ automatically generates the basic class definition and displays it in the Text Editor window. By default, the Text Editor window is displayed on the right.

In addition to creating a starting source code file, Visual J++ also displays the class (MyClass) under the project name (MyProject) in the ClassView pane. Notice that Visual J++ displays an icon next to the class name to help the programmer identify it as a class.

Classes in the FileView Pane

The FileView pane of the Project Workspace window displays the Java class source files for the open project. Figure 4.8 shows the FileView pane for the MyProject project.

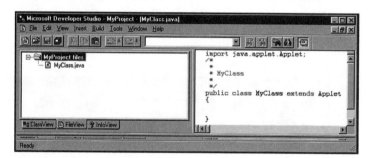

Figure 4.8:

The MyClass class in the FileView pane.

Additional files can be added to the FileView pane by accessing the Insert pull-down menu and choosing the Files Into Project option. You can use this option, for example, to add additional HTML and Java source code files to your projects.

Creating Methods

Visual J++ provides some useful functionality for adding methods to classes. When a user clicks the class name in the ClassView pane with the right mouse button, for example, a pop-up menu displays, as shown in figure 4.9.

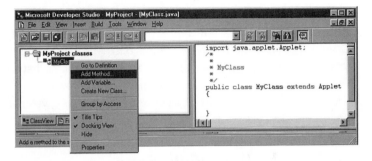

Figure 4.9:

Pop-up window for creating a new method.

After choosing Add Method from the pop-up menu, the Add Method dialog box displays, as shown in figure 4.10.

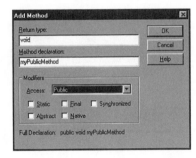

Figure 4.10:

The Add Method dialog box.

The Add Method dialog box provides the user with the options that are listed in table 4.4.

Table 4.4	Options in the Add Method Dialog Box
Option Name	**Option Description**
Return type	The data type of the value returned by the method.
Method declaration	The name of the method. The standard naming convention is to use a lowercase letter for the first character and uppercase characters for the first letters of any subsequent words in the method name.
Modifiers	Includes access modifiers (public, protected, or package) and the optional modifiers of static, final, synchronized, abstract, and native.

Synchronized and native methods are not discussed in this chapter. Synchronized methods are related to multithreading and are covered in Chapter 14, "Advanced Multithreading and Exception Handling." Native methods are typically platform-specific binary executables that are written in C or C++. Although Java programs can invoke native methods, this capability is not covered in this book because the ActiveX platform provides a more elegant technique for accessing native code.

Methods in the ClassView Pane

When the user clicks OK in the Create Method dialog box, a *public( )* method called *myPublicMethod( )* is created that does not return any value. Figure 4.11 shows the *myPublicMethod( )* method as displayed in the Visual J++ ClassView pane and the text editor.

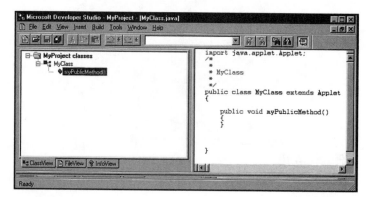

Figure 4.11:

The *myPublicMethod( )* method.

Notice the icon displayed next to the *myPublicMethod( )* method in the ClassView pane. Depending on whether the method has been defined with the public, private, protected, or package access modifier, a different icon displays. This is illustrated in figure 4.12, which shows what the project looks like after adding these three methods: *myPackageMethod( ), myPrivateMethod( ),* and *myProtectedMethod.*

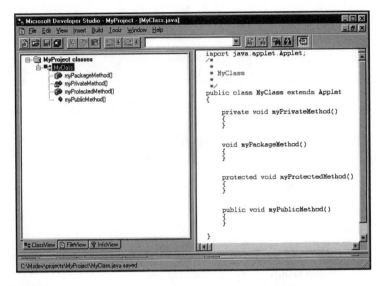

Figure 4.12:
Methods displayed in the ClassView pane and in the Text Editor.

As illustrated in figure 4.12, the ClassView pane displays the appropriate method icon next to the method name, depending on the access protection that is declared for the method.

Creating Variables

Variables can be added to a Java program in J++ just as easily as classes and methods. If you refer to figure 4.9, you will see that a variable could also be added by right-clicking the class. After clicking the Add Variable option in the pop-up menu, the Add Variable dialog box displays, as shown in figure 4.13.

The Add Variable dialog box provides the options that appear in table 4.5.

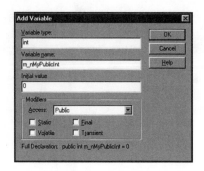

Figure 4.13:
The Add Variable dialog box.

Table 4.5 Options in the Add Variable Dialog Box

Option Name	Option Description
Variable type	One of the eight fundamental data types, an array or a class name (an object).
Variable name	Name given to the variable.
Initial value	Starting value of the variable.
Modifiers	Static, final, volatile, or transient (volatile and transient have been reserved by Java but have not yet been implemented).

When the user clicks OK in the Add Variable dialog box, a new variable called *m_nMyPublicInt*, with an initial value of 0, is created and added to the MyClass class.

Variables in the ClassView Pane and Text Editor

Just as Visual J++ provides special icons for methods, the declared access modifiers for variables are indicated by the variable icons, displayed in the ClassView pane. Figure 4.14 shows how Visual J++ represents variables with different access modifiers in the ClassView pane and in the text editor.

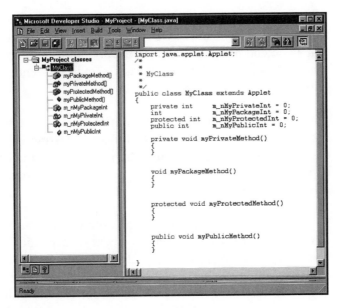

Figure 4.14:

Variables in the ClassView pane and in the Text Editor.

Summary

In Java, all functionality and variables must be defined within a class. Java and C++ classes are similar. They both have the following features:

➤ Constructors

➤ Data members and static data members

➤ Methods, abstract methods, and static methods

➤ The capability to inherit behavior and attributes

Classes can set the access levels of their data and methods by using the same access modifiers that are used in C++ —public, private, and protected. It is important, however, to remember that unlike C++, each declaration in Java requires its own access modifier. If you don't specify a modifier, then the default is package level access.

When working with methods, remember that all parameters in Java are passed by value. When working with objects, remember that all objects are created on the heap. Consequently, when you access an object, you are actually accessing a reference to the object.

The assignment operator (=) does not create a new object. Instead, it causes a variable to reference an existing object. In contrast, the default *clone( )* method creates a completely new copy of the original object. If you want to make a separate copy of an object, you should clone it.

The Visual J++ development environment provides some useful tools for working with Java classes. These tools include pop-up windows and dialog boxes that walk the user through the creation of classes, methods, and variables. The ClassView pane of the Project Workspace window provides a user-friendly graphical representation of a project.

Questions

1. What is the Java equivalent of the following C++ declaration?

```
class NewClass : public SuperClass

{

...

};
```

2. What is the C++ equivalent of an abstract class?

3. How is a constant variable declared in Java?

4. Can you modify the value of an int parameter from within a method?

5. How can an object pass itself to a method?

6. What is the result of not declaring an object's constructor as public?

7. How do you compare two objects for equality?

8. If no super class is specified in a Java class declaration, what will the class' super class be?

9. A *static()* method can access what type of variable?

10. What is the C++ equivalent of a Java class that is declared as final?

Answers

1. The Java equivalent is as follows:

```
public class NewClass extends SuperClass
{
...
};
```

2. The C++ equivalent of an abstract Java class is a class that contains one or more pure *virtual* methods.

3. A constant variable is declared as a *final* variable.

4. No. Java passes all fundamental data type parameters by value. Objects are essentially passed by reference because a value for the object's reference is passed.

5. An object can pass itself to a method using the *this* variable.

6. Only classes from the same package would be able to instantiate an object of that type.

7. If the object properly implements the *equals()* method, then the *equals()* method must be used. The == operator can be used, however, this operator only checks to see if both variables are referencing the same object instance.

8. The default super class for any Java class is the Object class, which is the base class of all Java classes.

9. *Static* methods can only access *static* variables.

10. C++ does not have an equivalent. When a Java class is declared as final, it cannot be extended. When you declare a class as final, you must make sure that it has all of the behavior and data required to perform its task.

Chapter 5

Java Interfaces and Packages

To anyone who intends to become proficient at developing systems in Java, understanding the concepts related to interfaces and packages discussed in this chapter is extremely important. Interfaces and packages are advanced topics. This chapter discusses how interfaces can be used to define class behavior, and how to create, access, and deploy Java packages.

This chapter covers the following topics:

- ➤ Creating and working with Java interfaces
- ➤ Java interfaces compared to C++ multiple inheritance
- ➤ Collection classes in C++ and Java
- ➤ Organizing classes into packages
- ➤ Working with packages in Visual J++
- ➤ Deploying packages on a web server

Interfaces

The public methods of a class are collectively known as a class's *public interface*. In Java, it is possible to formally declare a set of public methods and constants as an interface. An interface is similar to an abstract class in that it cannot be directly instantiated. Any data declared within an interface is—by definition—*public* and *final*. You cannot use the *extends* keyword to include an interface's characteristics within a class definition. Instead, you must declare the class so that it implements the interface.

A Java interface defines the ground rules for all classes that will implement the interface. By using an interface, you can define the methods and method signatures that must be present within any class that implements that interface.

Declaring an Interface

Interfaces are declared similar to the way that classes are declared. An interface called *Quadruped*, for example, is declared in listing 5.1.

Listing 5.1   The Quadruped Interface

```
public interface Quadruped
{
    int m_nNumberOfLegs = 4;

    void setLegLength(int nLegLength);
    void setLegDimensions(int nLegDimWidth, int
➥nLegDimLength);
}
```

The Quadruped interface contains two methods: *setLegLength( )* and *setLegDimensions( )*. Consequently, any class that implements the Quadruped interface must contain public *setLegLength( )* and *setLegDimensions( )* methods. The signatures of these methods must match the interface definition. The *setLegLength( )* method must take one integer parameter, and the setLegDimensions() method must take two integer parameters. Neither method should return any values.

Interface methods cannot be declared as *native, static, synchronized, final, private,* or *protected.*

Implementing an Interface

To implement an interface, a Java class must be declared by using the *implements* keyword in conjunction with the specific interface name. The following code shows how a class can be declared to implement the Quadruped interface:

```
public class Dog implements Quadruped
{
    // Class methods and data members go here
}
```

You could also declare a class to implement Quadruped with the following code:

```
Public class Chair implements Quadruped
{
    // Class methods and data members go here
}
```

Obviously, a Dog is not related to a Chair; however, both classes can share the characteristics of a Quadruped. Because the Dog class and the Chair class implement the Quadruped interface, they must contain public *setLegDimensions( )* and *setLegLength()* methods that match the signatures of those methods in the Quadruped interface.

Interfaces cannot have true variable data members; however, they can have constant data members. The m_nNumberOfLegs integer declared in listing 5.1, for example, is a constant with a value of 4. This makes sense because, by definition, all Quadrupeds have four legs. Because m_nNumberOfLegs is declared as part of the interface, this value will be available as a constant within any class that implements the Quadruped interface.

The Java compiler and interpreter will consider any data member declared within an interface *final* and *public*, regardless of whether these modifiers are used. Finally, any data member declared within an interface must be initialized or a compiler error will occur.

A class is of the type of any interface that it implements. If a class, for example, extends the Object class and implements the Quadruped interface, any instance of that class can be treated as an object of either the Object or Quadruped type.

Implementing Multiple Interfaces

A class can implement multiple interfaces. The Dog class, for example, can be declared as follows

```
public class Dog implements Quadruped, Mammal
{
    // Class methods and data members go here
}
```

Interfaces can be used to specify both Quadruped and Mammal characteristics for the Dog class. In the preceding code, the Dog class is defined as being of both the Quadruped type and the Mammal type. Therefore, all the following declarations are legal.

```
Dog d = new Dog();
Object o = new Dog();     // Dog extends Object
Quadruped q = new Dog();  // Dog implements Quadruped
Mammal m = new Dog();     // Dog implements Mammal
```

or

```
Quadruped dArray[] = new Quadruped[ 10 ];
dArray[ 0 ] = new Dog();
```

Java Interfaces versus C++ Multiple Inheritance

As previously mentioned, Java does not support multiple inheritance. Java interfaces, however, provide a mechanism that may be used to reap many of the same benefits. The creators of Java have made the language easier to learn by not including multiple inheritance. They also eliminated many of the complex class hierarchies that occur in C++ because of multiple inheritance.

Java interfaces do not provide implementations of methods. In C++ a derived class can inherit method implementations from the multiple base classes, but a Java interface only specifies the method names and signatures that must be present within any class that implements that interface. The actual method implementations must be defined within a Java class definition.

In the previous code example, the Dog class implements both the Quadruped and Mammal interfaces. In C++, you can declare the Dog class to be of the Quadruped type and the Mammal type by using multiple inheritance, as shown in the following code:

```
class Quadruped
{
    void setLegLength() = 0;
    void setLegDimensions() = 0;
};

class Mammal
{
    void breathAir() = 0;
};

class Dog : public Quadruped, public Mammal
{
    //Constructor(s) and methods go here
}
```

The Quadruped interface specifies that the *setLegLength()* and *setLegDimensions()* methods must be present in any class that implements the Quadruped interface. In the preceding C++ example, the Dog class would have to define its own implementation of these methods.

Collection Classes

Collection classes are used to manage collections of other objects. Some good candidates for collection classes are, for example, a hash table class and a sortable list class.

In C++, collection classes are defined by using parameterized classes known as templates. As discussed in the following sections, collection classes are easy to set up in Java without the use of templates. All object types in Java can be dealt with as generic objects or as objects of a specific interface type.

Using Templates to Create Collection Classes in C++

A C++ template is a generic class. The template can be used by a programmer to cause the compiler to create classes that are more specific. By creating these classes as C++ templates, you avoid having to recreate a new collection class for every object type that requires the same functionality.

As an example, suppose you need to implement a C++ template that will enable you to easily add objects to a stack. In this case, you could define the *Stack* template class as shown in the following C++ code:

```
template<class ElementClass> class Stack
{
     ElementClass m_Element;
public:
     Stack() {;};
     ~Stack() {;};
     long push(ElementClass &)
     {
```

```
        (code to add element to stack)
    }
    (code for other functions)
};
```

After defining the *Stack* template, you could include stack objects in other C++ programs with declarations such as the following:

```
Stack<SomeClass> SomeStackObject;
Stack<SomeOtherClass> SomeOtherStackObject;
```

In the preceding declarations, *SomeClass* and *SomeOtherClass* represent any two classes. SomeStackObject represents a stack that is created specifically to hold instances of SomeClass as elements. SomeOtherStackObject respresents another stack that is created specifically to hold instances of SomeOtherClass as elements. The important point is that even though both SomeStackObject and SomeOtherStackObject are declared as Stack, they are not of the same type.

After the program containing the SomeStackObject and SomeOtherStackObject declarations is compiled, the C++ compiler creates two new classes from the Stack template class. The new classes have the same code as Stack, except that ElementClass will be replaced with either SomeStackClass or SomeOtherStackClass.

Collection Classes in Java

C++ does not have a common ancestor for all classes. In contrast, all Java classes are related because they are all descendants of the Object class. This is a very important difference because it makes it possible to handle any Java object as a generic instance of the Object class.

In Java, for example, a stack can be defined as shown in the following line of code:

```
Stack aStack = new Stack();
```

The Stack class is provided by the Java environment in the `java.util` package. The Stack class is used as an example for convenience. You can, however, define your own classes to contain other generic objects.

To add an element to a stack, call the *push()* method provided by the Stack class. The *push()* method expects a parameter of the type Object to be passed to it. The following code shows how objects may be added to a stack in Java:

```
Stack aStack = new Stack();

SomeClass SomeObject = new SomeClass();
SomeOtherClass SomeOtherObject = new SomeOtherClass();

aStack.push(SomeObject)
aStack.push(SomeOtherObject);
```

In the preceding code example, two objects of different types are added to the aStack Stack object. Because the *push()* method only expects a parameter of the type Object, any object type can be added to the stack. By definition, all Java objects are of the Object type.

It is not possible to implement a collection class in C++ that would be able to handle generic objects. This is because C++ does not provide a base class from which all objects are derived. Consequently, templates are extremely useful when implementing collection classes in C++.

As the example in this section illustrates, templates are not required to implement collection classes in Java. It is possible in Java to define collection classes that are able to contain generic objects. This is because all Java objects are ultimately derived from the Object class.

Interfaces and Collection Classes

There may be situations when it is necessary to define specific characteristics for the objects handled by a collection class. Suppose, for example, that you need to implement a collection class for objects accessed by using a key. To accomplish this, you could define an interface as shown in the following code

```
public interface Indexable
{
    int getKey();
}
```

Any Java class that implements the *Indexable* interface must have a *getKey()* method that returns an integer value. You can define a collection class that handles any object of the Indexable type—any object that implements the Indexable interface.

When the objects to be contained in a collection class are required to have a specific method that is not provided by the Object class, define an interface that includes the appropriate method, then define the collection class so that it handles any object that implements that interface.

Packages

In Java, classes are grouped into *packages*. Java packages are similar to C++ class libraries. The standard Java package names are shown in table 5.1.

Table 5.1   Standard Java Packages

Package Name	Purpose
applet	Classes that are primarily used to create web page-based applets.
awt	The Abstract Windowing Toolkit contains classes used to create user interface components. Includes the peer and image subpackagesio Input/output classes used for file access.
net	Networking classes used for interprocess communications.
lang	Java language.
util	Java utilities.

The Java compiler and the interpreter must be able to access the appropriate packages to retrieve the Java classes required by a program. If a Java program, for example, instantiates an object to be used for file access, it has to access classes from the *io* package.

Packages are stored in a file system directory tree that matches the package hierarchy. The six standard Java packages are nested under the *java* directory. When you want to access the *io* package, for example, you must specify *java.io*. Figure 5.1 illustrates how the file structure of the standard Java packages appear in Windows Explorer.

Figure 5.1:

The standard Java packages.

A package file/directory hierarchy can also be stored in one compressed ZIP file. Storing the package hierarchy in a ZIP file saves storage space and simplifies file management because you only keep track of one file, instead of a hierarchy of directories and files.

Declaring Packages

It is possible to use a package statement to declare a class as part of a specific package. When doing so, the package statement must be the first statement in a Java source file. The following package statement specifies that the class is part of the *visualj* package:

```
package visualj;
```

It is possible to specify a package like this:

```
package visualj.shapes
```

The preceding package statement informs the Java compiler that the class is part of the *visualj.shapes* package. The *visualj.shapes* package must be located in the directory *visualj\shapes.*

Working with Packages in Visual J++

The Visual J++ environment provides facilities for creating and accessing packages. To enable the compiler to locate your packages, you must specify the appropriate options within the Visual J++ environment. The organization and locations of your classes have an impact on the way you configure your workstation's environment. The following sections discuss some important considerations.

Creating New Packages with Visual J++

You can specify the class's package when you create a new class in Visual J++. Figure 5.2 shows the Visual J++ Create New Class dialog box. See Chapter 4, "Java Classes and Objects," for information on how to create classes in Visual J++.

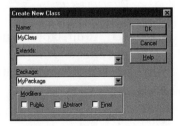

Figure 5.2:

Specifying a package.

In figure 5.2, the user specified the MyClass class to be part of the MyPackage package. In this case, Visual J++ creates a subdirectory called MyPackage within the existing project directory. The source file for the new class —MyClass.java—is created in the MyPackage subdirectory.

Setting the Directories Option

Whenever your Java program needs to access classes from packages other than standard Java packages, you must specify the directory that contains the package for the Visual J++ environment. This is accomplished by choosing the Options item from the Visual J++ Tools pull-down menu. When you choose this option, a tabbed Options dialog box appears. The directories containing other packages must be specified within this dialog box's Directories tab. Figure 5.3 shows an example of the Options dialog box Directories tab.

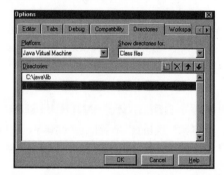

Figure 5.3:

The Options dialog box Directories tab.

In figure 5.3, the c:\java\lib directory is specified. The Visual J++ compiler will search that directory for packages. If the directories option, for example, is set as shown in figure 5.3 and a Java program includes the following import statement:

```
import mypackage.MyClass
```

then the preceding statement directs Visual J++ to locate the MyClass class in a directory called c:\java\lib\mypackage.

Using Packages

All standard Java packages listed in table 5.1 are guaranteed to be available on any platform that supports Java. If you create your own packages, or obtain additional packages from third parties, you need to make sure that these packages are accessible from your Java programs.

Classes in the java.lang package are automatically available to Java programs. Classes from other packages can be either explicitly referenced by using the package name or the package can be imported into the program.

A class within a specific package can be accessed by explicitly referencing the package. The following declaration creates an instance of the Circle class from the `visualj.shapes` package

```
visualj.shapes.Circle c;
```

A more convenient way to access a class contained in a package is to use an import statement. In the following code, the Circle class is imported from the `visualj.shapes` package. After the class has been imported, you can refer to it without the use of the package name.

```
import visualj.shapes.Cirle;
public class SomeClass
{
    Circle c;
}
```

Another option is to import an entire package by using the wild card character in place of the class name, as shown in the following line of code:

```
import visualj.shapes.*
```

When you use an asterisk (*), all the classes in the package are imported. A single import statement cannot import more than one package. You need at least one import statement for every package that your program needs to access.

Importing an entire package has no impact on the efficiency or size of a Java program. The main purpose of Java packages is to help avoid class name conflicts. It is usually easier to import entire packages, unless classes have the same name in two or more of the packages being imported.

Java package names should be chosen carefully to ensure uniqueness. A class name within a specific package is unique even if a class with an identical name is included within another package. To use two classes with identical names within a single program, you must explicitly reference each class's package. The following declarations of two different variables of the circle type illustrate this point:

```
visualj.shapes.circle c1;
somebodyelses.shapes.circle c2;
```

As long as no two class paths are identical, you can avoid the class name collisions.

Sun Microsystems recommends that you use your Internet domain name in reverse order as the root in your package hierarchy. A programmer who's company domain name is `www.worktechs.com` could adhere to Sun's package naming convention by calling the shapes package `com.worktechs.visualj.shapes`.

Setting the CLASSPATH Variable

Although the Visual J++ compiler uses the settings specified in the directories option, a browser such as Microsoft's Internet Explorer or Netscape's Navigator, uses the *CLASSPATH* environment variable to locate packages other than the standard Java packages. This is necessary because the bytecodes for any imported class files are loaded by the Java class loader at runtime. The class loader locates the imported classes by searching the directories specified in the CLASSPATH variable.

Under Windows 95, the CLASSPATH variable is typically set in the AUTOEXEC.BAT file. Under Windows NT, the CLASSPATH variable, and any other environment variable, can be set by using the control panel.

To enable a Java class loader to find a specific class, the class's package hierarchy must be rooted in a directory found in the CLASSPATH environment variable. If a package called visualj.shapes, for example, is in the directory D:\book\visualj\shapes, then the CLASSPATH environment variable must specify D:\book for the class loader to find visualj.shapes, such as CLASSPATH=C:\java;D:\book;.

When the CLASSPATH variable is set as it is in the previous example, the class loader searches the C:\java\visualj\shapes directory first and then it searches the D:\book\visualj\shapes directory.

CLASSPATH Settings for Using Sun's Compiler

The Visual J++ compiler was developed by Microsoft and is fully integrated into Visual J++. To use the original Java compiler for Windows, which is provided with Sun's Java Developer's Kit (JDK), you have to make sure that you set the CLASSPATH environment variable properly. The following line, for example, from an AUTOEXEC.BAT file shows how the CLASSPATH environment variable is specified when using the JDK.

```
SET CLASSPATH=.;C:\java\lib
```

Setting the CLASSPATH to period (.), makes it possible for the developer to compile Java programs from the command line and to resolve package names from the current directory. The CLASSPATH should be set to the C:\java\lib directory because this directory typically contains all the standard Java packages when the JDK is installed.

Setting Up Packages on Your Web Site

When you design a package, consider how the classes it contains will be accessed over a network from an end-user's workstation. Even if the user is on a private intranet, it is difficult to make sure that all of the proper environment variables are set and all the appropriate packages are installed. If the user is accessing your site over the Internet, you have almost no control over how their workstation is configured.

Fortunately, you can set up your Java packages so that your applets work regardless of how the end-user's workstation is configured. In fact, this capability is one of the main advantages of the thin client model of computing made popular by the web. No invasive software needs to be installed on the client computer—except for a Java-enabled browser. This also minimizes the probability of faulty client configurations that occur when, for example, the user's system software is out of date.

When you deploy Java programs that import additional packages, or packages other than the standard ones, the browser resolves the package hierarchy relative to the applet's directory on the web server. If the applet, for example, imports a class from the mypackages.special package, the browser attempts to locate the class in the `mypackages\special` directory. Alternatively, you can store all of your Java packages and class files in a separate directory. If you organize your packages in this way, you have to specify a CODEBASE parameter in all of the HTML pages that access your Java applets. Important Java-related HTML tags and parameters are covered in Chapter 7, "Building Your First Java Applet By Using Visual J++."

After you create new packages that must be accessed by production Java programs, you need to store them on your web site in a subdirectory that matches the package hierarchy. The root of this subdirectory must either be the directory location of the applet's HTML file, or the directory specified with the CODEBASE HTML parameter. In this way, the end-user's web browser is able to resolve the package hierarchy.

Storing Packages in Cab Files

With the release of the Internet Explorer 3.0 (IE3) browser, Microsoft has introduced the concept of storing Java classes and packages in what are known as *cab files*, which is short for cabinet files.

A *cab file* is an archive file that contains other files. Cab files are compressed by using the standard Lempel-Ziv algorithm. Microsoft uses the cab file format to distribute software such as Windows 95 and Windows NT. In addition, Microsoft is promoting the use of cab files to electronically distribute ActiveX controls and Java applets over a network.

Creating and using cab files is covered in Chapter 17, "Java and the ActiveX Platform."

Summary

Java packages are used to logically and physically to organize classes. An interface can be used to define the methods, method signatures, and constants that must be present in any class that implements that interface.

Java does not support multiple inheritance. Java interfaces, however, provide a less complicated and less error prone mechanism for defining the characteristics of a class. All methods declared in an interface are automatically *public*. Any variables declared in an interface must be initialized and are automatically *public* and *final*.

In C++, templates are typically used to create generic collection classes. In Java, however, collection classes can be defined to handle generic objects. This is possible because all Java classes are derived from the Object super class. For situations that require specialized class functions, collection classes can be defined to handle objects of a particular interface type.

In C++, classes are organized into class libraries. In Java, classes are organized into packages. The main purpose Java packages serve is to reduce class name conflicts and to promote the proper organization of classes. The `package` statement is used to specify the class's package.

The standard Java packages are guaranteed to be accessible from any Java-capable environment. A package's classes can be accessed explicitly, by using the package name as a prefix. Packages can be imported into a Java program. The Java compiler and the interpreter can access packages when they need to obtain information about classes.

Packages can be stored in compressed ZIP files on a client's workstation. When deploying packages on a web site, the package directory hierarchy can be stored on the server. The Microsoft Internet Explorer web browser can also access packages that are stored in compressed cabinet files, which are also known as cab files.

Questions

1. How many interfaces can be implemented by a Java class?

2. Is it possible to define method implementations in an interface?

3. What modifiers are automatically assigned to variables declared in an interface?

4. How can you specify that a Java class is part of a specific package?

5. Why are there packages in Java?

6. Why is it easier to create generic collection classes in Java than it is in C++?

7. For a web browser to find your additional packages on a workstation, what environment variable needs to be set?

Answers

1. The number of interfaces that you can implement by a Java class is not limited.

2. It is only possible to define method names and method signatures. You cannot include code for a method implementation within an interface definition. The method implementation must be included in any class that implements the interface.

3. Any variable declared in an interface is automatically *public* and *final*.

4. The package statement is used to specify that a class is part of a specific package.

5. The main purpose of packages in Java is to reduce name conflicts—classes with the same name.

6. It is easier to create collection classes of generic objects in Java because all Java objects are ultimately derived from the Object super class. Collection classes can be defined to handle generic objects of the Object type, which includes all objects in Java.

7. The CLASSPATH environment variable should be set to the root directory of any package that a Java program must access. Under Windows 95, the CLASSPATH is typically set in the AUTOEXEC.BAT file. Under Windows NT, the CLASSPATH can be set by using the control panel.

Part III

Building Java Programs

Chapter 6

Java Programming Architecture

This chapter discusses the basic architectures of stand-alone Java applications and web page-based applets. The concepts covered in this chapter are important because they will enable you to understand how Java programs interact with the Java environment.

The following topics are covered in this chapter:

➤ The applet security model

➤ The life cycle of an applet

➤ How to use basic threads in applets

➤ The life cycle of an application

➤ How to pass parameters to applications

Java Applets

A Java applet is a class designed to execute within a web browser, such as Microsoft's Internet Explorer. Because of this, all Java applets exhibit certain basic characteristics. The framework for these characteristics is defined by the Applet class, which is part of the java.applet package. When you create a Java applet, you must declare a class that extends the Applet class, as shown in the following code.

```
import java.applet.Applet;

public class MyApplet extends Applet
{
    // Class data member declarations and methods go here
}
```

All Java applets must be declared as *public*. This is because the web browser must be able to call the applet's constructor.

The Applet Security Model

One of the most highly debated topics concerning Java applets is the applet security model. The first implementations of Java-enabled web browsers took what has been termed a paranoid approach to security. This security model is frequently referred to as the sandbox. The sandbox prevents applets from doing anything that is potentially dangerous. Some of the more limiting applet security restrictions include:

➤ Applets cannot read from or write to the local file system.

➤ Applets cannot open a communications session with any host other than the one from which it was downloaded.

➤ Applets cannot invoke other executables on the user's workstation.

The paranoid approach was taken due to the fact that any executing program has the potential of damaging, destroying, or stealing information that is stored on a computer. Executables that perform these types of malevolent functions are commonly referred to as viruses or Trojan horses.

Viruses and *Trojan horses* are programs that destroy, steal, or otherwise corrupt information on a computer.

A *virus* is a program that is installed undetected because it is usually attached to another program or file. In addition, viruses can reproduce themselves and spread to other computers.

A *Trojan horse* is a program that appears to be harmless, but is not. A Trojan horse, for example, may be disguised as a useful utility; however, when run by a user, it actually does something bad, such as deleting all of the files on a computer's hard drive.

When shrink-wrapped software is purchased from a reputable retailer, the user should have a high degree of confidence that the software does not contain any viruses or Trojan horses. On the somewhat unruly web, however, users can download programs from thousands of sites that were developed by unknown authors with unknown motives.

How do you know that the dynamically downloaded program wasn't written by a couple of high school students that think it would be great fun to delete your hard drive? The sandbox, by severely restricting what Java applets can do, helps to ensure that things like this will not happen.

Breaking Out of the Sandbox

It may have occurred to you that the restrictions imposed by the sandbox make Java applets unusable for many sophisticated web-based applications. These limitations, however, can be avoided through the use of a technique known as *code signing*. Most Java-enabled browsers will be able to recognize signed code in the near future.

Signed code is a program that has been digitally stamped, or signed, by the software manufacturer. A valid signature proves the following with a high degree of certainty:

➤ The code signer's identity.

➤ The code has not been changed in transit between the creator and the user (a virus has not been inserted).

Because a digital signature proves the code's authenticity, signed code that you dynamically downloaded over the Internet is as secure as shrink-wrapped software that you purchase in a retail store. If you know that a program was developed by a company like IBM, for example, and it was not altered since it was created, you can feel relatively safe about running it on your workstation.

Browsers that can recognize signed code can be configured to enable the user only to run programs from a trusted source, such as Lotus or Microsoft. In this way, trusted applets can be freed from the restrictions imposed by the sandbox. These applets can be enabled to perform functions required to implement more robust applications. These functions might include writing to the hard drive, or communicating with more than one server.

Applet Security in Microsoft's Internet Explorer

Microsoft is one of the leading proponents of signed code and has made it an important part of the ActiveX platform. Internet Explorer 3.0 was the first Java-enabled web browser with the capability to recognize and authenticate digitally signed Java applets. Microsoft's code signing mechanism, known as *Authenticode*, is covered in Chapter 17, "Java and the ActiveX Platform."

When you use the latest version of Microsoft's Internet Explorer web browser or IE, an applet is "trusted" (allowed out of the sandbox) if it has been digitally signed by a trusted source. Internet Explorer gives the user the power to determine whether the creator of the applet is trusted.

Internet Explorer automatically trusts applets that are executed from within Visual J++, even when the applets are not signed. Microsoft designed Visual J++ and the Internet Explorer so that it is easy to test applets. If you try to execute any applet from outside of Visual J++, it will not be trusted unless it has a valid digital signature.

By making it possible to remove the restrictions of the sandbox, Microsoft has enabled developers to create more powerful Java applets. A trusted applet, for example, can perform useful functions, such as writing user preferences to the hard drive, or even extracting data out of an online report and writing the data to a local spreadsheet file.

Java applet security is a vast topic. The important thing to keep in mind is that although simple security is relatively easy to implement, ultimate security can only be achieved at an extremely high cost. You should take the time to familiarize yourself with security issues so that you can make an educated determination of the appropriate risk-to-cost tradeoff.

The Life Cycle of an Applet

Because all applets must execute within the context of a web browser, they must all behave in a consistent manner with regard to initializing, starting, stopping, and displaying. These behaviors are embodied within a set of methods that are inherited by all applets from the Applet class. Depending on the circumstances, the Java environment may call any or all of these methods automatically during the course of an applet's life cycle.

The *init()* Method

This method is typically used to initialize variables, get parameters, and instantiate objects. The Java environment always calls the *init()* method when an applet is first loaded. Unlike most of the other applet methods, the *init()* method is only called once during an applet's life cycle.

The *start()* Method

The *start()* method is typically used to create, start, and restart applet threads and to reinitialize any variables and objects before an applet resumes its execution. Applet threads are discussed in a later section of this chapter. The Java environment automatically calls the *start()* method immediately following the *init()* method. The *start()* method is called whenever a user returns to a previously opened web page containing an applet.

The *stop()* Method

The *stop()* method is typically used to release resources, such as suspending or stopping the execution of the applet's thread. The *stop()* method is the opposite of the *start()* method. The Java environment calls the *stop()* method whenever the user's browser leaves the web page containing the applet.

The *run()* Method

The *run()* method contains the main processing logic of a multithreaded applet. The Java environment calls the *run()* method after the *start()* method whenever an applet is executing on a separate thread.

The *paint()* Method

The paint() method is typically used to paint the applet's display area. The Java environment automatically calls the *paint()* method after the *start()* method. The *paint()* method can be called periodically by other methods, or by the browser, to update the applet's display area. If a pop-up window obscures part of an applet's display area, for example, the *paint()* method is called automatically by the browser when the pop-up window is removed.

The *destroy()* Method

The *destroy ()* method clears the applet from memory, as well as any objects and memory space used by the applet. The *destroy ()*

method is different from the more generalized *finalize()* method in that it is immediately called by the Java environment. You can never be sure when the *finalize()* method will be invoked because it is called by the Java garbage collection process, which runs on a low-priority thread. The Java environment calls the *destroy()* method whenever the browser is exited.

A *thread* is a processing task that executes independently of other tasks that are taking place at the same time.

Java Threads

By using threads, a program can perform more than one task at a time. Suppose, for example, that you were to write an applet that must read large files from another location across the Internet. If you implement the applet so that all other processing halts while the file is read, it would probably cause a long delay. Fortunately, you can code your applet so that it creates a separate thread for reading the files.

Adding Threads to an Applet

Threads are easy to implement by using the Java *Thread* class. The code for creating a thread in an applet is typically included in the *start()* method. The *start()* method is a convenient place to instantiate, start, and restart a thread because the Java environment calls this method automatically every time an applet's web page is accessed.

Any class that executes within its own thread must implement the *Runnable* interface. This interface ensures that the applet definition includes a *run()* method with the following signature:

```
public void run()
{
    // The main thread logic goes here
}
```

The following code provides an example of an applet that executes within its own thread.

```java
import java.applet.*;

public class MyThreadedApplet implements Runnable
{
    Thread m_AppletThread;

    // Other data member declarations go here

    // Other methods (e.g. init()) go here

    public void start()
    {
    if (m_AppletThread == null)
        {
            m_AppletThread = new Thread(this);
            m_AppletThread.start();
        }
            else if (m_AppletThread.isAlive())
            m_AppletThread.resume();
        }
    }

    public void stop()
    {
    if (m_AppletThread != null &&
    m_AppletThread.isAlive())
        m_AppletThread.suspend();
    }

    public void run()
    {
        // The main applet logic goes here
    }
}
```

In the preceding code example, a Thread object called m_AppletThread is instantiated in the *start()* method. The Thread object's constructor expects a parameter of the Runnable type. A reference to the applet itself is passed to the thread's constructor by using the *this* variable. Consequently, m_AppletThread is instantiated as the applet's execution thread. Next, the thread's *start( )* method is called to begin the thread's execution.

The Runnable interface specifies that any class that implements the Runnable interface must have a public *run()* method that returns no value (void). No other methods or member variables are defined by the Runnable interface.

When the user leaves the web page containing the MyThreadedApplet, the Java environment automatically calls the *stop( )* method. In this method, m_AppletThread's execution is suspended. If the user returns to the web page, the Java environment invokes the *start( )* method again. This time, however, m_AppletThread is not instantiated because it is not null. Instead, the execution of m_AppletThread is resumed.

Java Applications

The Java language has enjoyed an explosion in popularity due to the fact that it is especially suited for creating programs that can be dynamically downloaded and run over the Internet. Therefore, Java programs are more commonly implemented as web page-based applets. It is possible to implement Java programs as stand-alone applications. These applications can be executed from the command line by using a Java interpreter.

Both Microsoft and Sun have developed command line Java interpreters for Windows 95 and NT. Sun's *java* utility is included with the Java Developer's Kit (JDK). Microsoft's Java interpreter, *jview*, is included with the Windows 95 and NT operating systems. Sun's utility has also been implemented on other operating systems.

If you want to use either the *java* or the *jview* interpreters from the command line, you have to make sure that your computer's PATH environment variable points to the directory containing either the `java.exe` file or `jview.exe` file.

Perhaps the most well-known example of a Java application is the HotJava browser from JavaSoft. HotJava was the first browser capable of running Java applets.

Application Security Model

Because Java applications do not run within a web browser, the applications are not subject to the same security restrictions as applets. Java applications, for example, can communicate with several hosts and they can access the local file system.

Java applications have greater flexibility, but they can pose a greater threat to security applications, can send confidential information from the local system to a remote host, or write viruses to a workstation's hard disk. Presumably, these security risks are reduced because applications are typically installed on a computer, as opposed to being downloaded dynamically over the Internet.

Even though Java applications can be used to create viruses and Trojan horses, they are still arguably more secure than traditional executables that may have been written in C or C++. This is because the Java language does not support pointers; therefore, it is difficult to use a Java program to subvert the memory space of another program. Furthermore, the Java class loader performs a check of the Java bytecode to verify that the program does not perform anything suspicious.

Several security holes have been found in the Java class loader and in some browser vendors' implementation of the Java Virtual Machine (JVM). JavaSoft, along with the Java licensees, has been working hard to fix any potential security problems. As these problems are fixed, and as signed code becomes widely implemented by browser and system software vendors, Java is likely to become more popular as a general purpose language for implementing secure, mission-critical applets and applications.

The Life Cycle of an Application

The life cycle of a Java application can be very different from that of an applet. An application might not contain the Applet life cycle methods such as *init( )* and *paint( )*. For Java applications, the only method automatically invoked by the Java environment is the *main( )* method.

The *main()* Method

Classes that execute as a Java application, must contain a method with the following signature:

```
public static void main(String argv[])
```

The *main( )* method typically includes the main processing logic of a Java application. The Java environment automatically calls the *main( )* method whenever an application is executed. The String array parameter must be present and is used to pass command line arguments into the program. The following code shows the basic outline of a Java application.

```
Public class MyApplication
{
    // Class data member declarations go here

    public static void main(String argv[])
    {
        // The main processing loop goes here
    }

    // Other methods go here
}
```

It is possible to create a program that can execute as an application and as an applet. This can be accomplished by defining the application class so that it extends the Applet class and explicitly calls the appropriate applet methods (*init()*, *start()*, and so on) from the *main()* method.

Terminating an Application

Ordinarily, an application terminates when all of its threads have terminated. In an applet, the Java environment automatically calls the *destroy()* method and terminates the applet's execution when the user exits the web browser.

You are likely to encounter many situations where a Java application does not automatically terminate. If an application creates a frame, for example, and displays it to the user, the program does not terminate unless explicitly programmed to do so. You can terminate the application by calling the *exit()* method, provided by the System class. The *exit()* method has the following signature:

```
public static void exit(int status)
```

As indicated in the preceding method signature, the System class's *exit()* method expects an integer parameter. This parameter indicates the exit status. For normal program termination, the status should be set to 0, as shown in the following line of code.

```
System.exit(0);
```

You can also use non-zero values to represent various error conditions.

 The System class is a *public* and *final* class that is included in the *java.lang* package. The purpose of this class is to provide Java programs with platform-independent abstractions for accessing system functionality. The System object, for example, provides access to standard input, output, and error streams. These streams are declared within the *System* class and can be accessed, as shown by the following line of code.

```
System.out.println("This text will be written to standard
➥output.");
```

The Java environment automatically instantiates a System object when an applet or application executes. In many cases, you will need to call the System object's *exit()* method in response to an event. You would call the System object's *exit()* method when, for example, the user clicks on an Exit button. Event handling is covered in Chapter 10, "Handling Events."

Input Parameters

To pass command line arguments to a Java application, you must code your program's *main()* method so that it can accept parameters. Listing 6.1 contains the *MyApplicationWithParameters* class definition. This application prints out the first three parameters passed to it from the command line.

Listing 6.1   Passing Parameters to an Application

```
Public class MyApplicationWithParameters
{
    public static void main(String m_Parameters[])
    {
        System.out.println("");
        System.out.println("Parameter 1 = " + m_Parameters[0]);
        System.out.println("Parameter 2 = " + m_Parameters[1]);
        System.out.println("Parameter 3 = " + m_Parameters[2]);
    }
}
```

In listing 6.1, the *main()* method expects one or more parameters. The following output shows an example of how *MyApplicationWithParameters* can be executed from the command line:

```
C:\>jview MyApplicationWithParameters parameter1 param-
eter2 etc.
Microsoft (R) Visual J++ Command-line Interpreter Version
1.00.6194
Copyright (C)Microsoft Corp 1996. All rights reserved.
Paramter 1 = parameter1
Paramter 2 = parameter2
Paramter 3 = etc.
C:\>
```

Summary

Java applets are programs that run within the context of a web browser. An applet's class must be derived from the Java Applet class. Because a web browser calls an applet's constructor when an applet is executed, all applets must be declared as *public* classes. An applet's life cycle methods define how the applet behaves within the context of a web browser.

The Java environment automatically calls an applet's *init( )*, *start( )*, and *paint( )* methods every time the applet is executed. If the web browser leaves an executing applet's web page, the Java environment automatically calls the applet's *stop( )* method. If the browser returns to the web page, the Java environment calls the applet's *start( )* method again.

Threads perform a processing task, or set of tasks, independently of the rest of a program. By using the Thread class, applets can be implemented so that they run within their own execution thread. The code for creating, starting, or restarting an applet's execution thread is typically located in the applet's *start( )* method. The code for stopping or suspending an applet's execution thread is typically located in the applet's *stop( )* method.

Java programs can be implemented as stand-alone applications. Java applications must contain a *main( )* method. Arguments can be passed into an application's *main( )* method as String parameters. An applet can also run as an application by explicitly calling the appropriate applet life cycle methods from the *main( )* method.

Java applications are not subject to the same security restrictions that are imposed on applets by web browsers; this has the dual effect of making applications more flexible and potentially less secure than most applets.

Questions

1. What applet methods does the Java environment call automatically?

2. Why does the Java sandbox prevent applets from writing to a local hard drive?

3. What access modifier must be used when declaring an applet?

4. How can code signing be employed to enable applets to securely access a local hard drive?

5. What method is typically used to create an applet's execution thread?

6. What method is typically used to terminate or suspend an applet's execution thread?

7. What interface must be implemented by any applet that runs within its own execution thread?

8. What method does the Java environment automatically call when executing a Java application?

9. How can arguments be passed to Java applications?

10. How can a Java applet be implemented so that it can also be executed as an application?

Answers

1. The Java environment automatically calls an applet's *init()*, *start()*, and *paint()* methods every time the applet is executed. The *stop()* method is called whenever the web browser leaves the web page containing the applet, and the *start()* method is called whenever the web browser returns to the page. If an applet is executing within its own thread, the Java environment calls the applet's *run()* method every time the applet is executed.

2. Severe security restrictions were implemented to ensure that web page-based applets could not damage, steal, or destroy information located on a user's computer.

3. A Java applet must be declared by using the *public* modifier. This is because the browser must be able to call the applet's class constructor.

4. When a Java applet is digitally signed, it is possible for a web browser to automatically ascertain that the applet hasn't been corrupted, identify the applet's creator, and determine whether the creator is a trusted source. In this way, the browser can enable trusted applets to perform certain tasks, such as writing to a local hard drive, while maintaining a high level of security.

5. The *start( )* method is typically used to create, start, or restart an applet's execution thread. This is because the Java environment automatically calls an applet's *start( )* method every time a browser accesses the applet's web page.

6. The *stop( )* method is typically used to terminate or suspend an applet's execution thread. This is because the Java environment automatically calls an applet's *stop( )* method every time a browser leaves the applet's web page.

7. Any applet that executes within its own thread must implement the Runnable interface. Any class that implements Runnable must include a public *run( )* method.

8. The Java environment automatically calls an application's *main( )* method.

9. Arguments can be passed into a Java application's *main( )* method as a String array.

10. Java applets can also execute as applications as long as the appropriate applet life cycle methods are explicitly invoked from the *main( )* method.

Chapter 7

Building Your First Java Applet By Using Visual J++

At this point you should be familiar with the Applet class, the class from which all applets are derived. In addition, you should have an understanding of the way an applet interacts with its environment. The time has come for you to build your first multithreaded Java applet by using the tools provided by the Visual J++ development environment. This chapter describes how Visual J++ enables you to create Java applets and HTML files quickly and easily.

This chapter covers the following topics:

➤ Creating an applet's HTML page

➤ Passing parameters to an applet from HTML

➤ Using the Visual J++ Applet Wizard

➤ Working with the code generated by the Applet Wizard

This chapter walks you through the steps required to build a multithreaded Java applet called PartyText by using the Visual J++ Applet Wizard. In addition, this chapter provides instructions on how to compile and execute Java programs by using the tools that are provided by Visual J++.

The PartyText applet takes a string value from an HTML input parameter and displays it on a web page. In addition, PartyText animates the text by varying the colors and positions of each character. The character colors are set by using the functionality that is provided by the Color class. To enable the applet to create these animation effects, PartyText is executed as a separate thread.

After working with this example, the ease of implementing threads in Java will be apparent. You will see that the flow of control in an applet makes it easy to manage the execution of the applet's thread through the use of the *start()* and *stop()* methods.

HTML Tags and Parameters

Before creating the PartyText applet, you'll need to understand some basic Hypertext Markup Language (HTML). An HTML file, when loaded by a Java-enabled web browser, provides the browser with the instructions that are required to run and display an applet.

A *Java-enabled web browser* is a browser that is capable of executing Java applets that are embedded in an HTML page. Some well-known Java-enabled browsers are the Netscape Navigator (2.0 or higher) and the Microsoft Internet Explorer (3.0 or higher) browsers.

HTML is not a programming language. Instead, it is a rendering or page layout description language. Traditionally, HTML has been used to tell a web browser about the text and graphics contained in a page. The browser, on the other hand, makes most of the decisions regarding how to display the information. The

HTML tag `<strong>` tells the browser, for example, that an area of text should be emphasized over the surrounding text. It is up to the browser to decide whether to display the text with a larger font, boldface, or italics. In fact, it is possible that a browser may ignore some HTML tags altogether.

Listing 7.1 shows the HTML for a basic web page containing a Java applet called MyApplet.

Listing 7.1   A Basic HTML File Containing a Java Applet

```
<html>
<head>
<title>MyApplet's HTML page</title>
</title>
<body>
<applet code=MyApplet.class>
</applet>
</body>
</html>
```

Basic HTML Tags

Certain HTML tags are required to create a web page. When a web browser reads a file, for example, it knows that the file contains HTML rendering code when it encounters the `<html>` tag. Furthermore, the browser assumes that everything that comes after the `<html>` tag is HTML text, until it encounters a closing `</html>` tag. Table 7.1 provides a listing of the basic HTML tags required to create a web page.

Table 7.1   Basic HTML Tags Required to Create a Web Page

Tag	Meaning
`<html>`	Beginning of an HTML page
`</html>`	End of an HTML page
`<title>`	Beginning of the title section

continues

Table 7.1	Continued
Tab	**Meaning**
`</title>`	End of a title section
`<body>`	Beginning of the body section
`</body>`	End of the body section

The `<applet>` Tag

The `<applet>` tag is used to define an embedded Java applet. It is important to note that an `<applet>` tag must be accompanied by an `</applet>` tag, which serves as a delimiter. In fact, if you don't include an `</applet>` tag, the applet does not execute.

You can use the `<applet>` tag's attributes to specify applet characteristics, such as the location of the applet's executable files and the size and position of the applet's display area. The following attributes can be used with the `<applet>` tag:

➤ width

➤ height

➤ align

➤ hspace

➤ vspace

➤ code

➤ codebase

➤ id

➤ name

The width Attribute

The value of the width attribute tells the browser how wide, in pixels, the applet should appear on the web page. You should be careful not to over allocate horizontal space because this can result in part of the applet being drawn outside the page's boundary.

The height Attribute

The value of the height attribute tells the browser how long, in pixels, the applet should appear on a web page.

The align Attribute

The value of the align attribute determines how an applet's display area will be aligned in the client browser. Table 7.2 contains the possible values for this attribute.

Table 7.2   Possible Values of the Align Attribute

ALIGN Value	Effect
left	Places the applet at the left margin
right	Places the applet at the right margin
top	Aligns the applet with the topmost item in the line
texttop	Aligns the top of the applet with the top of the tallest character in the line
middle	Aligns the applet with the middle of the baseline of the adjacent text
absmiddle	Aligns the applet with the middle of the tallest character in the line
baseline	Aligns the applet with the bottom of the baseline of the adjacent text
bottom	Aligns the applet with the bottom of the baseline of the adjacent text
absbottom	Aligns the bottom of the applet with the lowest item in the line

The hspace Attribute

The hspace (horizontal space) attribute specifies the number of pixels between an applet and the text displayed on the left and/or right.

The vspace Attribute

The vspace (vertical space) attribute specifies the number of pixels between an applet and the text above or below.

The code Attribute

The code attribute specifies the name of the Java applet's executable class file. For example:

```
<applet code="MyApplet.class">
</applet>
```

The code attribute in the preceding example specifies that the Java class file called MyApplet.class, located in the same directory as the HTML file, should be executed. You should also note that the .class extension can be left out when specifying the code attribute; the Java environment looks for the .class file regardless.

The codebase Attribute

The codebase attribute is used when the Java class file is not stored in the same directory as the HTML file. For example:

```
<applet code="MyApplet.class" codebase="classdir">
</applet>
```

The codebase attribute in the preceding example specifies that the Java class file called MyApplet.class is in the classdir subdirectory. The Java class loader locates this subdirectory in the HTML file's directory.

```
<applet code="MyApplet.class" codebase="/maindir/classdir">
</applet>
```

The codebase attribute in the preceding example specifies that the Java class file MyApplet.class is in the /maindir/classdir directory. This directory name represents an absolute path, as opposed to a relative path.

The id Attribute

The id attribute is used to give the applet a name so that it can be referenced from VBScript. By using VBScript, you can control the applet. You can call applet methods, for example, from VBScript. This use of the id attribute for scripting is consistent with how the id attribute is used in conjunction with the `<object>` tag. The `<object>` tag is used to embed ActiveX controls in HTML files. ActiveX is covered in Chapter 1, "Overview of Visual J++ and Java," and in Chapter 17, "Java and the ActiveX Platform."

The name Attribute

JavaScript is another scripting language that can be used to script Java applets. JavaScript references applets by using the name attribute instead of the id attribute. The main advantage of JavaScript is that both IE and Netscape Navigator provide native support for it.

Passing Parameters to an Applet

Parameters can be passed to Java applets from an HTML file by using one or more `<param>` tags. The `<param>` tag must be placed between the `<applet>` and `</applet>` tags.

The following portion of HTML, for example, passes a parameter with a value of `"This string is being passed as a parameter."` to the MyApplet applet:

```
<applet code="MyApplet">
<param name=Parameter1 value="This string is being passed
➥as a parameter.">
</applet>
```

The attributes of the `<param>` tag are name and value. The name attribute specifies the name of the parameter. The name can be used by the Java applet to retrieve the string specified by the value attribute.

The parameter can be retrieved by the applet by using the *getParameter()* method provided by the Applet class. If a parameter was specified in an HTML file, for example, as shown in the previous code, the value attribute could be retrieved by a Java applet with the following line of code.

```
String parameter_value = getParameter("Parameter1");
```

The preceding line of Java code retrieves the HTML parameter with the name `Parameter1`, which is specified in the HTML code shown in this section. The result of the preceding line of code is to store the value `"This string is being passed as a parameter."` in a String object called parameter_value.

The cabbase Parameter

Cabinet files, which are also referred to as cab files, were briefly discussed in Chapter 5, "Java Interfaces and Packages." Microsoft built the capability to recognize cab files into the Internet Explorer 3.0 (and higher) (IE) browser. Cab files can be used to reduce the time it takes to load and reload Java applets. Because cab files are compressed, they take less time to download over a network. IE can access Java packages and individual class files that are stored in a cab file.

Creating cab files is covered in Chapter 17, "Java and the ActiveX Platform."

To instruct IE to look for your Java classes in a cab file, you must specify cabbase parameter in your applet's HTML file as shown in the following example:

```
<param name="cabbase" value="classfiles.cab">
```

If the cabbase parameter is specified as shown in the preceding example, the IE browser looks for the required Java class files in a cab file called `classfiles.cab`. When the cab file is located in a different directory from the HTML file, you can specify a path name for the cab file using the cabbase parameter. For example, if the cab file is located in a subdirectory called `cabdirectory`, the cabbase parameter could be specified as follows:

```
<param name="cabbase" value="cabdirectory/cabfile.cab">
```

Alternatively, you can use the codebase attribute of the `<applet>` tag to specify the cab file's directory, as shown in the following example:

```
<applet code="MyApplet.class" codebase="cabdirectory">
<param name="cabbase" value="cabfile.cab">
</applet>
```

In either of the two preceding examples, the IE browser would find the `cabfile.cab` file in the directory called `cabdirectory`.

If you use cab files, you should place the uncompressed class files in the applet's directory. This is because many people who access your applet, especially over the Internet, will not be using IE. Therefore, they won't be able to extract the applet from a cab file. Java-enabled browsers, other than IE, simply ignore the cabbase parameter and look for the applet as specified by the code attribute of the `<applet>` tag.

Catering for Java-Challenged Browsers

After you begin putting your Java applets on a web site, you might be surprised by how many electronic mail messages you get from people complaining that they can't use your applets. After investigating, you may discover that many of these individuals do not have a Java-enabled browser—not only are they unable to see your applets, they can't see any applets! You can save them and yourself some time by putting a descriptive message between the `<applet>` and `</applet>` tags, as shown in the following example:

```
<applet code="MyApplet.class" >
If you can see this message, your browser does not
➥support Java.
</applet>
```

Any browser capable of running Java applets ignores the text between the `<applet>` and `<applet>` tags. Other browsers, however, display the message to the user. If you want to be really nice, you can include a hotlink to a site from which the user can download a Java-enabled browser.

The Visual J++ Java Applet Wizard

One of the most powerful tools provided by the Visual J++ development environment is the Java Applet Wizard. This tool is similar to the Visual C++ AppWizard in that it enables programmers to quickly create starter code for a project. Based on the options chosen, the Applet Wizard creates the Java source code and HTML files. When it creates the Java source code file, the Applet Wizard automatically includes the appropriate references to the standard Java packages and classes.

The remainder of this chapter discusses how the Applet Wizard can be used to create a multithreaded applet called PartyText. In addition, this chapter also covers the Visual J++ tools that enable you to edit, compile, and execute Java programs.

Creating the PartyText Project with the Applet Wizard

Creating a generic project without the Applet Wizard is discussed in Chapter 4, "Java Classes and Objects." To use the Applet Wizard, you must start by creating a project. To accomplish this, choose New from the Visual J++ File pull-down menu. The New dialog box appears. The New dialog box can be used to create several file types, such as a text file, project workspace, resource template, or a bitmap file. When you choose project workspace, the New Project Workspace dialog box displays, as shown in figure 7.1.

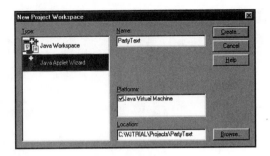

Figure 7.1:
You can start the Java Applet Wizard from the New Project Workspace dialog box.

In the dialog box, shown in figure 7.1, the user has already se-lected the Java Applet Wizard option and has specified the name of the project as PartyText. This name will be given to the project and the directory containing the project's files. By default, the same name will be given to the initial Java source code and HTML files created by the Applet Wizard. The Java Applet Wizard guides the user through up to five options dialog boxes. The Applet Wizard uses these options when it creates the project's starter files.

Applet Wizard Step 1

In Step 1 of the Applet Wizard, the user is presented with the dialog box shown in figure 7.2.

As shown in figure 7.2, the user can specify that the sample code generated by the Applet Wizard should run As an applet only or As an applet and as an application. If the user chooses to create the program as an applet only, the Java source code file is gener-ated with all of the appropriate applet life cycle methods (*init()*, *paint()*, and so on). If the user decides that the program should also run as an application, the applet source code will include a *main()* method in addition to the applet life cycle methods. The *main()* method will include calls to the appropriate applet methods.

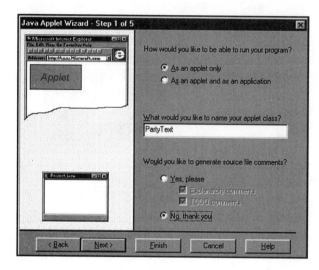

Figure 7.2:

Applet Wizard Step 1.

In Step 1, the user is given the option of changing the name of the initial Java source code file and class name. In figure 7.2, the user has left the default name, which is PartyText.

Finally, the user can choose whether to have the Applet Wizard include instructive comments within the applet's source code. Explanatory comments describe the functionality of the generated commands and methods (// A thread is created in the *start()* method). *TODO* comments instruct the programmer to add additional code (// Add class constructor code here) where necessary. In figure 7.2, the user has elected not to generate comments.

After clicking the Next> button in Step 1, the user is presented with the Applet Wizard's Step 2 options, as shown in figure 7.3.

The user can navigate through all of the options dialog boxes provided by the Applet Wizard by clicking on the appropriate navigation buttons (<Back and Next>) at the bottom of each dialog box.

At any time during the Applet Wizard setup process, you can decide to click the Finish button. This action causes all remaining options to be set to their default values. Before you use this feature, however, make sure you know what all the default values are.

Applet Wizard Step 2

In figure 7.3, the user selected the option that causes the Applet Wizard to generate a starter HTML file for the PartyText applet.

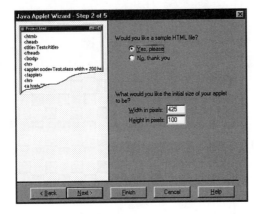

Figure 7.3:
Applet Wizard Step 2.

The user also specified that the applet's display area should be set to a width of 425 pixels and a height of 100 pixels. The applet's height and width are set in the starter Java program. In addition, the same dimensions are set in the applet's HTML file by using the height and width attributes of the <applet> tags.

After clicking the Next> button in figure 7.3, the Applet Wizard's Step 3 options display, as shown in figure 7.4.

Applet Wizard Step 3

In Step 3 of the Applet Wizard, the user specifies whether the applet is to be single or multithreaded and if the applet should include code for handling mouse events (see fig. 7.4).

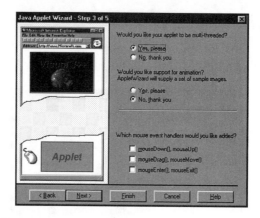

Figure 7.4:

Applet Wizard Step 3.

If the applet is to be multithreaded, the user can specify whether the Applet Wizard should generate code for a sample animation. The sample animation makes use of several techniques that are not required for the PartyText animation. Therefore, this option is not selected in figure 7.4. Animation is covered in detail in Chapter 16, "Fun with Sound and Animation."

In figure 7.4, the user specified that the applet should be multithreaded. Consequently, the generated applet will include the appropriate thread creation and management code in the *start()* and *stop()* methods. In addition, a *run()* method will be included in the applet.

After clicking on the Next> button in figure 7.4, the Applet Wizard's Step 4 options display, as shown in figure 7.5.

Applet Wizard Step 4

In Step 4, the user defines the parameters that are to be passed
into the applet from its HTML file. By using the Applet Wizard,
the user can define as many parameters as required. Note that the
dialog box for Step 4 provides two buttons near the upper-right
corner for creating and deleting parameter definitions. As shown
in figure 7.5, the following information regarding the parameters
can be specified in Step 4 of the Applet Wizard:

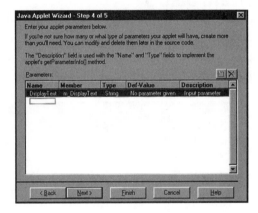

Figure 7.5:

Applet Wizard Step 4.

Table 7.3	Parameter Options in the Applet Wizard
Option	**Description**
Name	The name of the parameter. This name is defined in the applet's HTML file as an attribute of the `<param>` tag. The Applet Wizard generates the Java code required for the applet to get the parameter.
Member	The name of the class variable that ultimately holds the value of the parameter.
Type	The data type of the member. The default is a String object; however, this field provides a list box that enables the user to choose any valid data type.
Default Value	This is the value assigned to the member variable by the Java program when the parameter is not specified.
Description	A description of the parameter or its use.

In figure 7.5, an input parameter called DisplayText is defined. This parameter is used to specify the text passed into the applet from the HTML file. The PartyText applet retrieves this parameter and stores its value in a member variable called m_DisplayText.

After clicking the Next> button in figure 7.5, the Applet Wizard's Step 5 options display, as shown in figure 7.6.

Applet Wizard Step 5

The Applet Wizard automatically includes a public method, called *getAppInfo()*, in the generated Java applet code. In Step 5 of the Applet Wizard, the user specifies any text that would be useful to return from the *getAppInfo()* method.

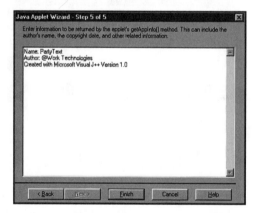

Figure 7.6:
Applet Wizard Step 5.

After the applet information is specified, the user can click the Finish button. The Applet Wizard then displays all of the options chosen in Steps 1 through 5 in the New Project Information dialog box, as shown in figure 7.7.

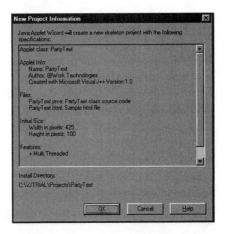

Figure 7.7:
The New Project Information dialog box shows all of the options specified for a project.

When the New Project Information dialog box displays, the user can change any of the options specified in Steps 1 through 5, by clicking the Cancel button. This action returns the user to Step 5 of the Applet Wizard. Any option can be changed by backing through the steps (clicking on the <Back button). Alternatively, if the user is satisfied with the information displayed in the New Project Information dialog box, she can click on the OK button, which causes the Applet Wizard to generate the appropriate Java and HTML files.

The PartyText Applet's Visual J++ Project

By using the same options that are specified in figures 7.1 through 7.7, the Applet Wizard automatically generates the following directory and files:

➤ PartyText. The project's directory.

➤ PartyText.java. The Java applet source code file.

➤ PartyText.html. An HTML file containing the PartyText applet.

➤ PartyText.mdp. The Microsoft Developer Studio Project file.

When you want to work with an existing project in Visual J++, you must open the project file for the project. Project files have a `.mdp` extension.

When you create a project in Visual J++, several files are created in addition to the applet and HTML files. For the PartyText applet, these other files include **PartyText.mak**, **PartyText.dep**, and **PartyText.ncp** files. Although all of these files are important for the project, this chapter only focuses on the code and HTML files that are required to execute the PartyText applet.

Figure 7.8 shows the PartyText project as displayed in Visual J++.

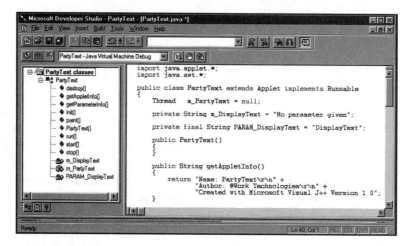

Figure 7.8:

The PartyText project displayed with the Project Workspace and the text editor windows visible.

As illustrated by the ClassView pane, shown in figure 7.8, the Applet Wizard automatically includes all of the required applet methods, namely *init()*, *start()*, *stop()*, *run()*, and *paint()*, in the Java source code file that it generates. In addition, the Applet Wizard also includes several other methods: *getAppletInfo()*, *getParameterInfo()*, and *destroy()*, as well as a class constructor.

Obviously, the Java Applet Wizard takes much of the front end work out of developing Java projects. The following sections discuss the HTML file and Java code that are generated by the Applet Wizard, and the changes that are required to create the final version of the PartyText applet.

The PartyText Applet's HTML File

Figure 7.9 shows the HTML file generated by the Applet Wizard for the PartyText applet in the text editor.

To access an HTML file in a Visual J++ project, switch to the FileView pane in the Project Workspace window.

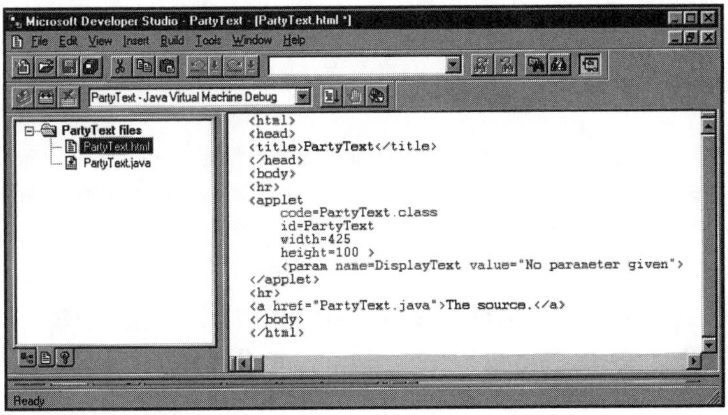

Figure 7.9:
The PartyText Applet's HTML file as generated by the Applet Wizard.

As shown in figure 7.9, the Applet Wizard automatically includes all the appropriate HTML tags and attributes in the HTML file that it generates. Notice also that the `<applet>` tag's width and height attributes are set in accordance with the options specified in Step 2 of the Applet Wizard (see fig. 7.3). In addition, a `<param>` tag is included in the HTML file for a parameter called DisplayText, which is set to the default value specified in Step 4 of the Applet Wizard (see fig. 7.5).

Editing HTML in the Visual J++ Text Editor

The Visual J++ text editor provides basic functionality for creating and editing HTML files. Just as the text editor automatically color-codes Java source code, it also color-codes HTML, making it easier to read the file as well as to spot errors. Table 7.4 provides a listing of the types of HTML text identified by the text editor.

Table 7.4 Default Text Editor HTML Colors

HTML Text	Default Color
tag text	purple
required attribute	pink
optional attribute	orange
attribute value	blue
normal text	black
<,>,/	blue

You can define customized settings and text types for the text editor by creating a user defined type file. For more information, see the Visual J++ Books Online User Guide.

Modifying the PartyText Applet's HTML File

Although the Applet Wizard automatically sets the default value of the DisplayText parameter in the PartyText applet's HTML file, this parameter can also be used to cause the applet to display a more interesting message. Therefore, in the interest of fun, the DisplayText parameter's value should be changed to something more festive. Figure 7.10 shows the HTML file with the DisplayText parameter's value set to `"It's time to have some fun!"` This value will be passed into the PartyText applet.

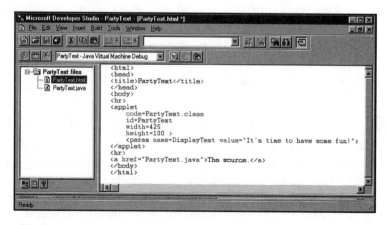

Figure 7.10:

A more festive message in the PartyText Applet's HTML File.

The Java Source Code Generated by the Applet Wizard

Listing 7.2 contains the full listing of the PartyText applet's Java source code file, as initially generated by the Applet Wizard.

Listing 7.2   The PartyText Applet as Generated by the Applet Wizard

```java
import java.applet.*;
import java.awt.*;

public class PartyText extends Applet implements Runnable
{
   Thread m_PartyText = null;

   private String m_DisplayText = "No parameter given";

   private final String PARAM_DisplayText = "DisplayText";

   public PartyText()
   {
   }

   public String getAppletInfo()
   {
      return "Name: PartyText\r\n" +
             "Author: @Work Technologies\r\n" +
             "Created with Microsoft Visual J++ Version 1.0";
   }

   public String[][] getParameterInfo()
   {
      String[][] info =
      {
         { PARAM_DisplayText, "String", "Input parameter" },
      };
      return info;
   }
```

continues

Listing 7.2   Continued

```java
public void init()
{
   String param;

   param = getParameter(PARAM_DisplayText);
   if (param != null)
      m_DisplayText = param;

   resize(425, 100);

}

public void destroy()
{
}

public void paint(Graphics g)
{
   g.drawString("Running: " + Math.random(), 10, 20);
}

public void start()
{
   if (m_PartyText == null)
   {
      m_PartyText = new Thread(this);
      m_PartyText.start();
   }
}

public void stop()
{
   if (m_PartyText != null)
   {
      m_PartyText.stop();
      m_PartyText = null;
   }
}
```

```
public void run()
{
   while (true)
   {
      try
      {
         repaint();
         Thread.sleep(50);
      }
      catch (InterruptedException e)
      {
         stop();
      }
   }
}
```

Required Packages

Because the PartyText class is an applet, the java.applet package must be imported. In addition, the java.awt package is imported into PartyText. The java.awt package—AWT stands for Abstract Windowing Toolkit—includes the classes required to draw on the applet's display area and to create a user interface.

Class Declaration and Constructor

The PartyText class is defined as a public class that extends the Applet class. All Java applets must be declared as public classes so that they can be instantiated by a web browser. Furthermore, the PartyText class implements the Runnable interface, which is required for the applet to execute on a separate thread.

The Applet Wizard automatically generates a class constructor for PartyText. Although this constructor is not required and has no code, it could become useful in the future. If the PartyText class, for example, is instantiated by another class, the *init()* method would never be called by the Java environment. In this case, the *PartyText()* class constructor could be used to perform the necessary initializations.

Variable Declarations

The Applet Wizard created declarations in the PartyText applet for the following variables:

➤ *PARAM_DisplayText*. The name of the applet's input parameter, as defined in the HTML file, is stored in this variable.

➤ *m_DisplayText*. The value of the input parameter, as defined in the HTML file, is stored in this member variable.

➤ *m_PartyText*. This Thread object is used for the applet's execution thread.

The *getAppletInfo()* Method

The Applet Wizard automatically creates a *getAppletInfo()* method. The PartyText applet's *getAppletInfo()* method overrides the *getAppletInfo()* method provided by the Applet class. This method can be called by another object (Java program or ActiveX control) to obtain information about the applet. This method returns a String value that contains the data defined in Step 5 of the Applet Wizard (see fig. 7.6). Carriage return (/r) and line feed (/n) characters are appended to the end of each line to ensure that when the string is printed, the lines appear in a proper format—on separate lines.

The *getParameterInfo()* Method

The Applet Wizard automatically creates a *getParameterInfo()* method. The PartyText applet's *getParameterInfo()* method overrides the one provided by the Applet class. Just as the *getAppletInfo()* method can be called from another object, the *getParameterInfo()* method can also be called in this manner. In the PartyText applet, the *getParameterInfo()* method returns a two-dimensional String array called info. This array consists of sets of three strings. In the PartyText applet, info[0][0] through info[0][2] is one set of String values. In a typical *getParameterInfo()* method, each set contains:

➤ The name of the parameter as specified in the HTML file

➤ The object or data type of the parameter

➤ A description of the parameter

If a second parameter had been passed to the PartyText applet called OtherDisplayText, for example, then the info array would be set as follows:

```
String[][] info =
{
    { PARAM_DisplayText, "String", "Input parameter" },
    { PARAM_OtherDisplayText, "String", "Other input
➡parameter" },
};
```

The *init()* Method

When an applet is executed, the Java environment calls the *init()* method first. In the PartyText applet, a String variable called param is declared in the *init()* method for the sole purpose of getting the input parameter. Next, the *getParameter()* method provided by the Applet class is invoked to retrieve the parameter and store its value in the param variable.

If no parameter is specified in the PartyText applet's HTML file, the *getParameter()* method returns a null value. Alternatively, if a value is specified in the HTML file, that value is stored in the member variable called m_DisplayText. Finally, the PartyText applet invokes the *resize()* method, which is provided by the Applet class, to size the applet's display area in accordance with the size options specified in Step 2 of the Java Applet Wizard (refer to figure 7.3).

The *destroy()* Method

The Applet Wizard automatically included a *destroy()* method when it created the PartyText applet. Although this method does not contain any code, it could be used to gracefully dispose of any resources when the user exits the web browser.

The *paint()* Method

The *paint()* method is used to update an applet's display area. It is the last method called automatically by the Java environment when an applet executes. The *paint()* method can be called, either automatically by the Java environment or explicitly by other methods, whenever the applet's display area must be refreshed or updated.

The standard *paint()* method expects a Graphics object as a parameter (The Graphics class is discussed in Chapter 9, "Working with Graphics, Fonts, and Colors.") In the case of the PartyText applet, the Graphics object passed to the *paint()* method is the Graphics context of the applet's display area. Therefore, when PartyText changes the display area, the user will see the change on the applet's web page.

When the Applet Wizard creates a Java applet, it automatically includes sample code in the *paint()* method. In the PartyText applet's *paint()* method, the *drawString()* method is called to draw a String object consisting of the text "Running: " concatenated with a random number that is generated by using the Math class. This string is drawn within the applet's display area at the x and y coordinates of 10 and 20 respectively. Although the *paint()* method generated by the Applet Wizard does not do exactly what the final version of PartyText is supposed to do, it does provide a good starting point in that it draws text to the applet's display area.

The *start()* Method

The Java environment automatically calls an applet's *start()* method whenever an applet's web page is accessed. In the PartyText applet's *start()* method, a Thread object, m_PartyText, is created if the applet's execution thread has not already been created—m_PartyText is null. After the Thread object is created, its *start()* method must be called to begin the Thread object's execution.

If you try to start the same thread more than once, you will generate an IllegalThreadStateException error.

The *stop()* Method

The Java environment automatically calls an applet's *stop()* method whenever the browser leaves the applet's web page. In the PartyText applet's *stop()* method, the applet's execution thread, m_PartyText, is stopped so that the applet does not continue to execute when a user leaves its web page. In addition, the m_PartyText Thread object is set to null. This causes the Java garbage collection process to automatically free any resources used by the previously allocated Thread object, because the object is no longer referenced by the applet.

In a multithreaded applet, the *start()* and *stop()* methods are highly dependent upon one another. Suppose PartyText, for example, had to perform a great deal of processing at startup. In that case you probably would not want to eliminate and recreate the applet's Thread every time the user leaves and returns to the applet's web page. Instead of stopping the PartyText applet's execution thread, you can just pause it. You can code the *stop()* method, for example, as follows:

```
public void stop()
{
   if (m_PartyText != null)
      m_PartyText.pause();
}
```

If you code the *stop()* method as shown in the preceding code, the *start()* method should be coded as follows:

```
public void start()
{
   if (m_PartyText == null)
   {
      m_PartyText = new Thread(this);
      m_PartyText.start();
   }
```

```
    else
        m_PartyText.resume();
}
```

When you code the *start()* method as shown in the preceding code, the applet's execution thread is only created when the m_PartyText Thread object is null. Therefore, when a user leaves the applet's web page, the execution thread is paused in the *stop()* method. When the user returns to the web page, the applet's execution thread is restarted or resumed. It is not necessary to create a brand new Thread object.

The *run()* Method

The *run()* method typically contains the main programming logic of a multithreaded applet. The PartyText applet's *run()* method creates an infinite loop that continually calls the *repaint()* method, provided by the Applet class. The *repaint()* method, in turn, calls the *update()* method, which is also provided by the Applet class. Finally, the *update()* method calls the *paint()* method, which updates the applet's display area.

You may ask why the *run()* method doesn't call the *paint()* method directly? The reason it doesn't is because when *repaint()* is called, the Java environment creates a separate thread and invokes the *update()* method. The *update()* method clears the screen and then calls the *paint()* method. Invoking the *paint()* method in this way causes it to execute on yet another thread. The benefit of this is that the applet can continue running instead of waiting for the *paint()* method to complete. This methodology for updating the applet's display area is especially useful for an applet that has a complex *paint()* method that takes a long time to execute.

The *run()* method employs exception handling. Don't be alarmed if the try and catch commands are not familiar to you. Exception handling is covered in Chapter 14, "Advanced Multithreading and Exception Handling." Exception handling had to be included in the *run()* method because it calls the Thread object's *sleep()*

method. The *sleep( )* method does not work without being enclosed within a try/catch block. This method is invoked to momentarily pause the applet's execution. Please note that the *sleep(50)* causes PartyText to pause for 50 milliseconds. In this way, the user can see the applet's animation effect. Without using the *sleep( )* method, the applet updates the screen far too quickly for the user to read the output of the *paint( )* method. Furthermore, by using the *sleep( )* method, the applet is prevented from overusing system resources.

Running the Code Generated by the Applet Wizard

At this point, you should be familiar with the sample code that is generated by the Visual J++ Java Applet Wizard. As you can see, the Applet Wizard is an extremely useful tool for creating an initial Java project. For the PartyText applet, most of the data members, code, and even the HTML can be generated automatically. Because PartyText is a complete applet, with all of the necessary files and code, you can execute it from within the Visual J++ environment.

Compiling the PartyText Applet

When you're ready to test a Java applet, you can execute it from within Visual J++. First, however, you must compile the applet and any new classes on which that applet depends. When you compile a Java program in Visual J++, Microsoft's Java compiler, which is referred to as the JVC (JVC.EXE), is invoked.

To compile the PartyText applet, you can choose one of the following functions from the Visual J++ Build pull-down menu:

➤ *Compile.* This function compiles the `PartyText.java` source code file only. This option is only available when the user is editing the source code file in the Visual J++ text editor and only compiles the file that is currently visible in the editor.

➤ *Build PartyText.* This function compiles the `PartyText.java` source file, as well as any other Java source files in the project. This function only compiles Java source files that have changed since the last build. In the case of the PartyText applet, however, only one Java source file exists.

➤ *Rebuild All.* This function compiles `PartyText.java`, as well any other Java source files in the project, regardless of whether the files have changed since the last build.

➤ *Batch Build.* This Function compiles `PartyText.java` in the background. This background job can be run as a build or as a rebuild all. In addition, the background build can create debug or release versions at the same time.

If the PartyText applet does not have any compile errors, the JVC creates a file called `PartyText.class` within the project's directory. For projects with more than one class, the JVC creates a separate class file containing Java bytecode for each Java class defined in the project. JVC messages are displayed in the Visual J++ Output window, which is typically positioned at the bottom of the Visual J++ application's display area. Figure 7.11 shows the messages generated by the JVC for a successful compile.

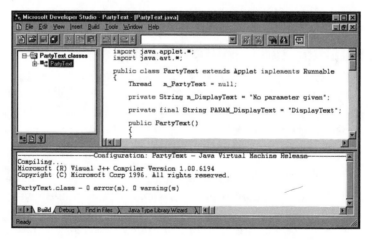

Figure 7.11:

The JVC messages generated by a successful compile in the Output window.

Fixing Compiler Errors

In a perfect world, there would never be such things as compiler errors, or any other programming error for that matter. Unfortunately, it's not a perfect world and compiler errors do occur frequently. Fortunately, however, Visual J++ and the JVC provides functionality that can help you quickly locate and fix these errors. Figure 7.12 shows an example of an error message put out by the JVC when it finds a compiler error in a Java program.

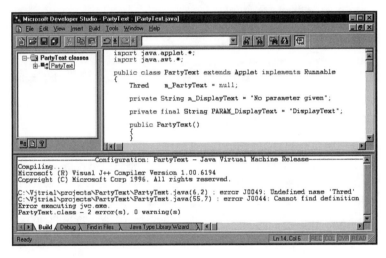

Figure 7.12:

An example of the JVC messages generated by a unsuccessful compile in the Output window.

As illustrated in figure 7.12, the JVC writes error messages to the Output window. These error messages indicate that the JVC could not find either a class or a fundamental data type called 'Thred'. This is a rather obvious, although not uncommon, typographical error. To fix the error, first the user must get to the source code line in which it occurs. When the user double-clicks an error message in the Output window, the Visual J++ text editor displays and indicates the line that caused the error. In most cases, after the error is found, it can be easily fixed. This process is illustrated in figure 7.13. After locating the erroneous line, the programmer can change 'Thred' to 'Thread'.

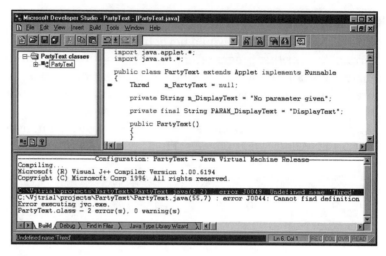

Figure 7.13:

By clicking on a error message in the Output window, the user can quickly locate the errant line of code.

In addition to assisting the programmer find the location of a line that causes a compiler error, Visual J++ also provides context-sensitive help. If the programmer clicks the line containing an error, as shown in figure 7.13, and presses the F1 key, a help window displays, showing information about the error.

Executing the PartyText Applet in Visual J++

After PartyText has been successfully compiled, the applet can be executed by choosing Execute PartyText from the Visual J++ Build menu. When the applet executes, the Internet Explorer displays the `PartyText.html` file created by the Applet Wizard (see fig. 7.10). Figure 7.14 shows the PartyText applet, as created by the Applet Wizard, executing in the Internet Explorer.

As you can see, the Applet Wizard can be used to create a complete multithreaded applet that draws text to its display area on a web page. The next section discusses how the PartyText applet can be modified to make it more interesting.

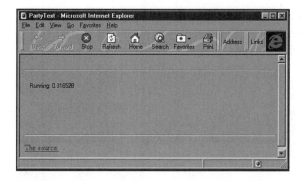

Figure 7.14:

The Applet Wizard PartyText applet executing in Internet Explorer.

Modifying the Code Generated by the Applet Wizard

Figure 7.15 shows what the final version of the PartyText applet should look like when running in the Internet Explorer.

Figure 7.15:

The final PartyText applet executing in Internet Explorer.

As you can see, although the code generated by the Applet Wizard provides an excellent starting point, the final PartyText applet is somewhat more interesting. To create the output shown in figure 7.15, the code generated by the Applet Wizard must be modified. Several new data members must be declared. In addition, changes must be made to both the *init()* and *paint()* methods.

Listing 7.3 shows the final PartyText applet. The code that was changed or added to the PartyText applet is shown in boldface. These changes are discussed in the next few sections.

Listing 7.3 The Final PartyText Applet

```java
import java.applet.*;
import java.awt.*;

public class PartyText extends Applet implements Runnable
{
    Thread m_PartyText = null;

    private String m_DisplayText = "No parameter given";

    private final String PARAM_DisplayText = "DisplayText";

    private Color[] m_TextColors =
        {Color.red, Color.black, Color.white, Color.yellow};

    private int m_nColorIndex;

    private int m_nCharIndex;

    private char[] m_SeparatedDisplayText;

    public PartyText()
    {
    }

    public String getAppletInfo()
    {
        return "Name: PartyText\r\n" +
               "Author: @Work Technologies\r\n" +
               "Created with Microsoft Visual J++ Version 1.0";
    }

    public String[][] getParameterInfo()
    {
        String[][] info =
        {
```

```
                { PARAM_DisplayText, "String", "Input parameter" },
        };
        return info;
    }

    public void init()
    {
        String param;

        param = getParameter(PARAM_DisplayText);
        if (param != null)
            m_DisplayText = param;

        resize(425, 100);

        m_SeparatedDisplayText =  new char
➥[m_DisplayText.length()];
        m_DisplayText.getChars(0,
➥m_DisplayText.length(),m_SeparatedDisplayText,0);

        setFont(new Font("TimesRoman",Font.BOLD,36));
    }

    public void destroy()
    {
    }

    public void paint(Graphics g)
    {
        int x_coord;
        int y_coord;
        for (m_nCharIndex = 0;
            m_nCharIndex < m_SeparatedDisplayText.length;
            m_nCharIndex++)
        {
            g.setColor(m_TextColors[m_nColorIndex]);
            if (m_nColorIndex == 3)
                m_nColorIndex = 0;
            else
                m_nColorIndex++;
```

continues

Listing 7.3   Continued

```
        x_coord = (int) (Math.random()*10+15*m_nCharIndex);
        y_coord = (int) (Math.random()*10+36);
        g.drawChars
➥(m_SeparatedDisplayText,m_nCharIndex,1,x_coord,y_coord);
    }
  }

  public void start()
  {
    if (m_PartyText == null)
    {
      m_PartyText = new Thread(this);
      m_PartyText.start();
    }
  }
  public void stop()
  {
    if (m_PartyText != null)
    {
      m_PartyText.stop();
      m_PartyText = null;
    }
  }

  public void run()
  {
    while (true)
    {
      try
      {
        repaint();
        Thread.sleep(50);
      }
      catch (InterruptedException e)
      {
        stop();
      }
    }
  }
}
}
```

Required Data Members

The final version of the PartyText applet introduces several effects that are not provided by the code generated by the Applet Wizard. To add this new functionality, the following data members were added to PartyText:

➤ *m_TextColors.* This data member is an array of Color objects used to set and reset the color of the text written to the applet's display area.

➤ *m_nColorIndex.* This integer is used as the index of the m_TextColors array.

➤ *m_SeparatedDisplayText.* The text passed into PartyText as a parameter is stored in this character array. When PartyText draws to its display area, it places each character of this array in a slightly different position. Consequently, the text appears to vibrate.

➤ *m_nCharIndex.* This integer is used as the index of the m_SeparatedDisplayText array.

Changes to the *init()* Method

Three lines of code must be added to the *init()* method generated by the Applet Wizard. First, the m_SeperatedDisplayText character array must be allocated; to allocate an array of the correct size, the *length()* method provided by the String class is used. In the PartyText applet, the *length()* method returns an integer value equal to the number of characters in the m_DisplayText String object. Next, the individual characters of the m_DisplayText String object are loaded into the m_SperatedDisplayText character array using the *getChars()* method provided by the String class. This method retrieves the individual characters of m_DisplayText, starting at position 0 and ending at the last character in the String object, and places the characters in the array starting at position 0.

The last operation performed in the *init()* method is to set the applet's default font by using the *setFont()* method provided by the Component class. An applet can access this method because the Applet class is derived from the Component class.

Changes to the *paint()* Method

The final PartyText applet's *paint()* method creates several effects when it displays text. First of all, instead of writing a random number to the display area, it writes the text specified by the input parameter in the applet's HTML file. Furthermore, each time that the final PartyText applet draws a character to the display area, it is shown in a completely different color and in a slightly different position. To achieve these effects, several changes must be made to the PartyText applet's *paint()* method.

In the final PartyText applet, a for loop is included in the *paint()* method. For each iteration of this loop, a different character from the m_SeparatedDisplayText array is drawn to the applet's display area by using the *drawChars()* method. In addition, the *paint()* method calls the *setColor()* method so that each character is drawn with a different color. The position of each character varies because the x and y coordinates that are set by using the random number that is generated by calling the Math class' *random()* method.

Finally, after all of the appropriate changes are made to PartyText, and the code has been successfully compiled, the applet can generate the animated output that was illustrated in figure 7.15.

Summary

To run a Java applet, its HTML page must include an `<applet>` tag with the appropriate attributes specified. The `<applet>` tag must always be accompanied by a closing `</applet>` tag. The code attribute defines the name of the Java class file to be executed. The height and width attributes define the size of the applet's display area in pixels. When you want to place your Java class files in a separate directory, you can use the codebase attribute to specify the directory.

Parameters can be passed into a Java applet from an HTML file by using the `<param>` tag. The `<param>` tag's name attribute can be used to identify the parameter to the Java applet and the value attribute specifies the value of the parameter. Microsoft's Internet Explorer 3.0 (and higher) can provide built-in support for the cabbase parameter. By using this parameter you can store all of your class files in a compressed cabinet file that the Internet Explorer can access. Cab files can be downloaded faster and can also be cached to your workstation's hard drive.

The Visual J++ Applet Wizard is similar to the Visual C++ AppWizard in that it enables programmers to quickly create starter files for a Java project. Based on the options specified, the Java Applet Wizard can create a source code file that provides sample code for an animation, uses multiple threads, and accepts input parameters from an HTML file. The Applet Wizard can also generate an applet's HTML file with all of the appropriate tags and attributes.

The Java compiler provided with Visual J++ is called the JVC. This utility is fully integrated with the Visual J++ environment. When you compile a Java program in Visual J++, the output of the JVC is displayed in the Output window. This output includes any compiler errors detected by the JVC. Double-clicking a compiler error message causes Visual J++ to display and indicate the line of code that caused the error in the text editor. In addition, context-sensitive help for JVC error messages can be accessed from Visual J++ by clicking the error message and pressing the F1 key.

Questions

1.   Which HTML tags are used to delimit a web page?

2.   Which applet life cycle methods are typically present in any multithreaded Java applet?

3.   In which applet method is the applet's execution thread typically created?

4.   Which method is used to get a parameter from an applet's HTML file?

5.   If an applet attempts to get a parameter that is not specified in its HTML file, what value is returned?

6. What does the Rebuild All function on the Visual J++ Build pull-down menu do?

7. What does the Build function on the Visual J++ Build pull-down menu do?

8. When you store your Java class files in a cabinet file, why should you also store the uncompressed class files in the same directory on your web server?

Answers

1. The <html> tag signifies the beginning of and HTML file and </html> signifies the end of an HTML file. These tags are understood by any standard web browser.

2. The most common life cycle methods in any applet are *init()*, *start()*, *stop()*, and *paint()*. The *run()* method is almost always present in a multithreaded applet.

3. An applet's execution thread is typically created in the *start()* method. This is because this method is called automatically by the Java environment whenever a user either visits or revisits the applet's web page.

4. The applet class provides a *getParameter()* method that can be used to retrieve an applet's parameter(s) from an HTML page.

5. A null value is returned by the *getParameter()* method when the parameter is not specified in the applet's HTML file.

6. The Rebuild All function on the Visual J++ Build pull-down menu compiles all of the Java source files in a Java project regardless of whether the files have changed since the last compile.

7. The Build function on the Visual J++ Build pull-down menu compiles any Java source files that have changed since the last compile.

8. When you use cab files, you should also store the uncompressed class files in the applet's code directory because not all web browsers can read cab files.

Chapter 8

The Visual J++ Debugger

The integrated Visual J++ debugger is a powerful tool that can help you create sophisticated Java applets and applications quickly, with minimum heartache. The debugger provides some extremely useful features, such as the capability to step through a project's code as it executes, set breakpoints, observe variable values, and view the method call stack. The purpose of this chapter is to discuss the most important debugging capabilities of Visual J++.

This chapter covers the following topics:

➤ Preparing a project for a debugging session

➤ Using the debug windows

➤ Setting and working with breakpoints

➤ Stepping through a project's code

➤ Handling exceptions in debug mode

➤ Debugging multithreaded programs

The debugging examples shown in this chapter use the PartyText applet created in Chapter 7, "Building Your First Java Applet By Using Visual J++." Although you do not learn how to write any Java code in this chapter, you do learn how to use an important tool that will greatly enhance your ability to quickly develop high-quality Java software.

The Debugging Process

The integrated Visual J++ debugger offers almost all of the features provided by the Visual C++ debugger. In addition, you can use the Visual J++ debugger to debug Java applets as they execute within a real web browser, the Internet Explorer. This capability can be quite useful because an applet may need to interact with other applets, ActiveX controls, and HTML scripts, all which can be part of the same HTML page.

Not only can you debug an applet as it executes within a web browser, you can use the Visual J++ debugger to debug a Java application as it executes within a stand-alone interpreter.

Visual J++ provides access to debugging commands via a dockable Debug toolbar, as well as a Debug menu, which is a submenu of the Build pull-down menu. When you debug a Java program, a series of debug windows are provided. You can use these windows, for example, to observe and change the values of variables on-the-fly as your program executes.

Preparing the Project for Debugging

Before you start a debugging session, it is important to do the following:

➤ Specify all the appropriate project settings for debugging

➤ Compile your project in debug mode so that the Visual J++ debugger will work properly

Project Settings

The project settings provide the debugger with important information about how you want to debug your project. You can access the Project Settings dialog box by choosing the Settings option from the Visual J++ Build pull-down menu.

From the Project Settings dialog box's Debug tab (see fig. 8.1), you can set several categories of options. The Debug categories that are available are:

➤ General

➤ Browser

➤ Stand-alone interpreter

➤ Additional classes

In all cases you must specify the general debug project settings. If you want to debug your project as an applet, you need to specify settings for the browser category. If you want to debug your project as an application, you need to specify the stand-alone interpreter settings. In some cases you need to specify both the browser and the stand-alone interpreter settings because you may want to debug a project as both an application and as an applet.

General Debug Project Settings

When you define the general debug project settings, you can specify the Java class to execute for debugging purposes and whether to automatically debug the program as an applet or as an application.

Notice that a folder tree is displayed on the left side of the Project Settings dialog box, shown in figure 8.1. By using this tree, you can specify whether the project settings you create are for release mode, debug mode, or both. For project settings in the Debug tab, however, the settings in this folder tree are irrelevant.

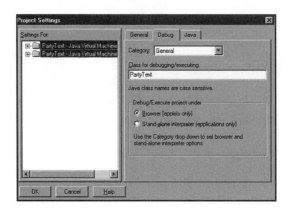

Figure 8.1:

Project Settings—General debug settings.

Browser Debug Project Settings

As mentioned previously, browser debug project settings must be specified correctly for you to debug your project as an applet.

The browser debug settings enable you to specify the browser that is to be used for debugging. At the time of this writing, only the Microsoft Internet Explorer 3.0 or higher can be used to debug a project in Visual J++. You can also specify whether the browser should load a specific HTML page when debugging an applet. That way, you can specify all the appropriate parameters in the HTML file. Alternatively, you can specify the applet's parameters in the Project Settings dialog box.

Stand-Alone Interpreter Debug Project Settings

When you want to debug your project as an application, you must make sure that the stand-alone interpreter debug project settings (see fig. 8.3) are correct.

The stand-alone category settings enable you to specify which interpreter you will use for debugging an application. At the time of this writing, only Microsoft's *jview* utility can be used to debug Visual J++ projects. In addition, you can define the command line arguments you want to pass to the stand-alone interpreter utility, as well as the arguments that you want to pass to your application. Because Visual J++ gives you the ability to specify arguments in the Project Settings dialog box, you don't have to exit to the command line when debugging Java applications.

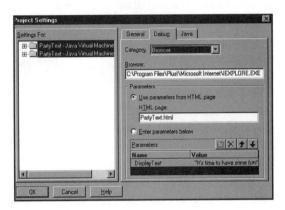

Figure 8.2:
Project Settings—Browser debug settings.

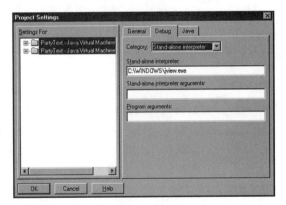

Figure 8.3:
Project Settings—Application debug settings.

Building a Project in Debug Mode

The final task that you need to complete before you debug a project is to compile it in debug mode. When you create a project, the compiler is set to debug mode by default. If for some reason, the Visual J++ compiler is set to release mode, you can change it back to debug mode via the list box located on the Project toolbar. Figure 8.4 shows the PartyText applet in Visual J++ just after it was compiled in debug mode. Notice that the compile option is set to Java Virtual Machine Debug.

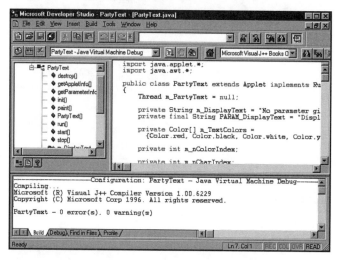

Figure 8.4:
Building the project in debug mode.

Starting a Debugging Session

After you have specified all the appropriate project settings and compiled your project in debug mode, you can start the integrated Visual J++ debugger by choosing Go, Step Into, or Run to Cursor from the Debug submenu of the Build pull-down menu. Figure 8.5 shows the PartyText applet being executed by the Visual J++ debugger after the Step Into command was issued. As indicated by a yellow arrow, the debugger is paused at the first line of code in the *init( )* method.

Figure 8.5:
Debugging the PartyText applet.

When the Visual J++ debugger pauses at a line of code, a yellow arrow, as shown in figure 8.5, indicates the current point of execution. The debugger also indicates the line of code that invoked the current method with a green arrow.

The Debug Toolbar

You can use the debug toolbar to execute common debugging commands and to display the various debugging windows available in Visual J++. This toolbar displays automatically when you initiate a debugging session, or when you explicitly display it by choosing the Toolbars option on the Visual J++ View pull-down menu. Figure 8.6 shows the Debug toolbar and indicates the functions performed by the various buttons.

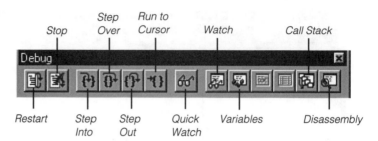

Figure 8.6:
The Debug toolbar.

In figure 8.6, two toolbar buttons are grayed out in Visual J++ because they are not applicable to Java. These buttons are used in Visual C++ to view Memory locations and system Registers. Although these options are not available in Visual J++, they were left on the toolbar for consistency.

Stepping Through a Project

When you start a debugging session in Visual J++, the debugger enables you to control how your program executes. One of the most important features of the debugger is its capability to step through a project.

The technique that you use to step through a project determines the next line that the debugger will pause at as your program executes. The following stepping commands are supported by the Visual J++ debugger.

➤ **Step Into.** This command executes the current line of code at which the debugger is paused. If the current line calls a method, the debugger pauses at the first line of code in the method.

➤ **Step Over.** This command executes the current line of code at which the debugger is paused. If the current line calls a method, the debugger invokes the method, but it does not pause until the point of execution reaches the line of code immediately following the current line.

➤ **Step Out.** This command executes all of the remaining lines of code in the current method and pauses at the first line of code of the method that invoked the current method.

➤ **Run to Cursor.** This command executes all of the lines of code in a project until the point of execution reaches the line of code that the cursor is positioned at in the Visual J++ text editor.

You can access the stepping commands from the Debug toolbar, the Debug pull-down menu, or the shortcut keys found in table 8.1.

Table 8.1   Stepping Shortcut Keys

Command	Shortcut Key
Step Into	F11
Step Over	F10
Step Out	Shift+F11
Run to Cursor	Ctrl+F10

If you access the Debug menu under the Build pull-down menu, you will see different stepping shortcut keys than those shown in table 8.1. The shortcut keys shown on the Debug menu are the keys that you can use to start a debug session. After you start debugging, the shortcut keys in table 8.1 can be used.

If you are familiar with Visual C++, you will notice that the Visual J++ shortcut keys in table 8.1 are the same.

The Debugger's Windows

When you debug a Java program, Visual J++ provides a great deal of useful information in a series of debugger windows that can be displayed as normal or docked windows. You can access all these windows, if not displayed, through the Visual J++ View pull-down menu.

The Variables Window

The Variables window (see fig. 8.7) lists the names and values of the variables used in the current method. By changing the method name in the Context list box, you can look at the variable names and values in the method that called the current method. The Variables window includes the following three tabs:

➤ **Auto.** Shows all the variables that are in scope for the current method.

➤ **Locals.** Shows local variables used in the current method.

➤ **this.** Shows the object pointed to by the *this* variable.

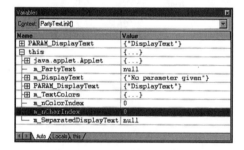

Figure 8.7:

The Variables window.

The Variables window can be used to modify variables of any fundamental data type. To change a variable's value, you must double-click it in the Variables window. When a variable's value changes during a debugging session it displays in red.

The Watch Window

The Watch window, shown in figure 8.8, can be used to monitor expressions and variables. You can add expressions and variables to any one of the four tabs in the Watch window by dragging-and-dropping them from the text editor, or by typing directly into the name field. Just as variables are shown in different colors in the Variables window when their values change, expressions and variables change color in the Watch window as their values change.

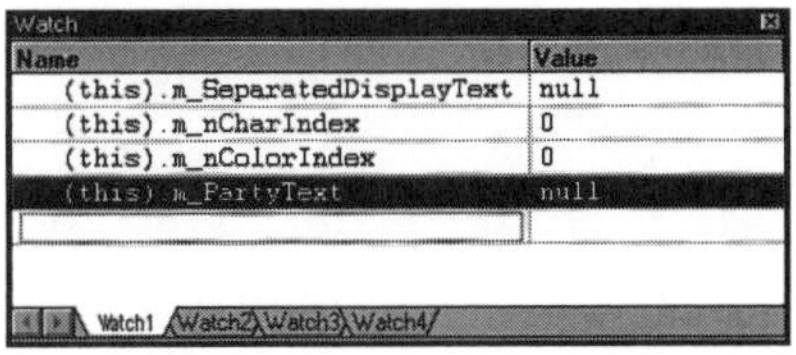

Figure 8.8:
The Watch window.

The Disassembly Window

By default, the Disassembly window, shown in figure 8.9, displays a project's source code and symbols as well as its compiled bytecode. This window can be useful for debugging a line of code that contains more than one command. Consider the following:

```
var1 = x; var2 = y; var3 = z;
```

When the text editor window has the focus, the debugger treats the preceding line of code as one line. In contrast, when the Disassembly window has the focus, you may step through each command separately.

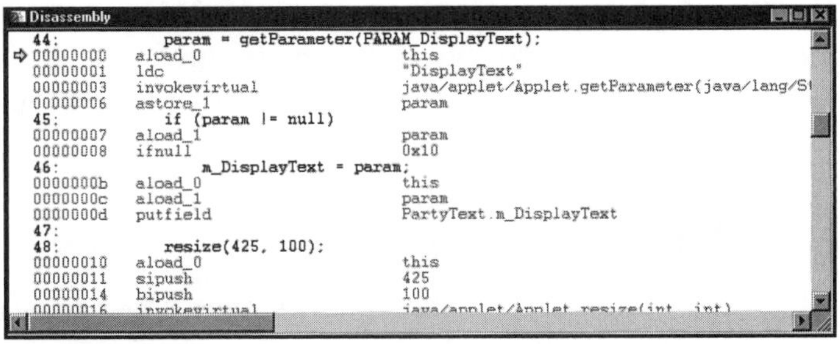

Figure 8.9:
The Disassembly window.

During a debugging session, it is possible to jump from the Visual J++ text editor to the Disassembly window by right-clicking in either window. This causes a pop-up menu to be displayed. When you're in the text editor, you can jump to the bytecode for the current line in the Disassembly window by using this pop-up command window and vice versa.

The Call Stack Window

The Call Stack window, shown in figure 8.10, shows a hierarchy of all the method calls that occur during a debugging session to bring you to the current point of execution. If you click on a method name in the Call Stack window and press F7, the debugger executes all the code in the project until it reaches that method. In addition, if you double-click a method name in the Call Stack window, the context of the source window and all the other debugger windows change to that method.

Figure 8.10:
The Call Stack window.

Viewing a Variable's Content

The QuickWatch dialog box and DataTips both provide a fast and convenient way to view the contents of variables and expressions during a debug session.

The QuickWatch Dialog Box

The QuickWatch dialog box, shown in figure 8.11, can be displayed by clicking the QuickWatch icon on the Debug toolbar, or by choosing QuickWatch from the Debug pull-down menu, which displays during a debugging session. When you display the QuickWatch dialog box, it shows the expression or variable that the cursor is positioned at in the text editor. If a variable or expression has been chosen in the text editor, it is displayed in the QuickWatch dialog box.

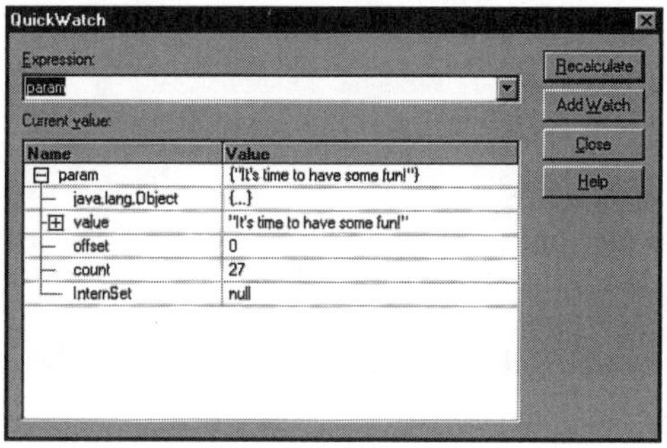

Figure 8.11:
The QuickWatch dialog box.

By using the QuickWatch dialog box, you can change the value of variables that are fundamental data types.

DataTips

DataTips provide a quick, easy way to look at a variable's value during a debugging session. They are similar to tool tips that are provided by many Windows applications when you hold the mouse pointer over a toolbar icon. Figure 8.12 shows a DataTip that would be displayed by holding the mouse pointer over the PartyText applet's *param* variable in the text editor.

Setting and Using Breakpoints

One feature provided by any good debugger is the capability to set breakpoints. When you use stepping commands, the debugger stops automatically. However, when you issue a Go command your program runs until it terminates or encounters a breakpoint. Visual J++ enables you to set location breakpoints and conditional location breakpoints.

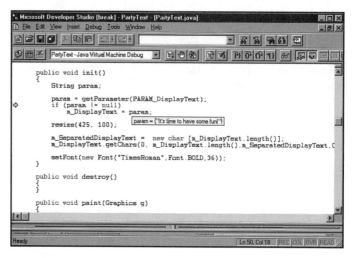

Figure 8.12:

Displaying a DataTip.

You can set a breakpoint by clicking the breakpoint icon in the Visual J++ Project toolbar (denoted by a hand raised with the palm forward), or by using the pop-up command window that displays when you right-click in the text editor. When you set a breakpoint, a red dot displays to the left of the line, as shown in figure 8.13.

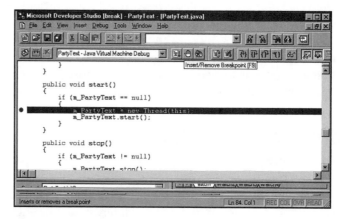

Figure 8.13:

A breakpoint, as shown in the text editor.

The Breakpoints Dialog Box

You can use the Breakpoints dialog box, shown in figure 8.14, to set both line and conditional breakpoints. Access this dialog box by choosing Breakpoints from the Visual J++ Edit menu.

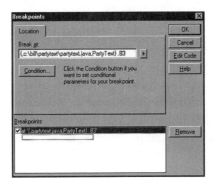

Figure 8.14:

The Breakpoints dialog box.

By using the Breakpoints dialog box, you can set breakpoints at the line at which the cursor is positioned in the text editor. Alternatively, you can access the Advanced Breakpoints dialog box by right-clicking the right arrow next to the Break at edit box. The Advanced Breakpoints dialog box enables you to set the location and context of a breakpoint. You can specify a condition for a location breakpoint by clicking the Condition button (see fig. 8.15). When you set a condition, the debugger only pauses at the line containing the breakpoint if the condition has been met.

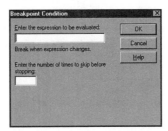

Figure 8.15:

Setting a conditional location breakpoint.

The Breakpoints dialog box lists all of the breakpoints that have been set in the project. An active breakpoint is shown with a check mark next to it. You can deactivate a breakpoint by removing this check mark. When a breakpoint is inactive, a hollow red dot is displayed to the left of its line in the text editor.

Debugger Exception Handling

The debugger notifies you of any exceptions that occur if the condition is not handled by your Java program—exceptions are usually abnormal or unexpected conditions. Exception handling is covered in Chapter 14, "Advanced Multithreading and Exception Handling." During a debugging session, you can access the Exceptions dialog box, shown in figure 8.16, by choosing Exceptions from the Debug pull-down menu. This dialog box is used to specify how a program responds to specific exception conditions during a debugging session.

At the time of this writing, the only system exception handled by the Visual J++ debugger was the Java Exception. You can, however, add user-defined exceptions to this dialog box. For each exception, you must specify the number and name of the exception and the action that you want the debugger to take.

If you choose the Stop if not handled option, the debugger writes a message to the Visual J++ Output window when the exception occurs. The debugger only stops the program and notifies you with a dialog box if no code was provided in the Java program to handle the exception.

If you choose Stop always for an exception's option, the debugger stops the program and notifies you immediately when any exception occurs.

You should specify Stop always for an exception's option if you want to debug the exception. If you use the Stop if not handled option, the debugger will immediately perform the exception's handling routine when it occurs. At that point, it will be too late to debug the exception.

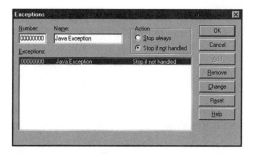

Figure 8.16:

The Exceptions dialog box.

Debugging Multithreaded Programs

During a debugging session, you can access the Threads dialog box by choosing Threads from the Debug pull-down menu. This dialog box displays all the threads that are currently active in an executing program. Figure 8.17 shows the Threads dialog box with two threads are executing; the first one is used by the Java environment and the second is used to execute the PartyText applet. The browser environment's thread is always executing. Therefore, in figure 8.17 only a single applet thread is executing.

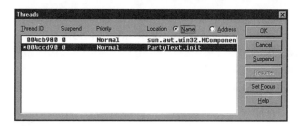

Figure 8.17:

The Threads dialog box with a single applet thread.

If you look at the Location column in the Threads dialog box that is shown in figure 8.17, you can see that the current line of the PartyText applet being executed by the debugger is in the applet's *init( )* method. Remember, the PartyText applet starts another thread in its *start( )* method. Consequently, when the *start( )* method is invoked, a new thread is created, as shown in figure 8.18. As you can see, when an applet starts a new thread, the control of the original thread is passed back to the browser and the applet executes on the new thread.

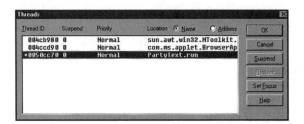

Figure 8.18:

The Threads dialog box after PartyText creates a new thread.

When a thread has the focus, it displays in the Threads dialog box with an asterisk to the left. In figure 8.18, for example, the third thread from the top has the focus. You can set the focus to another thread by double-clicking it in the Threads dialog box.

Other Debug Settings

In addition to the Project Settings, there are several other settings related to debugging that you should know. These settings are specified in the Options dialog box, which you can access from the Visual J++ Tools pull-down menu. Two of the tabs in this dialog box, Debug and Directories, are important for debugging.

The Options Dialog Box's Debug Tab

As shown in figure 8.19, the Options dialog box has a Debug tab. By using this tab, you can specify the following options:

➤ **Hexadecimal display.** When you choose this check box, variable values for fundamental data types are shown in hexadecimal representation in the Watch window, the Variables window, and the QuickWatch dialog box.

➤ **Disassembly window options.** As mentioned previously in this chapter, the default configuration for the Disassembly window is to display source code, symbols, and compiled bytecode. You can change what is displayed in the Disassembly window by changing these settings.

➤ **Call stack window.** You can use these settings to control whether the Call stack window displays parameter values and types.

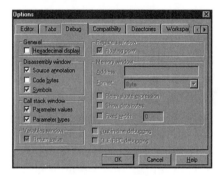

Figure 8.19:
The Options dialog box Debug tab.

The Options Dialog Box's Directories Tab

In addition to a Debug tab, the settings available in the Options dialog's Directories tab, as shown in figure 8.20, are important for debugging. In this tab, you should set the Directories for the Java Virtual Machine Source files to the directory on your workstation that contains the standard Java packages. When you set this option properly, the Java debugger can step into the source code for the standard Java packages and the Java source files in your project. In figure 8.20, notice that the Directories option is set to `C:\Windows\Java\Classes`. This is where the Visual J++ installation program stores the standard Java packages.

If you did not install the source code for the classes in the standard Java packages, the Visual J++ debugger cannot step into these classes. See Chapter 2, "Getting Started," to find out how to install the source code for these classes.

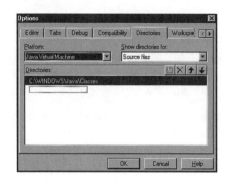

Figure 8.20:
The Options dialog box Directories tab.

Summary

The integrated Visual J++ debugger is a powerful tool that can help you to create highly sophisticated Java applets and applications. When you run a program in the debugger, you can set breakpoints, view and change variable values, and, if you're so inclined, see the project's compiled bytecode.

Before you can run a project in debug mode, you should make sure that the project settings are correct. The project settings can be used to control whether the debugger runs your project as an applet or as a stand-alone application. For the debugger to work properly, you must first compile your project in debug mode.

A debugging session can be initiated by choosing Go, Step Into, or Run to Cursor from the Debug submenu on the Visual J++ Build pull-down menu. The Visual J++ debugger provides commands that enable you to step into, out of, and over methods. You can use location breakpoints to pause the debugger at specific lines in your project. Conditional location breakpoints can be used to pause the debugger at a specific line when a condition is satisfied.

The Visual J++ debugger provides a great deal of information in the windows that are displayed during a debugging session. The Variables window displays the variable names and values used in the current method. The Watch window can be used to monitor the values of variables and expressions. The QuickWatch dialog box provides a fast and convenient way to view the value of variables or expressions during a debug session. Variable values are also provided by DataTips that pop-up when the mouse pointer is held over a variable in the text editor window. The Disassembly window shows the project's compiled bytecode. The Call stack window shows a hierarchy of all the method calls that have occurred during a debugging session to bring you to the current point of execution.

The Exceptions dialog box can be used to define how exceptions are to be handled during a debugging session. The Threads dialog box lists all of the Threads being used by an applet during a debugging session.

Questions

1. What two things should you do to prepare your project for a debugging session?

2. Suppose that you were debugging a Java program and the debugger paused at the following line of code:

   ```
   repaint();
   ```

   Which stepping command would you issue if you did not want the debugger to pause inside of the *repaint()* method?

3. Suppose that you want to initiate a debugging session for an applet and cause the debugger to pause at the first line of code in the *init()* method. Which command would you choose from the Debug submenu on the Build pull-down menu?

4. How can you tell that a variable's value has changed during a debugging session?

5. When a line of code contains more than one command, which debugger tool can be used to step through each command?

6. Which debugger window shows a hierarchy of the method calls that have occurred to bring you to the current point of execution?

7. Which Visual J++ dialog box can be used to specify a breakpoint that will pause the debugger when a specific condition is satisfied?

8. What should you do to make sure that you can step into a class that is part of one of the standard Java packages?

Answers

1. Before starting a debugging session, you should make sure that all of the options in the Project Settings dialog box are set properly. In addition, you must compile your project in debug mode.

2. The step over command would execute the *repaint( )* method and stop at the next line of code in the current method.

3. Step into can be used to start the applet. Because an applet's *init( )* method is the first method called by the browser environment, the step into command will cause the debugger to stop at the first line of code in the *init( )* method.

4. When a variable's value changes during a debugging session, it is displayed in red in the Debugger windows.

5. When a line of code contains more than one command, you can use the Disassembly window to step through each command in the line.

6. The Call stack window shows a hierarchy of the method calls that have occurred during a debug session to bring you to the current point of execution.

7. A conditional location breakpoint can be specified in the Breakpoints dialog box, which can be accessed from the Visual J++ Edit pull-down menu.

8. To be able to step into the code for a standard Java class, you should make sure that the Directories option, which is located in the Directories tab of the Option dialog box, points to the directory that contains the unpacked standard Java packages. In addition, if you did not install the source code for the classes in the standard Java packages, you must install these classes from the Visual J++ CD.

Chapter 9

Working with Graphics, Fonts, and Colors

Now that you know how to create Java applets, you'll want to be able to produce more than just text output on an applet's display area. The Graphics class, which is part of the Abstract Windowing Toolkit package (java.awt), provides methods for drawing text and shapes. This class is discussed briefly in Chapter 7, "Building Your First Java Applet By Using Visual J++." This chapter goes into greater detail about how to manipulate Graphics objects to achieve a variety of output effects.

This chapter covers the following topics:

➤ The Graphics class coordinate system

➤ Rendering lines, shapes, and text

➤   Using colors and fonts

➤   Controlling character spacing

➤   Using font information to position text

➤   Using Graphics methods to create a complete drawing

This chapter contains several code examples that demonstrate the drawing capabilities of Java. It is recommended that you experiment with the drawing methods provided by the Graphics class as you read through each section. After reading this chapter, you should be able to create Java programs that produce sophisticated output, such as bar charts and pie charts.

The Graphics Class

The Graphics class provides a set of methods that enable Java programs to draw text and shapes to a display area. A Java Graphics object is similar to the Microsoft Windows device-context in that both provide an abstraction layer between the program and the physical output device.

An applet's display area is the output window to which an applet can draw. The size of a display area is specified in the applet's HTML file by the height and width attributes of the `<applet>` tag. Basic applet HTML tags and attributes are covered in Chapter 7, "Building Your First Java Applet By Using Visual J++." The applet display area is equivalent to what is typically referred to as a *client area* by MS Windows programmers.

When executing a Java applet, the Java environment calls the applet's *paint()* method to update the display area. The Java environment passes the Graphics object for an applet when it calls the *paint()* method. To draw output to the display area, a Java program needs to draw to this Graphics object.

In some Java programs it is necessary to draw to the display area from other methods besides the *paint()* method. For these situations, the *getGraphics()* method can be called to obtain the

Graphics object for the applet's display area. By using this object, you can draw to the display area from any method. This may be necessary, for example, when you want to produce animation effects. Animation is covered in Chapter 16, "Fun with Sound and Animation."

Graphics objects utilize finite system resources. When your program is finished with a Graphics object, it should call that object's *dispose()* method.

The Graphics Coordinate System

As you are drawing with a Graphics object, the output is always positioned at specific x and y coordinates in the applet's display area. The origin (x,y = 0,0) is in the upper-left corner of the display area. The x value goes up as you move from left to right. The y value goes up as you move down. The values of the x and y coordinates within a display area are illustrated in figure 9.1.

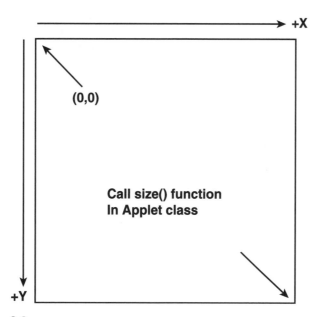

Figure 9.1:

The Graphics coordinate system.

You can determine the size of an applet's display area by using the *size()* method. This method returns a Dimension object that has width and height member variables. The width variable is equal to the display area's maximum x coordinate and the height variable is equal to the display area's maximum y coordinate. Both the height and width variable values are measured in pixels. The use of these variables is demonstrated in the following code:

```
// code to clear screen
public void paint(Graphics g)
{
    Dimension d = size();
    g.clearRect(0, 0, d.width, d.height);
}
```

The *clearRect()* method has the following signature:

```
void clearRect(int x, int y, int width, int height)
```

In the preceding code, the *size()* method returns a Dimension object. Next, the *clearRect()* method is called to clear a rectangle within the applet's display area. Because the rectangle being cleared starts at the origin (x,y = 0,0) and ends at the maximum x and y coordinates (x,y = d.width, d.height), the entire display area is cleared.

Working with Colors

The Graphics class utilizes the current color for all its drawing methods. The default current color is black; however, you can change it by using the *setColor()* method provided by the Graphics class. The *setColor()* method expects a Color object as a parameter. The Color class provides static member variables, which are also Color objects, for the most commonly used colors. The following list contains these standard color member variables.

➤ Color.black

➤ Color.blue

➤ Color.cyan

➤   Color.darkGray

➤   Color.gray

➤   Color.green

➤   Color.lightGray

➤   Color.magenta

➤   Color.orange

➤   Color.pink

➤   Color.red

➤   Color.white

➤   Color.yellow

The static data members in the preceding list can be passed to the *setColor()* method to change the current color, as demonstrated by the following example:

```
Graphics g = getGraphics();
g.setColor(Color.red);
```

The preceding code creates a Graphics object called *g*. Next *g*'s current color is set to red by using the *setColor()* method and a static member variable provided by the Color class. Any graphics or text subsequently drawn by using *g*, displays in red.

In addition to the standard colors, shown in the preceding list, new Color objects can be constructed. The Color class's constructor expects three values specifying the new color's red, green, and blue components, or RGB values. Integer values from 0 to 255, or float values from 0.0 to 1.0 can be passed to the Color class's constructor.

```
Color c = new Color(128, 192, 15);
```

or

```
Color c = new Color( (float)128/255, (float)192/255,
➥(float)15/255 );
```

When you create a custom color, remember that the actual color displayed to the end-user is limited by the capabilities of his display device. To be safe, stick to the standard colors. If you must create a custom color, make sure you test it with your display set to 256 colors. Exotic custom colors that look great on your high-end monitor may look terrible when displayed on less capable devices.

To sum things up, the following code shows how the current color can be set and reset.

```java
public void paint(Graphics g)
{
    // everything here is drawn in black

    g.setColor(Color.blue)

    // everything here is drawn in blue

    Color c = new Color(128, 192, 15);
    g.setColor(c);

    // everything here is drawn in a custom color
}
```

The Color class provides methods for converting RGB values to HSB (Hue, Saturation, Brightness) values and vice versa. In addition, the Color class provides functionality for constructing and decomposing RGB values and creating brighter and darker colors from a starting Color object.

Drawing and Filling Commands

The Graphics class provides many methods for drawing lines and geometric shapes. It also provides methods for drawing shapes that are filled with the current color. Remember that the current color determines the color of anything drawn on a Graphics object. Another important thing to remember is that the Graphics object does not keep track of where you are while you're drawing. Consequently, all drawing methods require that you specify the proper x and y coordinates of the starting point on the display area.

One limitation of the drawing methods, which are provided by the Graphics class, is their lack of a line thickness parameter. When drawing lines, you can get around this limitation by drawing one or more additional lines next to each other.

Lines

The *drawLine()* method is one of the most basic drawing methods. It provides functionality for drawing a line between two points. The *drawLine()* method takes four parameters, which are the coordinates of the line's starting and ending points. The *drawLine()* method has the following signature:

```
void drawLine(int startX, int startY, int endX, int endY)
```

The following code shows how to use the *drawLine()* method.

```
public void paint(Graphics g)
{
    g.drawLine(0, 0, 150, 150);
    g.drawLine(0, 150, 150, 0);
}
```

The output of the preceding code is shown in Figure 9.2.

Figure 9.2:

Line drawn by using the *drawLine()* method.

Rectangles

A rectangle can be used for many purposes, such as framing text and creating bar graphs. The Graphics class provides methods for drawing three different kinds of rectangles: plain, rounded, and three-dimensional. Each of these rectangle types can be drawn as a frame or they may be filled to create a solid shape.

Plain Rectangles

The Graphics class provides two methods that can be used to draw a normal rectangle: *drawRect()* and *fillRect()*. The *drawRect()* method draws the frame of a rectangle and the *fillRect()* method draws a solid rectangle. These methods have the following signatures:

```
void drawRect(int x, int y, int width, int height)
void fileRect(int x, int y, int width, int height)
```

The parameters for both *drawRect()* and *fillRect()* are the coordinates of the rectangle's starting point, followed by the rectangle's width and height. As with all drawing methods provided by the Graphics class, these methods utilize the current color. The following code, for example, draws one rectangle frame in black and another solid red rectangle.

```
public void paint(Graphics g)
{
    g.drawRect( 10, 10, 100, 100);

    g.setColor(Color.red);
    g.fillRect( 150, 10, 100, 100);
}
```

Figure 9.3 shows the output of the preceding code.

Figure 9.3:

Drawing rectangles.

Rounded Rectangles

Rounded rectangles are the same as plain rectangles except that their edges are rounded. Rounding a rectangle's edges is accomplished by drawing arcs instead of straight lines. The Graphics class provides two methods for drawing rounded rectangles—*drawRoundRect()* and *fillRoundRect()*. These methods have the following signatures:

```
void drawRoundRect(int x, int y, int width, int height,
➥int arcWidth, int arcHeight)
void fillRoundRect(int x, int y, int width, int height,
➥int arcWidth, int arcHeight)
```

The *drawRoundRect()* and *fillRoundRect()* methods use the same parameters as the *drawRect()* and *fillRect()* methods, with two additional parameters. The *arcWidth* parameter specifies the horizontal diameter of the arc drawn at the four corners of the rectangle. The *arcHeight* parameter specifies the vertical diameter of the arc at the four corners. In fact, if you make the *arcHeight* and *arcWidth* parameters large enough, you can draw a rounded rectangle that actually looks like a circle.

The following code draws two rounded rectangles. The parameters for the arc of the filled rectangle have been set so that the result is a circle.

```java
public void paint(Graphics g)
{
    g.setColor(Color.red);
    g.drawRoundRect( 10, 10, 100, 100, 75, 50);

    g.setColor(Color.blue);
    g.fillRoundRect( 150, 10, 100, 100, 100, 100);
}
```

Figure 9.4 shows the output of the preceding code.

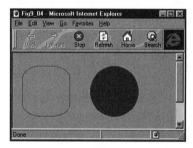

Figure 9.4:
Drawing rounded rectangles.

3D Rectangles

You can use the *draw3DRect()* and *fill3DRect()* methods to draw three-dimensional rectangles. These methods have the following signatures:

```java
void draw3DRect(int x, int y, int width, int height,
    boolean raised)
void fill3DRect(int x, int y, int width, int height,
    boolean raised)
```

Both methods take five input parameters. The first four are the same as the *drawRect()* method. The fifth parameter, raised, is a boolean value. If raised is *true*, the rectangle is drawn with a raised effect. If raised is *false*, the rectangle is drawn with a sunken effect.

The following code draws raised and sunken rectangles.

```
public void paint(Graphics g)
{
    g.setColor(Color.red);

    g.fill3DRect( 10, 10, 100, 100, false);

    g.fill3DRect( 150, 10, 100, 100, true);
}
```

Figure 9.5 shows the output of an applet of the preceding code.

Figure 9.5:
Rectangles drawn by using the *fill3Drect()* method.

At the time of this writing, 3D rectangles only worked correctly when the current color was set to *Color.lightGray*. When you use other colors, the edge colors of the rectangle are too thin to be seen. Hopefully, this will be fixed in a future implementation of Java. Until then, use *Color.lightGray*.

The following code draws a 3D rectangle after setting the current color to *Color.lightGrey*. This color produces a more noticeable 3D effect.

```
public void paint(Graphics g)
{
    g.setColor(Color.lightGray);

    g.fill3DRect( 10, 10, 100, 100, false);

    g.fill3DRect( 150, 10, 100, 100, true);
}
```

Figure 9.6 shows the output of the preceding code.

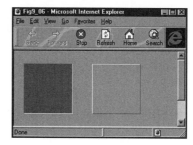

Figure 9.6:
A light gray 3D rectangle.

Polygons

Polygons are shapes consisting of any number of lines. The Graphics class provides two methods that can be used to draw polygons—*drawPolygon()* and *fillPloygon()*.

The *drawPolygon()* Method

The *drawPolygon()* method has the following signature:

```
void drawPolygon(int xPoints[], int yPoints[], int
➥nPoints)
```

To draw a polygon, you need two arrays. One array, *xPoints[]*, specifies the x coordinates of the points in each line of the polygon. The second array, *yPoints[]*, specifies all of the corresponding y values. The third parameter required by the *draw-Polygon( )* method, nPoints, specifies the total number of points.

A triangle is a good example of a polygon that can only be drawn by using either the *drawPolygon( )* or *fillPolygon( )* methods. The following code shows an example of drawing polygons.

```
public void paint(Graphics g)
{
    int xvals[] = { 75, 125, 25 };
    int yvals[] = { 10, 110, 110 };
    int numpts = xvals.length;

    g.drawPolygon(xvals, yvals, numpts);

    int xvals2[] = { 225, 275, 175, 225 };
    int yvals2[] = { 10, 110, 110, 10 };
    int numpts2 = xvals2.length;

    g.drawPolygon(xvals2, yvals2, numpts2);
}
```

Figure 9.7 shows the output of the preceding code.

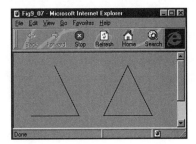

Figure 9.7:
Polygons drawn by using the *drawPolygon()* method.

In figure 9.7, notice that the endpoints of the first triangle are not connected. This illustrates an important point—in Java, you must start and end the polygon at the same point to achieve closure because polygons are not closed automatically. The second triangle is closed, because the proper ending point is specified.

The *fillPolygon()* Method

You can produce solid polygons with the *fillPolygon()* method. When a filled polygon is drawn, the polygon is automatically closed.

The following code creates filled polygons.

```java
public void paint(Graphics g)
{
    int xvals[] = { 75, 125, 25 };
    int yvals[] = { 10, 110, 110 };
    int numpts = xvals.length;

    g.setColor( Color.black );
    g.fillPolygon(xvals, yvals, numpts);

    int xvals2[] = { 225, 275, 175, 225 };
    int yvals2[] = { 10, 110, 110, 10 };
    int numpts2 = xvals2.length;

    g.setColor( Color.yellow );
    g.fillPolygon(xvals2, yvals2, numpts2);
}
```

Figure 9.8 shows the output of the preceding code.

In the previous example, the polygon is defined by two arrays of integers. If a Java program needs to produce many polygons, keeping track of arrays can get messy. As an alternative, Java provides a Polygon class that encapsulates all the points of a polygon. In addition to the method signatures discussed

previously, the *drawPolygon( )* and *fillPolygon( )* methods support
the following signatures:

```
drawPolygon(Polygon p)
fillPolygon(Polygon p)
```

Figure 9.8:
Drawing a filled polygon.

Because the *drawPolygon( )* and *fillPolygon( )* methods can accept
Polygon objects as parameters, you can simplify your Java programs that
handle many polygons by creating an array of Polygon objects.

Ovals

Ovals are circles that can be stretched either horizontally or
vertically. The *drawOval( )* and *fillOval( )* methods have the
following signatures:

```
void drawOval(int X, int Y, int width, int height)
void fillOval(int X, int Y, int width, int height)
```

As you can see, these methods take the same parameters as
drawRect( ). With the *drawRect( )* method these parameters
defined the size of a rectangle. In the case of the *drawOval( )* and
fillOval( ) methods, however, these parameters define the size of
the bounding rectangle within which the oval is drawn.

The following code draws a regular oval by using *drawOval( )* and
a solid red oval, which uses the *fillOval( )* method:

```
public void paint(Graphics g)
{
    g.drawOval( 10, 10, 75, 100);

    g.setColor(Color.red);
    g.fillOval( 150, 10, 100, 75);
}
```

Figure 9.9 shows the output of the preceding code.

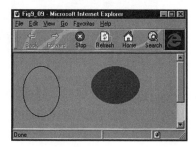

Figure 9.9:

Drawing ovals.

Arcs

Arcs can best be described as partial ovals. To draw an arc, you can use the *drawArc()* or *fillArc()* methods. These methods have the following signatures.

```
void drawArc(int X, int Y, int height, int width, int
⟶startAngle, int arcAngle)
void fillArc(int X, int Y, int height, int width, int
⟶startAngle, int arcAngle)
```

Both methods take six parameters, the first four parameters are the same as *drawOval()*. The fifth parameter specifies the starting angle of the arc and the sixth specifies how far to draw around the oval. Both the fifth and sixth parameter values are measured in degrees. Figure 9.10 shows the orientation of the arc angles.

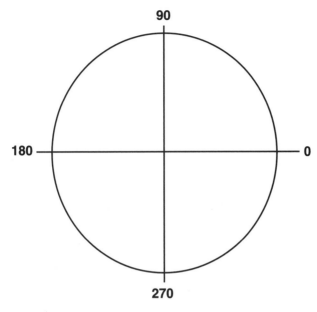

Figure 9.10:

Arc angle orientation.

The following code shows how a pie chart can be produced by drawing two arcs.

```
public void paint(Graphics g)
{
    g.setColor(Color.blue);
    g.fillArc( 10, 10, 100, 100, 90, 270);

    g.setColor(Color.red);
    g.fillArc( 10, 10, 100, 100, 0, 90);
}
```

Figure 9.11 shows the output of the preceding code.

In figure 9.11, both arcs are drawn within the same oval. Each arc, however, is drawn by using different starting and ending angles. The first arc, which is blue, is drawn starting from the top of the oval—an angle of 90 degrees—and ending at an angle of 0 degrees. Because a positive number (270) is used to specify the ending angle's distance from the starting angle, the arc is drawn in a clockwise direction. In contrast, if the arc distance were specified as –270, the blue arc would be drawn in a counterclockwise manner. Consequently, the blue arc would be partially obscured by the red arc, which would have been drawn over the blue arc.

Figure 9.11:

A pie chart drawn by using arcs.

When positive angle values are used to create an arc, it is drawn in a clockwise direction. When negative angle values are used to draw an arc, it is drawn in a counterclockwise direction.

Working with Text

In addition to drawing shapes, the Graphics class provides methods for drawing text to a display area. In more sophisticated applications, it is often necessary to use different typefaces, font sizes, and character placement. This section covers the text display capabilities of the Graphics class, which include:

➤ Drawing text

➤ Setting the current font

➤ Utilizing font information—also known as *font metrics*

Drawing Text

The Graphics class contains two methods that draw text to the applet window, these methods are *drawString()* and *drawChars()*. The *drawString()* method is used for writing an entire String object to a specific location in an applet window. The *drawChars()* method enables you to specify a subset of characters from a character array, which is to be written to an applet window.

The *drawString()* Method

The *drawString()* method has the following signature:

```
void drawString(String str, int x, int y)
```

The parameter for the *drawString()* method includes a String object (str) and the x and y coordinates of the text's position. The text is drawn from left to right from the starting point. The x coordinate specifies the starting point and the y coordinate is used as the baseline for the text.

The following code illustrates the use of the *drawString()* method. Remember that in Java a string constant is treated as a String object:

```
public void paint(Graphics g)
{
    g.setColor( Color.gray );
    g.drawLine(10, 50, 300, 50);

    g.setColor( Color.black );
    g.drawString("Please, no more hello world
➥programs!", 50, 50);
}
```

Figure 9.12 shows the output of the preceding code.

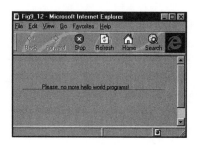

Figure 9.12:
Drawing text with a baseline.

In figure 9.12, a gray line is drawn at the same y coordinate as the output string. This line represents the baseline of the string. Notice that the letters *p* and *g* extend below the baseline; this is known as the *descent* of the font. The portion of the letters that extend above the baseline is known as the *ascent* of the font. The font's height is the sum of the ascent and the descent. It is important to take the font's descent into account when trying the place a string onto the applet display area.

The *drawChars()* Method

The *drawChars()* method provides functionality for outputting one character at a time to a specific location within a display area.

In the previous chapter, the final version of the PartyText applet repeatedly calls the *drawChars()* method to make the letters of its output text move about the applet's display area. A more serious application could be to use the *drawChars()* method to control output *kerning*.

Kerning has to do with controlling the distance between characters while displaying a string.

The *drawChars()* method has the following signature:

```
drawChars(char data[], int offset, int length, int x,
➥int y)
```

To use the *drawChars()* method, you must create an array of characters (*char data[]*). To do this, use the *getChars()* method to obtain the individual characters from a String object. The following code demonstrates how the *drawChars()* method can be used to control kerning.

```
public void paint(Graphics g)
{
    char sepChars[];
    String s;

    s = "Kerning at work";
    sepChars =  new char [s.length()];

    s.getChars(0,s.length(),sepChars,0);

    for(int i=0;i<sepChars.length;i++)
    {
        g.drawChars(sepChars, i,1, 10 + (15*i), 50);
    }
}
```

Figure 9.13 shows the output of the preceding code.

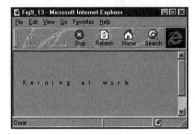

Figure 9.13:
The output of the kerning example.

In the previous code, both the *s* String and the *sepChars* character arrays are initialized at the start of the *paint()* method. The *sepChars* array is then filled with the individual characters from *s*, by calling the *getChars()* method provided by the String class. The contents of the *sepChars* array are then displayed, one character at a time with a separation of 15 pixels.

The output kerning can be controlled by setting the x coordinate specified in the *drawChars()* method's parameter list. If, for example, the call to *drawChars()* method were changed to read:

```
g.drawChars(sepChars, i,1, 10 + (5*i), 50);
```

Then the resulting characters would be drawn five pixels apart as shown in figure 9.14.

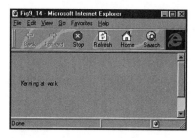

Figure 9.14:
Kerning—small spacing output.

Working with Fonts

A Java applet always has a default output font. For Windows 95, the default Java font is the Dialog font with a point size of 12. There may be many cases, however, where the default font will not be adequate. It is important for you to understand how to change the current font and font size.

The *setFont()* Method

The Graphics class provides a *setFont()* method, which is used to change the current font of a Graphics object. The *setFont()* method expects a Font object as a parameter. Before you can set the current font, you must create a Font object with the appropriate typeface, attributes, and point size.

The following code, for example, sets the current font of the *g* Graphics object to TimesRoman, bold, with a point size of 14. Any text, subsequently drawn to *g*, will be displayed in this font. Next, a new Font object is created that is used to reset the current font, replacing the BOLD attribute with PLAIN.

```
public void paint(Graphics g)
{
    Font f = new Font("TimesRoman", Font.BOLD, 14);
    g.setFont(f);
    // text drawn here will be bold

    f = new Font("TimesRoman", Font.PLAIN, 14);
    g.setFont(f);
    // text draw here will be normal

}
```

In the preceding code, notice that the *f* Font object is set twice. Although coding a program in this manner would waste memory resources in other programming languages, it does not in Java. This is because the Java garbage collection thread is intelligent enough to know that the first Font object is no longer being referenced. It can free up and reclaim memory as needed.

Picking and Using Typefaces

The typefaces supported by Java include Dialog, TimesRoman, Helvetica, and Courier. Because these typefaces are part of the Java specification, they must be present in any Java implementation. Some platforms and browsers may also support other typefaces.

A Java applet can obtain a list of supported typefaces by using a Toolkit object. The default Toolkit represents the native implementation of the Java environment. This object's *getFontList( )* method returns a String array containing the names of all font typefaces that are supported on a particular platform. The following code demonstrates how the default Toolkit can be used to determine the supported font typefaces.

```java
public void paint(Graphics g)
{
    g.drawString("Font Listing:", 10, 10);

    Toolkit t = Toolkit.getDefaultToolkit();
    String s[] = t.getFontList();
    for(int i=0; i<s.length; i++)
    {
        g.drawString(s[i], 75, 20+(i+1)*20);
    }
}
```

When run in Internet Explorer under Windows 95, the preceding code produces the output shown in Figure 9.15.

Figure 9.15:

Windows 95—font listing output.

Although any one platform may support additional fonts, it is a good idea to stick with the four basic fonts so that your applet produces consistent results on all platforms. If you use a font that is not available on a particular platform, Java substitutes the closest font available, which usually is the Courier font.

Font Attributes

Just as the Color class provides variables representing the most common colors, the Font class provides static variables for basic font attributes. The font attribute variables provided are *Font.PLAIN*, *Font.BOLD*, and *Font.ITALIC*.

The *Font.BOLD* and *Font.ITALIC* attributes can be combined by adding the two variables together—*Font.BOLD+Font.ITALIC*. The point size can be any positive integer. The following code shows an example of how font attributes can be set:

```
public void paint(Graphics g)
{
    Font f = new Font("TimesRoman", Font.BOLD +
Font.ITALIC, 25);
    g.setFont(f);
    g.drawString("Visual J++ Java Programming", 25, 25);

    f = new Font("TimesRoman", Font.PLAIN, 15);
    g.setFont(f);
    g.drawString("Introduction", 35, 50);
    g.drawString("Summary", 35, 75);
}
```

Figure 9.16 shows the output of the preceding code.

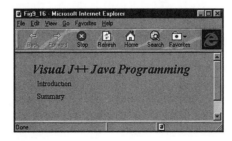

Figure 9.16:

Changing font attributes.

Getting and Using Font Information

When drawing text with the Java Graphics class methods, discussed previously in this chapter, you can only control the position and kerning of the characters. If, however, your Java applets make extensive use of text output, it is likely that you will need to control other aspects of how text is drawn. If you have multiple lines of text output, for example, you will need to make sure that the lines are spaced properly and given a particular font size. Another example is when you want to center text on an applet's display area. For these situations, you need to obtain information about the font being used and the size of the display area being drawn on.

The Graphics class provides a *getFont( )* method that returns the current font for a Graphics object. You can then get all the information that you need regarding the current font by passing the Font object as a parameter to the Graphics object's *getFont-Metrics( )* method. As you probably expect, this method returns a FontMetrics object. The FontMetrics object provides several methods that enable you to get information about the current font. The FontMetrics class, for example, provides a *string-Width( )* method that returns the width, in pixels, of a String object passed to it as a parameter. The following code uses the *stringWidth( )* method to center text of various fonts in the output display area:

```
private int getXVal( Graphics g, String s)
{
    Font f = g.getFont();

    FontMetrics fm = getFontMetrics(f);

    int nXVal = (size().width - fm.stringWidth(s)) / 2;

    return nXVal;
}

public void paint(Graphics g)
{
```

```
    g.setColor(Color.white);
    g.fillRect( 0, 0, size().width, size().height);

    g.setColor(Color.black);
    Font f = new Font("TimesRoman", Font.BOLD, 25);
    g.setFont(f);

    String s = "Centered TimesRoman";
    g.drawString(s, getXVal(g, s), 40);

    f = new Font("Helvetica", Font.PLAIN, 15);
    g.setFont(f);

    s = "Centered Helvetica";
    g.drawString(s, getXVal(g, s), 75);
}
```

Figure 9.17 shows the output of an applet that uses the preceding code to display centered text.

Figure 9.17:

Drawing centered text by using the FontMetrics class.

In the preceding example, even though the current font changes, you can use the *getXVal()* method to calculate the starting x coordinate for the applet's display area, given the current font. To accomplish this, get the width of the applet window that uses the *size()* method, subtract the length of the string in the current font and divide by two. A FontMetrics object can provide the height of the font, which can be used for vertical alignment.

Putting It All Together

Now that the various drawing methods made available by the Graphics class have been discussed, you can see that they are very useful for generating charts, graphs, and other effects. The capabilities of the various drawing methods can be combined to produce more sophisticated output. Figure 9.17, for example, shows Pauly, the Promising Politician, making his infamous quote.

Figure 9.18:

Pauly's infamous quote.

The following code shows how the methods are used to produce the drawing in figure 9.18.

```
public void paint(Graphics g)
{
    Font f = new Font("TimesRoman", Font.PLAIN, 20);
    g.setFont(f);

    // draw quote box
    g.drawRoundRect(75, 20, 150, 75, 20, 20);

    // draw quote text
    g.drawString("Don't Quote Me!", 85, 60);

    // draw line to connect head to quote box
    g.drawLine(120, 150, 175, 95);
```

```
    // draw head
    g.drawOval(70, 115, 45, 45);

    // draw two eyes
    g.fillRoundRect( 80, 125, 8, 15, 7, 10);
    g.fillRoundRect( 95, 123, 8, 15, 7, 10);

    // draw mouth
    g.drawArc(80, 140, 22, 15, 160, 235);
}
```

As you can see in the preceding code, Pauly is broken down into parts that are drawn at designated coordinates.

The standard drawing methods provided by the Graphics class are not typically used to produce high-quality graphic images. The Graphics class, however, does provide a *drawImage()* method that can be used to draw predrawn images of various graphic file formats, such as GIF and JPEG images. Therefore, you can create high-quality images by using a graphics application, such as Adobe's Photoshop, and then use the *drawImage()* method to render these images on a display area. The *drawImage()* method is covered in Chapter 16, "Fun with Sound and Animation."

Summary

The Graphics class encapsulates all the basic drawing methods required to render shapes, colors, and text on a display area. The Graphics coordinate system originates at the x,y coordinates of 0,0. The x coordinate increases as you move to the right of the display area, and the y coordinate increases as you move down. Each increment of a coordinate represents one pixel.

The *paint( )* method receives a Graphics object as its parameter. This Graphics object can be used to draw to the display area. The *paint( )* method is called by the Java environment when an applet's display area needs to be drawn or redrawn.

The Graphics class provides methods for drawing lines, rectangles, circles, arcs, polygons, and text. Any shape drawn to a Graphics object is rendered in the object's current color. Any text drawn to a Graphics object is rendered in the current color and current font. The Graphics class provides *setColor( )* and *setFont( )* methods that can be used to set a Graphics object's color and font respectively.

The Color class provides a set of Color objects as static variables, representing the most commonly used colors. These Color objects can be passed to the *setColor( )* method. In addition, you can define new colors by creating a Color object and specifying the desired RGB values as parameters passed to the Color class constructor.

The Font and FontMetrics classes provide access to font attributes and behavior. A FontMetrics object can be obtained by calling the *getFontMetrics( )* method of the Graphics class. The FontMetrics class provides a means to get the width and height of a String when drawn in the current font. The typefaces supported by Java are TimesRoman, Helvetica, and Courier. Remember that Java might not support some fonts on a particular platform. Consequently, to get consistent results, you should try to use the Java-supported fonts.

Questions

1. What method should be called to obtain a Graphics object for an applet's display area?

2. What three types of rectangles are supported by Java?

3. What method is used for drawing plain rectangles? What about filled rectangles?

4. How can you make sure that polygons that you draw in Java are displayed as closed shapes?

5. What two methods are used by the Graphics class to draw text?

6. What is kerning?

7. Why is it a good idea to use basic fonts when creating Java applets?

8. You can determine a font's typeface, point size, and attributes by using the *getFont()* method. If additional information is needed, such as the width of a string object, what object should a Java program get?

Answers

1. The *getGraphics()* method returns a Graphics object for an applet's display area.

2. The Graphics object can draw plain, rounded, and three-dimensional rectangles.

3. The *drawRect()* method is used to draw a plain rectangle, and the *fillRect()* method is used to draw a filled rectangle.

4. The last point in the polygon definition must be the same as the first to ensure that it will be drawn as a closed shape.

5. The *drawChars()* and *drawSting()* methods are used to render text in a Java applet's display area.

6. Kerning is the spacing of the characters in text output.

7. By using only the basic fonts, you can be sure that your applet will always look the same. This is because not all platforms support all of the Windows fonts.

8. The program must retrieve a FontMetrics object to determine the width of an output String when displayed in the current font.

Chapter 10

Handling Events

One of the most exciting things about Java is that it is especially designed to enable you to create interactive programs that can be dynamically delivered over a network. "But wait a minute!" you might say. "So far, none of the programs covered in this book are interactive." Well, your patience is about to pay off! This chapter covers a key requirement for interactive applications—the capability to handle *events*. An event is an occurrence that your program is required to recognize. When a user clicks on OK , for example, an event is generated and the program should react accordingly. Therefore, event handling capability is an absolute requirement for any interactive program.

This chapter covers the following topics:

- ➤ The Java Event class
- ➤ The event delivery system
- ➤ Mouse event handling
- ➤ Keyboard event handling

> ➤ User Interface (UI) component event handling

> ➤ Window event handling

This chapter covers the Various types of events that may occur in Java, how these events are delivered, and how you can code event handling capability into your Java programs.

Working with Events

Events are typically generated by a user's actions. Therefore, event handling enables your program to react to user's commands. When a user moves the mouse or presses a key, for example, events are generated and delivered to the Java program. The program must process and respond to the event. Events may be generated by the operating system and by other classes used by your Java program.

In the Java environment, all events are delivered as Event objects; these are instances of the Event class. The Event class encapsulates all the information that is necessary to properly handle events.

The Event Class

The *Event* class is a platform-independent class that provides an abstraction layer for events generated by the user's native Graphical User Interface (GUI) environment, for example Windows, Mac, and so on. The Event class is part of Java's Abstract Windowing Toolkit package (java.awt) and is derived from the Object class.

Event Class Constructors

Although Event objects are usually created and delivered automatically by the Java environment, they can also be constructed. To construct an Event, you must use one of the following constructor forms:

```
Event(Object target, long when, int id, int x, int y, int
➥key, int modifiers, Object arg)
Event(Object target, long when, int id, int x, int y, int
➥key, int modifiers)
Event(Object target, int id, Object arg)
```

All Event class constructors accept parameters for the target component and the event type (*id*). Depending on the nature of the event, you may also need to specify the x,y coordinates, keyboard key, state of the modifier keys, and an object reference (*arg*). These parameters correspond to the Event class member variables discussed in the next section.

Member Variables

The Event class has the following member variables.

> **Object target.** This specifies the UI component that triggered the event, for example a list box. It is set to null if the event was not triggered by a UI component.

> **long when.** This records the time stamp of the event.

> **int id.** This integer value represents the type of event.

> **int x.** This is the x display coordinate of the event.

> **int y.** This is the y display coordinate of the event.

> **int key.** If the event was generated by the keyboard, this variable indicates the specific key that triggered the event. It is set to 0 for nonkeyboard events.

> **int modifiers.** This specifies the state of the Ctrl, Shift, Alt, and Meta keys.

> **int clickCount.** This records the number of consecutive mouse clicks. This field is only relevant for MOUSE_DOWN events. It is set to 1 for single-clicks, 2 for double-clicks, and so on. A value of 0 indicates any other type of event.

➤ **Object arg.** This variable contains additional information regarding the event. The information provided by this object depends on the event and the component that generated it.

➤ **Event evt.** This specifies the next event. This variable is used to link custom events in a list.

Methods

The following methods enable you to query and set the various attributes of an Event object.

➤ *void translate(int dx, int dy).* This method adds the integer values dx and dy to event's x and y member variables respectively. The dx parameter represents the change in the x member variable and dy represents the change in the y member variable.

➤ *boolean shiftDown( ).* This method returns *true* if the shift key is down; otherwise, this method returns *false*.

➤ *boolean controlDown( ).* This method returns *true* if the control key is down; otherwise, this method returns *false*.

➤ *boolean metaDown( ) method.* This method returns *true* if the meta key is down; otherwise, this method returns *false*.

Static Member Variables

The Event class contains many static member variables that represent the values of standard Java events, common function keys (F1 for example), and the state of modifier keys, which are Alt, Shift, and so on. These static member variables can be grouped into the following categories.

➤ Mouse events

➤ Keyboard events

➤ Keyboard function key values

➤ Keyboard modifier key status

➤ User Interface (UI) component events

➤ Window events

The static member variables of the Event class are discussed, where appropriate, throughout this chapter.

Using the *handleEvent()* Method

The handling of an event involves two main tasks:

➤ Identifying the type of event that has occurred.

➤ Invoking the appropriate Java code to respond to the event.

The Java environment provides default event processing for many common events. This makes event handling a little easier for the programmer. Java does this by implementing a series of default event handler methods. These methods are invoked by the *handleEvent()* method, which is provided by the Component class. Because all UI component classes are derived from the Component class, they all inherit Component's event handling behavior.

When an event occurs, the Java environment creates an Event object and calls the *handleEvent()* method of the component in which the event occurred. The *handleEvent()* method, in turn, invokes the appropriate event handler method. When you derive new classes from a UI class, you can provide your own event handling behavior by overriding the *handleEvent()* method or any default event handler method invoked by *handleEvent()*.

Listing 10.1 shows the default *handleEvent()* method.

Listing 10.1 Default *handleEvent()* Method

```
public boolean handleEvent(Event evt) {

    switch (evt.id) {
      case Event.MOUSE_ENTER:
        return mouseEnter(evt, evt.x, evt.y);

      case Event.MOUSE_EXIT:
        return mouseExit(evt, evt.x, evt.y);
```

continues

Listing 10.1   Continued

```
        case Event.MOUSE_MOVE:
          return mouseMove(evt, evt.x, evt.y);

        case Event.MOUSE_DOWN:
          return mouseDown(evt, evt.x, evt.y);

        case Event.MOUSE_DRAG:
          return mouseDrag(evt, evt.x, evt.y);

        case Event.MOUSE_UP:
          return mouseUp(evt, evt.x, evt.y);

        case Event.KEY_PRESS:
        case Event.KEY_ACTION:
          return keyDown(evt, evt.key);

        case Event.KEY_RELEASE:
        case Event.KEY_ACTION_RELEASE:
          return keyUp(evt, evt.key);

        case Event.ACTION_EVENT:
          return action(evt, evt.arg);

        case Event.GOT_FOCUS:
          return gotFocus(evt, evt.arg);

        case Event.LOST_FOCUS:
          return lostFocus(evt, evt.arg);
      }
    return false;
    }
```

The flow of execution of the *handleEvent()* method depends on the value of the Event.id variable. The `switch` statement at the beginning of the code calls the appropriate event handler method based on the value of the Event.id member variable. If the Event.id variable, for example, is equal to `Event.MOUSE_ENTER`, the *mouseEnter()* method is called to handle the event.

To provide special processing for a specific event, you can override the default event handler method for that event. You can create your own *mouseDown( )* method, for example, that increments a counter each time a mouse button is pressed. If your program requires event handling for events that are not called by the default *handleEvent( )* method, you can override this method to invoke your customized event handlers.

Event Propagation

An event is *propagated* when it is passed from a component to the component's container. Events can either be handled by a UI component object, or events can be passed from the component to the container. An event generated by a Button UI component in an applet, for example, can be handled by the Button object or passed to the applet.

To illustrate the component-container relationship, figure 10.1 shows an applet that contains a button. In this case, the Applet is the container and the Button is the component in the container.

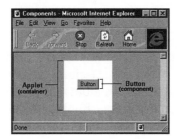

Figure 10.1:

A Button component in an Applet container.

When a user clicks on the Button, the Button component receives the mouse click event first. The Button component can either process the mouse click event, or it can delegate the responsibility of handling the event to the Applet.

If the Button component's *handleEvent( )* method returns a *false* value, the event is propagated, or passed, to the Applet. If the Button's *handleEvent( )* method returns a *true* value, the event is not propagated. Figures 10.2 and 10.3 illustrate how events can be propagated based on the return value of the *handleEvent( )* method.

Figure 10.2:
A Button event propagating to an Applet container.

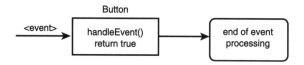

Figure 10.3:
An event that does not propagate.

You control event propagation where you handle events in your program. It may be more logical to handle some events within the individual components. Many events, however, are best handled centrally in the container. Deciding where to handle an event is a design decision that you should make based on reuse and efficiency considerations. You should include specialized event handling in a UI component class when, for example, you know that this customized class will be reused in other applets or applications. Alternatively, you should put your event handling code for a UI component in the component's container class when this functionality is unlikely to be needed in other programs.

Components are covered in Chapter 11, "Building a User Interface." Containers are covered in Chapter 12, "More AWT Containers."

Handling Mouse Events

The capability to point and click a mouse is a key feature of a user-friendly GUI. When a Java applet executes within a web browser, it uses the native GUI of the host platform. Therefore, to interact with the user, it is often necessary to add mouse event handling capability to your Java applets.

There are six types of mouse events defined in the Java environment. The Event class provides static data members for these events. Each data member contains an integer value corresponding to a specific event (see table 10.1).

Table 10.1   Static Member Variables that Represent Mouse Events

Static Data Member	Event Description
MOUSE_DOWN	A mouse button is pressed.
MOUSE_UP	A mouse button is released.
MOUSE_MOVE	The mouse pointer is moved within a component's display area.
MOUSE_DRAG	The mouse pointer is moved within a component's display area while a mouse button is held down.
MOUSE_ENTER	The mouse pointer is moved into a component's display area.
MOUSE_EXIT	The mouse pointer is moved out of a component's display area.

The following mouse event handler methods are provided by the Component class.

```
mouseDown(Event evt, int x, int y)
mouseUp(Event evt, int x, int y)
mouseMove(Event evt, int x, int y)
mouseDrag(Event evt, int x, int y)
mouseEnter(Event evt, int x, int y)
mouseExit(Event evt, int x, int y)
```

The preceding method signatures illustrate that all mouse event handler methods receive an Event object as well as the x,y coordinates of the event. The x,y coordinates indicate the location of the mouse pointer within the component's display area when the event occurred. The x,y coordinates of the event are also contained within the Event object.

To customize the handling of mouse events, you must override the appropriate mouse event handler methods. The following code shows how to override the *mouseDown()* method.

```java
public boolean mouseDown(Event evt, int x, int y)
{
    // TODO: processing for mouseDown event

}
```

Using Center and Right Mouse Buttons

A popular misconception about Java is that Java programs cannot detect the center and right mouse buttons. This is not true. The problem is that some computing platforms don't support these mouse buttons. Therefore, you must be careful when adding mouse event handling for the right and center buttons. It may be useful, for example, to add specific event handling for the center mouse button. Before you add this functionality, however, you should make sure that your intended users are able to take advantage of it. A Macintosh user, for example, will only have a one-button mouse.

 With a three-button mouse, the buttons are referred to as the left, center, and right mouse buttons. With a two-button mouse, the buttons are referred to as the left and right mouse buttons. With a single-button mouse, the button is referred to as the left mouse button.

It is a good habit to design programs so that they degrade gracefully. A program may increase its longevity by including various means of accessing functionality. In the Microsoft Windows environment, for example, the right mouse button commonly provides a context-sensitive command menu. When adding this kind of behavior to a Java applet, you should make sure that this functionality is available by some other means, such as a pull-down menu. This maintains the applet's utility to users with only single-button mouse.

To detect the center and right mouse buttons, a Java program must check the value of the *Event.modifiers* member variable. This variable is set to the value of Event.ALT_MASK when the center mouse button is pressed, and it is set to the value of Event.META_MASK when the right mouse button is pressed.

The *Event.modifiers* member variable is used to differentiate between the mouse buttons. It is set while the mouseDown event is taking place. Consequently, the code that determines the occurrence of a left, center, or right mouse button click should be placed within the *mouseDown( )* method.

The following code identifies the mouse button that was clicked.

```
public boolean mouseDown(Event evt, int x, int y)
{
    if( (evt.modifiers & Event.META_MASK) != 0 )
    {
        // TODO: process right mouse button click
    }
    else if( (evt.modifiers & Event.ALT_MASK) != 0)
    {
        // TODO: process center mouse button click
    }
    else
    {
        // TODO: process left mouse button click
    }
    ...
}
```

Detecting Double-Clicks

Double-clicking the left mouse button is commonly used to activate objects, such as opening a folder in the Windows 95 Explorer. Although Java does not have a double-click event, it is possible to detect double-clicks by overriding the *mouseDown( )* method and inspecting the value of the *clickCount* variable provided by the Event class. If *clickCount* is equal to two, a double-click has occurred.

The following code detects a double-click mouse event.

```
public boolean mouseDown(Event evt, int x, int y)
{
    if( evt.clickCount = 2 )
    {
        // TODO: processing for mouse double click
    }

}
```

This mechanism can be used, for example, to activate an object when the user double-clicks on an object.

Mouse Event Handling: The FloatingBoxes Applet

Figure 10.4 shows the output of the FloatingBoxes applet when executed in the Internet Explorer web browser. This applet provides working examples of the various mouse event handling techniques that may be added to your interactive Java applets and applications.

The FloatingBoxes applet is included on the CD that comes with this book.

FloatingBoxes handles all mouse events. When you run this applet, double-click your mouse to create a box shape anywhere in the applet's display area. In addition, any box turns red when you position the mouse pointer over the box. You can move boxes by using a drag-and-drop technique. FloatingBoxes also responds to the right and center mouse button events.

If the FloatingBoxes applet doesn't respond to your center mouse button, this may be because you don't have a three-button mouse driver installed on your computer.

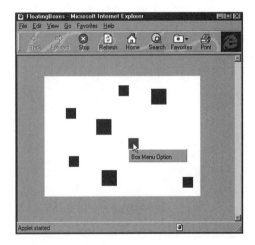

Figure 10.4:

The FloatingBoxes applet.

The following listing contains the code for the FloatingBoxes applet.

Listing 10.2 The FloatingBoxes Applet

```
import java.applet.*;
import java.awt.*;
import java.util.*;

public class FloatingBoxes extends Applet
{
```

continues

Listing 10.2 Continued

```java
    final    int    BOX_SIZE = 21;
    final    int    BOX_OFF = (BOX_SIZE - 1) / 2;
    final    int    BOX_GROW_SIZE = (BOX_OFF / 2);

    final    int    HELP_BOX_WIDTH = 120;
    final    int    HELP_BOX_HEIGHT    = 26;

    Vector         m_Boxes;

    Rectangle      m_HotBox;

    Point          m_DragStart;
    Point          m_DragCurrent;
    Rectangle      m_DragBox;

    Rectangle      m_HelpBox;

    public FloatingBoxes()
    {
    }

    public String getAppletInfo()
    {
        return "Name: FloatingBoxes\r\n" +
               "Author: @Work Technologies\r\n" +
               "Created with Microsoft Visual J++ Version
➥1.0";
    }


    public void init()
    {
        // If you use a ResourceWizard-generated "control
➥creator" class to
        //  arrange controls in your applet, you may want to
➥call its
        // CreateControls() method from within this method.
➥Remove the following
        // call to resize() before adding the call to
```

```
CreateControls();
        // CreateControls() does its own resizing.
        //---------------------------------------------------

        resize(320, 240);

        m_Boxes = new Vector();
        setBackground( Color.gray );
    }

    public void destroy()
    {
    }

    public void paint(Graphics g)
    {
        int     index;
        int     listSize = m_Boxes.size();
        Rectangle r;

        g.setColor( Color.black );

        if( listSize == 0 )
        {
            g.drawString("Double-click anywhere to create a
➥box.", 50, 50);
            return;
        }

        for( index = 0; index < listSize; index++ )
        {
            if( (r = (Rectangle)m_Boxes.elementAt(index))
➥!= null )
            {
                g.fillRect( r.x, r.y, r.width, r.height);
            }
        }

        if(     m_HotBox != null )
```

continues

Listing 10.2   Continued

```
        {
            g.setColor( Color.red );
            g.fillRect( m_HotBox.x, m_HotBox.y,
                        m_HotBox.width,
➥m_HotBox.height);
        }

        if(    m_HelpBox != null )
        {
            g.setColor( Color.lightGray );
            g.fill3DRect( m_HelpBox.x,
                        (m_HelpBox.y+m_HelpBox.height+1),
                        HELP_BOX_WIDTH,
➥HELP_BOX_HEIGHT, true );

            g.setColor( Color.black );
            g.drawString("Box Menu Option", m_HelpBox.x+6,
                (m_HelpBox.y+m_HelpBox.height+1+HELP_BOX_HEIGHT-
➥6));
        }

        if( m_DragBox != null )
        {
            int     dx = m_DragCurrent.x - m_DragStart.x;
            int     dy = m_DragCurrent.y - m_DragStart.y;

            g.setColor( Color.blue );
            g.drawRect( m_DragBox.x+dx, m_DragBox.y+dy,
                        m_DragBox.width,
➥m_DragBox.height );
        }
    }

    public void start()
    {
    }

    public void stop()
    {
```

```
        }

    public boolean mouseDown(Event evt, int x, int y)
    {
        Rectangle hitBox = getBoxAt( x, y );

        if( m_HelpBox != null )
        {
            m_HelpBox = null;
            repaint();
        }

        if( (evt.modifiers & Event.META_MASK) != 0 )
        {
            if( hitBox == null ) return true;

            m_HelpBox = hitBox;
        }
        else if( (evt.modifiers & Event.ALT_MASK) != 0)
        {
            if( hitBox == null ) return true;

            if( hitBox.width == BOX_SIZE )
            {
                hitBox.grow( BOX_GROW_SIZE, BOX_GROW_SIZE
➥);
            }
            else
            {
                hitBox.grow( (-BOX_GROW_SIZE), (-
➥BOX_GROW_SIZE) );
            }
        }
        else
        {
            if( evt.clickCount > 1 )
            {
                Rectangle r = new Rectangle( x-BOX_OFF, y-
➥BOX_OFF,
```

continues

Listing 10.2   Continued

```
                                                      BOX_SIZE,
➥BOX_SIZE );
                  m_Boxes.addElement( r );
            }
            else if( hitBox != null )
            {
                  m_DragBox = hitBox;
                  m_DragStart = new Point( x, y );
                  m_DragCurrent = new Point( x, y );
            }
            else
            {
                  return true;
            }
        }

        repaint();

        return true;
    }

    public boolean mouseUp(Event evt, int x, int y)
    {
        if( m_DragBox == null )        return true;

        m_DragBox.translate( (x-m_DragStart.x), (y-
➥m_DragStart.y) );

        m_DragBox = null;
        m_DragStart = null;
        m_DragCurrent = null;

        repaint();

        return true;
    }

    public boolean mouseMove(Event evt, int x, int y)
    {
```

```
        Rectangle hitBox = getBoxAt( x, y );

        if( hitBox == m_HotBox ) return true;

        m_HotBox = hitBox;
        repaint();

        return true;
}

public boolean mouseDrag(Event evt, int x, int y)
{
        if( m_DragBox == null )      return true;

        m_DragCurrent.move( x, y );
        repaint();

        return true;
}

public boolean mouseEnter(Event evt, int x, int y)
{
        setBackground( Color.white );
        repaint();

        return true;
}

public boolean mouseExit(Event evt, int x, int y)
{
        setBackground( Color.gray );
        repaint();

        return true;
}

public Rectangle getBoxAt( int x, int y )
{
        int     index;
```

continues

```
Listing 10.2   Continued

          int     size = m_Boxes.size();
          Rectangle r;

          for( index = 0; index < size; index++ )
          {
              if( (r = (Rectangle)m_Boxes.elementAt(index))
➡!= null )
              {
                  if( r.inside( x, y ) ) return r;
              }
          }

          return null;
    }
}
```

FloatingBoxes Member Variables

In addition to the final data members (these variables are declared by using the *final* modifier) the FloatingBoxes applet declares the following member variables:

➤ *m_Boxes.* This vector object is used to store all the Rectangle objects representing squares displayed by the applet. A vector can be thought of as a growable array. Consequently, you can continually add objects to the vector without having to allocate a large chunk of memory beforehand.

➤ *m_Hot.* This references the Rectangle object that is currently under the mouse cursor.

➤ *m_DragStart.* This Point object represents the location of the mouse pointer when a drag motion begins.

➤ *m_Drag.* This specifies the Rectangle object that was selected for dragging.

➤ *m_Help.* This indicates the Rectangle object that was selected for help.

init() Method

When the *FloatingBoxes* method executes, the first method called by the Java environment is the *init( )* method. In the *init( )* method, the m_Boxes vector is created and the applet's display area background is set to gray.

paint() Method

After the *init( )* method, the Java environment automatically calls the *paint( )* method. Notice, however, that the *repaint( )* method, which is provided by the Applet class, is called by each of the mouse event handling methods in the FloatingBoxes applet. The *repaint( )* method ultimately causes the *paint( )* method to be invoked. Consequently, whenever a mouse event occurs, the applet's display area is updated; this update reflects the mouse event handling performed by FloatingBoxes.

The first time the *paint( )* method is invoked, it displays the beginning instruction—Double-click anywhere to create a box. Any other time that the *paint( )* method is called, it is a result of a mouse event. If any boxes exist, they are redrawn by the *paint( )* method. If there is a hot box—a box that the user is pointing at with the mouse—it is drawn in red.

If the right mouse button is being held down, the *paint( )* method displays a pseudo help menu. If a box is being dragged, the *paint( )* method draws its outline in blue at the appropriate location.

mouseDown() Method

When the user clicks on a mouse button, the *mouseDown( )* method is invoked. The *mouseDown( )* method locates the box that is currently under the mouse pointer. Next, the *mouseDown( )* method clears any help menu that may be on the applet's display area.

If the user clicks on the right mouse button, the help menu is displayed at the appropriate coordinates. If the user clicks on the left mouse button, the indicated box is marked as a possible drag. If the user double-clicks with the left mouse button, a new box is drawn at the mouse pointer's position.

Boxes can be drawn in two sizes—normal and large. If the user clicks on a normal sized box with the center mouse button, the box is redrawn as a large box. When the user clicks on a large box with the center mouse button, it is drawn at the normal size.

mouseUp() Method

The *mouseUp( )* method only performs special processing when the left mouse button is released at the end of a drag. When this situation occurs, the *mouseUp( )* method updates the *m_DragBox* member variable with the location of the mouse pointer. It then calls *repaint( )*.

mouseMove() Method

When the mouse cursor moves, the *mouseMove( )* method is called. This method checks the position of the mouse pointer to determine whether it is positioned over a box. If the cursor is over a box, the *m_HotBox* variable is set and *repaint( )* is called.

mouseDrag() Method

This method is called when the user moves the mouse cursor while holding down the left mouse button. The *mouseDrag( )* method updates the *m_DragCurrent* variable's x,y coordinates and calls *repaint( )*. Subsequently, when the *paint( )* method executes, it draws the box being dragged at m_DragCurrent's coordinates.

mouseEnter() Method

The *mouseEnter( )* method sets the applet's background color to white when the mouse pointer enters the applet's display area.

mouseExit() Method

The *mouseExit( )* method sets the applet's background color to gray when the mouse pointer exits the applet's display area.

getABox() Method

This returns the first box in the m_Boxes vector that contains the point, which is represented by the x,y coordinates, within the boundaries of the box.

Handling Keyboard Events

Another category of event handling methods are related to keyboard events. Although the keyboard is not as intuitive as the mouse, it is the primary mechanism that enables human-computer interaction. You can provide special processing based on user actions by adding keyboard event handling to your Java programs. Table 10.2 lists the keyboard events delivered by the Java environment.

Table 10.2   Keyboard Events—Static Member Variables

Static Data Member	Event Description
KEY_PRESS	A key is pressed.
KEY_RELEASE	A key is released.
KEY_ACTION	The same as KEY_PRESS.
KEY_ACTION_RELEASE	The same as KEY_RELEASE.

The default *handleEvent( )* method provided by the Component class responds to two types of keyboard events. The *keyDown( )* method is called when a key is depressed, and the *keyUp( )* method is called when a key is released. These methods have the following signatures:

```
keyDown(Event evt, int key)
keyUp(Event evt, int key)
```

Both the *keyUp( )* and *keyDown( )* methods expect two parameters—the Event object (evt) and the key that triggered the event (key). You can define special processing for specific keyboard events by overriding the *keyUp( )* and *keyDown( )* methods.

One constructive use of keyboard events is to provide context-sensitive help. In most Microsoft Windows applications, for example, the user can get context-sensitive help by pressing the F1 key. Similar functionality can be implemented in Java.

The following code tests if the F1 key is being pressed:

```
public boolean keyDown(Event evt, int key)
{
    if( key == Event.F1)
    {
        // TODO: generate context specific help
        return true;
    }
    ...
}
```

The key parameter of the *keyDown( )* method is tested against the static member variable Event.F1. The Event class provides definitions, in the form of static member variables, for function keys and navigation keys. See Table 10.3 for a list of the standard key definitions in the Event class.

Table 10.3   Keys—Static Member Variables

Member Variable	Description
DOWN	down arrow key
UP	up arrow key
LEFT	left arrow key
RIGHT	right arrow key
HOME	home key

Member Variable	Description
END	end key
PGUP	page up key
PGDN	page down key
Fx	function key x, where x is 1 through 12

Situations will arise when your Java program must be able to detect keys that do not have standard Event class definitions. The Tab key, for example, is frequently used to move the cursor from one window control to the next. The following code checks whether or not the tab key is pressed:

```
public boolean keyDown(Event evt, int key)
{
    int nTabKey = 9; // ASCII value of the Tab key

    if( key == nTabKey )
    {
        // TODO: place Tab key processing here
        return true;
    }
    ...
}
```

Checking for Modifier Keys

Modifier keys (for example, Alt, Shift, and Ctrl) change the behavior of other keys. In most Windows applications, for example, if you hold down the Shift key and simultaneously press the Insert key, the contents of the clipboard are pasted into the application. In this example, the Shift key is the modifier because it changes the behavior of the Insert key.

The Event class provides methods that test the modifier key's status—this is whether a modifier key is being held down. The methods are *shiftDown( )*, *controlDown( )*, and *metaDown( )*; all these return a *true* boolean value when the key is held down, and they return *false* when the key is not pressed.

The following code determines whether the Ctrl key is pressed.

```
public boolean keyDown(Event evt, int key)
{
    if( evt.controlDown() )
    {
        // TODO: processing for CTRL key
        return true;
    }
    ...
}
```

Alt Key Processing

The Alt key modifier is not delivered to Java applets. This is because, for some platforms, including Microsoft Windows, the Alt key is captured by the web browser to activate its pull-down menu options.

Although the Event class does not provide a method for checking the Alt key modifier's status, it can provide information about the status of the Alt key; this is detailed in the following portion of code:

```
public boolean keyDown(Event evt, int key)
{
    if( evt.modifiers & Event.ALT_MASK )
    {
        // TODO: processing for Alt Key
        return true;
    }
    ...
}
```

In the preceding code, if the result of the expression (evt.modifiers & Event.ALT_MASK) is *true*, then the Alt key is being held down. This test can be performed for the other modifier keys by using the appropriate static member variable (SHIFT_MASK, CTRL_MASK, and so on) instead of ALT_MASK.

Table 10.4   Key Modifiers—Static Member Variables

Member Variable	Description
SHIFT_MASK	The shift modifier constant.
CTRL_MASK	The control modifier constant.
META_MASK	The meta modifier constant.
ALT_MASK	The alt modifier constant.

Some function keys—such as Shift, Ctrl, Num Lock, Insert, Scroll Lock, Pause, Print Scrn, and Caps Lock—generate a KEYUP event, but they never generate a KEYDOWN event.

Keyboard Event Handling: The KeyTester Applet

Figure 10.5 shows the output of the KeyTester applet when executed in the Internet Explorer web browser. This applet provides working examples of the various keyboard event handling techniques that you may want to add to your interactive Java applets. The KeyTester applet is included on the CD that comes with this book.

Although FloatingBoxes handles most mouse events, the KeyTester applet handles all keyboard events. When you run this applet, it lists keyboard events as they occur. This applet is useful for observing the result of different keyboard actions. It is also useful in determining the ASCII value of special keys that are not defined within the Event class. Figure 10.5 shows the KeyTester applet before it is activated and figure 10.6 shows the KeyTester applet after it is activated.

Figure 10.5:

The KeyTester applet before it is activated.

Figure 10.6:

The KeyTester applet after it is activated.

The source code for the KeyTester applet is shown in listing 10.3.

Listing 10.3   The KeyTester Applet

```
import java.applet.*;
import java.awt.*;

public class KeyTester extends Applet
{
    boolean  m_bGotFocus = false;

    Event    m_evtList[];

    public String getAppletInfo()
    {
        return "Name: KeyTester\r\n" +
                "Author: @Work Technologies\r\n" +
                "Created with Microsoft Visual J++ Version
➥1.0";
    }

    public void init()
    {
        resize(320, 240);

        m_evtList = new Event[10];
    }

    public void paint(Graphics g)
    {
        Font font;

        g.setColor( Color.lightGray );
        g.draw3DRect( 1, 1, size().width-4, size().height-4,
➥true );
        g.setColor( Color.black );

        if( !m_bGotFocus )
        {
            font = new Font("TimesRoman", Font.BOLD, 20);
            g.setFont(font);
            g.drawString("(Click here to start KeyTester)",
➥70, 150);
```

continues

Listing 10.3   Continued

```
            return;
        }

        font = new Font("TimesRoman", Font.BOLD, 12);
        g.setFont(font);

        g.drawString("Key", 20, 50);
        g.drawString("Event", 80, 50);
        g.drawString("Modifiers", 140, 50);
        g.drawString("Key", 240, 50);
        g.drawString("Event", 270, 50);
        g.drawString("Modifiers", 310, 50);

        for( int i = 0; i < m_evtList.length; i++ )
        {
            if( m_evtList[i] != null )
                showEvent( g, m_evtList[i], 80+(i*20) );
        }
    }

    public void showEvent( Graphics g, Event evt, int row )
    {
        Font   font = new Font("TimesRoman", Font.PLAIN,
12);
        String outputStr = "";
        char   ch;

        g.setFont(font);

        if( evt.key == 32 )
            outputStr = "<space>";
        else if( evt.key > 32 && evt.key < 127 )
            outputStr = ""+(char)evt.key;
        else if(evt.key >= evt.HOME && evt.key <= evt.F12)
            outputStr = getFunctionKeyString( evt.key );
        else
            outputStr = "<n/a>";

        g.drawString(outputStr, 20, row);
```

```
            if( evt.id == evt.KEY_PRESS ¦¦ evt.id ==
➥evt.KEY_ACTION )
                outputStr = "KeyDown";
            else if( evt.id == evt.KEY_RELEASE ¦¦ evt.id ==
➥evt.KEY_ACTION_RELEASE )
                outputStr = "KeyUp";
            else
                outputStr = "";

            g.drawString(outputStr, 80, row);

            outputStr = "";
            if( evt.controlDown() )
                outputStr += "CTRL ";
            if( evt.shiftDown() )
                outputStr += "SHIFT ";
            if( evt.metaDown() )
                outputStr += "META ";
            if( (evt.modifiers & Event.ALT_MASK) != 0 )
                outputStr += "ALT ";

            g.drawString(outputStr, 140, row);


            outputStr = ""+evt.key;
            g.drawString(outputStr, 240, row);

            outputStr = ""+evt.id;
            g.drawString(outputStr, 270, row);

            outputStr = ""+evt.modifiers;
            g.drawString(outputStr, 310, row);
        }

    public String getFunctionKeyString(int key)
    {
        String keyStrings[] =
➥{"HOME","END","PGUP","PGDN","UP","DOWN",
```

continues

Listing 10.3   Continued

```
                    "LEFT","RIGHT","F1","F2","F3","F4","F5",
                    "F6","F7","F8","F9","F10","F11","F12"};

    int    keyOffset = key - Event.HOME;

    if( keyOffset < 0 ¦¦ keyOffset >= keyStrings.length )
        return "<n/a>";

    return keyStrings[(key-Event.HOME)];
}

public boolean gotFocus(Event evt, Object arg)
{
    m_bGotFocus = true;
    repaint();
    return true;
}

public boolean lostFocus(Event evt, Object arg)
{
    m_bGotFocus = false;
    repaint();
    return true;
}

public boolean keyDown(Event evt, int key)
{
    addEvent( evt );
    return true;
}

public boolean keyUp(Event evt, int key)
{
    addEvent( evt );
    return true;
}

public void addEvent(Event evt)
{
```

```
        for( int i = (m_evtList.length-1); i > 0; i— )
            m_evtList[i] = m_evtList[i-1];

        m_evtList[0] = evt;
        repaint();
    }
}
```

KeyTester Applet Methods

In the KeyTester applet's *init( )* method, an array of Event objects, called m_evtList, is allocated. When the *paint( )* method is called, it draws a three-dimensional frame around the applet's display area. If the applet does not have the focus, *paint( )* draws the message Click here to start KeyTester. If the applet has the focus, *paint( )* draws the event list heading and calls the *showEvent( )* method to display information related to keyboard events. Starting at the top of the applet's display area, *showEvent( )* lists events in order from the most recent to the least recent.

Both the *keyUp( )* and *keyDown( )* methods call *addEvent( )* to add the event to the m_evtList array. The *gotFocus( )* and *lostFocus( )* methods set the focus flag accordingly and call the *repaint( )* method.

Handling UI Component Events

Another category of events are those generated by UI components. UI components are covered in detail in Chapter 11, "Building a User Interface." These components generate events when the user affects them in a significant way, such as clicking on a Button component. Like mouse and keyboard events, UI component events are represented in the Event class by static data members. Table 10.5 contains a listing of these data members.

Table 10.5 UI Component Event—Static Member Variables

Static Data Member	Event Description
ACTION_EVENT	An action event.
GOT_FOCUS	A component gained the input focus.
LOST_FOCUS	A component lost the input focus.
LIST_SELECT	The item select List event.
LIST_DESELECT	The item deselect List event.
SCROLL_LINE_UP	The line up scroll event.
SCROLL_LINE_DOWN	The line down scroll event.
SCROLL_PAGE_UP	The page up scroll event.
SCROLL_PAGE_DOWN	The page down scroll event.
SCROLL_ABSOLUTE	The absolute scroll event.

The most common UI event processed by the default event handler is the action event, which is represented by the ACTION_EVENT static data member. Whenever a UI component event occurs, an ACTION_EVENT is generated and the default event handler calls the *action()* method.

As demonstrated in the KeyTester applet, the default event handler calls the *gotFocus()* method when the component has input focus. It calls the *lostFocus()* method when the component looses input focus. These methods are important when processing keyboard input because the component must have input focus to receive keyboard events.

The *action()*, *gotFocus()*, and *lostFocus()* methods all take two parameters. One parameter is the Event object. The other parameter provides additional information regarding the event.

Most UI components only generate an ACTION_EVENT. Therefore to add your own event processing for these UI components, you must override the *action()* method. This is shown in the following code.

```
public boolean action( Event evt, Object arg )
{
    // TODO: add processing
    return true;
}
```

Some UI components generate events that are not processed by the default *handleEvent( )* method. A List component, for example, generates a LIST_SELECT event when items are selected. LIST_DESELECT is generated when items are deselected. To handle these events, the default *handleEvent( )* method must be overridden. The following code details this technique.

```
public boolean handleEvent(Event evt)
{
    if(evt.id == LIST_SELECT)
    {
        // TODO: check selected value and set the
➥applet's color
        return TRUE;
    }
}
```

There is a problem with the *handleEvent( )* method shown in the preceding code. Because it overrides the default *handleEvent( )* method, none of the default event processes can occur. The mouse event handling methods, for example, are not called. You can remedy this situation by including a call to the default, or super, *handleEvent( )* method at the end of your own *handleEvent( )* method. This technique is demonstrated in the following code.

```
public boolean handleEvent(Event evt)
{
    if(evt.id == LIST_SELECT)
    {
        // do special processing
```

```
            return TRUE;
    }

    return super.handleEvent( evt ); // call default
handleEvent()
    }
```

In the preceding code, the new *handleEvent( )* method processes all LIST_SELECT events. All other events are passed to the default *handleEvent( )* method. Therefore, you can override the default *handleEvent( )* method to process specific events without having to rewrite the entire code already included in the default *handleEvent( )* method.

The specific events generated by each type of UI component is covered in Chapter 11, "Building a User Interface."

Determining Which UI Component Generated an Event

When you use the *action( )* method to handle UI component events, it is usually necessary to determine which UI component generated the event. The processing performed when an OK button is pressed, for example, is different from the processing performed for a Cancel button.

When a UI Component generates an event, the *target* member variable of the Event class references the component that generated the event. Therefore, you can code special processing for each UI component or handle all components of a specific type in the same manner.

The following code shows how the *target* member variable can be used to handle UI component events.

```
public boolean action( Event evt, Object arg )
{
    if(evt.target instanceof TextField)
    {
        // TODO: processing for text fields
        return true;
    }
    else if( evt.target == OkButton )
    {
        // TODO: processing for the OK button
        return true;
    }
    else if( evt.target == CancelButton )
    {
        // TODO: processing for the Cancel button
        return true;
    }
    ...
}
```

In the preceding code, the instanceof keyword enables the same processing for all UI components of a generic type. This type of processing, for example, enables the applet to spell check all TextField objects.

It is also possible to perform specific event handling for individual components. In the preceding code, for example, both the OkButton and CancelButton objects have their own event processing.

The Event.arg Variable

The value of the *Event.arg* variable provides additional information about the UI component event that has occurred. When a button is pressed, for example, the *arg* variable is set to the button's text. The following code retrieves a Button component's text and performs special processing when the Button's text is "OK."

```
public boolean action( Event evt, Object arg )
{
    if(evt.target instanceof Button)
    {
        String ButtonText = evt.arg.toString();
        if( ButtonText.compareTo( "OK" ) == 0 )
        {
            // do special processing for the OK button
        }
        ...

        return true;
    }
    ...
}
```

Handling Window Events

In Java, window events are delivered to stand-alone GUI-based Java applications and pop-up applet windows. Classes derived from the Applet class do not receive any window events because an applet's display area is embedded within a web page. GUI-based Java applications, pop-up windows, and window events are discussed in Chapter 12, "More AWT Containers."

Table 10.6 contains a list of the window events delivered by the Java environment.

Table 10.6   Window Event—Static Member Variables

Member Variable	Event Description
WINDOW_DESTROY	The destroy window event.
WINDOW_EXPOSE	The expose window event.
WINDOW_ICONIFY	The iconify window event.
WINDOW_DEICONIFY	The de-iconify window event.
WINDOW_MOVED	The move window event.

Window events are not handled by the default *handleEvent( )* method. Therefore, to handle window events, you must override the *handleEvent( )* method. The most important window event is the WINDOW_DESTROY event. If your Java applications don't handle the WINDOW_DESTROY event properly, users are not able to close the application gracefully.

When you use the Visual J++ Applet Wizard to generate an application, it creates starter code that implements the proper window event handling. The following *handleEvent( )* method was generated by the Visual J++ Applet Wizard for an application.

```
public boolean handleEvent(Event evt)
{
    switch (evt.id)
    {
        case Event.WINDOW_DESTROY:
            dispose();
            System.exit(0);
            return true;

        default:
            return super.handleEvent(evt);
    }
}
```

In the preceding code, the *handleEvent( )* method calls the *system.exit( )* method in response to a WINDOW_DESTROY event. The WINDOW_DESTROY event is typically triggered when the user chooses the Exit option from an application's File pull-down menu; it can also be triggered when the user clicks on the standard window close button on the upper-right side of a window.

The WINDOW_ICONIFY event is delivered when the user minimizes an application, and the WINDOW_DEICONIFY is delivered when the application is restored from iconic form. The WINDOW_EXPOSE event is delivered when an obscured portion of your application window is no longer obscured. The

WINDOW_MOVED event is delivered whenever the main application window is moved on the windows desktop. All these events must be handled from within the *handleEvent( )* method of the Java application's Frame class. Frames are covered in Chapter 12, "More AWT Containers."

Summary

To be interactive, Java programs must be able to react to events. The Event class provides all of the information required to handle events. Java automatically creates an instance of the Event class and calls the *handleEvent( )* method when an event occurs. The *handleEvent( )* method can be overridden to customize or redefine default event handling. Events can be generated by either a user or the system. Users generate mouse, keyboard, UI component, and window events.

Mouse events occur when a user clicks, moves, or alters the state of the mouse attached to a workstation. Although Java runs on a wide variety of hardware platforms, it is possible to code programs to handle platform-specific events. Java programs can detect a right mouse button click in Windows, for example, by checking if the Event.META_MASK bit is set in the *Event.Modifiers* member variable.

Keyboard events occur when a user presses or releases a key on the workstation's keyboard. Modifier keys change the effect of other keys. Java provides methods, including *shiftDown( )* and *controlDown( )*, that make it easy to check whether a modifier key is being pressed.

UI components generally generate ACTION events. The Java environment also delivers GOT_FOCUS and LOST_FOCUS events; these events indicate the status of the component's input focus.

Window events are only delivered to pop-up applet windows and stand-alone GUI-based Java applications.

Questions

1. What two actions are performed by the Java runtime library when an event occurs?

2. When overriding the default *handleEvent( )* method, what line of code must be included in the new *handleEvent( )* method so that the default *handleEvent( )* method is still invoked?

3. How can a Java program identify the component that generated an event?

4. After a button is pressed, what member variable of the Event class contains the text of the button?

5. Can the ALT key modifier be detected by an applet?

6. What modifier keys never generate KEYDOWN events?

7. How can you know when a component has the input focus?

8. Are window events delivered to classes derived from the Applet class?

Answers

1. The runtime library creates an Event object and calls the *handleEvent( )* method.

2. The following line of code can be used to call the default *handleEvent( )* method from within the method that overrides it:

```
/* handleEvent() method: */ return super.handleEvent(
➥evt );
```

3. The *Event.target* member variable of the Event class references the component that generated the event. The following if statement, for example, can be used to determine whether the Cancel button generated a UI component event:

```
if ( evt.target == CancelButton )
{
    // do special processing
    return true;
}
```

4. After a button is pressed the *Event.arg* variable contains the text of the button.

5. No. The ALT key modifier is only delivered to Java applications. With applets, the ALT event is captured and used by the browser to invoke the pull-down menus.

6. The Shift and Ctrl keys never generate KEYDOWN events.

7. The Java environment delivers a GOT_FOCUS event.

8. No. Window events are only delivered to pop-up windows and GUI-based Java applications.

Chapter 11

Building a User Interface

User interface (UI) components are the buttons, text fields, lists, and other essential visual elements that enable users to interact with applets and applications. The previous chapter includes a discussion of how the *action( )* method can be used to handle events for UI components.

This chapter provides a detailed discussion of the UI component classes, which are part of Java's Abstract Windowing Toolkit (AWT) package (the java.awt package). After you have mastered these classes, you will be able to create Java programs that offer the standard graphical user interface features required for any serious business application.

This chapter covers the following topics:

➤ An overview of the Java AWT

➤ AWT UI component classes

➤ How to create custom UI components

➤ How to use layout managers to structure a user interface

If you read this chapter carefully, you should be able to attain a firm grasp on the functionality provided by the standard AWT classes. When you read Chapter 13, "Working with UI Components in Visual J++," you'll also learn how to generate standard Java code for UI components by using the Visual J++ Resource Editor and the Resource Wizard.

Overview of the Java Abstract Windowing Toolkit

The Abstract Windowing Toolkit (AWT) was aptly named because the actual drawing of components is hidden from the developer. The benefit of this is that programmers do not need to be concerned with platform-specific windowing toolkits. User interfaces built by using the AWT have a consistent look and feel.

The AWT provides UI components, containers for those components, an event delivery system (event handling is discussed Chapter 10, "Handling Events")and layout managers for controlling the placement of UI components within containers.

Java AWT *containers* are display areas into which UI components are placed.

Containers can contain other containers. It might be useful, for example, to create a container with a standard grouping of UI components. This container could be re-used by nesting it within other containers.

The discussion in this chapter focuses on the use of applets as container for UI components. Other container classes are covered in Chapter 12, "More AWT Containers."

Figure 11.1 shows the various Java UI components.

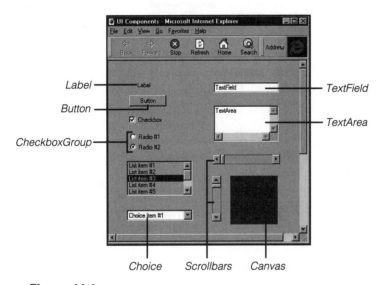

Figure 11.1:

UI components.

Figure 11.2 illustrates the class hierarchy of Java UI Component classes.

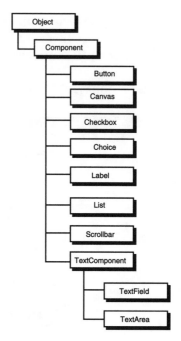

Figure 11.2:

UI components class hierarchy.

Creating and Customizing AWT Components

When you use the UI component classes provided by the Java AWT package, you gain the benefit of a great deal of functionality that has already been coded into these classes. Buttons and list boxes, for example, provide the generic appearance and behavior that is expected in these types of components. By extending these classes, you can create new components with customized behavior. The following sections discuss the AWT's UI component classes and how to utilize them to build powerful Java programs.

Adding UI Components to Your Java Applets

As previously mentioned, a container is an object, such as a Panel, that can hold UI components. Because the Applet class is derived from the Panel class, applets can hold UI components. To place a UI component within your applet, you need to use the *add( )* method. For simple applets you should place the code for adding UI components within the applet's *init( )* method.

The following code shows how a Label component can be created in an applet's *init( )* method.

```
public void init()
{
    ...

    Label l = new Label("This is a label");
    add(l);
    ...
}
```

Some complex applets require a lot of processing in the *init()* method. Consequently, adding UI code may make the *init()* method too lengthy. In these cases, you should consider implementing a separate method that creates and positions UI components.

The following code shows how a separate *CreateUI()* method could be implemented.

```
public void init()
{
    ...
    CreateUI();
    ...
}
private void CreateUI()
{
    Label l = new Label("This is a label");
    add(l);
}
```

Although it does require a little more work, implementing a separate *CreateUI( )* method may make your code more understandable and much easier to maintain.

UI Component Placement

By default, UI components are placed in an applet's display area from left to right and from top to bottom. When all of the space in a row is used, the next UI component is placed on the next row. Usually this will not create the desired user interface. Initially, you will be working with this form of UI component layout. The last part of this chapter focuses on how the Java *layout manager* classes can be used to control UI component placement and sizing.

Layout managers are Java classes that control the placement and dimensions of UI components within a container.

Because Java programs can be displayed on a wide variety of monitors with different sizes and resolutions, user interface appearance can vary greatly. Layout managers give you greater control over how UI components are placed on the display. Components, for example, can be laid out from left to right, in a grid, or around the edges of an applet's display area.

UI Component Size

Without deriving new classes from the AWT classes, UI component size can only be modified by either changing the current font or by changing the layout manager that is used. The Java layout manager classes use the *preferredSize( )* and *minimumSize( )* methods to determine the proper placement and size of each component within a container.

If you need more control over the size of each AWT UI component, you can create your own subclassed component and override both the *preferredSize( )* and *minimumSize( )* methods as shown in the following code:

```
public class MyLabel extends Label
{
    public Dimension preferredSize
    {
        return minimumSize();
    }
    public Dimension minimumSize
    {
        return new Dimension(100, 75);
    }
    ...
}
```

The method illustrated above will enable you to control the size of your UI components. It is important to remember that Java is cross-platform. Consequently, you should always test the changes you have made in your subclass on as many platforms as possible. Doing this will help to ensure consistency in your applet's UI.

Some AWT UI components, such as *TextField*, have more specific *preferredSize()* and *minimumSize()* methods.

The Components

If you have had any exposure to graphical user interface development, many of the UI components described in the following sections should be familiar to you. This section covers each UI component's behavior, attributes, and the methods used to control both. As you read this section, it may be useful for you to refer back to the screen shot of UI components shown in figure 11.1 as well as the UI component class hierarchy shown in figure 11.2.

The following paragraphs discuss the primary behavior, constructors, class variables, class methods, and event handling capabilities of each UI component. If these attributes are not listed, it is because they do not apply to the UI component in question. Event handling for Label components, for example, is not discussed because a Label does not generate any events.

Label Component

The most basic UI component is the *Label*. A Label is a text string that is usually used to indicate the name of other UI components. Label components can be assigned an arbitrary text string and alignment attribute. After a Label has been created, the text string and alignment can be queried and modified.

Constructors

To construct a Label component, you may use one of the following constructor forms:

➤ *Label( )*—Constructs an empty Label.

➤ *Label(String text)*—Constructs a new Label with the specified *text*.

➤ *Label(String text, int alignment)*—Constructs a new Label with the specified *text* and the specified *alignment*.

Static Data Members

The following static definitions are provided by the Label class to be used in specifying the alignment of the text within the Label component's display area:

➤ LEFT—left alignment of the text

➤ CENTER—center alignment of the text

➤ RIGHT—right alignment of the text

Class Methods

The following methods enable you to query and to set the various attributes of a Label component.

➤ *int getAlignment( )*—Gets the current alignment of the Label.

➤ *String getText( )*—Gets the text of the Label.

➤ *void setAlignment(int alignment)*—Sets the alignment for the Label to the specified alignment that is defined by a static data member.

➤ *void setText(String text)*—Sets the text for the Label to the string specified by the *text* parameter.

Button Component

A *Button* is one of the most common UI components. A Button can be constructed with a text string and will trigger a user event when pressed.

Constructors

To construct a Button object, you can use one of the following constructor forms:

➤ *Button( )*—Constructs a Button with no label.

➤ *Button(String text)*—Constructs a Button with a string label.

Class Methods

The following methods enable Java programs to query and to set the various attributes of the Button component:

➤ *String getLabel( )*—Gets the label text of the Button.

➤ *void setLabel(String text)*—Sets the Button label with the string value specified by the *text* parameter.

Event Handling

The Button component only generates one event, ACTION_EVENT, which is triggered when a Button is pressed.

After the event is generated, the Event member variable *Event.arg* will contain the Button's label text. This value can be extracted into a String object as demonstrated by the following line of code:

```
String myarg = evt.arg.toString();
```

Checkbox Component

The *Checkbox* UI component has two states: *true,* or selected, and *false,* or deselected. Checkbox components trigger user events when selected and deselected. When more than one Checkbox appears within a container, they can either be independently selected or they can be exclusive of each other. When only one Checkbox component in a group can be selected at one time, the Checkbox components in the group are usually referred to as radio buttons. In Java, Checkbox components can be given the behavior of radio buttons by associating each component with another object called a CheckboxGroup.

Constructors

To construct a Checkbox object, you may use one of the following constructor forms:

➤ *Checkbox( )*—Constructs a Checkbox initialized to a false state with no label text and no CheckboxGroup association.

➤ *Checkbox(String text)*—Constructs a Checkbox initialized to a false state with the specified label text and no CheckboxGroup association.

➤ *Checkbox(String text, CheckboxGroup cbg, boolean state)*—Constructs a Checkbox with the specified label text, specified CheckboxGroup, and specified boolean state.

Class Methods

The following methods enable you to query and to set the various attributes of the Checkbox component:

➤ *CheckboxGroup getCheckboxGroup( )*—Returns the CheckboxGroup associated with the Checkbox.

➤ *String getLabel( )*—Gets the label text of the Checkbox.

➤ *boolean getState( )*—Returns the boolean state of the Checkbox.

➤ *void setCheckboxGroup(CheckboxGroup cbg)*—Sets the CheckboxGroup to the specified CheckboxGroup object.

➤ *void setLabel(String text)*—Sets the label *text* of the Checkbox to the specified String.

➤ *void setState(boolean state)*—Sets the Checkbox to the specified boolean state—*true* if selected or *false* if deselected.

Event Handling

The Checkbox component only generates one event— ACTION_EVENT. This event is triggered when a Checkbox is selected or deselected

After the event is generated, the Event member variable *Event.arg* will be *true* if the Checkbox is checked or *false* if the Checkbox is not checked. This value can be extracted into a boolean as demonstrated in the following code.

```
String myargtemp = evt.arg.toString();
boolean myarg = new Boolean(myarg).booleanValue();
```

CheckboxGroup

A *CheckboxGroup* is not a UI component. As mentioned in the last section, however, it can be used to create an association between a collection of Checkbox components. When you instantiate a CheckboxGroup object and use it to create a set of Checkbox controls, only one of those Checkbox controls can be selected at a time. Therefore, you can only use a CheckboxGroup when one choice is possible out of a group.

Constructors

To construct a CheckboxGroup object, you may use the following constructor form:

➤ *CheckboxGroup( )*—Constructs a CheckboxGroup object.

Class Methods

The following methods enable you to query and to set the various attributes of the CheckboxGroup object:

➤ *Checkbox getCurrent( )*—Gets the Checkbox component in the group that is currently selected.

➤ *void setCurrent(Checkbox cbox)*—Sets the specified Checkbox to *true*. If another Checkbox within the CheckboxGroup was previously set to *true*, it is set to *false.*

Choice Component

The *Choice* component generates a drop-down list. The Choice component enables one item to be selected at a time. An event is triggered when an item is selected. The Choice component does not have sorting capabilities, therefore, items are positioned in the Choice list in the order that they were added.

Constructors

To construct a Choice component, you may use the following constructor form:

➤ *Choice( )*—Constructs a new Choice component.

Class Methods

The following methods enable you to query and to set the various attributes of the Choice component:

➤ *addItem(String item)*—Adds an item to the Choice list.

➤ *int countItems( )*—Returns the number of items in the Choice list.

➤ *String getItem(int index)*—Returns the *String* at the specified index within the Choice pull-down list.

➤ *int getSelectedIndex( )*—Returns the index of the currently selected Choice item.

➤ *String getSelectedItem( )*—Returns a *String* representation of the selected Choice item.

➤ *void select(int item)*—Selects the Choice item with the specified position.

➤ *void select(String text)*—Selects the Choice item with the specified text.

Event Handling

The Choice component generates only one event— ACTION_EVENT. The event is triggered when an item is selected or deselected.

After the event is generated, the Event member variable *Event.arg* will contain the text of the selected item. This value can be extracted into a String object as demonstrated by the following line of code:

```
String myarg = evt.arg.toString();
```

List Component

The *List* component displays a number of selectable items in a multiline list box. The number of rows to display in a list can be specified in the constructor. A List can be defined to enable a user to select one item at a time, or more than one item at a time. The List component triggers user events when items are selected or deselected.

Constructors

To construct a List component, you can use one of the following constructor forms:

➤ *List()*—Creates a new scrolling list initialized with no visible lines and no multiple selections.

➤ *List(int lines, boolean multsel)*—Creates a new scrolling list initialized with the specified number of visible lines and a boolean value that indicates whether multiple selections are allowed or not.

Class Methods

The following methods enable you to query and to set the various attributes of a List component:

➤ *void addItem(String item)*—Adds the specified item to the end of the scrolling List.

➤ *void addItem(String item, int index)*—Adds the specified item at the index given. If index is greater than the List length, the item is added to the end of the scrolling List.

➤ *boolean allowsMultipleSelections()*—Returns *true* if this List enables multiple selections.

➤ *void clear()*—Clears the List.

➤ *int countItems()*—Returns the number of items in the List.

➤ *void delItem(int index)*—Deletes an item from the List.

➤ *void delItems(int start, int end)*—Deletes a range of items from the List.

➤ *void deselect(int index)*—Deselects the item at the specified index.

➤ *String getItem(int index)*—Gets the item at the specified index.

➤ *int getRows()*—Returns the number of visible lines in the List.

➤ *int getSelectedIndex()*—Gets the index of the selected item on the list or –1 if no item is selected.

➤ *int[] getSelectedIndexes()*—Returns the indices of the selected items in the List as an *int* array.

➤ *String getSelectedItem()*—Returns the selected item on the List or the value of *null* if no item is selected.

➤ *String[ ] getSelectedItems()*—Returns the selected items on the List in a *String* array.

➤ *int getVisibleIndex()*—Returns the index of the item that was last made visible by the *makeVisible()* method.

➤ *boolean isSelected(int index)*—Returns *true* if the item at the specified index has been selected; otherwise, it returns a value of *false.*

➤ *void makeVisible(int index)*—Forces the item at the specified index to be visible in the List.

➤ *Dimension minimumSize(int rows)*—Returns the minimum dimensions needed for the amount of rows in the List.

➤ *Dimension preferredSize(int rows)*—Returns the preferred dimensions needed for the List with the specified number of rows.

➤ *void replaceItem(String item, int index)*—Replaces the item at the specified index with the specified item.

➤ *void select(int index)*—Chooses the item at the specified index.

➤ *void setMultipleSelections(boolean bMuliSel)*—Sets whether this List enables multiple selections or not.

Event Handling

The following events can be generated by the List component:

➤ *LIST_SELECT*—Triggered when an item is selected in a List control.

➤ *LIST_DESELECT*—Triggered when an item is deselected in a List control. This only occurs when the List has multiple selection turned on.

After an event has been generated, the Event member variable *Event.arg* will contain the index of the item that was selected or deselected as a zero-based number. This value can be extracted into an *int* variable as demonstrated by the following line of code:

```
int myarg = ((Integer)evt.arg).intValue();
```

TextComponent Component

As illustrated in figure 11.2, the *TextComponent* component is the super class of the TextField and TextArea classes. These classes provide methods that make it possible to get and set both the full text within the UI component and the currently selected text within the component. All the TextComponent methods are available for both the TextField and TextArea classes.

Class Methods

The following methods enable you to query and to set the various attributes of the TextComponent component:

➤ *String getSelectedText( )*—Returns the selected text contained in the TextComponent.

➤ *int getSelectionEnd( )*—Returns the selected text's end position.

➤ *int getSelectionStart( )*—Returns the selected text's start position.

➤ *String getText( )*—Returns the full text contained in the TextComponent.

➤ *boolean isEditable( )*—Returns a boolean value that indicates whether this TextComponent is editable.

➤ *void select(int start, int end)*—Selects the text found between the specified *start* and *end* character locations within the TextComponent.

➤ *void selectAll( )*—Selects all the text in the TextComponent.

➤ *void setEditable(boolean bEditable)*—Sets whether the TextComponent is editable.

➤ *void setText(String text)*—Sets the text of the TextComponent.

TextField Component

The *TextField* component enables the user to enter information into a text field. TextField components can be created as empty or with an initial string. TextField components can be defined to have an initial number of columns.

If you do not define an initial number of columns, then the layout manager may use the TextField component's initial text value to determine the TextField component's appropriate length. The TextField component inherits most of its functionality from TextComponent.

Constructors

To construct a TextField component, you can use one of the following constructor forms:

➤ *TextField()*—Constructs a new TextField.

➤ *TextField(int cols)*—Constructs a new TextField initialized with the specified number of columns.

➤ *TextField(String text)*—Constructs a new TextField initialized with the specified text.

➤ *TextField(String text, int cols)*—Constructs a new TextField initialized with the specified text and number of columns.

Class Methods

The following methods enable you to query and to set the various attributes of the TextField component:

➤ *boolean echoCharIsSet()*—Returns *true* if the TextField has been defined to echo a specific character to the screen when a user types into the field.

➤ *int getColumns()*—Returns the number of columns in the TextField.

➤ *char getEchoChar()*—Returns the character that has been defined to be used for echoing.

➤ *Dimension minimumSize(int cols)*—Returns the minimum size dimensions needed for the TextField with the specified number of columns.

➤ *Dimension preferredSize(int cols)*—Returns the preferred size dimensions needed for the TextField with the specified number of columns.

➤ *void setEchoCharacter(char echoChar)*—Sets the echo character for the TextField.

An echo character is the character displayed in the TextField when a key is pressed. The echo character, for example, for a password text field is frequently an asterisk.

Event Handling

The TextField component generates only one event, ACTION_EVENT. The event is triggered when the Enter key is pressed in the TextField component.

After the event is generated, the Event member variable *Event.arg* will contain the content of the TextField. This value can be extracted into a String object as demonstrated by the following line of code:

```
String myarg = evt.arg.toString();
```

TextArea Component

The *TextArea* component can contain multiple lines of text. Like the TextField component, TextArea components can also be created either empty or with an initial string. TextArea components can be defined with an initial number of rows and columns. The TextArea component inherits most of its functionality from TextComponent.

Constructors

To construct a TextArea component, you can use one of the following constructor forms:

➤ *TextArea( )*—Constructs a new TextArea.

➤ *TextArea(int rows, int cols)*—Constructs a new TextArea with the specified number of rows and columns.

➤ *TextArea(String text)*—Constructs a new TextArea with the specified text displayed.

➤ *TextArea(String text, int rows, int cols)*—Constructs a new TextArea with the specified text, number of rows, and number of columns.

The constructors for the TextArea component provide a high degree of flexibility to the developer. In most cases, you should try to use the constructor that accepts the highest level of detail. If your program, for example, can determine the required columns, rows, and text at the time that it creates a TextArea object, you should utilize this information by using the appropriate constructor. That way, the UI presented to the end-user will not have to change the proportionate amount of display space allocated to the TextArea component.

Class Methods

The following methods enable you to query and to set the various attributes of the TextArea component:

➤ *void appendText(String text)*—Appends the specified text to the end of the TextArea's existing text.

➤ *int getColumns( )*—Returns the number of columns in the TextArea.

➤ *int getRows( )*—Returns the number of rows in the TextArea.

➤ *insertText(String text, int index)*—Inserts the specified text at the specified position within the TextArea's existing text.

➤ *Dimension minimumSize(int rows, int cols)*—Returns a Dimension object defining the minimum size of the TextArea given the specified number of rows and columns.

➤ *Dimension preferredSize(int rows, int cols)*—Returns a Dimension object defining the preferred size of the TextArea given the specified number rows and columns.

➤ *void replaceText(String text, int rows, int cols)*—Replaces the existing text from the indicated start to end positions with the new text specified.

A Dimension object defines the size of an entity, typically in pixels. The TextArea class methods, *minimumSize()* and *preferredSize()*, both translate a specified number of rows and columns in a TextArea object to the appropriate dimensions measured in pixels.

Event Handling

The TextArea component generates only one event, ACTION_EVENT. The event is triggered when the Enter key is pressed in the TextArea component.

After the event is generated, the Event member variable *Event.arg* will contain the contents of the TextArea. This value can be extracted into a String object as demonstrated by the following line of code:

```
String myarg = evt.arg.toString();
```

Scrollbar Component

The *Scrollbar* component is used to enable the user to choose an arbitrary value between a minimum and maximum. The Scrollbar's values are changed by using either the line increment, page increment, or thumb control.

The following line of code would generate the Scrollbar control shown in figure 11.3:

```
Scrollbar(Scrollbar.HORIZONTAL, 35, 0, 1, 100);
```

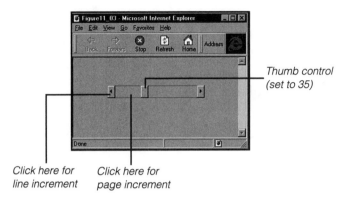

Thumb control
(set to 35)

Click here for
line increment

Click here for
page increment

Figure 11.3:
The Scrollbar control.

Constructors

To construct a Scrollbar component, you can use one of the
following constructor forms:

➤ *Scrollbar()*—Constructs a new Scrollbar. By default, it will
have a vertical orientation.

➤ *Scrollbar(int orientation)*—Constructs a new Scrollbar with
the specified orientation (horizontal or vertical).

➤ *Scrollbar(int orientation, int value, int SizeofThumb, int
min, int max)*—Constructs a new Scrollbar with the specified orientation, value, size of the thumb control, minimum
value, and maximum value.

In most cases it is advisable to explicitly define the state of the
Scrollbar at the time your program instantiates a Scrollbar object.
If the Scrollbar being created, for example, must have a vertical
orientation, you could use the constructor that provides the
minimal amount of information—*Scrollbar()*. If, however you
explicitly define the orientation in the constructor, your code will
be more easily understood by another developer. You can use the
constructor that provides the maximum amount of detail when

you need finite control over the state of the Scrollbar. A Scrollbar component that controls brightness, for example, could be set to a default value.

Static Data Members

The following static definitions are provided by the Scrollbar class and can be used to specify, or determine, the orientation of a Scrollbar:

➤ *HORIZONTAL*—The horizontal Scrollbar variable.

➤ *VERTICAL*—The vertical Scrollbar variable.

Class Methods

The following methods enable you to query and to set the various attributes of the Scrollbar component:

➤ *int getLineIncrement( )*—Gets the line increment for the Scrollbar.

➤ *int getMaximum( )*—Returns the maximum value of the Scrollbar.

➤ *int getMinimum( )*—Returns the minimum value of the Scrollbar.

➤ *int getOrientation( )*—Returns the orientation of the Scrollbar.

➤ *int getPageIncrement( )*—Returns the page increment of the Scrollbar.

➤ *int getValue( )*—Returns the current value of the Scrollbar.

➤ *int getVisible( )*—Returns the visible amount of the Scrollbar.

➤ *void setLineIncrement(int LineInc)*—Sets the line increment for the Scrollbar. When the user clicks on the arrow on either end of the Scrollbar, the Scrollbar's value changes by the amount specified by *LineInc.*

➤ *setPageIncrement(int PageInc)*—Sets the page increment for the Scrollbar. When the user clicks on the area on either side of the slider, the value of the Scrollbar will change by the value specified by the *PageInc* variable.

➤ *setValue(int value)*—Sets the value of the Scrollbar to the specified *value*. If a Scrollbar's value, for example, can be from 1 to 100, and the *setValue( )* method is used to set the value at 50, the slider will be positioned exactly in the middle of the Scrollbar.

➤ *setValues(int value, int PageInc, int min, int max)*—Sets the value, page increment, minimum value, and maximum value of the Scrollbar.

Event Handling

The following events can be generated by the Scrollbar component:

➤ *SCROLL_LINE_UP*—Triggered when the Scrollbar's left or top line increment control is pressed.

➤ *SCROLL_LINE_DOWN*—Triggered when the Scrollbar's right or bottom line control is pressed.

➤ *SCROLL_PAGE_UP*—Triggered when the Scrollbar's left or top page increment is pressed.

➤ *SCROLL_PAGE_DOWN*—Triggered when the Scrollbar's right or bottom page increment is pressed.

➤ *SCROLL_ABSOLUTE*—Triggered when the Scrollbar's thumb control is dragged.

After an event is generated, the Event member variable *Event.arg* will contain the value of the Scrollbar. This value can be extracted into an *int* data type as demonstrated by the following line of code:

```
int myarg = ((Integer)evt.arg).intValue();
```

Canvas Component

If you are going to create a custom UI control, the Canvas class is the base class you want to extend. The Canvas class has only one method, *paint(Graphics g)*. Because the Canvas class is derived from the Component class, you can use it to trap all mouse and keyboard events. You can also use the Canvas class to create any type of control you desire with minimum effort. Of course, to use Canvas effectively, you have to derive a class from it.

Constructors

To construct a Canvas object, you can use the following constructor form:

➤   *Canvas( )*—Constructs a new Canvas.

Class Variables

The Canvas class does not contain any class-specific variables.

Class Methods

The following method is available for the Canvas component:

➤   *paint(Graphics g)*—Paints the Canvas by using the default background color. You can customize the Canvas component by overriding the *paint( )* method.

Event Handling

The Canvas component passes all mouse and keyboard events to the container. Because the Canvas component gets all the events first, however, you can use it to create customized components. You can, for example, trap all events except for the MOUSE_UP event and reset the *Event.id* variable to ACTION_EVENT, thus simulating a button.

After an event is generated, the Event member variable *Event.arg* will contain a null value for a Canvas component. This value can be set to any information relevant to the custom component. This is done in the *handleEvent()* method of your Canvas-derived class by setting the *Event.arg* variable to any valid data object. When you put a value in *Event.arg*, you must obey the Java casting rules—casting rules are discussed in Chapter 4, "Java Classes and Objects." If, for example, you put a String value in *Event.arg*, you should extract it into a String data type.

The following code shows the *handleEvent( )* method of a customized Canvas component that only generates the ACTION_EVENT. The *Event.arg* variable will always contain the string "Custom Value".

```
public boolean handleEvent(Event evt)
{
    evt.arg = new String("Custom Value");
    if( evt.id == Event.MOUSE_UP )
    {
        evt.id = Event.ACTION_EVENT;
        return false; // forward this event to the
➥container
    }

    return true; // do not forward this event to the
➥container
}
```

Custom UI Components

The code in listing 11.1 shows how a basic custom UI component, called the HelloComponent, can be created by extending the Canvas class. Figure 11.4 shows the output of the new component.

Listing 11.1   The Hello Custom UI Component

```
class HelloComponent extends Canvas
{
    public void paint(Graphics g)
    {
        g.setColor(Color.white);
        g.fillRect(0,0,size().width,size().height);
        g.setColor(Color.red);
        g.drawString("Hello", 40, 50);
    }

    public boolean handleEvent(Event evt)
    {
        evt.arg = new String("Hello");
        if( evt.id == Event.MOUSE_UP )
        {
            evt.id = Event.ACTION_EVENT;
            return false; // forward this event to the
➡container
        }

        return true; // do not forward this event to the
➡container
    }
    public Dimension preferredSize()
    {
        return minimumSize();
    }

    public Dimension minimumSize()
    {
        return new Dimension(100,100);
    }
}
```

Figure 11.4:

The Hello custom UI component.

Most UI components generate only one event, ACTION_EVENT. Therefore, it is possible to handle most UI component generated events by
overriding the *action()* method.

UI Component Placement and Layout Managers

Because Java supports many operating systems, the mechanisms
provided for UI component placement must offer a great deal of
flexibility. A container's layout manager controls the placement
and sizing of a UI component within the container. As mentioned
earlier in this chapter, layout managers are Java classes that help
define the position and dimensions of UI components. The
following layout manager classes are provided in the AWT:

➤ FlowLayout

➤ GridLayout

➤ BorderLayout

➤ CardLayout

➤ GridBagLayout

In addition to the standard AWT layout managers, you can create
your own customized layout manager, use no layout manager, or

use the DialogLayout layout manager provided when you generate components by using the Visual J++ Java Resource Wizard. The Java Resource Wizard is covered in Chapter 13, "Working with UI Components in Visual J++."

The following paragraphs discuss the various options available to you for controlling UI component layout in Java applets and applications.

FlowLayout Layout Manager

All the previous examples shown in this book have used the FlowLayout layout manager. FlowLayout is the default layout manager for the Panel class, which is the super class of the Applet class. Therefore, when placing components within an applet's display area, FlowLayout is used by default.

The FlowLayout class places UI components on the screen from left to right and from top to bottom. When a row is completely filled, a new one will be started.

The FlowLayout class has several constructors that enable you to effect component alignment as well as gaps.

Constructors

To construct a FlowLayout object, you can use one of the following constructor forms:

➤ *FlowLayout( )*—Constructs a FlowLayout object with a centered alignment—all UI components will be aligned to the center of the display area.

➤ *FlowLayout(int alignment)*—Constructs a FlowLayout object with the specified alignment as defined by one of the *FlowLayout* static data members.

➤ *FlowLayout(int alignment, int HorzGap, intVertGap)*— Constructs a FlowLayout object with the specified alignment and gap values. The horizontal gap is to the left or right of a UI component in pixels. The vertical gap is the area above or below the UI component in pixels.

Static Data Members

The following static definitions are provided by the FlowLayout class to be used in specifying the alignment of UI components:

➤ *CENTER*—The center alignment variable.

➤ *LEFT*—The left alignment variable.

➤ *RIGHT*—The right alignment variable.

FlowLayout Examples

The following code sets the layout manager to the FlowLayout constructor and adds eight buttons to the container:

```java
import java.awt.*;

public class FlowApp extends java.applet.Applet
{
    public void init()
    {
        setLayout(new FlowLayout());
        add(new Button("1"));
        add(new Button("2"));
        add(new Button("3"));
        add(new Button("4"));
        add(new Button("5"));
        add(new Button("6"));
        add(new Button("7"));
        add(new Button("8"));
    }
}
```

The `setLayout(new FlowLayout());` line in the previous code example is unnecessary because FlowLayout is the default layout manager. It was used to illustrate the setting of a layout manager and to be consistent with the other examples.

Figure 11.5 shows a view of the FlowApp applet's output with its default window size.

Figure 11.5:

FlowLayout—default size.

Figure 11.6 shows the applet after resizing it to a smaller window size.

Figure 11.6:

FlowLayout—small size.

The default for alignment and gap values can be changed by using the following FlowLayout constructor:

```
setLayout(new FlowLayout(FlowLayout.LEFT, 30, 15));
```

Figure 11.7 shows the placement of the UI components by using the new alignment and gap parameters.

Figure 11.7:

FlowLayout.

GridLayout Layout Manager

The GridLayout class enables you to divide a Panel into a specified number of rows and columns. When you use *GridLayout,* the UI components are placed in each cell from left to right and from top to bottom.

The GridLayout class has two constructors that enable you to effect the number of rows and columns and the gaps between the components.

Constructors

To construct a GridLayout component, you may use one of the following constructor forms:

➤ *GridLayout(int rows, int cols)*—Creates a GridLayout with the specified rows and columns.

➤ *GridLayout(int rows, int cols, int hgap, int vgap)*— Creates a GridLayout with the specified rows, columns, horizontal gap, and vertical gap.

GridLayout Examples

The following line of code shows how to construct a GridLayout object with two rows and four columns:

```
setLayout(new GridLayout(2,4));
```

Figure 11.8 is an example of the output that would be produced by using the GridLayout layout manager as defined by the preceding line of code.

Figure 11.8:

GridLayout.

Notice that GridLayout will expand the sizes of the buttons to fill in the entire area of the Panel. The horizontal and vertical gap defaults are both zero.

The gaps between the buttons can be changed by using the following GridLayout constructor:

```
setLayout(new GridLayout(2,4,30,15));
```

Figure 11.9 shows the output that would be produced by using the GridLayout defined in the preceding line of code.

Figure 11.9:

GridLayout with gaps.

The horizontal and vertical gap effects the space between the components, not the space between a component and the edge of the panel
display area.

BorderLayout Layout Manager

The *BorderLayout* class enables you to place UI components
within a Panel based on the following navigational directions:

➤ *North*—Places the component on the top of the Panel.

➤ *South*—Places the component on the bottom of the Panel.

➤ *East*—Places the component on the right side of the Panel.

➤ *West*—Places the component on the left side of the Panel.

➤ *Center*—Places the component in the center of the Panel.

The BorderLayout class has two constructors that enable you to
effect the gap between components.

Constructors

To construct a BorderLayout object, you can use one of the
following constructor forms.

➤ *BorderLayout( )*—Constructs a new BorderLayout.

➤ *BorderLayout(int hgap, int vgap)*—Constructs a BorderLayout
with the specified gaps between UI components.

BorderLayout Examples

When UI components are added to a Panel with a BorderLayout,
the UI component's navigational direction must be a String
object as demonstrated by the following code:

```
setLayout(new BorderLayout());

add("North",new Button("North"));
add("South",new Button("South"));
add("East",new Button("East"));
add("West",new Button("West"));
add("Center",new Button("Center"));
```

Figure 11.10 shows the output that would be produced by this code.

Figure 11.10:

BorderLayout.

If a navigational direction is not used, that area of the window will not be reserved and will be used by the other UI components. If, for example, the *North* button was not specified in the preceding example, the *East, West,* and *Center* buttons would expand to take up the unused space.

The default horizontal and vertical gaps can be changed by using the following constructor:

```
setLayout(new BorderLayout(30,15));
```

Figure 11.11 shows the output that would be produced by using a BorderLayout as defined in the previous line of code. The horizontal gaps are set to 30 pixels and the vertical gaps are set to 15 pixels.

Figure 11.11:

BorderLayout with gaps.

CardLayout Layout Manager

The *CardLayout* class is very different from the layout managers discussed so far. The CardLayout class enables you to separate one set of UI components from another. By using this capability, you can create a tabbed dialog box in Java.

When you use the CardLayout class, you add the UI component to the Panel with a name for the component. The name can be used to refer to the UI component later.

Constructors

To construct a CardLayout object, you can use one of the following constructor forms:

➤ *CardLayout( )*—Constructs a new CardLayout.

➤ *CardLayout(int hgap, int vgap)*—Constructs a CardLayout with the specified gaps.

Class Methods

The following methods enable you to navigate through the UI components in the CardLayout:

➤ *show(Container cntr, String CompName)*—Displays the named UI component in the container.

➤ *first(Container cntr)*—Displays the first UI component added to the container.

➤ *last(Container cntr)*—Displays the last UI component added to the container.

➤ *next(Container cntr)*—Displays the next UI component in the container.

➤ *previous(Container cntr)*—Displays the previous UI component in the container.

CardLayout Examples

The example code in listing 11.2 shows how the CardLayout class can be used to switch between different UI components.

Listing 11.2   CardLayout Example

```
import java.awt.*;

public class CardApp extends java.applet.Applet {
    CardLayout cl;

    public void init()
    {
        cl = new CardLayout();
        setLayout(cl);

        add("1", new Button("Show Chart"));
        add("2", new Button("Show Graph"));
        add("3", new Button("Show Document"));

        cl.first(this);
    }

    public boolean keyUp(Event evt, int key) {
        cl.next(this);
        return true;
    }
}
```

When you execute the preceding applet, each time you press a key, a different button will be displayed. Figure 11.12 shows the CardApp applet's initial display area.

Figure 11.12:

CardLayout—initial display.

Figure 11.13 shows the CardApp applet after the first time a key is pressed.

Figure 11.13:

CardLayout—after pressing a key.

To simulate a tabbed dialog box, the CardLayout class should be set with multiple Panels. Each Panel should contain its own UI components. Then, by using CardLayout methods, entire Panels can be switched and displayed.

GridBagLayout Layout Manager and GridBagConstraints

The *GridBagLayout* class can be used to define more precise placement of UI components in Java applets. The GridBagLayout, however, is the most complex and difficult layout manager available.

GridBagLayout is similar to the GridLayout layout manager because the Panel is divided into a grid of cells with rows and columns. The UI components are added from left to right and from top to bottom. In GridBagLayout, however, the number of rows and columns is based on the UI components, their placement, and their relative sizes.

Constructors

To construct a GridBagLayout object, you can use the following constructor:

➤ *GridBagLayout( )*—Constructs a new GridBagLayout.

To use GridBagLayout, information must be provided describing the size and layout of each UI component. The helper class GridBagConstraints holds all the information needed by the GridBagLayout class to properly position and size each UI component. The GridBagConstraints class is more of a data structure than a class because it only has a few methods but many data members.

GridBagConstraints Class Variables

The following is a list of the GridBagConstraints member variables and their default values that are used to define UI component placement:

➤ *weightx, weighty*—Specifies how the GridBagLayout should distribute space. If you do not specify a weight for at least one UI component in a row (*weightx*) and column (*weighty*), the UI components will cluster together in the middle of the Panel. The default for both *weightx* and *weighty* is zero.

➤ *gridwidth, gridheight*—Specifies the number of cells across or down in a UI component's display area. The default for both variables is one.

➤ *fill*—Specifies how a UI component will fill a cell if that cell is larger than the UI component. The default is to leave UI component size unchanged. The following static data members can be used as valid values for the fill member variable:

GridBagConstraint.NONE—This is the default and it does not change the component's size.

GridBagConstraint.HORIZONTAL—Makes the component wide enough to fill its display area horizontally, but doesn't change its height.

GridBagConstraint.VERTICAL—Makes the component tall enough to fill its display area vertically, but doesn't change its width.

GridBagConstraint.BOTH—Makes the component fill its display area entirely.

➤ *Insets*—Specifies the top, left, bottom, and right gap space between UI components. The default value is zero.

➤ *gridx, gridy*—Specifies the cell in which to place the UI component. This is normally not changed because the default values enable each UI component to be placed just to the right of or just below the last UI component added. If you use the *GridBagConstraints.RELATIVE* static data member to specify the value of *gridx*, the component will be placed just to the right of the last component that was added to the container. If you specify the value of *gridy* as *GridBagConstraints.RELATIVE*, the component will be placed just below the last component that was added to the container.

The following variables only effect the layout if fill is not set to GridBagConstraint.BOTH static data member:

➤ *anchor*—Specifies where to place the UI component in the cell, if the cell is larger than the UI component. The default is to put the UI component in the center of the cell. The following static data members can be used as valid values for *anchor*:

GridBagConstraints.NORTH

GridBagConstraints.NORTHEAST

GridBagConstraints.EAST

GridBagConstraints.SOUTHEAST

GridBagConstraints.SOUTH

GridBagConstraints.SOUTHWEST

GridBagConstraints.WEST

GridBagConstraints.NORTHWEST

➤ *ipadx, ipady*—Specifies the amount to change the minimum width and height of each UI component. Actually, this will add either 2*ipad$x$ to the minimum width or 2*ipad$y$ to the minimum height because the extra space is added to both the left and right (ipad$x$) or both the top and bottom (ipad$y$). The default value for ipad$x$ and ipad$y$ is zero.

Even though the list of GridBagContraints class variables is a bit daunting, don't despair—the default values for most of these variables will suffice for most applets.

GridBagLayout Example

Finally, it's time to take a look at how UI components may be added to a Panel by using GridBagLayout as the layout manager. To associate a constraint with a particular UI component the *setConstraints( )* method must be used. The following code shows how a button may be added to a panel by using GridBagLayout and GridBagConstraints:

```
GridBagLayout gridbag = new GridBagLayout();
GridBagConstraints c = new GridBagConstraints();
setLayout(gridbag);
Button button = new Button("hello");
c.weightx = 1.0;
gridbag.setConstraints(button, c);
add(button);
```

The next step is to put it all together with an example. Figure 11.14 shows the output of an applet that uses GridBagLayout. Note that it would be impossible to create this effect with any other layout manager because each UI component has a specific placement and size.

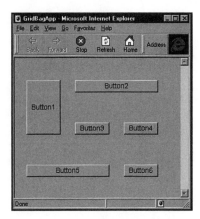

Figure 11.14:

GridBagLayout.

Listing 11.3 contains the applet code that would produce the output shown in figure 11.14.

Listing 11.3   GridBagLayout Example

```
import java.util.*;
import java.awt.*;
import java.applet.Applet;

public class GridBagApp extends Applet
```

continues

Listing 11.3 Continued

```
{
    public void init()
    {
        setFont(new Font("Helvetica", Font.PLAIN, 14));
        GridBagLayout gridbag = new GridBagLayout();
        GridBagConstraints c = new GridBagConstraints();
        setLayout(gridbag);

        // these values will not change
        c.insets = new Insets(30,15,30,15); // change gap
                                            // between
                                            // UI components
        c.fill = GridBagConstraints.BOTH;   // UI components
                                            // will be
                                            // adjusted
                                            // to fill cells
        c.weightx = 1.0;                    // UI components
                                            // will fill
                                            // Panel
                                            // left to right
        c.weighty = 1.0;                    // UI components
                                            // will fill
                                            // Panel
                                            // top to bottom

        c.gridheight = 2;                   // make twice as
                                            // tall
        makebutton("Button1", gridbag, c);

        c.gridheight = 1;                   // back to
                                            //normal
        c.gridwidth = GridBagConstraints.REMAINDER; // end
                                                    // row
        makebutton("Button2", gridbag, c);

        c.gridwidth = GridBagConstraints.RELATIVE; // next-
                                                   // to-
                                                   // last
                                                   // in
                                                   // row
```

```
          makebutton("Button3", gridbag, c);

          c.gridwidth = GridBagConstraints.REMAINDER; // end
                                                      // row
          makebutton("Button4", gridbag, c);

          c.gridwidth = 2; // make twice as wide
          makebutton("Button5", gridbag, c);

          c.gridwidth = GridBagConstraints.REMAINDER; // end
                                                      // row
          makebutton("Button6", gridbag, c);
     }

     protected void makebutton(String name, GridBagLayout
➡gridbag,
            GridBagConstraints c)
     {
          Button button = new Button(name);   // create button
          gridbag.setConstraints(button, c);  // set grid
                                              // constraints
          add(button);                        // add button to
                                              // Panel

     }
}
```

In the *init( ) method,* GridBagLayout and GridBagConstraints
objects are created and the container's layout manager is set to
the GridBagLayout.

Next, values are set in the GridBagConstraints object that are to
be constant for all UI components. These values include the
spacing between UI components, the fill value, as well as the x
and y weight.

Looking ahead in the code, the *makebutton( )* method performs
the task of creating a new Button component, setting the constraints of that button, and adding the button to the applet.

When *Button1* is created, the *gridheight* is adjusted to define the component to be two cell units in height. Next, the applet calls the *makebutton()* method to create and add the *Button1*.

To create *Button2*, the *gridheight* is reset and the *gridwidth* is set to specify that the *Button2* component should use the remaining space in its row. This is done by setting the *gridwidth* class variable to REMAINDER.

Button3 is created with the *gridwidth* variable set to RELATIVE, which makes the control's dimensions dependent on the next component in its row. *Button4* is created after setting *gridwidth* to REMAINDER. The result is that the size of both buttons will be the same and each will use half the space remaining in their respective rows.

Lastly, the *gridwidth* of *Button5* is set to be two cell units and *gridwidth* is reset before adding *Button6*.

It is important to remember that, when you use GridBagLayout, the cell size is determined on a row-by-row basis and is effected by the natural width and height of the components on a row. Figure 11.15 illustrates this by replacing some of the buttons with other controls. Notice that the size of the controls have changed because the natural size of the new controls are different.

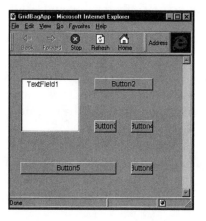

Figure 11.15:
GridBagLayout—not all buttons.

Nested Panels

In many cases, the exact layout of your UI components will require the use of several Panels, each with its own layout manager. Listing 11.4 shows a *CreateUI( )* method that would generate the UI shown in figure 11.16.

Listing 11.4   Nested Panels

```
public void CreateUI()
{
    setLayout(new BorderLayout());
    Panel p1 = new Panel();
    p1.setLayout(new FlowLayout(FlowLayout.LEFT));
    p1.add(new Label("Left Side"));
    p1.add(new Scrollbar(Scrollbar.HORIZONTAL, 1, 0, 1,
➥100));
    add("North",p1);

    Panel p2 = new Panel();
    p2.setLayout(new FlowLayout(FlowLayout.RIGHT));
    p2.add(new Label("Right Side"));
    p2.add(new Scrollbar(Scrollbar.HORIZONTAL, 1, 0, 1,
➥100));
    add("South",p2);
}
```

Figure 11.16:

Nested panels.

To create the desired UI, two panels are required. The first Panel is defined with a left aligned FlowLayout layout manager and the second is defined with a right aligned FlowLayout layout manager. Next, the applet's layout manager is set to BorderLayout. Finally, the two panels are added, one North and one South.

Where and when to nest panels is a skill that can be improved with experience. If certain UI components, for example, are likely to appear frequently together within several different containers, you might want to consider creating a Panel for these components and nesting the entire Panel with other containers when necessary.

Customized Layout Managers

If none of the preceding layout managers meet your needs, you can always create your own. To do this, create a class that implements the LayoutManager interface.

Interface Methods

To create a customized layout manager that implements the LayoutManager interface, you must include the following methods in your class:

➤ *addLayoutComponent(String name, Component comp)*— Adds the specified component with the specified name to the layout.

➤ *layoutContainer(Container cntr)*—Lays out the specified container with this layout.

➤ *minimumLayoutSize(Container cntr)*—Calculates the minimum size dimensions for the specified container given the components in the specified container.

➤ *preferredLayoutSize(Container cntr)*—Calculates the preferred size dimensions for the specified container given the components in the specified container.

➤ *removeLayoutComponent(Component comp)*—Removes the specified component from the layout.

The Visual J++ CD contains the source code for all the standard layout managers. Use this code as a guide when you create your own layout manager.

UI Component Placement Without a Layout Manager

It is possible to place and size UI components within a container without a layout manager. If fact, without a layout manager, you can gain absolute control over the placement and sizing of UI components. The only problem is, without a layout manager, you have no choice but to explicitly define the size and placement of UI components. The reason for layout managers is to make the UI for Java applets and applications flexible enough to run on many different platforms, which support a multitude of screen resolutions and capabilities. Although you have more control without a layout manager, the UI of your Java programs will loose the capability to dynamically adjust to the capability of the user's hardware.

To add UI components to a container without a layout manager, you must take the following steps:

1. Set the layout manager to *null* by using the *setLayout( )* method.

2. After adding a component by using the *add( )* method, reposition and resize the component by calling the component's *reshape( )* method.

The *reshape( )* method is provided by the Component class. This method has the following signature:

➤ *reshape(int x, int y, int width, int height)*—Specifies the component's x,y coordinates within the container and the components width and height in pixels.

The *NoLayout* applet shown in listing 11.5 demonstrates how UI components can be placed and sized without a layout manager:

Listing 11.5 NoLayout Manager

```java
import java.applet.*;
import java.awt.*;

public class NoLayout extends Applet
{

    public void init()
    {
        Button Sun     = new Button("Sun");
        Button Mercury = new Button("Mercury");
        Button Venus   = new Button("Venus");
        Button Earth   = new Button("Earth");
        Button Moon    = new Button("Moon");

        setLayout(null);

        add(Sun);
        Sun.reshape(5,50,90,90);

        add(Mercury);
        Mercury.reshape(115,73,45,45);

        add(Venus);
        Venus.reshape(225,70,50,50);

        add(Earth);
        Earth.reshape(340,68,55,55);

        add(Moon);
        Moon.reshape(355,165,30,30);
    }

}
```

The NoLayout applet creates a series of buttons that imitate the size and positioning of the first three planets in the solar system. The output of the NoLayout applet in listing 11.5 is shown in figure 11.17.

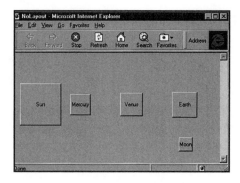

Figure 11.17:

UI components placed without a layout manager.

As you can see by looking at figure 11.17, when you use no layout manager, you can gain a great deal of control over the sizing and positioning of UI components within a container.

When you layout components in a container without a layout manager, the user interface that you create will frequently not look correct when run with a different font size or screen resolution. This is because, in the absence of a layout manager, the Java program cannot automatically adjust the layout of components.

Figure 11.18 shows the results of running the NoLayout example applet when you use a slightly larger font. As you can see, without a layout manager, the applet does not display the buttons correctly even though the font is only slightly larger.

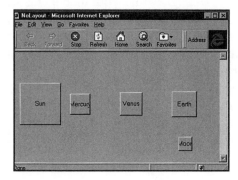

Figure 11.18:

UI components placed without a layout manager.

When Not to Use a Layout Manager

Working without a layout manager is a viable alternative when you are sure that your program's users will have a specific screen resolution and default font size. Another situation where not using a layout manager might work well is when you are creating a highly graphics-oriented UI. When you display a UI component as an image, for example, you can be sure of the absolute size, in pixels, of the component that will remain the same regardless of the dispaly resolution.

Microsoft's DialogLayout Layout Manager

Chapter 13, "Working with UI Components in Visual J++," provides a discussion of the Visual J++ Resource Wizard. This tool can be used to automatically generate code for both UI components and a layout manager. Although the specifics of the Resource Wizard are covered in Chapter 13, it is important for you to understand the functionality of the layout manager class that it generates, which is called DialogLayout.

Microsoft wrote the DialogLayout class to address what many see as a shortcoming of the AWT layout managers. Specifically, it is extremely difficult to have precise control over how the AWT layout managers place and size components. Consequently, the DialogLayout layout manager places control over the user interface layout back in the hands of the programmer.

Working the DialogLayout layout manager is similar to using no layout manager in that you can specify a size and position for components. At the same time, however, DialogLayout addresses the disadvantages of using no layout manager in that components are automatically resized and repositioned, in proportion to the original layout, based on the screen resolution and the container's default font. DialogLayout has this flexibility because it lays out components by using a resolution independent unit of measurement called dialog logical units (DLU) instead of pixels.

DialogLayout dynamically maps DLUs to pixels at runtime. The x coordinate DLU is defined as 25 percent of the average character width. A y coordinate DLU is defined as 12.5 percent of the character height used in the container.

Constructors

To instantiate the DialogLayout layout manager, you can use one of the following constructor forms:

➤ *DialogLayout(Container cntr, int width, int height)*— Constructs a DialogLayout object for the *cntr* container. The dimensions of *cntr* are calculated based on the *cntr* parameter's default font, the number of vertical DLUs specified by the *height* parameter and the number of horizontal DLUs specified by the *width* parameter.

➤ *DialogLayout(Container cntr, Dimension dim)*—Constructs a DialogLayout object for the *cntr* container. This constructor works the same way as the preceding constructor, however, the height and width values are extracted from the Dimension object.

Normally, you will use the constructor that takes the height and width integers as parameters. There may be times, however, when the values for height and width that you want to use are held in a Dimension object, you can pass that object to the constructor for DialogLayout.

Methods

The most important method in the DialogLayout class is the *setShape( )* method. This method is similar to the *reshape( )* method provided by the Component class except that it works with DLUs instead of pixels. The *setShape( )* method can be invoked by using one of the following method signatures.

➤ *setShape(Component comp, int x, int y, int width, int height)*—Places the *comp* component at the DLU position specified by the x,y coordinates and sizes the component based on the rectangle defined by the width and height parameters.

➤ *setShape(Component comp, int x, int y, Rectangle rect)*—
Works the same way as the preceding method signature,
except that the height and width values are taken from the
rect parameter.

DialogLayout Example

The MSLayout applet shown in listing 11.6 uses the DailogLayout
layout manager to layout buttons representing the Sun and the
first four planets in the solar system. This example is essentially
the same example that is used in this chapter to demonstrate no
layout manager. By using DialogLayout, however, the user
interface appears the same regardless of the screen resolution
and default font size.

Listing 11.6   DialogLayout Manager

```
import java.applet.*;
import java.awt.*;
import DialogLayout;

public class MSLayout extends Applet
{
    DialogLayout m_Layout;

    Button Sun     = new Button("Sun");
    Button Mercury = new Button("Mercury");
    Button Venus   = new Button("Venus");
    Button Earth   = new Button("Earth");
    Button Moon    = new Button("Moon");

    public void init()
    {
        m_Layout = new DialogLayout(this, 350, 199);
        setLayout(m_Layout);

        add(Sun);
        m_Layout.setShape(Sun, 5, 35, 60, 60);

        add(Mercury);
```

```
          m_Layout.setShape(Mercury, 80, 53, 30, 30);

          add(Venus);
          m_Layout.setShape(Venus, 150, 52, 35, 35);

          add(Earth);
          m_Layout.setShape(Earth, 222, 50, 40, 40);

          add(Moon);
          m_Layout.setShape(Moon, 235, 120, 22, 22);
     }

}
```

As mentioned previously, the code for the DialogLayout class is automatically generated by the Visual J++ Resource Wizard and placed in a project directory. Consequently, you should either import the DailogLayout class, as shown in listing 11.6, or place the class in one of your own packages and import that package.

The result of the MSLayout applet is shown in figure 11.19.

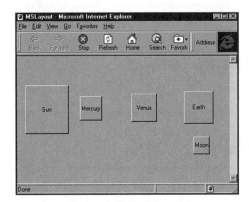

Figure 11.19:
UI components placed by using DialogLayout as the layout manager.

Dynamic Resizing with the DialogLayout Layout Manager

In contrast to the example that uses no layout manager, when the user's screen resolution changes, or when a different default font size is used for the container, the MSLayout applet resizes the components and proportions used to layout its user interface. This is made possible because the layout proportions are given in DLUs that are recalculated at runtime.

Figure 11.20 illustrates how DialogLayout would layout the planet buttons for a slightly larger default font.

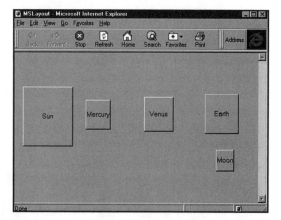

Figure 11.20:

UI components placed by using DialogLayout as the layout manager.

Summary

The Abstract Windowing Toolkit (AWT) provides the functionality required to implement cross-platform Java applets with sophisticated and interactive user interfaces. The AWT includes containers, which are display areas. Containers can hold other containers and UI components. AWT UI components are the visual objects that can be placed within containers by using the *add( )* method. The Applet class is derived from the Panel container class. Consequently, Java applets are containers.

In most cases, you should extend the Canvas class when you want to create your own custom UI component. You can create your own event types and handle the member variable *Event.arg* differently for each event.

Most UI components only generate one event, ACTION_EVENT. Therefore, it is possible to handle most UI component events by overriding the *action( )* method.

The AWT provides classes, called layout managers, that enable developers to control the placement and size of UI components within containers. The default layout manager for the Applet class is FlowLayout. This layout manager places UI components from left to right and from top to bottom. The GridBagLayout class provides the most control over UI component placement, however, it is the hardest layout manager to use. A customized layout manager can be created by developing a class that implements the LayoutManager interface. Nested panels can be used to combine the effects of several different layout managers into one UI.

You can work without a layout manager when you want to have absolute control over how UI components are sized and positioned within a container. When you don't use a layout manager, however, your components will probably not look right when displayed at different resolutions or at different font sizes. Fortunately for developers who use Visual J++, Microsoft has provided a layout manager class called DialogLayout that enables you to position and size components within a container by specifying resolution-independent dialog logical units (DLU) instead of pixels.

Questions

1. What method is used to include UI components in an applet?

2. What methods are used by Java layout managers to size UI components?

3. Can you use the Java Button class to create radio buttons?

4. What is a layout manager?

5. By using the FlowLayout layout manager and a TextField component, how does the layout manager determine the size of the component to be displayed?

6. What is the most common event generated by UI components?

7. What TextField component method can be used to echo a specified character to the display when a user types in a TextField?

8. Can the Canvas class be used to create a custom control with event processing?

9. What is the default layout manager for the Applet class?

10. What interface must a custom layout manager class implement?

11. When should nested panels be used for UI component placement?

12. What are the basic steps that you need to take to layout UI components without a layout manager?

13. What is the advantage of using Microsoft's DialogLayout layout manager?

Answers

1. The *add( )* method is used to add UI components to a container.

2. The Java layout managers use the *preferredSize( )* and *minimumSize( )* methods to size UI components.

3. No. The Java Button component cannot be used to create a radio button. You can, however, use the Java Checkbox and CheckboxGroup classes to create radio buttons.

4. Layout managers are classes provided in the AWT package (java.awt) that help the developer control the placement and sizing of UI components within a container.

5. If an initial length of TextField is defined, the layout manager will display a TextField by using this length. If an initial length is not defined, but an initial string is specified, the layout manager will attempt to size the TextField component displayed by using the initial string.

6. The ACTION_EVENT is the most common event generated by UI components.

7. The *setEchoCharacter( )* method can be used to specify the character that is echoed to the display when a user types into a TextField component.

8. Yes. Because the Canvas class is derived from the Component class—it gets all events. Consequently, a custom UI component that extends Canvas can trap the appropriate events and perform special processing.

9. The Applet class is derived from the Panel class. Because the default layout manager for the Panel class is FlowLayout, it is also the default layout manager for the Applet class.

10. A custom layout manager must implement the LayoutManager interface.

11. Nested panels are helpful when you need to create a UI that combines the capabilities of different layout managers or when certain UI components frequently appear grouped together in different containers.

12. To layout components without a layout manager, you must set the layout manager to *null* by using the *setLayout( )* method of the container. You must call the *reshape( )* method for each component so that you can specify the absolute size of the component as well as its position within the container.

13. Microsoft's DialogLayout layout manager enables the programmer to place UI components within a container by using Dialog Logical Units (DLU) instead of pixels. Because DLUs are resolution independent, they can be recalculated at runtime. Consequently, when you use DialogLayout for your container's layout manager, the user interface you create will provide a consistent appearance at all resolutions and at all default font sizes.

Chapter 12

More AWT Containers

The discussion of Abstract Windowing Toolkit (AWT) containers in Chapter 11, "Building a User Interface," is limited to applets. The Applet class is derived from the Panel class, which is derived from the Container class. This chapter discusses the other AWT classes that are derived from Container, which in addition to Panel, include the Window, Frame, Dialog, and FileDialog classes.

The following topics are covered in this chapter:

- ➤ Overview of the Container class
- ➤ Working with the Window, Frame, and Dialog classes
- ➤ Creating and customizing menus
- ➤ Accessing files with the FileDialog class
- ➤ Using the AWT in stand-alone applications

After reading this chapter, you will know how to build a user interface in Java that utilizes pop-up windows and menus. In addition, you will know how to use Container-derived classes and AWT components to develop stand-alone Java applications that feature graphical user interfaces.

The Container Class

The Container class, and its derived classes, can be used to create AWT components that are capable of containing other AWT components. Because containers are user interface (UI) components, Container-derived components can contain other Container-derived components. Nested panels, for example, are containers that are placed within other containers.

Most of the methods used to control UI components within a container, such as the *add()*, *setLayout()*, and *preferredSize()* methods, are provided by the Container class. In most cases, you should not derive new containers directly from the Container class. Instead, use either the Panel, Dialog, or Frame classes. These classes provide more functionality than the Container class. Figure 12.1 illustrates the hierarchy of all Container-derived classes provided in the AWT.

Pop-up Windows

Figure 12.1 illustrates the two AWT classes derived directly from Container: Panel and Window. The Panel class is generally used to create a display area within a web browser, while the Window class is used to create a new display area, such as a pop-up dialog box.

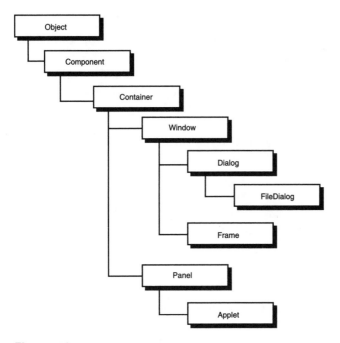

Figure 12.1:

AWT container class hierarchy.

When an untrusted Java applet is executed by the Internet
Explorer (IE) web browser, pop-up windows created by the applet
display the message, Warning: Applet Window (see fig. 12.2).

Figure 12.2:

A Pop-up Window.

A warning message is displayed to alert the user that the window has been created by an applet. This makes it more difficult for a sinister programmer to access information with a Trojan horse. A common Trojan horse, for example, is a dialog box that looks like a login screen. The dialog box's actual purpose is to steal the passwords of unsuspecting users.

When an applet is trusted, the applet window warning message is not displayed by the IE web browser. As explained in Chapter 6, "Java Programming Architecture," IE trusts applets that are digitally signed by someone that the user has designated as a trusted source. For testing purposes, Java applets that are executed from Visual J++ are inherently trusted, regardless of author signature.

The Window Class

In most cases, you should not derive new classes directly from the Window class. Use the Window-derived classes, Dialog and Frame, because these classes provide additional functionality. Both the Frame and Dialog classes, for example, provide a title bar on a window, whereas the Window class does not provide a title bar.

The Window class, however, provides the base functionality for both the Frame and Dialog classes. Consequently, the Window class methods described in the following sections are often used with Frame and Dialog objects.

The *show()* Method

To make a Window object visible, the *show()* method must be called. The *show()* method provided by the Window class is similar to the *show()* method that is provided by the Component class; however, the Window class's *show()* method causes an obscured window to come to the forefront of the screen.

The *hide()* method makes a Window object disappear. The *hide()* method, however, is not unique to the Window class; it is inherited from the Component class.

The *dispose()* Method

The *dispose()* method removes a window from the screen and releases all the resources that are used by the window.

The *pack()* Method

The *pack()* method is usually called after UI components are added to a window. This ensures that the window is drawn correctly.

The *resize()* Method

The *resize() method,* provided by the Window class, enables a program to change the dimensions of a window. The following method signature describes how the *resize()* method can be used to redefine the width and height of a window:

```
resize(int width, int height);
```

The *move()* Method

The *move()* method, provided by the Window class, enables the repositioning of a Window object within a display area. The following method signature describes how the *move()* method can be used to reposition a window at a new location, defined by the specified x,y coordinates:

```
move(int x, int y);
```

The *setResizable()* Method

By default, a Window object is user-resizable. This characteristic can be controlled with the *setResizable()* method. The following line of code, for example, makes it impossible for a user to resize the window.

```
w.setResizable(false);
```

Conversely, the window could be made resizable again with this code:

```
w.setResizable(true);
```

The Frame Class

The Frame class can be used to create a standard window with a configurable menu and cursor selection. The Frame class provides methods for obtaining the attributes of the window, such as the window's title and whether the window can be resized.

The following constructor creates a Frame object without a title:

```
Frame f = new Frame();
```

Figure 12.3 displays the frame created by the preceding line of code.

Figure 12.3:

An Untitled frame.

By default, Java sets the frame's title to Untitled. Alternatively, a frame can be created with a specific title. The following line of code, for example, creates a Frame object with the title `"This Frame has a title!"`:

```
Frame f = new Frame("This Frame has a title!");
```

The frame created by the preceding line of code is shown in figure 12.4.

Figure 12.4:
A frame with a title.

When a Frame object is first created, it is invisible. To make the Frame object visible, the *show()* method must be called.

The *setCursor()* Method

Changing the cursor is easy to accomplish with a Java Frame object. The *setCursor()* method can be used to change the default cursor to any of the following predefined cursors.

CROSSHAIR_CURSOR

DEFAULT_CURSOR

E_RESIZE_CURSOR

HAND_CURSOR

MOVE_CURSOR

NE_RESIZE_CURSOR

NW_RESIZE_CURSOR

N_RESIZE_CURSOR

SE_RESIZE_CURSOR

SW_RESIZE_CURSOR

S_RESIZE_CURSOR

TEXT_CURSOR

WAIT_CURSOR

W_RESIZE_CURSOR

The following code creates a Frame object with a crosshair cursor.

```
Frame f = new Frame("Figure 12.5 - Frame with a crosshair
↪cursor");
f.setCursor(Frame.CROSSHAIR_CURSOR);
```

The frame created by the preceding code is shown in Figure 12.5.

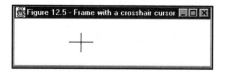

Figure 12.5:

Frame with a crosshair cursor.

Creating a Menu

An important characteristic of a Frame object is its capability to support menus. This functionality is provided by three classes: MenuItem, Menu and MenuBar. These classes support standard menu items and menu items that may be checked or unchecked. Separators can be placed between menu items.

To create a menu, an instance of a MenuBar object must first be created and passed to the *setMenuBar()* method of the frame that will contain the menu. The following code shows how this can be accomplished:

```
MenuBar mb = new MenuBar();
f.setMenuBar(mb);
```

The Menu class holds a first level menu item (for example, File or Edit) and a list of subordinate menu items. The MenuItem class holds individual menu items that are represented by String variables. Separators can be added to a menu item list by adding a hyphen as a menu item.

The following code shows how to create a MenuBar object that includes two Menu objects, File and View, with menu items under each:

```
Frame f = new Frame("Figure 12.6 - Menu Example");
MenuBar mb = new MenuBar();
f.setMenuBar(mb);

Menu m = new Menu("File");
m.add("New");
m.add("Open");
m.add("-");
m.add("Exit");
mb.add(m);

m = new Menu("View");
m.add(new CheckboxMenuItem("Display Everything"));
m.add(new CheckboxMenuItem("Hide Nothing"));
mb.add(m);

f.resize(250,150);
f.show();
```

Figure 12.6 shows the menu created by the preceding code.

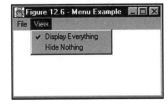

Figure 12.6:
A frame with a menu.

Processing Menu Events

The easiest way to process menu selections is to override the *action( )* method of the Frame class. In the *action( )* method, the Event object must be inspected first to determine if it is a menu event.

The ShowFonts applet in listing 12.1 creates a frame with a menu
and includes code that handles menu events:

Listing 12.1   The ShowFonts Applet

```java
import java.awt.*;

public class ShowFonts extends java.applet.Applet
{

    public void init()
    {
        Frame f = new NewFrame("Figure 12.7: The ShowFonts
Applet");
        MenuBar mb = new MenuBar();
        f.setMenuBar(mb);

        Menu m = new Menu("Font");
        m.add("TimesRoman");
        m.add("-");
        m.add("Arial");
        m.add("-");
        m.add("Courier");
        mb.add(m);

        f.resize(350,200);

        f.show();
    }

}

class NewFrame extends Frame
{
    Font fnt = new Font("TimesRoman", Font.BOLD,18);
    String label = "TimesRoman";
    NewFrame(String title)
    {
        super(title);
    }
```

```
    public boolean action(Event evt, Object arg)
    {
        if (evt.target instanceof MenuItem)
            {
                label = (String)arg;
                if (label.equals("TimesRoman"))
                    fnt = new Font("TimesRoman",
➥Font.BOLD,18);
                else if (label.equals("Arial"))
                    fnt = new Font("Arial", Font.BOLD,18);
                else if (label.equals("Courier"))
                    fnt = new Font("Courier", Font.BOLD,18);
                repaint();
                return true;
            }
        else return false;
    }

    public void paint(Graphics g)
    {
        g.setFont(fnt);
        g.setColor(Color.blue);
        g.drawString("This is the " + label + " Font", 30,
➥100);
    }
}
```

Figure 12.7 shows the frame and menu created by the ShowFonts applet.

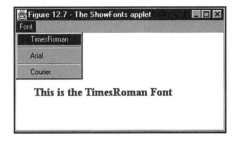

Figure 12.7:

Event handling in the ShowFonts applet.

When a user chooses a font from the ShowFonts Font menu, a text string is displayed in the frame in the correct font. Notice that to process menu events, the NewFrame class has been derived from the Frame class and the *action()* method has been overridden.

Menu selection events can also be trapped by overriding the *handleEvent()* method, checking for the ACTION_EVENT, and then checking whether the *event.target* variable is an instance of MenuItem.

The Dialog Class

The Dialog class is used to create a standard dialog box window. Windows created by the Dialog class are very similar to windows created by the Frame class. In most cases, you use the Dialog class to create pop-up windows for displaying messages or inputting data. Methods are provided to obtain and set the Dialog object's title. A dialog box can be defined to be modal or nonmodal as well as resizable or nonresizable.

Modal windows are common in Java and MS-Windows applications. A modal window must be closed before the user can access any other window in the application.

To create a Dialog object, you must first create a Frame object. A Dialog object can be created by using the following constructors.

➤ *Dialog(Frame frame, boolean modal).* This creates a Dialog object that is associated with the specified frame. The Dialog object is either modal (modal = true) or nonmodal (modal = false).

➤ *Dialog(Frame frame, String title, boolean modal).* This creates a Dialog object that is associated with the specified frame. The Dialog object is either modal or nonmodal, depending on the specified boolean value. The title of the Dialog object is set to the specified String value of the title parameter.

The following code demonstrates how a Dialog object can be created and displayed.

```
Frame f = new Frame();
Dialog d = new Dialog(f, "Choose Next Option", true);
d.show();
```

The parameters passed to the Dialog class in the preceding code include the Frame object, a String value for the title, and a boolean value. Specifying a true boolean value causes the dialog box to be modal. The last line of code invokes the *show()* method to display the dialog box. Even though it is necessary to associate the Dialog object with a Frame object, note that it is not necessary to display the Frame object.

Dialog Example

The TipOfTheDay applet in listing 12.2 creates a dialog box that displays a useful message.

Listing 12.2   The TipOfTheDay Applet

```
import java.awt.*;

public class TipOfTheDay extends java.applet.Applet
{
    Dialog d;

    public void init()
    {
        Frame f = new Frame();
        d = new NewDialog(f, "Tip of the day", false);
        d.setLayout(new GridLayout(2,1,15,1));
        d.add(new Label("Don't bet on the races!"));
        d.add(new Button("OK"));
        d.resize(190,100);
        d.show();
    }
}
```

continues

Listing 12.2   Continued

```java
class NewDialog extends Dialog
{
    NewDialog(Frame f, String title, boolean m)
    {
        super(f, title, m);
    }

    public boolean action(Event evt, Object arg)
    {
        if (evt.target instanceof Button)
        {
            String label = (String)arg;
            if (label.equals("OK"))
                this.dispose();
            return true;
        }
        else return false;
    }
}
```

The TipOfTheDay applet creates the Dialog shown in figure 12.8.

Figure 12.8:
The TipOfTheDay applet.

The TipOfTheDay applet first creates a Frame object in the *init( )* method. Next, the applet creates a Dialog object. At the same time, the applet associates the Dialog object with the Frame object, sets Dialog object's title to Tip of the Day, and specifies the Dialog object as nonmodal.

The applet sets the Dialog object's layout manager to GridLayout. Two UI components, a Button and a Label, are added to the Dialog object. Finally, the applet calls the *show( )* method to display the dialog box. Notice that the frame is never displayed.

To respond to events, the NewDialog class extends the Dialog class and overrides the *action( )* method. When the user clicks on OK, the Java runtime environment calls the *action( )* method to remove the dialog box from the display area and to release the Dialog object's resources.

The FileDialog Class

The FileDialog class can be used to create a standard open and save file dialog box. The FileDialog class is similar to the Dialog class because it too must always be associated with a Frame object. The frame associated with the FileDialog must be displayed at least once before the FileDialog can be shown. Unlike the Dialog class, the FileDialog class always creates a modal window.

It may not be a good idea to use the FileDialog class in your applets because security measures provided by many web browsers prevent Java applets from reading and writing local files.

As mentioned previously in this chapter, IE has the capability to recognize signed code. If an applet is signed by a trusted source, IE enables it to access the local hard drive. In the future, most browsers will also have the capability to recognize signed code. For now, however, if most of your target audience is not using IE, the FileDialog class is likely to be more useful in Java applications than in applets.

A FileDialog object can be created with the following constructors:

➤ **FileDialog**(*Frame frame, String title*). This creates an open FileDialog object associated with the specified frame. The title of the FileDialog object is set to the specified title.

➤ **FileDialog**(*Frame frame, String title, int mode*). This creates a FileDialog object that is associated with the specified frame. The title of the FileDialog object is set to the specified title. The mode argument specifies whether the dialog is used for loading or saving files. The valid mode values are FileDialog.LOAD and FileDialog.SAVE.

Selecting Directories and Files

You can use the *setFile( )* and *setDirectory( )* methods to set the current file and directory prior to using the *show( )* method to display a FileDialog object.

The code after the *show( )* method will not be executed until the FileDialog object's window is closed. After the window is closed, the *getFile( )* and *getDirectory( )* methods can be used to determine the name of the directory and file that the user selected.

A FileDialog Example

The following code demonstrates how a FileDialog object could be created and displayed:

```
Frame f = new Frame();
FileDialog fd =
    new FileDialog(f, "This was invoked by a Java
➥program");
f.show();
fd.show();
```

Figure 12.9 shows the FileDialog object created by the preceding code when run under Windows 95.

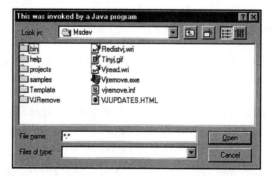

Figure 12.9:

A FileDialog object displayed in Windows 95 by a Java program.

As Figure 12.9 illustrates, when created under Windows 95, a FileDialog object invokes the standard operating system file open\save dialog box. When a Java program creates a FileDialog object while running on other operating systems, the native file open\save dialog box is used if it is available.

Window Events

The Java Event class defines the following window events:

➤ **WINDOW_DESTROY.** This event is generated when a use clicks on the window destroy button.

➤ **WINDOW_DEICONIFY.** This event is generated when a user indicates that a window should be restored from an icon. A user can generate this event, for example, by double-clicking on an iconified window.

➤ **WINDOW_EXPOSE.** This event is generated when an obscured window is brought to the forefront.

➤ **WINDOW_ICONIFY.** This event is generated when a user indicates that a window is should be iconified. A user can generate this event, for example, by clicking on a window's minimize button.

➤ **WINDOW_MOVED.** This event is generated when a window is moved.

Normally, you would expect a window to be automatically destroyed when a user generates a WINDOW_DESTROY event by clicking on a destroy button. The default behavior, however, of the both the Frame and the Dialog classes is to ignore the WINDOW_DESTROY event.

You should override the *handleEvent( )* method so that it calls the *dispose( )* method whenever a WINDOW_DESTROY event occurs. The following code shows how to accomplish this.

```
class MyFrame() extends java.awt.Frame
{

public boolean handleEvent(Event evt)
```
continues

```
        {
            if(evt.id == Event.WINDOW_DESTROY)
                {
                    dispose();
                    return true;
                }
            else
                    return false;
        }
    }
```

The browser does not automatically remove Frame objects and Dialog objects when the user moves from one HTML page to another. Therefore, override the *start( )* and *stop( )* methods of the Applet class, as shown in the following code:

```
public class MyFrameApp extends java.applet.Applet
{
    MyFrame f;
    // Other declarations and applet code goes here

    public void start()
    {
        f = new MyFrame();
        f.show();
    }

    public void stop()
    {
        f.dispose();
    }
}
```

Or implement the following:

```
public class MyFrameApp extends java.applet.Applet
{
    MyFrame f;
    // Other declarations and applet code goes here
    public void init()
```

```
{
    // Additional initialization code goes here
    f = new MyFrame();
    f.show();
}

public void start()
{
    f.show();
}

public void stop()
{
    f.hide();
}
}
```

Stand-Alone Applications

It is possible to use AWT containers and AWT UI components within stand-alone Java applications and in web-page based applets. As you should already know, to implement a stand-alone Java application, a *main()* method must be included in your program. The *main()* method in stand-alone Java applications should be defined as follows:

```
public static void main(String argv[])
{
    // The main application logic goes here.
}
```

Hybrid Applets-Applications

It is possible to create a single set of Java source code that can run either as an applet or application. To accomplish this, the following steps are necessary:

1. Set a flag in the *main()* method to ensure that the program does not attempt to read HTML parameters when the program runs as a stand-alone application.

2. Explicitly call the *init( )* and *start( )* methods (if appropriate) from the *main( )* method.

Applet-Application Example

The FriendlyGreeting program, shown in listing 12.3, can run as either a stand-alone application or as an applet. When FriendlyGreeting is executed as an application, it accepts a command line argument. When it executes as an applet, it reads a parameter from its HTML file.

Listing 12.3   The FriendlyGreeting Applet/Application

```
import java.awt.*;

public class FriendlyGreeting extends
java.applet.Applet
{

    boolean m_bApplication;
    Label m_label;

    public static void main(String argv[])
    {

        Frame f = new NewFrame("Friendly Greeting
➥Application");

        FriendlyGreeting fg = new FriendlyGreeting();
        fg.CreateLabel(argv[0]);
        fg.m_bApplication = true;
        fg.init();
        fg.start();

        f.add("Center", fg);
        f.resize(250,100);
        f.show();
    }

    public void init()
```

```
        {

            if (this.m_bApplication != true)
            {
                CreateLabel(getParameter("name"));
                this.add(m_label);
            }
            else
            {
                this.add(m_label);
                this.add(new Button("Close Application"));
            }

        }

    public void CreateLabel(String name)
    {
        m_label =
            new Label("It's great to see you again " +
➡name + "!");
    }

}

class NewFrame extends Frame
{

    NewFrame(String title)
    {
        super(title);
    }

    public boolean action(Event evt, Object arg)
    {

        if (evt.target instanceof Button)
        {
            String label = (String)arg;
            if (label.equals("Close Application"))
                System.exit(0);
```

continues

Listing 12.3   Continued

```
                return true;
        }
        else return false;
    }
}
```

Executing FriendlyGreeting

If FriendlyGreeting is set up as a Visual J++ project, you can execute it as an application from within Visual J++. Be sure that the appropriate settings are specified in the Project Setting dialog box's Debug tab. For the General Category options, the Debug/Execute project under option should be set to stand-alone interpreter. The stand-alone interpreter options should specify jview.exe as the stand-alone interpreter, and a name, such as Jimmy, should be specified for the Program arguments option.

Alternatively, you could execute FriendlyGreeting as an application from the MS-DOS command line as follows:

```
jview FriendlyGreeting Jimmy
```

Figure 12.10 shows how FriendlyGreeting looks when it executes as an application.

Figure 12.10:

FriendlyGreeting as an application.

After you try running FriendlyGreeting as an application, you might want to try running it as an applet. You can do this by using the same FriendlyGreeting executable (`FriendlyGreeting.class`). Running the program as an applet can be accomplished by including the following tags in an HTML file:

```
<APPLET CODE="FriendlyGreeting.class" WIDTH=300
➡HEIGHT=75>
<PARAM NAME=name VALUE="Jimmy">
</APPLET>
```

The message displayed by the preceding applet appears in the
Internet Explorer, as shown in figure 12.11.

Figure 12.11:
FriendlyGreeting as an applet.

When FriendlyGreeting is invoked as an application, the *main()*
method is called. The first task the *main()* method performs is
the creation of a Frame object. The Frame object will serve as a
container for the AWT UI components used in the application. It
is important to note that when executing an application, the Java
runtime environment does not automatically instantiate the
Applet class. Consequently, the *main()* method in the
FriendlyGreeting program must explicitly create a instance
of the FriendlyGreeting class. Furthermore, references to the
FriendlyGreeting class variables and methods must specify the
appropriate instance. Otherwise, a compiler error occurs.

When executing as an application, FriendlyGreeting passes the
argv[0] command line argument to the *CreateLabel()* method.
When running as an applet, the program gets the name HTML
parameter and passes it to the *CreateLabel()* method.

The *main()* method simulates an applet by calling the *init()* and
start() methods. In this case, the start method is not overridden.

The main( ) method sets the application boolean variable to indicate to the *init( )* method that the program is executing as an application.

The NewFrame class extends the Frame class. This is necessary because the *action( )* method must be overridden to add event processing for the Close Application button. This is only important when FriendlyGreeting executes as an application. When the button is clicked, the *action( )* method is invoked and calls *System.exit( )* method with an argument of 0, causing the application to terminate. The *dispose( )* method could also be used; however, this method only disposes the Frame object, while the application continues to execute.

Summary

The Java Applet class is derived from the Panel container class. The Java AWT also provides the Window, Frame, Dialog, and FileDialog container classes. You should not derive new containers directly from the Window class because the Window-derived Frame and Dialog classes offer more functionality.

The Frame and Dialog classes are similar; they both create a pop-up window, and they both inherit many of their methods from the Window class. A Dialog object, however, must always be associated with a Frame object.

A MenuBar object can only be added to a Frame object. To process menu events, the *action( )* method or *handleEvent( )* method must be in your Frame-derived class.

The FileDialog class always creates a modal dialog box. Like a Dialog object, a FileDialog object must always be associated with a Frame object. When a FileDialog object is created by a Java program executing under Windows 95, the standard operating system file open\save dialog box is invoked. The FileDialog class will most likely be used in stand-alone applications rather than web page-based applets because of the severe security restrictions imposed by many web browsers.

AWT containers and UI components can be used in Java stand-alone applications as well as applets. You can write Java programs that can run as both a Java applets and applications if you take into account how the Java runtime environment handles both types of programs. The *main( )* method, for example, is automatically executed in applications. In contrast, the *init( ), start( )* and *stop( )* methods are automatically executed in applets. Therefore, you will have to code your applet/application so that the appropriate processing takes place in either case.

Questions

1. With what type of container object must a Dialog object or FileDialog object always be associated?

2. Why shouldn't you derive a custom container from the Window class?

3. What method is automatically called when you run a Java program as a stand-alone application?

4. Why are you more likely to use the FileDialog class in stand-alone applications rather than in applets?

5. Can you define a layout manager for a Container object when the container is not derived from the Panel class?

6. Why is a warning message displayed in the pop-up windows created by untrusted applets?

7. What method eliminates a Window object and releases the memory resources used by that object?

8. What type of Container object can hold a Menu object?

9. How do you create a Menu object that displays items in separate logical groups?

Answers

1. A Dialog object and FileDialog object must always be associated with a Frame object.

2.   The Window object creates a simple pop-up window. The Window object, for example, does not have a title bar. The Frame and the Dialog classes provide more of the functionality that you are likely to need in your program.

3.   The *main( )* method always runs when you execute a Java program as an application.

4.   Due to security considerations, most web browsers prevent untrusted Java applets from accessing local files.

5.   Yes. The TipOfTheDay applet in listing 12.2, for example, sets the layout manager of a Dialog object to GridLayout.

6.   This security precaution makes it difficult for a programmer to disguise an applet window as a different type of window, such as a login dialog box. Unscrupulous individuals frequently create fake programs, also known as Trojan horses, intending to steal secret data.

7.   The *dispose( )* method eliminates a Window object and frees-up its resources.

8.   A Frame object can hold a Menu object.

9.   Add a hyphen to a Menu object as a MenuItem. This creates a separator between items in the menu.

Chapter 13

Working with UI Components in Visual J++

The Visual J++ Dialog and Menu Resource Editors enable developers to visually define user interfaces and to save these definitions in resource templates. The Java Resource Wizard can be used to automatically generate standard Java code from these templates.

Now that you are familiar with most of the classes that compose the Java Abstract Windowing Toolkit (AWT) package, it's time to learn how to use the tools provided by Visual J++ that will help you to rapidly produce code that utilizes these classes. Mastering the use of the Resource Editors and the Java Resource Wizard can significantly boost your productivity as a Java developer by enabling you to produce user interfaces for your Java programs much faster than writing all the code from scratch.

This chapter covers the following topics:

➤ Creating a dialog resource with the Dialog Resource Editor

➤ Creating a menu resource with the Menu Resource Editor

➤ Generating code with the Java Resource Wizard

➤ Using the Wizard-generated code in a project

This chapter provides examples for the purpose of illustrating the practical benefits of using the Resource Editor and the Java Resource Wizard to create a user interface.

Using Resources in Java Programs

To create an application's user interface, Windows programmers typically create resource templates (.rct) and compiled resource files (.res). These resources are maintained separately from the application's source code. In Java, the user interface for an applet or application is generated by code that utilizes the Java AWT classes. So, if you're a Windows programmer and you've already created a slew of resource templates, you won't be able to use any of them for developing in Java, correct? Fortunately, this is not the case because Visual J++ not only provides the same Resource Editor used by Visual C++ developers, but it also provides a Java Resource Wizard that can turn your Windows resources into standard Java code. In other words, the resource templates that you define in Developer Studio are language-independent when it comes to migrating to a Java environment.

A *resource* is a visual item, such as a pull-down menu or a dialog box containing user interface (UI) components, that can be used to generate a graphical user interface.

Creating a Dialog Resource

This section describes how to create a dialog resource by using the Visual J++ Dialog Resource Editor.

The easiest way to create a resource is to choose Resource from the Visual J++ Insert pull-down menu. This causes the Insert Resource dialog box to be displayed as shown in figure 13.1.

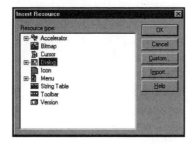

Figure 13.1:

The Insert Resource dialog box.

A *dialog resource* defines the layout and size of the elements, such as the display area, push-buttons, static text, and so on, which make up a user interface. A dialog resource should not be confused with the Java Dialog class, which is just one of the classes that can be used to create a container for UI components.

To create a dialog resource, choose Dialog from the Insert Resource dialog box as shown in figure 13.1. This causes the Dialog Resource Editor to be displayed as shown in figure 13.2.

When the Dialog Resource Editor displays, a default dialog resource is created automatically with two standard button controls, OK and Cancel.

To maintain consistency with other Developer Studio programming languages, such as Visual C++, the term *control* is used when discussing UI components, such as a button or a list box, in the Visual J++ Dialog Resource Editor.

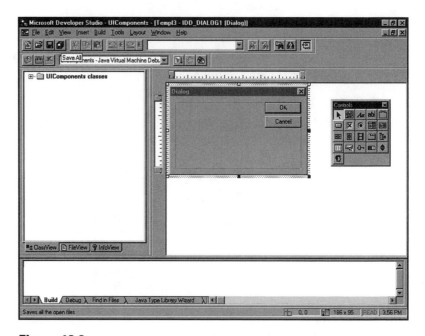

Figure 13.2:
The Dialog Resource Editor.

Adding Controls to a Dialog Resource

As shown in figure 13.2, the Developer Studio Controls toolbar displays when you invoke the Dialog Resource Editor. To add controls to your dialog resource, you must first click on the appropriate icon in this toolbar. You can then either drag the control into the display area, or click on the position within the dialog where you want to insert the component.

The only controls supported by the Visual J++ Java Resource Wizard are the ones that have corresponding Java AWT UI component classes. Figure 13.3 shows the Visual J++ Controls toolbar and the following list details each control's corresponding Java class.

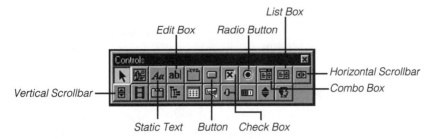

Figure 13.3:
The Visual J++ Controls toolbar.

➤ **Static Text control button.** The Java Resource Wizard will generate a Label UI component from a static text control in a dialog resource.

➤ **Edit Box control button.** The Java Resource Wizard will generate TextField and TextArea UI components from an edit box control in a dialog resource, when the edit box is multiline.

➤ **Button control.** The Java Resource Wizard will generate a Button UI component from a button control in a dialog resource.

➤ **Check Box control button.** The Java Resource Wizard will generate a Checkbox UI component from a check box control in a dialog resource.

➤ **Radio Button control.** The Java Resource Wizard will generate a Checkbox UI component from a radio button control in a dialog resource.

➤ **List Box control button.** The Java Resource Wizard will generate a List UI component from a list box control in a dialog resource.

➤ **Combo Box control button.** The Java Resource Wizard will generate a Choice UI component from a combo box control in a dialog resource.

➤ **Horizontal Scrollbar control button.** The Java Resource Wizard will generate a Scrollbar UI component from a horizontal scrollbar control in a dialog resource.

➤ **Vertical Scrollbar control button.** The Java Resource Wizard will generate a Scrollbar UI component from a vertical scrollbar control in a dialog resource.

Sizing Dialog Controls

When you insert a control in a dialog resource, you have the option to accept the default size of the control or to specify a different size by holding down the left mouse button and dragging the mouse pointer diagonally across the dialog's display area. When sizing a control in this manner, the editor draws the outline of a rectangle. This rectangle defines the boundaries or size of the control being inserted. Figure 13.4 illustrates how this technique can be used to insert an oversized button into a dialog resource.

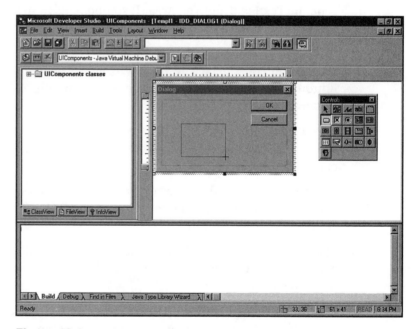

Figure 13.4:
Inserting and sizing a control.

Inserting and sizing a button control as illustrated in figure 13.4 creates an oversized button in the Dialog Resource Editor as shown in figure 13.5.

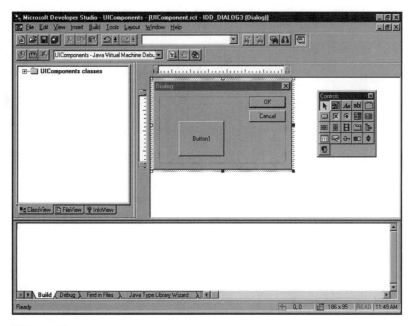

Figure 13.5:

An oversized button.

You can resize a control after it has been inserted in a dialog resource by choosing it with the mouse pointer and then dragging the handles displayed on the edges of the control to the new size of your choice. Figure 13.6 illustrates how the oversized button from figure 13.5 looks after being resized with this technique.

You can also resize a control, such as a button, in proportion to its content, for example, its label. To do this, choose the Size to Content option from either the Visual J++ Layout pull-down menu, or the context-sensitive command menu that displays when you right-click inside the Dialog Resource Editor.

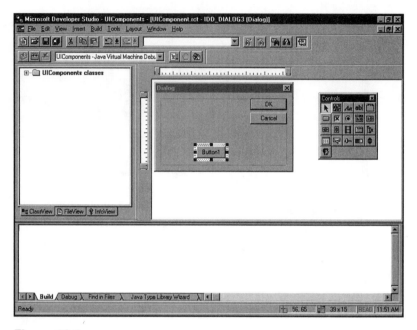

Figure 13.6:

Resizing a control.

Setting Control Properties

You can specify a number of properties that define a control's appearance. The properties associated with a control depend on the control type. A label, for example, can be left justified, centered, or right justified. It is possible to change the properties of individual controls as well as the properties of a dialog itself, when editing a dialog resource. You can accomplish this by choosing a control or the dialog and then choosing the Properties option from either the Edit pull-down menu or from the context-sensitive help menu that displays when you right click on a control. The Push Button Properties dialog box in figure 13.7 is associated with the OK button.

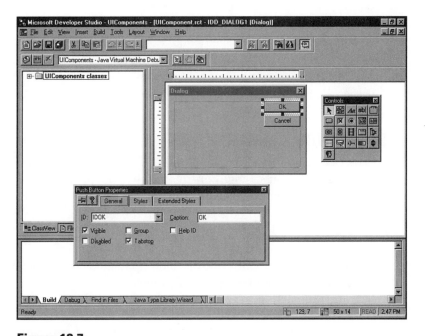

Figure 13.7:

Push Button Properties dialog box.

When the Java Resource Wizard generates code, it uses many of the settings specified in the Push Button Properties dialog box; however, not all the properties that you can specify for a control are supported by the Java Resource Wizard. In release 1.0 of Visual J++, for example, if you specify list items for a combo box control, the Resource Wizard will not include the appropriate source code required to add items to the Java Choice component that it generates.

To change the properties for multiple controls, you can use the push-pin in the upper left corner of the Push Button Properties dialog box as shown in Figure 13.7. When the pin is pushed in, the dialog box remains displayed even when the focus shifts to another window. Consequently, you will not have to invoke the Push Button Properties dialog box for each control you choose.

The Java Resource Wizard uses the default font size of eight points as specified in the dialog resource's Push Button Properties dialog box when it generates code. If eight points is not desirable for your applet or application, you can change this value in the General tab of the Push Button Properties dialog box.

Positioning Controls

The Dialog Resource Editor provides a number of mechanisms that can help you arrange controls within a dialog resource. Before you can change the position of a control you must choose it by either clicking on the control with the left mouse button or by clicking and dragging the mouse pointer over the control. This outlines a rectangular selection area. Releasing the mouse button chooses any and all the controls encompassed by this selection area. Figure 13.8 illustrates how this technique selects both the OK and Cancel buttons in the Dialog Resource Editor.

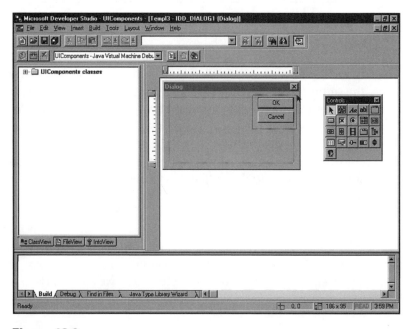

Figure 13.8:
Selecting multiple controls in the Dialog Resource Editor.

When choosing multiple controls, you can use the Dialog Resource Editor's alignment commands from the Layout pull-down
menu to arrange the controls within a display area. Any re-
alignment of controls is based on the position of the *dominant*
control. Figure 13.9, for example, shows two buttons and one
radio button control in the Dialog Resource Editor. The radio
button (Radio1) is the dominant control, as denoted by the solid
handles around it.

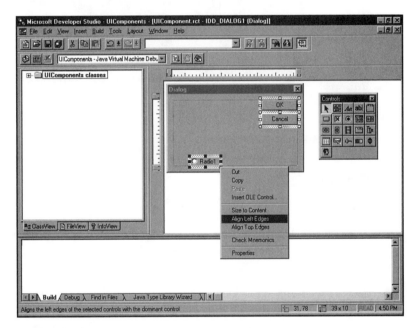

Figure 13.9:

The Radio1 button is the dominant control.

To align the controls within the dialog resource's display area,
you can choose the correct alignment command from the Visual
J++ Layout pull-down menu, or as demonstrated in figure 13.9,
you can invoke the Dialog Resource Editor's context-sensitive
command menu by right-clicking and choosing the appropriate
alignment command. Figure 13.9 shows the Dialog Resource
Editor as the user is about to choose the Align Left Edges command. The result of this alignment command is shown in figure
13.10.

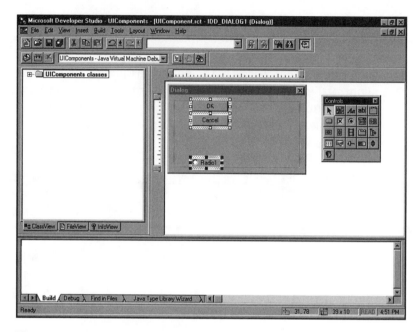

Figure 13.10:

Buttons left aligned on the dominant Radio1 button.

When more than one control is already selected, you can make one of the controls dominant by holding down the Ctrl key and clicking on the control.

You can also set the dominant control by choosing more than one control at a time by using a mouse drag technique. In this case, the control that you drag the mouse pointer over first will become the dominant control.

Positioning Controls with Guides

The Dialog Resource Editor can also provide guides to help you position controls within a dialog resource. You invoke the Guide Settings dialog box from the Visual J++ Layout pull-down menu. The Guide Settings dialog box is shown in figure 13.11.

Figure 13.11:

The Guide Settings dialog box.

The Guide Settings dialog box enables you to specify the type of layout guides displayed by the Dialog Resource Editor. You can use these guides to position controls precisely within a display area. You can elect to have no layout guides by choosing the None option, which enables you to place controls anywhere within the dialog resource without the benefit, or encumbrance, of grids and rulers. Unless your goal is to create a haphazard-looking user interface, however, you will probably be better off choosing either the Rulers and Guides option or the Grid option. The tools for positioning controls within a dialog resource give you a great deal of flexibility. In most situations, the tool you use will depend on your personal preference.

Aligning Controls with Rulers and Guides

The Rulers and Guides option displays the rulers as shown in figure 13.12. You can add more guides by clicking on the vertical or horizontal rulers. Figure 13.12 shows two vertical guides and two horizontal guides along which the two push-buttons and two radio buttons have been aligned. A control can be attached to a guide by clicking and dragging it to the guide. When you want to reposition all the controls that have been attached to a guide, all you need to do is drag the guide to the desired position—all the controls will move along with it.

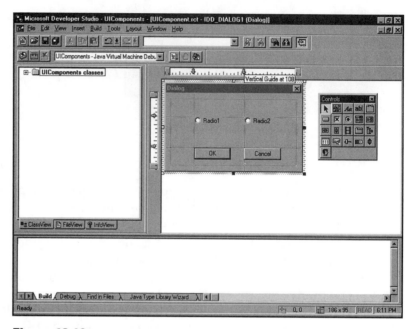

Figure 13.12:
Rulers and guides.

Aligning Controls with Grids

As an alternative to rulers and guides, you can set the Layout guides option to Grid. The Grid, as shown in figure 13.13, enables you to arrange controls based on dialog logical units (DLUs). Because the actual number of pixels in a DLU is calculated at runtime and based on the font size that is used, the proportionate space between controls should remain the same regardless of font size and display resolution. By setting the Grid spacing options in the Guide Settings dialog box, you can control the number of horizontal and vertical DLUs between each grid point.

The default font in Java is the Dialog font. A good chance is that this font will not be supported by the Dialog Resource Editor. Consequently, when you add UI components to a Dialog Resource, you should leave enough room between components to provide for slight variations between the font used by the Dialog Resource Editor and your Java program.

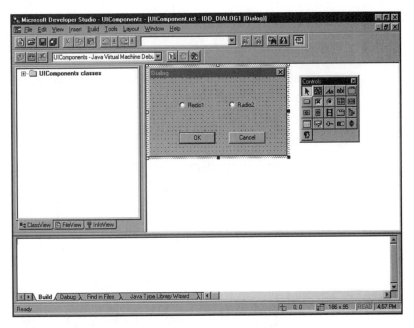

Figure 13.13:
Grid.

The Dialog Toolbar

Although all the commands necessary to position controls within a dialog resource can be accessed from the Visual J++ Layout pull-down menu, you may find that it is more convenient to use Developer Studio's Dialog toolbar as shown in figure 13.14. You can display this toolbar from the Toolbar dialog invoked from the Visual J++ View pull-down menu.

As illustrated in figure 13.14, the Dialog toolbar provides easy point-and-click access to the following types of commands:

➤ *Testing*—This tool displays the dialog resource in test mode so you can see how it will look when it is running in a program.

➤ *Alignment*—These tools can be used to align controls (right, left, top, bottom) based on the dominant control.

➤ *Centering*—These tools can be used to center one or more controls horizontally or vertically within a dialog resource's display area.

➤ *Spacing*—These tools can be used to space a group of controls evenly, either horizontally or vertically.

➤ *Sizing*—These tools can be used to make a group of controls the same height, width, or size as the dominant control.

➤ *Toggle Grid*—This tool puts the editor into the Grid mode.

➤ *Toggle Guides*—This tool puts the editor into the Rulers and Guides mode.

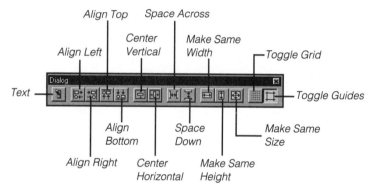

Figure 13.14:
The Dialog Toolbar.

Most of the commands accessible from the Dialog toolbar also have shortcut keys. You can find out what these shortcut keys are from the small pop-up windows (also known as *tooltips*) that automatically display when you hold the mouse cursor over a toolbar icon.

A Dialog Resource Example

To demonstrate the use of the Visual J++ Dialog Resource Editor and the Java Resource Wizard, this section discusses how these tools can be used to create a registration form. In the following example, the Java Dialog Resource Editor creates a template and

the Java Resource Wizard generates source code. The final code
for this example can be found in the RegistrationApp project on
the accompanying CD.

Creating a Registration Form

After creating an initial project and shell code for the main applet
class, invoke the Dialog Resource Wizard as described previously
in this chapter. By using the Controls toolbar, a user interface can
be laid out as shown in figure 13.15.

Creating a Visual J++ project is covered in Chapter 4, "Java Classes and
Objects."

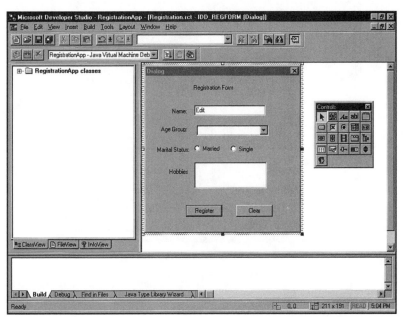

Figure 13.15:

A Dialog resource for a Registration Form.

When you create a dialog resource in Visual J++, the Dialog Resource
Editor assigns default IDs to the dialog resource and to the individual
controls. This is important because the Java Resource Wizard uses the ID

continues

values when it assigns names to the corresponding Java classes that it generates. Although this works fine, you may want to consider changing the default IDs to something that is more meaningful to you and the other developers that need to look at your code. The ID of the dialog resource in figure 13.15, for example, was changed from IDD_DIALOG1 to IDD_REGFORM and the static text at the top of the dialog resource was changed from IDC_STATIC1 to IDC_FORM_TITLE. You can change the ID of dialog resources and controls in the Properties dialog box.

The controls in figure 13.15 are not aligned very well. To create a more professional appearance, you should use guides and rulers to align the controls as illustrated in figure 13.16.

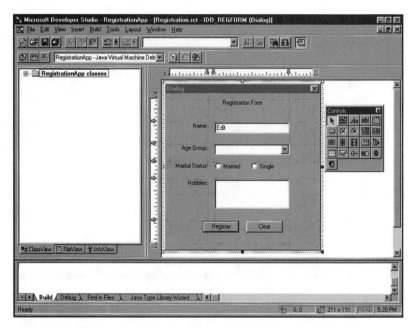

Figure 13.16:

Using rules and guides to align controls in the Registration Form.

As shown in figure 13.16, horizontal guides can be used to position the controls on this particular form. Notice, however, that vertical guides were not used to position the form's title (the "Registration Form" static text control) or the Register and Clear buttons at the bottom of the form. Instead, these controls were aligned to the horizontal center of the dialog resource.

After the dialog resource has been laid out, you can save it to a resource template (`.rct`) file. By default, Visual J++ saves the resource template in a centralized directory such as:

```
c:\msdev\template
```

If the template is specific to a particular applet or application, you may want to save it directly in the project directory. This is a good idea because when the Java Resource Wizard generates code from a template, it saves the source files in the template's directory. Then, when these source files are compiled, the compiler stores the bytecode (`.class`) files in the same directory as the source code. The location of the bytecode files is important because these files must be accessible from your program at runtime.

If a class that is used by your project is not stored in the project's directory, your program can access the class as long as the class file's directory is specified in the Options dialog box's Directories tab. The Options dialog box can be accessed from the Visual J++ Tools pull-down menu.

Running the Java Resource Wizard

After you create a dialog resource in the Dialog Resource Editor, you use the Java Resource Wizard to generate Java code that creates an interface. You can access the Java Resource Wizard from the Visual J++ Tools pull-down menu. Running the Java Resource Wizard is a simple, two-step process. First, you need to specify a resource template file. The easiest way to do this is to browse to the directory containing the template you created in the Dialog Resource Editor. Figure 13.17 shows the dialog box displayed in Step 1 of the Java Resource Wizard.

The second and last step of the Java Resource Wizard displays all the dialog and menu resources found in the Resource Template file. As mentioned previously, the Java Resource Wizard names the Java source code file based on the ID specified in its Properties dialog. At this point in the Resource Wizard process, the user has another chance to change the name of the Java class file about to be created. Figure 13.18 shows the dialog displayed in Step 2 of the Java Resource Wizard.

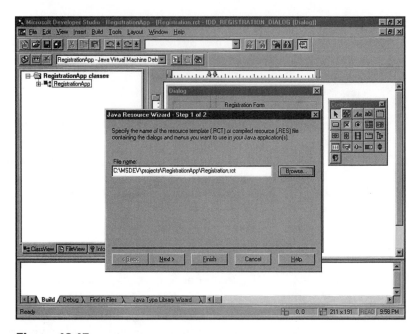

Figure 13.17:

Step 1 of the Java Resource Wizard.

Figure 13.18:

Step 2 of the Java Resource Wizard.

When the user clicks on the Finish button, the Java Resource Wizard creates the appropriate Java source files and displays a confirmation message to the user as shown in figure 13.19.

Figure 13.19:
Source code created by the Java Resource Wizard.

Wizard-Generated Java Source Code

As indicated in figure 13.19, the Java Resource Wizard creates the following Java source code files from the dialog resource used in listing 13.1.

➤ *IDD_REGFORM.java*—This Java class instantiates and adds AWT UI component classes to a Java container object such as Panel, Frame, and so on. In addition, this class sets the layout manager of the container object to DialogLayout. The code generated for the IDD_REGFORM class is shown in listing 13.1.

➤ *DialogLayout.java*—This class is a layout manager that was developed by Microsoft. The DialogLayout class and the AWT layout managers are discussed in Chapter 11, "Building a User Interface." The key advantage of this layout manager is that it sizes and positions UI components based on resolution-independent dialog logical units (DLU).

Listing 13.1   The IDD_REGFORM Class Generated by the Java Resource Wizard

```
//----------------------------------------------------------------
// IDD_REGFORM.java:
//          Implementation of "control creator" class
➥IDD_REGFORM
```

continues

Listing 13.1 Continued

```
//------------------------------------------------------------
import java.awt.*;
import DialogLayout;

public class IDD_REGFORM
{
        Container     m_Parent      = null;
        boolean       m_fInitialized = false;
        DialogLayout m_Layout;

        // Control definitions
        //------------------------------------------------------------
        Button          ID_REGISTER;
        Button          IDCLEAR;
        Label           IDC_FORM_TITLE;
        TextField       IDC_NAME;
        Label           IDC_NAME_LABEL;
        Choice          IDC_AGE_GROUP;
        Label           IDC_AGE_GROUP_LABEL;
        CheckboxGroup group1;
        Checkbox        IDC_MARRIED;
        Checkbox        IDC_SINGLE;
        Label           IDC_MARITAL_STATUS_LABEL;
        List            IDC_HOBBIES;
        Label           IDC_HOBIES_LABEL;


        // Constructor
        //------------------------------------------------------------
        public IDD_REGFORM (Container parent)
        {
                m_Parent = parent;
        }

        // Initialization.
        //------------------------------------------------------------
```

```
        public boolean CreateControls()
        {
                // CreateControls should be called only once
                //--------------------------------------------
                if (m_fInitialized || m_Parent == null)
                return false;

                // m_Parent must be extended from the Container
➥class
                //--------------------------------------------
                if (!(m_Parent instanceof Container))
                        return false;

                // Because a given font may not be supported
➥across all platforms, it
                // is safe to modify only the size of the font,
➥not the typeface.
                //---------------------------------------------
                Font OldFnt = m_Parent.getFont();
                if (OldFnt != null)
                {
                        Font NewFnt = new Font(OldFnt.getName(),
➥OldFnt.getStyle(), 8);

                        m_Parent.setFont(NewFnt);
                }

                // All position and sizes are in dialog logical
➥units, so we use a
                // DialogLayout as our layout manager.
                //---------------------------------------------
                m_Layout = new DialogLayout(m_Parent, 211, 191);
                m_Parent.setLayout(m_Layout);
                m_Parent.addNotify();

                Dimension size   = m_Layout.getDialogSize();
                Insets     insets = m_Parent.insets();
```

continues

Listing 13.1   Continued

```
             m_Parent.resize(insets.left + size.width  +
➡insets.right,
                 insets.top  + size.height +
➡insets.bottom);

         // Control creation
         //-----------------------------------------------
         ID_REGISTER = new Button ("Register");
         m_Parent.add(ID_REGISTER);
         m_Layout.setShape(ID_REGISTER, 51, 156, 50, 14);

         IDCLEAR = new Button ("Clear");
         m_Parent.add(IDCLEAR);
         m_Layout.setShape(IDCLEAR, 111, 156, 50, 14);

         IDC_FORM_TITLE = new Label ("Registration Form",
➡Label.CENTER);
         m_Parent.add(IDC_FORM_TITLE);
         m_Layout.setShape(IDC_FORM_TITLE, 78, 7, 55, 8);

         IDC_NAME = new TextField ("");
         m_Parent.add(IDC_NAME);
         m_Layout.setShape(IDC_NAME, 67, 35, 103, 14);

         IDC_NAME_LABEL = new Label ("Name:",
➡Label.RIGHT);
         m_Parent.add(IDC_NAME_LABEL);
         m_Layout.setShape(IDC_NAME_LABEL, 30, 35, 28,
➡8);

         IDC_AGE_GROUP = new Choice ();
         m_Parent.add(IDC_AGE_GROUP);
         m_Layout.setShape(IDC_AGE_GROUP, 67, 62, 103,
➡30);

         IDC_AGE_GROUP_LABEL = new Label ("Age Group:",
➡Label.RIGHT);
         m_Parent.add(IDC_AGE_GROUP_LABEL);
```

```
            m_Layout.setShape(IDC_AGE_GROUP_LABEL, 16, 62,
➥42, 8);

            group1 = new CheckboxGroup ();
            IDC_MARRIED = new Checkbox ("Married", group1,
➥false);
            m_Parent.add(IDC_MARRIED);
            m_Layout.setShape(IDC_MARRIED, 67, 84, 37, 10);

            IDC_SINGLE = new Checkbox ("Single", group1,
➥false);
            m_Parent.add(IDC_SINGLE);
            m_Layout.setShape(IDC_SINGLE, 117, 84, 35, 10);

            IDC_MARITAL_STATUS_LABEL = new Label ("Marital
➥Status:", Label.RIGHT);
            m_Parent.add(IDC_MARITAL_STATUS_LABEL);
            m_Layout.setShape(IDC_MARITAL_STATUS_LABEL, 12,
➥84, 46, 8);

            IDC_HOBBIES = new List (1, true);
            m_Parent.add(IDC_HOBBIES);
            m_Layout.setShape(IDC_HOBBIES, 67, 105, 103,
➥36);

            IDC_HOBIES_LABEL = new Label ("Hobbies:",
➥Label.RIGHT);
            m_Parent.add(IDC_HOBIES_LABEL);
            m_Layout.setShape(IDC_HOBIES_LABEL, 26, 105, 32,
➥8);

            m_fInitialized = true;
            return true;
    }
}
```

Using the Wizard-Generated Code in a Project

This section discusses how the code generated by the Java Resource Wizard can be utilized in a Visual J++ project containing an applet called RegistrationApp.

To use the wizard-generated code, you should insert the source code files into the project by choosing the Files into Project option from the Visual J++ Insert pull-down menu. After the IDD_REGFORM and DialogLayout source code files have been inserted into the project, the main applet must be updated so that it instantiates an IDD_REGFORM object.

As shown in listing 13.1, the IDD_REGFORM class has the following constructor form:

```
IDD_REGFORM(Container parent)
```

Consequently, when an IDD_REGFORM object is instantiated, a Container object (parent) must be passed to the class constructor.

The IDD_REGFORM class has a single method called *CreateControls()* that sets the layout manager of the parent container object to DialogLayout and adds the appropriate AWT UI components. The code for these components is generated by the Java Resource Wizard based on the controls included in the dialog resource.

The code in listing 13.2 shows how the IDD_REGFORM class could be included in the RegistrationApp applet.

Listing 13.2   The RegistrationApp Applet

```
import java.applet.*;
import java.awt.*;

public class RegistrationApp extends Applet
{
```

```
IDD_REGFORM m_Form;

public void init()
{
    m_Form = new IDD_REGFORM(this);
    m_Form.CreateControls();

    // Add Age Groups
    m_Form.IDC_AGE_GROUP.addItem("Under 20");
    m_Form.IDC_AGE_GROUP.addItem("20 to 30");
    m_Form.IDC_AGE_GROUP.addItem("Over 30");

    // Add Hobbies
    m_Form.IDC_HOBBIES.addItem("Baseball");
    m_Form.IDC_HOBBIES.addItem("Basketball");
    m_Form.IDC_HOBBIES.addItem("Reading");
}

}
```

Notice that to create the user interface within the applet's display area, the *this* variable, which represents the applet itself, is passed to the IDD_REGFORM class constructor.

After the *CreateControls( )* method is called, the RegistrationApp applet adds several items to the IDC_AGE_GROUP Choice component.

Even though the Dialog Resource Editor enables the user to enter items for the IDC_AGE_GROUP control in the Properties dialog box, the Java Resource Wizard does not generate the code required to add these items to the Choice AWT component that it generates.

The RegistrationApp applet also adds items to the IDC_HOBBIES List component. You can specify whether the List control generated by the Java Resource Wizard should support multiple selections in the Properties dialog box. The IDC_HOBBIES component supports multiple selections because an individual could have more than one hobby.

After the appropriate code has been added to the RegistrationApp applet, it can be compiled by choosing either Build or Rebuild All from the Visual J++ Build pull-down menu. When executed, the applet displays a registration form as shown in figure 13.20.

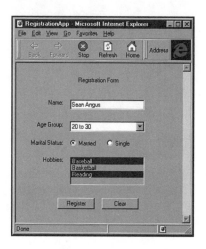

Figure 13.20:
The RegistrationApp applet.

Creating a Menu Resource

Another tool that you can use to create Java code is the Menu Resource Editor. By using the Menu Resource Editor, you can define pull-down menus and save your definitions in a resource template file. After you define a menu resource, you can use the Java Resource Wizard to generate code from your menu resources.

Just as you can invoke the Dialog Resource Editor by choosing Dialog from the Insert Resource dialog box, you can invoke the Menu Resource Editor by choosing the Menu as the resource type. The user interface for the Menu Resource Editor is shown in figure 13.21.

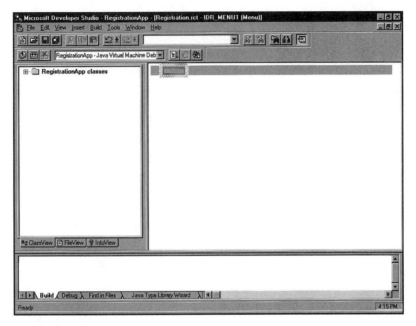

Figure 13.21:

The Menu Resource Editor.

The Menu Resource Editor provides fewer options, and is therefore less complicated than the Dialog Resource Editor. To create menu item, you must define a first-level menu to appear on a Java Frame object's toolbar. (Remember, in Java you can only add a menu to a Frame object.) You can create a first-level menu by typing in the item name. This action displays the Menu Item Properties dialog box as shown in figure 13.22. The menu name is entered in the Caption field. After a menu is entered, you can either enter menu items under the menu, or create the next first-level menu.

Figure 13.22:

The Menu Item Properties dialog box.

You can also display the Menu Item Properties dialog box by taking any of the following actions.

1. Double-clicking on the appropriate menu item.

2. Choosing Properties from the Visual J++ Edit menu.

3. Choosing Properties from the Menu Resource Editor's context-sensitive command menu that is displayed when the right mouse button is clicked.

When you create a menu resource, you cannot specify the font that will ultimately be used to display the menu. This is because a menu's font is determined by your workstation's operating system at runtime.

Cascading Menus

Cascading menus are menus that pop-up when you hold the mouse cursor over a menu item. You can create cascading menus (submenus under menu items) by choosing the Pop-up option in the Menu Item Properties dialog box as shown in figure 13.23.

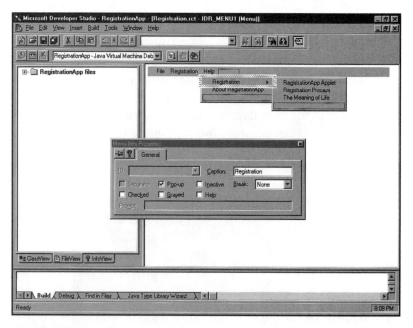

Figure 13.23:
Creating cascading menus.

As you can see in figure 13.23, when the Pop-up option is selected in the Registration Menu Item Properties dialog box, it becomes possible to enter submenu items.

Adding a Menu to the RegistrationApp Applet

A menu resource can be saved in a resource template file along with other resources or it can be saved in its own template file. The Java Resource Wizard can then be used to generate source code to create the menu. This can be accomplished by following the exact same procedure required to generate Java code from a dialog resource by using the Java Resource Wizard. Figure 13.24 shows an example of the source code files generated by the Java Resource Wizard from a template file that contains both a dialog and a menu resource.

When you save more than one resource in a resource template file, you can use the Java Resource Wizard to generate source code from multiple resources at a time.

Figure 13.24:

Menu and dialog code files generated by the Java Resource Wizard.

In addition to the code generated from the dialog resource, the Java Resource Wizard also generates a Java source code file for a class called IDR_MENU1 that contains the code required to create the menu specified in the Menu Resource Editor. This code is shown in listing 13.3.

Listing 13.3   The IDR_MENU1 Class Generated by the Java Resource Wizard

```java
//----------------------------------------------------------------
// IDR_MENU1.java:
//          Implementation for menu creation class IDR_MENU1
//
//----------------------------------------------------------------
import java.awt.*;

public class IDR_MENU1
{
      Frame    m_Frame       = null;
      boolean m_fInitialized = false;

      // MenuBar definitions
      //------------------------------------------------------
      MenuBar mb;

      // Menu and Menu item definitions
      //------------------------------------------------------
      Menu m1;         //
      Menu m2;         // File
      MenuItem ID_FILE_OPENUSERPROFILE;       // Open User
➡Profile
      MenuItem ID_FILE_EXIT; // Exit
      Menu m5;         // Registration
      MenuItem ID_REGISTRATION_REGISTER;      // Register
      MenuItem ID_REGISTRATION_CLEAR;         // Clear
      Menu m8;         // Help
      Menu m9;         // Registration
      MenuItem ID_HELP_REGISTRATION_REGISTRATIONAPPAPPLET; //
➡RegistrationApp Applet
      MenuItem ID_HELP_REGISTRATION_REGISTRATIONPROCESS;   //
➡Registration Process
      MenuItem ID_HELP_REGISTRATION_THEMEANINGOFLIFE;      //
➡The Meaning of Life
      MenuItem ID_HELP_ABOUTREGISTRATIONAPP;       // About
```

```
➡RegistrationApp

        // Constructor
        //--------------------------------------------------------
        public IDR_MENU1 (Frame frame)
        {
                m_Frame = frame;
        }

        // Initialization.
        //--------------------------------------------------------
        public boolean CreateMenu()
        {
                // Can only init controls once
                //------------------------------------------------
                if (m_fInitialized ¦¦ m_Frame == null)
                        return false;

                // Create menubar and attach to the frame
                //------------------------------------------------
                mb = new MenuBar();
                m_Frame.setMenuBar(mb);

                // Create menu and menu items and assign to
➡menubar
                //------------------------------------------------
                m1 = new Menu("");
                mb.add(m1);
                m2 = new Menu("File");
                mb.add(m2);
                        ID_FILE_OPENUSERPROFILE = new
➡MenuItem("Open User Profile");
                        m2.add(ID_FILE_OPENUSERPROFILE);
                        ID_FILE_EXIT = new MenuItem("Exit");
                        m2.add(ID_FILE_EXIT);
```

continues

```
Listing 13.3   Continued
                m5 = new Menu("Registration");
                mb.add(m5);
                    ID_REGISTRATION_REGISTER = new
➡MenuItem("Register");
                    m5.add(ID_REGISTRATION_REGISTER);
                    ID_REGISTRATION_CLEAR = new
➡MenuItem("Clear");
                    m5.add(ID_REGISTRATION_CLEAR);
                m8 = new Menu("Help");
                mb.add(m8);
                    m9 = new Menu("Registration");
                    m8.add(m9);
                    ID_HELP_REGISTRATION_REGISTRATIONAPPAPPLET
➡= new MenuItem("RegistrationApp Applet");
                        m9.add(ID_HELP_REGISTRATION_REGISTRATIONAPPAPPLET);
                        ID_HELP_REGISTRATION_REGISTRATIONPROCESS
➡= new MenuItem("Registration Process");
                        m9.add(ID_HELP_REGISTRATION_REGISTRATIONPROCESS);
                        ID_HELP_REGISTRATION_THEMEANINGOFLIFE
➡= new MenuItem("The Meaning of Life");
                        m9.add(ID_HELP_REGISTRATION_THEMEANINGOFLIFE);
                    ID_HELP_ABOUTREGISTRATIONAPP = new
➡MenuItem("About RegistrationApp");
                    m8.add(ID_HELP_ABOUTREGISTRATIONAPP);

            m_fInitialized = true;
            return true;
        }
}
```

To implement the menu in the RegistrationApp applet, you need to insert the IDR_MENU1 source code file into the project. Next, you need to add code to the applet to instantiate an IDR_MENU1 object. As shown in listing 13.3, the IDR_MENU1 class has the following constructor form:

```
IDR_MENU1(Frame frame)
```

This constructor is quite similar to the IDD_REGFORM class's constructor. The only difference is that the container (the frame parameter in this case) must be a Frame object. Consequently, the applet itself cannot be used as the container because the Applet class is derived from the Panel class and not the Frame class.

After the RegistrationApp applet instantiates an IDR_MENU1 object, the *CreateMenu( )* method provided by the IDR_MENU1 class must be called to create the menu. This version of the RegistrationApp applet, shown in listing 13.4, uses the IDR_MENU1 class to create a menu.

Listing 13.4 The RegistrationApp Applet with a Menu

```
import java.applet.*;
import java.awt.*;

public class RegistrationApp extends Applet
{
    IDD_REGFORM m_Form;

    IDR_MENU1 m_Menu;

    Frame m_Frame;

    public void init()
    {
        m_Frame = new Frame("Registration Form");
        m_Frame.setFont(new Font("Dialog", Font.PLAIN, 10));

        m_Menu = new IDR_MENU1(m_Frame);
        m_Menu.CreateMenu();

        m_Form = new IDD_REGFORM(m_Frame);
        m_Form.CreateControls();

        // Add Age Groups
        m_Form.IDC_AGE_GROUP.addItem("Under 20");
        m_Form.IDC_AGE_GROUP.addItem("20 to 30");
        m_Form.IDC_AGE_GROUP.addItem("Over 30");
```

continues

Listing 13.4 Continued

```
        // Add Hobbies
        m_Form.IDC_HOBBIES.addItem("Baseball");
        m_Form.IDC_HOBBIES.addItem("Basketball");
        m_Form.IDC_HOBBIES.addItem("Reading");

        m_Frame.show();
    }

}
```

Remember to set the Frame object's font! If the font is not set, a null pointer exception will be thrown when the IDD_REGFORM class's *CreateControls()* method is called.

In addition, although the RegistrationApp applet in listing 13.4 sets the font size of the m_Frame Frame object to 10, the *CreateControls()* method resets the font size to whatever was specified in the dialog resource's Properties dialog box. If you want to use a different font size, you will have to modify the code for the IDD_REGFORM class or edit the dialog resource and rerun the Java Resource Wizard.

Figure 13.25 shows the user interface created by the RegistrationApp applet in listing 13.4.

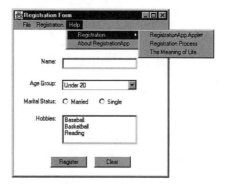

Figure 13.25:

The Registration applet with a menu.

Adding Event Handling Code to the RegistrationApp Applet

The final task required to complete the registration applet's user interface is to add event handling capabilities. You can accomplish this by extending the Frame class and overriding the *action( )* method. Listing 13.5, for example, contains a version of the RegistrationApp applet that responds to a user event. Specifically, when the user chooses the Exit item from the File pull-down menu, the Frame object's *dispose( )* method is called which causes the form to be exited.

Listing 13.5   The RegistrationApp Applet with Event Handling

```
import java.applet.*;
import java.awt.*;

public class RegistrationApp extends Applet
{
    IDD_REGFORM m_Form;

    IDR_MENU1 m_Menu;

    Frame m_Frame;

    public void init()
    {
    m_Frame = new NewFrame("Registration Form");
    m_Frame.setFont(new Font("Dialog", Font.PLAIN, 10));

    m_Menu = new IDR_MENU1(m_Frame);
    m_Menu.CreateMenu();

    m_Form = new IDD_REGFORM(m_Frame);
    m_Form.CreateControls();

    // Add Age Groups
    m_Form.IDC_AGE_GROUP.addItem("Under 20");
    m_Form.IDC_AGE_GROUP.addItem("20 to 30");
    m_Form.IDC_AGE_GROUP.addItem("Over 30");
```

continues

```
Listing 13.5    Continued

        // Add Hobbies
        m_Form.IDC_HOBBIES.addItem("Baseball");
        m_Form.IDC_HOBBIES.addItem("Basketball");
        m_Form.IDC_HOBBIES.addItem("Reading");

        m_Frame.show();
        }

}

class NewFrame extends Frame
{
    NewFrame(String title)
    {
        super(title);
    }

    public boolean action(Event evt, Object arg)
    {
        if (evt.target instanceof MenuItem)
        {
            String itemname = (String)arg;
            if (itemname.equals("Exit"))
                this.dispose();
        return true;
        }
        else return false;
    }
}
```

Summary

In Developer Studio, a resource is a definition of a visual item,
such as a dialog box or a pull-down menu. The same resource can
be used to generate a user interface for both Windows and Java-
based programs. Visual J++ provides Resource Editors that enable
developers to visually define resources and save these definitions

in resource template files. The Java Resource Wizard can then be used to automatically generate standard Java code that utilizes AWT UI component classes.

The Developer Studio Dialog Resource Editor has a number of features that enable developers to quickly lay out controls, which are analogous to Java UI components, within a display area. These features include a series of commands that can be used to size and arrange controls. The Java Resource Wizard can only generate code for controls that have corresponding AWT UI component classes. Many of the options available in the Properties dialog box for a control can be used to set the characteristics of the UI component that is generated from it.

The Developer Studio Menu Resource Editor can be used to define a pull-down menu resource. A cascading menu can be defined in the Menu Resource Editor by choosing the Pop-up option in the Menu Item Properties dialog box.

Menu and Dialog resources can be saved in the same resource template file. Subsequently, the Java Resource Wizard can then generate standard Java code from the template. When incorporated into a Java project, this code produces the UI components and menus defined in the Resource Editors.

When the Java Resource Wizard generates code from a dialog resource, two source code files are produced. One is a layout manager class called DialogLayout. The main advantage of this layout manager is that it determines the position of UI components within a display area based on resolution-independent dialog logical units (DLUs). The other class produced by the Java Resource Wizard sets the parent container's layout manager to DialogLayout and adds the appropriate UI components to the container.

When you use the code generated by the Java Resource Wizard to add a menu to your program's user interface, you must make sure that the container is a Frame object because only Frame objects can hold a menu.

Questions

1. Why are visual elements, such as buttons and text boxes, called controls in the Dialog Resource Editor and not UI components?

2. Suppose you want to size a button to be just large enough for its label. What Dialog Resource Editor command enables you to do this easily?

3. In what situation will the Java Resource Wizard generate code that adds a Checkbox component to a CheckboxGroup?

4. In what situation will the Java Resource Wizard generate code that produces a TextArea component?

5. When you select multiple controls in the Dialog Resource Editor, how do you know which control is the dominant control?

6. Why is the value of the ID option specified in a control's Properties dialog box important?

7. Suppose you are attempting to use the Java Resource Wizard-generated code to create a user interface within a Frame object. When you execute your program, you find that the font used for the user interface is too small, even though you set it to a larger size. What is the most likely cause of this?

8. Can a Java program set the font for a menu resource?

9. When the Java Resource Wizard generates code from a dialog resource, why does it always generate a source code file called `DialogLayout.java`?

Answers

1. The term control has always been used to describe an element of a dialog resource in Developer Studio. Remember, the same resource template used to generate Java code

can also be used to generate a user interface for a Windows application that is written in Visual C++. The term control is used in Visual J++ for consistency.

2. You can use the Size to Content command to make a button just large enough to hold its label.

3. The Java Resource Wizard generates code that creates a Checkbox component and adds it to a Checkbox group object when the dialog resource contains a radio button control.

4. The Java Resource Wizard generates code that creates a TextArea component when the dialog resource contains a multiline Edit Box control.

5. When multiple controls are selected in the Dialog Resource Editor, the dominant control is displayed with solid handles around it.

6. The value of a control's ID is important because the Java Resource Wizard uses this value to name the corresponding UI component variable when it generates code.

7. The *CreateControls( )* method that is included in the wizard-generated code for a dialog resource sets the default font size of all UI components that it creates to the font size specified in the dialog resource's Properties dialog box. If you want to change the font size, you'll have to regenerate the code using the Resource Wizard or modify the *CreateControls( )* method yourself.

8. You cannot set the font of a menu resource because it is automatically set by the operating system at runtime.

9. `DialogLayout.java` contains the source code for the DialogLayout class, which is a layout manager that positions and sizes UI components based on resolution-independent DLUs. The Dialog Resource Editor also lays out controls based on DLUs. Therefore, by setting the layout manager of a container object to DialogLayout, a user interface is produced that corresponds to the layout defined in a dialog resource.

Chapter 14

Advanced Multithreading and Exception Handling

Although multithreading and exception handling are not particularly related, they are both advanced topics that you will need to understand if you are to develop efficient and stable programs in Java.

The first part of this chapter discusses exception handling. When something exceptional happens in a program, it's not necessarily a good thing. For better or worse, however, it is a simple fact of life that unexpected, abnormal, and/or unwanted things happen, even in Java. Therefore, for you to write well-behaved Java applets and applications, you will have to learn how to detect, handle, and, if necessary, create exceptions. The exception handling topics covered in this chapter include:

➤ An overview of Java exceptions

➤ Handling exceptions by using try/catch

➤ Throwing exceptions

➤ Creating custom exceptions

The other advanced topic covered in this chapter is multi-threading. You have already been exposed to the techniques for implementing multiple threads to create an animation in a Java applet (basic applet threads are covered in Chapter 6, "Java Programming Architecture" and Chapter 7, "Building Your First Java Applet By Using Visual J++"). This chapter delves into more advanced multithreading issues. The multithreading topics covered in this chapter include:

➤ Extending the Thread class

➤ Coordinating multithreaded access to shared resources

➤ Avoiding deadlock

➤ Coordinating interdependent threads

➤ Creating well-behaved threads

By definition, any good Java program handles exceptions when it is appropriate and properly manages any threads that it creates. Therefore, the concepts that you learn in this chapter will help round out your Java programming skills. When you're finished, you should be able to create Java applets and applications that are more problem-free, robust, and efficient.

Java Exceptions

When an exception occurs, an Exception object is created either implicitly by the Java environment, or explicitly by the Java program. Java defines a great many exceptions that are all derived from the Exception class. The Exception class is part of the java.lang package and is derived from the Throwable class. Figure 14.1 illustrates the class hierarchy of the exceptions provided in the java.lang package.

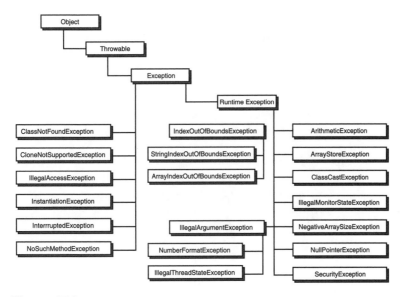

Figure 14.1:

Class hierarchy of the java.lang package exceptions.

In addition to the exceptions shown in figure 14.1, other Java packages also include exceptions. The IOException class, for example, is part of the java.io package.

As indicated by the names of the exceptions shown in figure 14.1, the Java-defined exceptions cover a great many conditions that can occur implicitly within a Java program. You can define your own exception types by extending the Exception class. Java's exception delivery mechanism is triggered by issuing a Throw command, which is discussed later in this chapter.

Exception Handling

When an Exception object is created, it signals that a situation—typically an unexpected error—has occurred. Exception handling involves the mechanism used to trap an exception and the propagation of the exception up through the call stack. Therefore, with exception handling, a program can trap an error and deal with it accordingly or pass it to the calling method.

In Java, exceptions are caught with a try/catch block. The following code shows an example of exception handling.

```
try
{
    char small_array[] = new char[2];
    small_array[4] = "A";
}
catch (ArrayIndexOutOfBoundsException e)
{
    System.out.println("Exception Handled: " +
e.getMessage());
    e.printStackTrace();
}
```

A method *catches* an exception when the method contains a try/catch block that handles the exception condition.

The preceding code attempts to access memory outside the bounds of the allocated array. This results in the generation and delivery of an Exception object. The exception is handled by printing an error message associated with the exception along with the program stack. In this particular case, the program will continue to execute after the exception has been caught.

Catching Multiple Exceptions

More than one catch statement can be used in conjunction with a try statement to enable the program to differentiate between the types of exceptions. The following pseudo-code shows how this may be accomplished.

```
try
{
    // open a file
    // read contents into array
    // process array
    // close file
    // other program code goes here
}
```

```
catch (FileNotFoundException e)
{
    // handle File error
}
catch (ArithmeticException e)
{
    // handle Arithmetic error
}
finally()
{
    // close file
}
```

By using this technique, the program can differentiate between a File Not Found error and an arithmetic error.

Using the finally Clause to Perform Cleanup Operations

If you've done any C++ programming, the try/catch syntax should be familiar to you; however, if you look at the pseudo-code in the previous section, you may notice that a *finally( )* statement is used to identify the last code block. The code in this block executes regardless of whether an exception is thrown or not.

The finally block comes in handy when your program needs to perform cleanup operations. Closing a file opened in the try block is a good example of a cleanup chore. Without a finally block, you would have to add cleanup code to both the catch block and the body of the method.

Although it is generally considered good programming practice to free up resources, such as closing open files and releasing graphics contexts, when appropriate, it is less of an issue in Java because the Java garbage collection process automatically cleans up objects that are no longer referenced by any other object.

Printing Information about an Exception

It is useful to discover the cause of an exception. When you know the cause of an exception, it makes it easier to fix programming bugs as soon as they are discovered. Because all exceptions are derived from Throwable, they all support the following methods provided by the Throwable class.

➤ *getMessage()*—Returns a detailed message regarding a Throwable object.

➤ *printStackTrace()*—Outputs the current call stack when the Throwable object was caught.

➤ *toString()*—Returns a string representation of a Throwable object. This method overrides the *toString()* method provided by the Object class.

The example code in Listing 14.1 shows how the Throwable methods can be used to print information about an exception object.

Listing 14.1 The ShowException Application

```
public class ShowExceptionInfo
{

    public static void main(String argv[])
      {
      try
      {
         int b = 0;
         int a = 2/b;
      }
      catch(Exception e)
      {
         e.printStackTrace();
         System.out.println("getMessage: "+e.getMessage());
         System.out.println("toString: "+e.toString());
      }
      System.out.println("Program continues");
   }

}
```

The ShowExceptionInfo application generates an exception condition because it attempts to divide an integer with value of 2 by 0. In this case, the ShowExceptionInfo application implicitly throws an exception because the Java environment automatically creates an exception condition whenever a program attempts to divide by 0. Because this divide operation is performed within a try block, the exception that it creates will be caught by the catch statement immediately following the try block. Because the catch block catches a generic Exception object, it handles any exception condition. The catch block prints out the method call stack, the exception's message, and a string value representing the exception. After the code in the catch block executes, the program continues processing at the line of code following the catch statement.

When the ShowExceptionInfo application is run from the command line by using Microsoft's jview utility, it produces the following output.

```
C:\>jview ShowExceptionInfo
Microsoft (R) Command-line Loader for Java (tm) Version
1.00.6211
Copyright (C) Microsoft Corp 1996. All rights reserved.
java.lang.ArithmeticException
        at ShowExceptionInfo.main
getMessage: null
toString: java.lang.ArithmeticException
Program continues
C:\>
```

As demonstrated in the preceding output when the ShowExceptionInfo application attempts to perform a divide by 0 operation, an ArithmeticException occurs. The first error message in the listing is the method call stack which indicates that the ArthmeticException was thrown in the ShowExceptionInfo application's *main()* method. The output listing indicates that the catch block executed after the exception condition occurred. There was no error message associated with the exception (getMessage: null) and the exception object generated was an instance of the java.lang.ArithmeticException class. After the catch block executed, the program continued at the line of code following the catch block (Program continues).

The first release of the Microsoft Java Virtual Machine (JVM) provides a minimal amount of information to the Throwable methods. However, if you run the ShowException program under the Sun JVM for Windows, you would get some useful additional information, such as a message describing the exception as well as the line number of the source code file that caused the exception. The following output shows the results of the ShowExceptionInfo program when it is run with the Sun's Java interpreter.

```
C:\>java ShowExceptionInfo
java.lang.ArithmeticException: / by zero
        at
ShowExceptionInfo.main(C:\Msdev\projects\ShowExceptionInfo\
ShowExcept
ionInfo.java:9)
getMessage: / by zero
toString: java.lang.ArithmeticException: / by zero
Program continues
C:\>
```

Notice that in both output listings, the application will continue to execute even after the exception is thrown. This happens because the program's exception handling mechanism—the catch block—prints the exception information and continues processing. If the exception was not caught, it would propagate up through the method call stack and the Java environment would ultimately terminate the program.

Throwing Exceptions

Although it is important to understand how you can catch and deal with exceptions that are thrown implicitly by the Java environment, it is also important for you to know how to create programs that explicitly throw exceptions when it is appropriate. You can do this by using the throw command as shown in the following line of code.

```
throw SomeException;
```

The preceding line of code shows that SomeException is an object derived from the Throwable class. When an exception is thrown, program control immediately transfers to the nearest catch clause that handles that exception. In most cases, when you use the throw command, you will either have to include a try/catch block within the same method or include a throws keyword as part of the method signature as shown in the following example.

```
public void throwSomeException() throws SomeException
{
    throw new SomeException();
}
```

The signature of the *throwSomeException()* method signals to any method that calls it that it may throw a SomeException object. Consequently, the calling method has to catch SomeException or pass SomeException to its calling method by including yet another throws clause in its method declaration.

If an exception is derived from the RunTimeException class, your program can throw it without catching it or identifying it in the method signature. A RuntimeException can be handled automatically by the Java environment.

In general, a RuntimeException results from a programming error. A NullPointerException, for example, is a an exception that is derived from RunTimeException. A NullPointerException occurs when a program attempts to access a variable that has a null value. Because you are not required to catch a RunTimeException, you don't have to enclose all your program code in a try/catch block.

Creating a Custom Exception

By using custom exceptions, you can define and handle very specific conditions in your Java programs. The example code given in listing 14.2 shows how to create a custom exception and how to use both the throws clause and the throw statement.

Listing 14.2   The ThrowCustom Applet

```java
public class ThrowCustom extends java.applet.Applet
{

    public void init()
    {
      try
      {
          noNegativeNumbers( -1 );
      }
      catch(DontBeNegativeException e)
      {
          System.out.println("Exception:
➥"+e.getMessage());
          System.out.close();
      }

    }

    public void noNegativeNumbers(int i) throws
➥DontBeNegativeException
    {
        if (i < 0)
        {
            throw new DontBeNegativeException();
        }
    }
}

class DontBeNegativeException extends Exception
{
```

```
public DontBeNegativeException()
{
    super("No negative numbers allowed.");
}

}
```

A custom exception class called DontBeNegative is created in listing 14.2 by extending the Exception class. The new exception does not do anything special; it calls the class constructor of the Exception class that takes a String parameter for a descriptive message. You can also call the Exception class constructor without specifying any parameters.

Calling the *noNegativeNumbers()* method is the first thing that happens in the *init()* method of the ThrowCustom applet. The method signature of *noNegativeNumbers()* indicates that the method may throw a DontBeNegativeException. Because of this, the invocation of the *noNegativeNumbers()* method must be enclosed within a try/catch block.

To cause the *noNegativeNumbers()* method to throw an exception, an integer value of –1 is passed to it as a parameter. Consequently, the *noNegativeNumbers()* method creates a DontBeNegativeException object and simultaneously throws it. This transfers the program control back to the catch clause in the *init()* method, which prints an error message and continues processing.

The error message generated by the ThrowCustom applet is printed to the `System.out` object. The Java environment provides this object and typically links it to standard output. In a Java application, text printed to `System.out` is printed to the display. When running an applet in Internet Explorer under Windows 95, text printed to `System.out` is written to a file called `C:\windows\java\javalog.txt`. To test applets that write to `System.out`, you may find it more convenient to put a shortcut to this file on your desktop or to save it as a Favorite in Internet Explorer.

You should be aware that instead of throwing the custom DontBeNegative exception, the ThrowCustom applet's *noNegativeNumbers()* method could have thrown an IllegalArgumentException in response to receiving a −1 value as a parameter. Furthermore, if the applet was coded to throw an IllegalArgumentException, the Throws clause in the method declaration and the try/catch block could have been left out altogether. This is because IllegalArgumentException is a subclass of RuntimeException, and is therefore, exempt from the normal Java exception handling requirements. In this case, the programmer would have the option of explicitly catching the exception with a try/catch block or passing the exception to the calling method.

Multithreading in Java

The multithreading capability of Java makes it possible for a program to perform more than one task at a time. The PartyText applet from Chapter 7, "Building Your First Java Applet By Using Visual J++," utilizes multithreading to create an animation. The following code from the PartyText applet's *start()* method instantiates and starts the applet's execution thread.

```
m_PartyText = new Thread(this);
m_PartyText.start();
```

In the preceding code, the m_PartyText Thread object is instantiated by calling the Thread class constructor that accepts a Runnable object as a parameter. When this constructor form is used, the Thread object calls the Runnable object's *run()* method. By using the *this* variable to pass a reference to the applet itself, the m_PartyText Thread object executes the PartyText applet's *run()* method. (The PartyText applet implements the Runnable interface).

The only purpose of the Runnable interface is to specify that any class that implements Runnable, must have a public *run()* method.

Using a generic thread to execute a Runnable object is a simple and convenient way to enable a program such as an applet to execute its own thread. Another way to implement multithreading is to create a new class that extends the Thread class. This enables a single program to create many threads. Because each Thread-derived object executes as a separate task, a program can use this technique to perform functions simultaneously, and as a result, more efficiently. The remainder of this chapter discusses how to create and manage your own thread objects.

Extending the Thread Class

As mentioned previously, you can create a separate thread by instatiating an object that is derived from the Thread class; however, to actually execute the thread, you must also do the following:

1. In your Thread-derived class, override the Thread class's *run()* method. It is here that you must put the main processing logic of the class.

2. In your main program, create an instance of your Thread-derived class.

3. Call the *start()* method of your Thread-derived object.

When your program calls the *start()* method provided by the Thread class, the *run()* method of your new class will be invoked. Therefore, the *run()* method should contain the main processing logic of your thread-derived object. After the *run()* method terminates, so does the object's execution thread.

The program in listing 14.3 shows a simple example of an application that creates multiple execution threads by using a class called DelayPrintThread, which extends the Thread class.

Listing 14.3   The ThreadExample Application

```java
public class ThreadExample
{
   public static void main(String args[])
   {
      DelayPrintThread thread1,thread2,thread3;

      thread1 = new DelayPrintThread();
      thread2 = new DelayPrintThread();
      thread3 = new DelayPrintThread();

      thread1.start();
      thread2.start();
      thread3.start();

      try
      {
         Thread.sleep( 10000 );
      } catch(InterruptedException e){} // Do nothing
   }

}

class DelayPrintThread extends Thread
{
   private static int threadCount = 0;
   private int threadNumber = 0;
   private int delay;

   public DelayPrintThread()
   {
      delay = (int)(Math.random()*5000);
      threadCount++;
      threadNumber = threadCount;
   }

   public void run()
   {
      try
      {
```

```
      sleep( delay );
   }
   catch ( InterruptedException e ) {} // do nothing

   System.out.println( "This is Thread# "+threadNumber+
                       " with a delay of "+delay+"." );
   }
}
```

The DelayPrintThread class's constructor sets the delay period (the *delay* variable) to a randomly generated number that will always be between one and five seconds. The processing performed in the *run()* method is quite simple; it sleeps for the delay period, prints its message, and then terminates.

Notice that in the ThreadExample class's *main()* method, three execution threads are created by instantiating three DelayPrintThread objects. Each thread begins executing when its *start()* method is called. Because each DelayPrintThread represents a separate thread, they all execute at the same time.

The output of the ThreadExample program will be different every time it executes because each of the three threads will sleep for a delay period that is randomly generated. As this example demonstrates, by using the Thread class a Java program can create multiple objects that execute as independent tasks.

Multithreading Issues

Although Java makes it easy to create and control threads, it does not eliminate the potential problems related to multithreading. The three main issues that you should consider are:

➤ Coordinating shared resources among threads

➤ Avoiding thread deadlock

➤ Coordinating interdependent threads

The following sections discuss these issues, as well as the solutions to the problems that may result from the use of multithreading.

Coordinating Shared Resources Among Threads

Because many threads can be created in one program, it is not unusual for multiple threads to share the same resource, such as a member variable. A concurrency problem may occur when two or more threads access a shared resource at the same time. The result can be a lost update or an incorrect value returned from a check.

The code in listing 14.4 illustrates an example of a resource that can cause problems when it is shared by more than one thread.

Listing 14.4   The BankAccount Shared Resource

```
class BankAccount
{
   int balance = 100;

   boolean withdraw(int amount)
   {
      if( balance >= amount ) // do not allow an overdraft
      {
         balance -= amount;
         return true;
      else
         return false;
      }
   }
}
```

The BankAccount class, as defined in listing 14.4, can cause concurrency problems in a multithreaded environment because there is nothing to stop more than one thread from calling the *withdraw()* method at the same time. If a BankAccount object has a balance of 100, for example, and two threads withdraw 80 at the same time, the balance is likely to become overdrawn. The first thread checks the balance and finds that there is a balance of 100, which is enough to make a withdrawal of 80. If a second thread checks the balance before the first thread completes its transaction, it determines that the account balance is 100. In this way, both threads pass the availability test (balance > amount); however, by the time both transactions are completed, the account will be overdrawn.

There is also another, more subtle concurrency problem. If both threads attempt to subtract 80 from a balance of 100 at the same time, the result might be a balance of 20. This is possible because in a true multithreaded environment, such as Windows NT, the subtraction of an amount from a balance could be interrupted in the middle of the operation when the operating system executes another thread. To illustrate this point, consider the following line of Java code from the BankAccount object:

```
balance =- amount;
```

When compiled, the preceding Java instruction results in the following bytecode instructions:

```
iload_1                    balance
iload_2                    amount
isub
istore_1                   balance
```

You can use the Visual J++ debugger's Disassemble window (the debugger is covered in Chapter 8, "The Visual J++ Debugger") to see the bytecode created from any Java instruction.

As you can see from the preceding bytecode, one line of Java source code does not necessarily map to one machine instruction, or even one bytecode instruction. The preceding bytecode commands load the balance and amount integers (`iload_1` and `iload_2`), perform the subtraction (`isub`), and then move the resulting value back to the balance variable (`istore_1`). Now suppose two threads attempt to subtract an amount from balance at the same time. After the first thread executes the `iload_1` instruction, the time slice allocated by the operating system for the first thread ends and the thread's execution is temporarily suspended. The second thread then performs the entire operation and stores (`istore_1`) the result of the operation (100 – 80 = 20) back in the balance variable. Finally, the first thread is woken up by the operating system and completes its subtraction operation (100 – 80) and stores the result (20) in balance. In this situation, 80 has been subtracted twice from the initial balance of 100; however, the balance has a value of 20 instead of –60.

The Windows NT operating system has true multithreading capability because it allocates time slices to tasks and can preemptively switch execution between threads. Both Sun's and Microsoft's Java Virtual Machine (JVM) implementations on Windows NT take advantage of the threading capabilities of the underlying operating system. The Sun JVM 1.0 for Solaris, however, implements what are known as green threads, which only permit switching between threads when the executing thread yields. Solaris's green threading is similar to the cooperative multitasking provided by Windows 3.1—a thread has to enable another thread to take over the processor.

For reasons illustrated by the BankAccount example, the probability of thread coordination problems is higher with true multithreaded environments.

Coordinating Threads Using the synchronized Clause

Java provides a simple mechanism for preventing concurrent access to variables within a class. When you declare a method by using the synchronized clause, any thread that calls the method must acquire a lock on the current object before the method executes.

In Java every object is associated with one lock. Therefore, when an object is *locked*, any thread that attempts to obtain a lock on the object must wait until the object is unlocked.

To solve the concurrency problem in the Balance class, for example, the *withdraw( )* method could be declared as follows:

```
boolean synchronized withdraw(int amount)
{
    if( balance >= amount ) // do not allow an overdraft
    {
        balance -= amount;
        return true;
    else
        return false;
    }
}
```

By declaring the *withdraw()* method as synchronized, a thread
has to obtain a lock on the BankAccount object before it can
execute the method. Therefore, only one thread can withdraw
from the object's balance variable at a time.

Coordinating Threads Using the synchronized Statement

Although declaring a method as synchronized is an easy way to
solve the problem of concurrency for a multithreaded program, it
could have an undesirable impact on performance because each
thread must wait its turn. The performance penalty can be even
more significant for complex methods that may take a long time
to complete. To reduce the impact of synchronized methods on a
program's performance, you can use the synchronized statement
instead.

The synchronized statement locks an object while a block of code
is executing. In this way, the lock does not remain in effect for the
entire execution of the method and thus the program is likely to
be more efficient.

The following code shows the syntax of a synchronized block:

```
synchronized( this )
{
    if( balance >= amount ) // do not allow overdraw
    {
```

```
        balance -= amount;
        return true;
    }
    else
        return false;
}
```

As you can see by the preceding example, the synchronized statement is different from the *synchronized( )* method in that the lock does not need to be in effect for the entire time it takes a method to execute. Notice that the synchronized statement requires an object as its argument. This object locks this section of code, and therefore prevents access by multiple threads. In the preceding code, the current object is locked. The object is unlocked when the code in the synchronized block finishes executing.

Protecting a Static Data Member

In the BankAccount class shown in listing 14.4, each instance of the class has a *balance* instance variable. In that case, synchronizing the *withdraw( )* method prevents concurrency on the balance instance variable by locking the BankAccount object. If a class contains a static variable, however, a different approach must be taken to prevent concurrency because, by definition, all instances of the class share the same static variables. Therefore, a concurrency problem can still occur if two or more instances of the same class attempt to update a static variable, even from within a synchronized method or code block.

Suppose, for example, that you tried to code a class so that it protects a static variable as follows:

```
class MyCounter
{
 private static int count;

 public synchronized void updateCount()
 {
```

```
        count += 1;
    }
}
```

In the MyCounter class, the synchronized keyword locks the current MyCounter object when accessing the *updateCount()* method. If, however, there are more than one MyCounter objects, the synchronized keyword will not stop another MyCounter object from updating the *count* variable because a static variable is shared between multiple instances of the class and the synchronized keyword only locks the current instance. Any MyCounter object can call its own *updateCount()* method. Because count is shared by all instances of MyCounter, this situation could result in an erroneous update.

To avoid this problem, you must lock the Class object instead of just a single instance of the class. Because only one Class object exists for any given Java class, you can ensure proper updating of the count variable by using the synchronized statement in conjunction with the *getClass()* method to lock the Class object.

The following code shows how a class can be locked.

```
public void updateCount()
{
 synchronized(getClass())
 {
        count += 1;
 }
}
```

Locking the class prevents other objects from updating the count static variable until the synchronized code block is completed.

Avoiding Deadlock

If a locked object is never unlocked, a thread waiting to put a lock on it will wait indefinitely. This condition, known as *deadlock*, occurs when two or more threads are permanently frozen because each is waiting for a lock that is already held by the other.

The danger of deadlocks is usually not very great in simple programs; however, the risk increases in proportion to the number of threads and shared resources.

The following sequence of steps explains how a classic deadlock situation might occur.

1. Thread #1 obtains a lock on Object #1 when it calls one of the object's synchronized methods.

2. Thread #2 obtains a lock on Object #2 when it calls one of the object's synchronized methods.

3. The synchronized method in Object #1, which is still locked by Thread #1, calls a synchronized method in Object #2. Because Object #2 is already locked by Thread #2, Thread #1 must wait until Object #2 is unlocked.

4. The synchronized method in Object #2, which is still locked by Thread #2, calls a synchronized method in Object #1. Because Object #1 is already locked by Thread #1, Thread #2 must wait until Object #1 is unlocked.

A deadlock has occurred because both threads have locked an object that the other needs to continue processing.

If your program uses a great many threads, a deadlock can occur easily. Unfortunately, Java does not provide a mechanism for automatically detecting and resolving deadlocks. You can, however, greatly reduce the probability of this condition if you take the following precautions:

➤ Avoid calling a synchronized method from within another synchronized method or block of code. If you must nest synchronized methods, always call them in the same order.

➤ Always try to minimize access to shared resources when you design your classes.

Coordinating Interdependent Threads

When you create multithreaded programs, it is likely that you will run into situations where one thread is required to wait until another thread changes the state of an object or variable. Suppose, for example, that one thread attempts to withdraw money from a bank account that does not have enough funds available. One way to handle this situation is to code your program so that the thread will fail and throw a customized FundsNotAvailableException, for example. Throwing an exception for a relatively normal situation like this one, however, is probably not desirable. If you think about it, the thread tries to perform a perfectly normal operation. If the thread had waited a few seconds, perhaps another thread would have deposited enough money into the account.

Alternatively, you could use a simple thread coordination technique to handle these types of situations. The following sections demonstrate the collision problem that may result from uncoordinated threads and how this problem may be addressed through thread coordination.

An Uncoordinated Multithreading Example

Listing 14.5 contains a code listing for an applet called UnrulyIntersection. This program creates an animation by using multiple threads that are not coordinated. The animation simulates two cars driving through a traffic intersection.

Listing 14.5   The UnrulyIntersection Applet

```
import java.applet.Applet;
import java.awt.*;


public class UnrulyIntersection extends Applet implements
➥Runnable
{
    Thread    AnimThread = null;
```

continues

Listing 14.5   Continued

```
ICar      LRcar;
ICar      TBcar;

public void init()
{
    resize( 400, 400 );

    LRcar = new ICar( ICar.leftToRight, 16 );
    TBcar = new ICar( ICar.topToBottom, 17 );

} // End of init()

public void start()
{
    if(AnimThread == null)
    {
        AnimThread = new Thread(this);
        AnimThread.start();

        if( LRcar != null && TBcar != null )
        {
            LRcar.start();
            TBcar.start();
        }
    }
    else
    {
        AnimThread.resume();

        if( LRcar != null ) LRcar.resume();
        if( TBcar != null ) TBcar.resume();
    }
} // End of start()

public void stop()
{
    AnimThread.suspend();

    if( LRcar != null ) LRcar.suspend();
    if( TBcar != null ) TBcar.suspend();

} // End of stop()
```

```
public void run()
{
    while (true)
    {
        try
        {
            Thread.sleep(50);
        }
        catch (InterruptedException e)
        {}

        repaint();
    }
} // End of run()

public void paint(Graphics g)
{
    Color saveColor = g.getColor();

    g.setColor( Color.black );

    g.fillRect( 0, 180, 400, 40 );
    g.fillRect( 180, 0, 40, 400 );

    LRcar.drawCar( g );
    TBcar.drawCar( g );

} // End of paint()

public void update(Graphics g)
{
    // If the view has been invalidated, call paint to
    // do a complete redraw

    if( !isValid() )
    {
        paint( g );
        return;
    }
```

continues

Listing 14.5   Continued

```java
            LRcar.updateCar( g );
            TBcar.updateCar( g );

    } //Ends of update()

} // End of UnrulyIntersection Applet

class ICar extends Thread
{
    public     int     lastPos = -1;
    public     int     carPos = 0;
    public     int     speed = 10;
    public     int     direction = 1;

    public final static int leftToRight = 1;
    public final static int topToBottom = 2;

    public ICar( int direction, int speed )
    {
        this.speed = speed;
        this.direction = direction;
    }

    public void run()
    {
        while( true )
        {
            carPos += speed;
            if (carPos >= 400)
            carPos = 0;

            try
            {
                Thread.sleep(100);
            }
            catch (InterruptedException e)
            {}

        }
    }
```

```
    public void drawCar( Graphics g )
    {
        if( direction == ICar.leftToRight ) // draw Left-Right
➡Car
        {
            if( lastPos >= 0 )
            {
                g.setColor( Color.black );
                g.fillRect( 0+lastPos, 185, 40, 32 );
            }

            g.setColor( Color.gray );
            g.fillOval( 2+carPos, 185, 10, 10 );
            g.fillOval( 26+carPos, 185, 10, 10 );
            g.fillOval( 2+carPos, 205, 10, 10 );
            g.fillOval( 26+carPos, 205, 10, 10 );

            g.setColor( Color.green );

            g.fillRect( 0+carPos, 190, 40, 20 );

            lastPos = carPos;
        }
        else // draw Left-Right Car
        {
            if( lastPos >= 0 )
            {
                g.setColor( Color.black );
                g.fillRect( 185, 0+lastPos, 32, 40 );
            }

            g.setColor( Color.gray );
            g.fillOval( 185, 2+carPos, 10, 10 );
            g.fillOval( 185, 26+carPos, 10, 10 );
            g.fillOval( 205, 2+carPos, 10, 10 );
            g.fillOval( 205, 26+carPos, 10, 10 );

            g.setColor( Color.blue );

            g.fillRect( 190, 0+carPos, 20, 40 );
```

continues

Listing 14.5   Continued

```
        lastPos = carPos;
    }
}

public void updateCar( Graphics g )
{
    if( lastPos != carPos )
    {
        drawCar(g);
    }
}
}
```

When you execute the UnrulyIntersection applet, it creates two car objects traveling at the same speed, but in different directions. The *start()* method starts all threads in the applet and the *run()* method, which executes indefinitely, periodically calls the *repaint()* method. The *paint()* method draws the intersection and car objects. The result is an animation that simulates two cars progressing through an intersection.

Each car object represents a separate execution thread and each has its own speed and position on the road. If you look at the listing, you can see that the *run()* method of the ICar object periodically updates the position of the car. If an ICar object passes the border of the applet, its position is reset to the beginning and the process starts over. Because the car threads are not coordinated, there will be periodic collisions at the intersection as shown in figure 14.2.

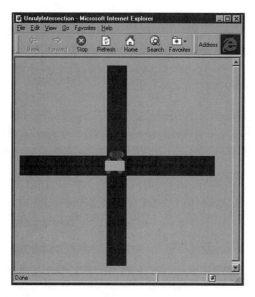

Figure 14.2:

Collision in the UnrulyIntersection applet.

Coordinating Threads with the *wait()* and *notify()* Methods

Unless you were the type of kid that liked to make your toy trains collide in a cataclysmic crash, you probably agree that it is not desirable for the cars to collide in the UnrulyIntersection applet. Fortunately, you can use the *wait()* and *notify()* methods (provided by the Object class) to coordinate the threads.

The *wait()* method must be called from within a synchronized method or code block. Therefore, the thread must already have a lock on the current object. Calling the *wait()* method results in the thread releasing its lock. At this point, it becomes possible for another thread to lock the current object and to continue processing. The thread that called *wait()* will be suspended until another thread notifies it with a call to either the *notify()* method or the *notifyAll()* method. The waiting thread will then wake up and attempt to re-obtain ownership of a lock on the object. If the thread cannot perform its function because of the state of the object (for example, there is still not enough money in the BankAccount object to make a withdrawal), it can call the *wait( )* method again. This process can be repeated until the thread can complete its task.

A Coordinated Multithreading Example

What the UnrulyIntersection applet needs is a traffic cop that manages the applets car threads. Listing 14.6 contains a new version of the intersection simulation called the OrderlyIntersection applet. This version uses a new class called TrafficCop. A TrafficCop object's sole function is to prevent collisions of ICar threads.

Listing 14.6   The OrderlyIntersection Applet

```
import java.applet.Applet;
import java.awt.*;

public class OrderlyIntersection extends Applet implements
➥Runnable
{
    Thread      AnimThread = null;

    ICar            LRcar;
    ICar            TBcar;

    TrafficCop      tCop;


    public void init()
    {
        resize( 400, 400 );

        tCop = new TrafficCop();

        LRcar = new ICar( tCop, ICar.leftToRight, 16 );
        TBcar = new ICar( tCop, ICar.topToBottom, 17 );

    } // End of init()
```

```
public void start()
{
    if(AnimThread == null)
    {
        AnimThread = new Thread(this);
        AnimThread.start();

        if( LRcar != null && TBcar != null )
        {
            LRcar.start();
            TBcar.start();
        }
    }
    else
    {
        AnimThread.resume();

        if( LRcar != null ) LRcar.resume();
        if( TBcar != null ) TBcar.resume();
    }
} // End of start()

public void stop()
{
    AnimThread.suspend();

    if( LRcar != null ) LRcar.suspend();
    if( TBcar != null ) TBcar.suspend();

} // End of stop()

public void run()
{
    while (true)
    {
        try
        {
            Thread.sleep(50);
        }
        catch (InterruptedException e)
        {}
```

continues

Listing 14.6   Continued

```java
            repaint();
        }
    } // End of run()

    public void paint(Graphics g)
    {
        Color saveColor = g.getColor();

        g.setColor( Color.black );

        g.fillRect( 0, 180, 400, 40 );
        g.fillRect( 180, 0, 40, 400 );

        LRcar.drawCar( g );
        TBcar.drawCar( g );

    } // End of paint()

    public void update(Graphics g)
    {
        // If the view has been invalidated, call paint to do
➡a complete redraw

        if( !isValid() )
        {
            paint( g );
            return;
        }

        LRcar.updateCar( g );
        TBcar.updateCar( g );

    } //Ends of update()

} // End of OrderlyIntersection Applet

class ICar extends Thread
{
    public    int    lastPos = -1;
    public    int    carPos = 0;
```

```
public    int    speed = 10;
public    int    direction = 1;

public    TrafficCop    tCop;


public final static int leftToRight = 1;
public final static int topToBottom = 2;


public ICar( TrafficCop tCop )
{
    this( tCop, ICar.leftToRight, 10 );
}

public ICar( TrafficCop tCop, int direction, int speed )
{
    this.tCop = tCop;
    this.speed = speed;
    this.direction = direction;
}

public void run()
{
    while( true )
    {
        tCop.checkAndGo( carPos, speed );
        carPos += speed;
        if( carPos >= 400 )
        {
            carPos = 0;
        }

        try
        {
            Thread.sleep(100);
        }
        catch (InterruptedException e)
        {}
```

continues

Listing 14.6   Continued

```java
        }
    }

    public void drawCar( Graphics g )
    {
        if( direction == ICar.leftToRight ) // draw Left-Right
Car
        {
            if( lastPos >= 0 )
            {
                g.setColor( Color.black );
                g.fillRect( 0+lastPos, 185, 40, 32 );
            }

            g.setColor( Color.gray );
            g.fillOval( 2+carPos, 185, 10, 10 );
            g.fillOval( 26+carPos, 185, 10, 10 );
            g.fillOval( 2+carPos, 205, 10, 10 );
            g.fillOval( 26+carPos, 205, 10, 10 );

            g.setColor( Color.green );

            g.fillRect( 0+carPos, 190, 40, 20 );

            lastPos = carPos;
        }
        else // draw Left-Right Car
        {
            if( lastPos >= 0 )
            {
                g.setColor( Color.black );
                g.fillRect( 185, 0+lastPos, 32, 40 );
            }

            g.setColor( Color.gray );
            g.fillOval( 185, 2+carPos, 10, 10 );
            g.fillOval( 185, 26+carPos, 10, 10 );
            g.fillOval( 205, 2+carPos, 10, 10 );
            g.fillOval( 205, 26+carPos, 10, 10 );
```

```
            g.setColor( Color.blue );

            g.fillRect( 190, 0+carPos, 20, 40 );

            lastPos = carPos;
        }
    }

    public void updateCar( Graphics g )
    {
        if( lastPos != carPos )
        {
            drawCar(g);
        }
    }
}

class TrafficCop
{
    private    boolean    IntersectionBusy = false;

    public synchronized void checkAndGo( int carPos, int speed
)
    {
        if( carPos+40 < 180 && carPos+40+speed >= 180 &&
➥carPos+speed <= 220 )
        {
            while( IntersectionBusy )
            {
                try
                {
                    wait();
                }
                catch ( InterruptedException e ) { }
            }

            IntersectionBusy = true;
        }

        if( carPos+speed > 220 )
```

continues

Listing 14.6   Continued

```
    {
        IntersectionBusy = false;
    }

    notify();
}
}
```

In the OrderlyIntersection applet, both ICar objects share a *TrafficCop* object. The *run()* method of OrderlyIntersection differs slightly from UnrulyIntersection because it calls the TrafficCop object's *checkAndGo()* method which enables only one ICar object to pass through the intersection at a time.

The TrafficCop class is the coordinating class, which is sometimes referred to as a monitor class. This class contains a boolean flag, called IntersectionBusy, that indicates whether a car is currently in the intersection. The synchronized *checkAndGo()* method is called by each thread when moving the car in the applet's display area.

The *checkAndGo()* method first determines whether the current ICar object (the object that called the method) is entering the intersection. If it is, the method determines whether the IntersectionBusy flag is set to *true*. If the intersection is busy, the thread's execution is suspended by calling the *wait()* method. The thread waits until the other thread (the ICar object already in the intersection) sets the IntersectionBusy flag to *false* and calls the *notify()* method. After the waiting thread is notified, it wakes up and attempts to reobtain a lock on the current object. If successful, it proceeds into the intersection and sets the IntersectionBusy flag to *true* to prevent the other ICar object from entering the intersection.

If the intersection is not busy, the ICar does not wait. The IntersectionBusy flag is set to *true* if the ICar object enters the intersection. After an ICar object passes the intersection, the IntersectionBusy flag is set to *false* and the *notify()* method is called so that, if the other thread is waiting, it will wake up and proceed through the intersection.

Figure 14.3 shows the top-to-bottom car waiting at the intersection for the left-to-right car to pass.

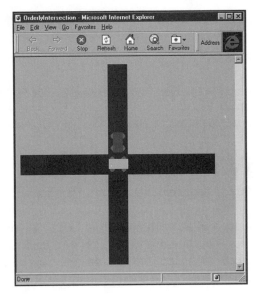

Figure 14.3:

The OrderlyIntersection applet.

The *notify()* method only resumes the thread that has been waiting the longest. In a program where there are more than two threads and you need to wake them all, you can use the *notifyAll()* method. This method resumes all waiting threads. The one that actually begins executing first is determined by the Java scheduler, which is discussed later in this chapter.

As demonstrated by the OrderlyIntersection applet, the implementation of a coordinating object is a relatively simple procedure enabling your program to create interdependent threads. The *wait()* and *notify()* methods can be used for purposes other than creating a coordination class. Suppose, for example, that you wrote a program that provides two buttons—pause and continue. You can code your program so that when a user presses the pause button, the program calls the *wait( )* method for each thread object. Subsequently, when the user presses continue, your program can call the *notifyAll( )* method to resume all waiting threads.

For programs that need to create and manage many threads, it may be more convenient to use the ThreadGroup class. A ThreadGroup object can include thread objects as well as other ThreadGroup objects. You can use a ThreadGroup object to simultaneously control all the threads in the group. If your program calls the *stop()* method for a ThreadGroup, for example, all its threads will stop executing. For more information on the ThreadGroup class, see the Visual J++ Books Online documentation.

Creating Well-Behaved Threads

An important issue related to multithreading is how much processor time is allocated to each thread. A well-behaved thread does not prevent other threads from being executed by hogging the processor. Although you might expect each thread to get an equal amount of processor time, this may not be true depending on the capabilities of the operating system and the design of your program.

Thread Scheduling

Every multithreaded operating system has a thread scheduler. In Windows 95 and NT, each process has a priority class that is shared by all threads created from that process. The priority level within the class can be modified dynamically by the user or the operating system. The priority of a process greatly influences how it is scheduled.

The Java Virtual Machine (JVM) assigns priorities to thread objects. In Java, the priority of a thread is expressed as an integer value between 1 and 10. The Thread class defines the final static data members MIN_PRIORITY, NORM_PRIORITY, and MAX_PRIORITY to represent the minimum, normal, and

maximum priorities respectively. All threads are created with
NORM_PRIORITY by default. A thread's priority can be adjusted
by using the *setPriority()* method. The following line of code, for
example, sets the priority of a Thread object, called MyThread, to
the maximum priority possible.

```
MyThread.setPriority(Thread.MAX_PRIORITY);
```

When it is time to execute a new thread, the Java scheduler
executes the waiting thread with the highest priority. In this way,
the priority values of your program's threads tells the Java environment how to distribute processor time.

How Java Threads Are Scheduled

The Java scheduler is responsible for allocating processor time to
each thread in an applet or application. In the Java Developer's
Kit (JDK) 1.0, the Java thread scheduler functions differently
under different operating systems. The scheduler provides either
preemptive multithreading or *nonpreemptive* multithreading.

When the scheduler is preemptive, a time slice is computed for
each thread based on the thread's priority. Then, each thread
occupies the processor for its allocated time slice, after which the
scheduler suspends the running thread, putting it at the end of
the wait queue, and starts the thread with the highest priority in
the wait queue. This type of scheduling makes life much easier for
the developer because it eliminates the need to specify when
each thread can be interrupted.

When the scheduler is nonpreemptive, the threads are queued by
priority and each thread is run either to completion, or until it
yields to other threads. The danger of this is that a selfish thread
(a thread that never gives other threads a chance to run) could
run forever. In other words, if it doesn't yield to other threads, it
will never be interrupted by the scheduler! Under this type of
scheduling, the programmer must ensure that any executing
thread periodically yields to other threads. When you design your
Java programs, you should consider the type of scheduling used
on the target platforms on which your programs may execute.

The SchedulerTest application creates two threads with low-priority and two threads with high-priority. Each thread prints its identity continuously. If the scheduler on the target platform is preemptive, each thread should get a chance to execute; however, if the scheduler is nonpreemptive, the first thread to be executed will run indefinitely.

The SchedulerTest application in listing 14.7 runs indefinitely unless you interrupt it by pressing Ctrl+C.

The code in listing 14.7 illustrates the type of scheduling implemented on any given target platform.

Listing 14.7   SchedulerTest Application

```
public class SchedulerTest
{
    public static void main(String strargv[])
    {
        Thread1 t1 = new Thread1("thread one");
        t1.setPriority(Thread.MIN_PRIORITY);
        t1.start();

        Thread1 t2 = new Thread1("thread two");
        t2.setPriority(Thread.MIN_PRIORITY);
        t2.start();

        Thread1 t3 = new Thread1("thread three");
        t3.setPriority(Thread.MIN_PRIORITY);
        t3.start();

        Thread1 t4 = new Thread1("thread four");
        t4.setPriority(Thread.MAX_PRIORITY);
        t4.start();

    }
}

class Thread1 extends Thread
{
```

```
    String m_s;
    Thread1(String s)
    {
        m_s = s;
    }

    public void run()
    {
        while(true)
        {
            System.out.println(m_s);
        }
    }
}
```

Under Windows NT, the Java scheduler is preemptive, therefore the two threads with MAX_PRIORITY will take most, but not all, of the processor's time. You can use this program on different operating systems and change the priorities of each thread to see how it affects the scheduler.

Yielding to Other Threads

Because Java is cross-platform, you should design your programs to function properly on all possible target operating systems. When it comes to multithreading, it is safest to assume that your program must be well-behaved when executed by a nonpreemptive Java scheduler. Therefore, you should design your programs so that each executing thread periodically yields control to the other thread that might be waiting for the processor.

A thread provides other threads with a chance to execute whenever the Thread class's *yield( )*, *sleep( )*, *stop( )*, or *suspend( )* methods are called. A thread also relinquishes control whenever the Object class's *wait( )* method is called for the current object.

Although these methods make it possible for other threads to take over the processor, in most cases it makes the most sense to call the *yield( )* method when all you want to do is to make a thread more suitable for a nonpreemptive Java scheduler. This is because *yield( )* does nothing but give other threads a chance to execute.

The following code demonstrates how either the *sleep( )* method or the *yield( )* method can be used to give other threads a chance to execute.

```
try
{
    sleep(1000);       // Always stop for 1000 milliseconds
➥and let
                       // other threads execute if any are
➥waiting
{
catch(InterruptedException e) {}

yield();               // Yield the processor only if
➥another thread is
                       // waiting. If not, keep on
➥chugging!
```

The comments in the preceding code describe how the *sleep( )* method always stops the execution of a thread for the specified interval, whereas the *yield( )* method has no impact on a thread's performance unless another thread is waiting.

If a thread makes many input/output (I/O) calls, it may not be necessary to yield because the I/O call itself suspends the thread's execution until the operation has completed.

Although one of the primary advantages of developing programs in Java is that they can execute on almost any computer, you have to remember that some implementations of the Java Virtual Machine may be limited by the capabilities of the underlying operating system. When you create multithreaded Java programs, you must keep in mind that some target machines may not support true multithreading. Therefore, if you want to address the widest possible audience with your Java programs, you should design them to be well-behaved.

Summary

Exception handling is vital to writing stable code that will perform predictably even in unpredictable circumstances. In Java, exceptions are caught by using a try/catch block. Programs that throw exceptions must handle the exception with a try/catch block or pass the exception to its calling method by including a throws clause in the method declaration. The only exceptions exempt from Java's exception handling requirements are RuntimeExceptions. A finally block can be used to clean up resources for both normal and exception conditions. You can define custom exceptions by deriving classes from the Exception class or one of its subclasses.

Chapter 7, "Building Your First Java Applet By Using Visual J++," introduced the concept of using Java's multithreading capabilities to create an animation in an applet. Multiple threads can also be created in a program by defining a class that extends the Thread class.

Sometimes threads must share resources such as variables. For these situations, you can use a synchronized clause in a method declaration to lock the current object. When an object is locked by a thread, no other thread can lock it. To minimize the performance penalty that may result from synchronization, you can use the synchronized statement to lock an object for a block of code instead of locking it for an entire method. When you need to protect a static variable in a multithreaded program, it is important that you remember to use the *getClass()* method to lock the entire class instead of just an instance of the class.

If you're not careful, synchronized resources can cause a condition known as deadlock. This situation occurs when two threads are suspended because they are waiting to obtain a lock held by the other. You can reduce the probability of deadlock by minimizing shared resources, never nesting synchronized code, and always accessing shared resources in the same order.

In Java, the thread scheduler determines when, and for how long, each thread gets executed. The Java scheduler may not always be preemptive on the target platform. Therefore, you should design your Java programs so that any executing thread periodically yields so that other threads can execute. The least disruptive way for a thread to yield is to call the *yield()* method.

Questions

1. Is it possible to derive a custom exception class?

2. Can you avoid handling an exception that is not derived from RuntimeException?

3. How can you ensure that only one thread at a time can update an instance variable?

4. What object must be locked to ensure proper shared access to a static variable?

5. If threads are scheduled differently on different platforms, what should you do to ensure that your program's threads are well-behaved on all platforms?

6. How do you resume the execution of a thread that was suspended by calling the *wait()* method?

Answers

1. Yes. Custom exceptions can be derived from the Exception class or one of its subclasses.

2. No. Exceptions that are not derived from RuntimeException must be handled. You can, however, defer the handling of the exception by including a throws clause for the exception in your method declaration. The exception will then have to be handled by the method that called your method, or passed on again to its calling method by using another throws clause.

3. You can ensure that only one thread at a time can update an instance variable by putting the update code in a synchronized method or code block of the object that holds the variable. When you do this, any thread that attempts to update the variable will have to lock the current object that holds the variable. Because only one thread at a time can have a lock on an object, only one thread at a time can update a locked variable.

4. The Class object for the current class must be locked to ensure proper shared access to a static variable by multiple threads. You can do this by using the *getClass()* method in conjunction with a synchronized statement.

5. You should code your multithreaded programs assuming that the Java scheduler will be nonpreemptive. Therefore, you should ensure that any executing thread periodically yields to other threads.

6. The *notify()* or *notifyAll()* methods can be used to resume either the oldest suspended thread or all the suspended threads respectively.

Chapter 15

Working with IO Streams and Sockets

This chapter focuses on the fundamental concepts that will help you get started creating Java programs that can access and interact with other programs and resources over a network. The classes discussed in this chapter are provided in the java.io and java.net packages. When used in combination, these classes make it possible to create powerful client-server Java applets and applications. This chapter covers the following topics:

➤ Accessing Internet resources with the URL class

➤ Controlling a web browser from an applet

➤ Working with input and output streams

➤ Creating client and server programs by using sockets

In many cases, a Java applet is constrained by the security requirements imposed by the web browser within which it is running. Because Java applications are not subject to the same restrictions, most of the examples used in this chapter are applications.

The URL Class

The URL class is provided in the java.net package. This class makes it possible to create an object that represents a network-based resource.

A *URL*, or *Uniform Resource Locator* (sometimes referred to as a Universal Resource Locator) represents a unique identifier for a resource on either the public Internet or a private intranet.

You've probably already heard people talk about URLs. Most companies and many individuals have their own URLs. At one time it was considered cool to just have an e-mail address on your business card. Now, everyone wants to know your URL as well.

A URL is composed of several parts. The URL `http://www.worktechs.com/index.html`, for example, is the home page for @Work Technologies. The first part of the URL, `http`, specifies the protocol that must be used to connect to the resource. The second part, `www.worktechs.com`, specifies the host name. Finally, `index.html` specifies the file name.

Most web servers will default to `index.html` when a directory is specified but no file name is given.

The most common way to create a URL object is to use the constructor that takes a single String object as shown in the following code.

```
URL  u = null;

try
{
   u = new URL("http://www.microsoft.com");
}
catch (MalformedURLException e)
{
   System.out.println("Bad URL: http://
➥www.microsoft.com");
}
```

After being instantiated, the URL object provides a valid address for a particular resource. The functionality provided by this class can be used to specify a URL to other programs, open a stream for reading or writing, discussed later in this chapter, or validate a URL entered by the user.

The AppletContext Interface

The AppletContext interface corresponds to the environment in which an applet is running. The environment can be a Java-enabled web browser or some web browser simulator such as the appletviewer, which is provided with the Java Developer's Kit (JDK) from Sun. Any Java-enabled browser creates an object that implements that AppletContext interface. Consequently, the functionality provided by this object can be utilized by any applet.

The Applet class provides the *getAppletContext()* method that can be used to get the current AppletContext object. The AppletContext object provides methods that enable Java applets to control certain functions performed by the web browser. In addition, the AppletContext object provides methods that enable Java applets to communicate with other applets while running within the same HTML page.

Controlling the Web Browser

The *showDocument( )* method provided by the AppletContext object can be used to make a web browser display a specific web page.

The following two forms of the *showDocument( )* method make the browser connect to and display a URL.

➤ *showDocument(URL document)*—Causes the browser to display the document indicated by the specified URL.

➤ *showDocument(URL document, String target)*—Causes the browser to display the document indicated by the specified URL in a specific target window or frame. This method accepts the following target strings:

  ➤ *self*—Shows the document in the current window.

  ➤ *parent*—Shows the document in the parent window.

  ➤ *top*—Shows the document in the top-most window.

  ➤ *blank*—Shows the document in a new, unnamed top-level window.

  ➤ *window_name*—Shows the document in a new top-level window and gives the window the name specified by the `window_name` target string.

Finding the Applet's Directory

The *getCodeBase( )* method provided by the Applet class returns a URL object corresponding to the location from which the Java applet was read. It may be useful to know this before accessing another URL.

Finding the HTML Page's Directory

The *getDocumentBase( )* method provided by the Applet class returns a URL object corresponding to the location from which the current HTML page containing the Java applet was read.

Displaying a Status Message

At times it may be necessary to display information to the user in the form of a status message. This can be useful, for example, when an applet is waiting for a file to be read across a network. The *showStatus( )* method provided by the AppletContext object can be used to display a message to the user on a web browser's status bar. The following line of code, for example, displays an informative message to the user.

```
showStatus("Loading http://www.microsoft.com, one moment
➥please...");
```

You should not rely exclusively on the *showStatus( )* method to display important information to the user. In some situations the status bar may not be visible. The Internet Explorer, for example, can be configured so that the status bar is not displayed at all. Alternatively, you could display a message by using a Label UI component on the applet's display area.

Applet to Applet Communication

The AppletContext object provides the *getApplet( )* and *getApplets( )* methods that make it possible for an applet to see other applets on the same HTML page. These methods return Applet objects, or a null value if no Applet objects are found.

The *getApplet( )* and *getApplets( )* methods can be useful when multiple applets need to share information, or when a master applet needs to control the processing of other applets.

Getting an Applet by Name

The *getApplet( )* method gets an applet by name. For your browser to distinguish one applet from another, you must include the appropriate NAME parameter in your HTML file.

The following HTML tags, for example, define an applet called *main* and another called *other*.

```
<APPLET CODE=MainApplet WIDTH=500 HEIGHT=500 NAME=main>
</APPLET>
< APPLET CODE =OtherApplet WIDTH =500 HEIGHT =500 NAME
↪=other>
</APPLET>
```

As long as a NAME parameter is specified as shown in the preceding HTML code, the *getApplet()* method can be used to gain access to the OtherApplet object and its public methods. The following code, for example, could be used by the MainApplet to invoke the OtherApplet's *repaint()* method.

```
Applet other = getAppletContext.getApplet("other");
if(other != null)
    other.repaint();
```

By enabling you to call applet methods from other applets, the *getApplet()* method provides you a great deal of flexibility when you design web-based Java applets. You can, for example, create a master toolbar applet that controls the behavior of all the other applets on the web page.

Enumerating Through All Applets on an HTML Page

For situations where you have more than one applet on a web page that need to communicate with each other, it may be more convenient to use the *getApplets()* method instead of the *getApplet()* method. The *getApplets()* method is similar to the *getApplet()* method; however, instead of returning a single Applet object, the *getApplets()* method returns an object that implements the Java Enumeration interface. This object contains a list of all the Applet objects within an HTML page. The applets can be accessed by enumerating through the object.

An object that implements the *Enumeration* interface generates a series of elements that can be accessed one at a time. You can access the next element in a series by calling the Enumeration object's *nextElement()* method.

The following code shows how to access an Enumeration object containing a list of all available applets.

```
Enumeration e = getAppletContext().getApplets();
for(;e.hasMoreElements();)
{
    Applet app = (Applet)(e.nextElement());
    // do something with the applet
}
```

The *nextElement()* method returns an object. After the object is obtained, it can be cast to an Applet object, or to a more specific subclass of the Applet class. After it has been cast as an Applet object, the program can call any of its public methods. Casting objects and fundamental data types is covered in Chapter 4, "Java Classes and Objects."

Streams

Streams provide a useful abstraction in Java for accessing data such as files or information provided by other programs over a network. The Java stream classes can be used by a Java program to read from a source and write to a destination. The java.io package includes classes for both input and output streams.

A *stream* is a communications path between a source of information, such as a URL, and a destination. A stream can be used by Java programs to access resources, such as files, over a network.

Streams can be thought of as generic input/output devices that provide uniform access to data no matter what the source or destination. The Java streams classes are similar to C++ input/

output streams; however, Java streams have the added capability of being able to access network-based resources over an intranet or the Internet.

A stream can be attached to a keyboard, file, URL, and so on. In Java, reading from and writing to a stream is performed through a standard set of methods. This level of abstraction makes it easier to incorporate new technologies. Some of the examples in previous chapters use the standard output stream to display information, such as the *System.out.println( )* method. This section provides a more detailed discussion of the functionality available through streams.

Because streams are defined in the java.io package, you will either have to specify stream objects by using the java.io prefix or import the java.io package into your program.

When a program uses an output stream, the program is the source of the data. Conversely, input streams enable a program to get data from another source, such as a file. The following sections discuss the types of stream classes available in Java.

It is important to remember that most stream methods can throw an IOException. Therefore, any time you access a stream, you should enclose the code within a try/catch block. Exception handling is discussed in Chapter 14, "Advanced Multithreading and Exception Handling."

Input Streams

The java.io package provides the *InputStream* abstract class. This class is derived from the Object class and is the parent of all input stream classes.

The input stream classes, as the name implies, provide methods for reading data, such as a URL, from a source. In addition, the InputStream-derived classes provide a great deal of additional functionality such as the capability to mark a position within an input stream.

InputStream-Derived Classes

The following classes are derived from the InputStream class:

➤ *ByteArrayInputStream*—Enables bytes of data to be transferred in memory.

➤ *StringBufferInputStream*—Holds a String in memory.

➤ *FileInputStream*—Enables access to the contents of a file.

➤ *SequenceInputStream*—Joins two or more objects derived from InputStream. Reads applied to a SequenceInputStream alternate between each merged stream. If a SequenceInputStream contains, for example, two streams, the first read accesses the first stream, the second read accesses the second stream, and the third read starts over with the first stream.

➤ *PipedInputStream*—Used in combination with a *PipedOutputStream* to facilitate communication between threads. The PipedInputStream class provides all the functionality required to managed threads and streams.

➤ *FilterInputStream*—Extends an input stream's functionality by wrapping it within another input stream.

FilterInputStream-Derived Classes

As mentioned in the previous section, the FilterInputStream class can be used to wrap, or nest, an input stream within another input stream. As you should already know, Java does not support multiple inheritance. By wrapping one input stream within another, however, the resulting object can inherit functionality from multiple InputStream-derived classes. Therefore, the FilterInputStream class can be used to create a rather unique Java object. The following code shows how the FilterInputStream class, for example, can be used to create a nested input stream object.

```
URL u                    = new URL("http://
➥www.worktechs.com");
InputStream in           = u.openStream();
BufferedInputStream in1  = new BufferedInputStream(in);
DataInputStream in2      = new DataInputStream(in1);

String MyLine = in2.readLine();
```

The preceding code shows an InputStream nested within both a BufferedInputStream object and a DataInputStream object. Consequently, the call to the *readLine()* method provided by the DataInputStream class reads a full line of data from the URL. At the same time, the data read is automatically buffered because of the functionality provided by the BufferedInputStream class. As this example demonstrates, method calls applied to a nested input stream are passed up through the chain of nested stream classes.

Although the FilterInputStream class is not explicitly defined as abstract, it is similar to an abstract class because you will most likely not create direct instances of it. This is due to the fact that the only additional functionality implemented by the FilterInputStream class is the capability to be nested.

In Java, you cannot directly instantiate objects of a class that are declared as *abstract*. You can only use the functionality provided by an abstract class by deriving a new class from it. Abstract classes are covered in Chapter 4, "Java Classes and Objects."

The following classes are derived from the FilterInputStream class:

➤ *BufferedInputStream*—Provides a buffer to hold information from the nested input stream. By buffering data, the number of reads can be reduced. This is the only stream that supports marks, which are discussed a little later in this chapter, see the section entitled "Marking an Input Stream."

➤ *DataInputStream*—Provides methods for reading data into primitive variable types, such as boolean or String, rather than in bytes.

➤ *LineNumberInputStream*—Provides a method that calculates the current line number by counting end-of-line characters Under Windows, the end-of-line is denoted by "/n".

➤ *PushbackInputStream*—Provides a method that reads back one byte of data after it has already been read from the stream. This class is useful for parser functions that need to read ahead.

Reading from an Input Stream

The InputStream-derived classes provide a series of methods that enable you to get information from an input stream. The most fundamental of these methods is the *read()* method. The *read()* method extracts one or more bytes from an input stream. If the bytes are not ready, the read command will wait until they are available. This is known as synchronized access. When the input stream has reached its end, the *read()* method returns a –1 instead of the number of bytes read. The *read()* method can be invoked by using the following method signatures.

➤ *read()*—Returns the next byte read from an input stream.

➤ *read(byte[] input)*—Returns the appropriate number of bytes from an input stream into the byte array specified by *input.*

➤ *read(byte[] input, int start, int end)*—Returns the appropriate number of bytes into the byte array specified by *input,* starting at position *start* and ending at position *end* in the input stream.

If a Java program invokes a *read()* method to access data and the data is not available, the entire applet will go into a wait state. This situation may occur frequently, especially if you're accessing files over the Internet. You can avoid this problem by creating a thread for each stream that your Java program attempts to read. That way, your program can continue processing while it is waiting for the data it needs.

Bytes can be read one at a time or many at once. The following code shows how to read one byte at a time with the *read()* method.

```
InputStream is;
byte b;

while( (b = (byte)is.read()) != -1)
{
    // process b
}
```

When it is not necessary to process individual bytes, the read method can read an entire array of bytes. The following code shows how to use of the *read()* method to read an array of bytes at one time. This method is more efficient when retrieving a large amount of data because less overhead is involved with issuing one read to retrieve many bytes than reading one byte at a time.

```
InputStream s;
int length = 512;
byte[] buffer = new byte[512];

int bytesread = s.read(buffer);
```

Skipping Bytes in an Input Stream

The *skip()* method skips over the specified number of bytes in an input stream. You should use the *skip()* method when the data you need is located at a specific position within an input stream. Suppose, for example, your program needed to read the fifth record in an input stream. If the records have a known fixed length, you could use the *skip()* method to skip over the first four records. It is important to remember that, even though the skipped bytes are not used, skipping may cause a delay if the bytes are not ready. The following code shows how to invoke the *skip()* method.

```
long readAhead = 1000;
MyInputStream.skip(readAhead);
```

This code reads past the next 1000 bytes in an input stream called MyInputStream.

In release 1.0 of the Java environment, skips larger than a number that can fit into an *int* variable will not work correctly because a *long* variable is converted to an *int* by the Java environment. If you want to work around this, you will have to derive your own input stream class and write the code yourself, or you can just make multiple calls to the *skip()* method.

Calculating the Bytes Available in an Input Stream

The *available()* method returns the number of bytes currently available in an input stream.

The base InputStream class will always return a zero when the *available()* method is applied to it. Therefore, if you create your own input stream by extending InputStream and you want to check for the number of bytes available, you will have to code this functionality yourself.

Marking an Input Stream

The *mark()* method saves a position in an input stream. This capability is useful, for example, for parsing data in a stream. Parsing may require that your program read ahead in the stream and then return to a specific position.

After creating a mark, the *reset()* method can be used to return to the marked position. The *markSupported()* method returns a boolean value indicating whether or not the input stream supports this feature. The only input stream class that supports the *mark()* and *reset()* methods is the BufferedInputStream class.

When you use the *mark()* method, you must specify the maximum number of characters beyond the current position that you plan to read. The input stream class will then create a buffer of the size you specified and copy the corresponding number of bytes into it. If your program reads more than the specified number of bytes before calling the *reset()* method, the mark will become invalid and any subsequent invocation of the *reset()* method will throw an IOException.

The following code shows a basic example of how the *mark( )* and *reset( )* methods can be used.

```
URL u                  = new URL("http://
➥www.worktechs.com");
InputStream s          = u.openStream();
BufferedInputStream bs = new BufferedInputStream(s);

if( bs.markSupported() )
{
   byte[] readAhead = new byte[256];

   bs.mark(512); // mark the current position, buffering
➥512 bytes

   bs.read( readAhead ); // read less than 512 bytes

   bs.reset(); // go back to original position
}
```

The preceding code instantiates a URL object (u). The code then calls the URL object's *openStream( )* method, which returns an InputStream object (s) for the file represented by the URL. The code wraps the InputStream object within a BufferedInputStream object (BS) so that the stream can be marked. If marks are supported by the BufferedInputStream, the code creates an array of 256 bytes (readAhead). The code marks the BufferedInputStream object at position zero and buffers the next 512 bytes. This enables the program to read ahead up to 512 bytes. Next, the code reads 256 bytes from the input stream into the byte array. At this point the code is positioned at byte 256 in the BufferedInputStream object. Finally, the code returns to byte zero in the BufferedInputStream object by calling the reset( ) method.

In the interest of brevity, exception handling was left out of the preceding code; however, you should always code exception handling (try and catch) when you use streams.

Closing an Input Stream

Whenever an input stream object is no longer needed (that is, no longer referenced), Java's garbage collection process closes an input stream and recovers the memory used by its internal data structures. It is still a good idea, however, to call the *close( )* method whenever you're finished with a stream. By doing this, you ensure that the resources used by the stream are freed immediately and can be used by other streams. Even if an input stream method has thrown an exception, your program can still close the stream by using the *finally* clause, as discussed in Chapter 14, "Advanced Multithreading and Exception Handling." Of course, you should only close an input stream if it has been opened successfully.

Using Streams to Read a URL

Streams are typically used in conjunction with the URL class to read information from a location on the Internet. The URL class has a method called *openStream( )* that returns an InputStream object. You can then call the *read( )* method to read bytes from that URL. You could also read the data from a URL one line at a time; however, you would have to nest an InputStream object within a DataInputStream to accomplish this.

In the Internet Explorer 3.0, only trusted applets (digitally signed applets) are permitted read and write local files. In addition, unless the applet is trusted, it will not be permitted to access a URL from a host other than the one from which the applet came.

Any applet, however, can read URLs from its own web server. If an attempt is made to read from another host, a security violation occurs. As mentioned previously, Java applications are not subject to the same constraints as applets—they can do just about anything even if they're not signed.

The sample application in listing 15.1 opens a URL and reads the contents. The contents of the URL are then printed to standard output. When running this example program, remember that you must be connected to the Internet. This is required because the program is attempting to access an Internet-based URL. This program outputs the HTML code sent by the HTTP (Hypertext Transfer Protocol) server at the specified Internet location.

Due to the complexity of the subject matter in this chapter, all the code listings have been numbered to facilitate code walkthroughs.

Listing 15.1   The ReadURL Application

```
01  import java.io.*;
02  import java.net.*;
03
04  public class ReadURL
05  {
06     public static void main(String args[])
07     {
08        URL u = null;
09        InputStream in= null;
10
11        try
12        {
13           System.out.println("Creating URL...");
14           u = new URL("http://www.worktechs.com");
15
16           System.out.println("Opening Stream...");
17           in = u.openStream();
18           DataInputStream buffer = new DataInputStream(in);
19
20           System.out.println("Reading data...");
21           System.out.println("-----------------");
22
```

```
23          String lineOfData;
24          while( (lineOfData = buffer.readLine()) != null )
25          {
26              System.out.println("LINE: "+lineOfData);
27          }
28
29          System.out.println("-----------------");
30      }
31      catch( MalformedURLException e)
32      {
33          System.out.println("Bad URL");
34      }
35      catch( IOException e)
36      {
37          System.out.println("IO Error"+e.getMessage());
38      }
39      finally
40      {
41          if(in != null)
42          {
43              try
44              {
45                  in.close();
46                  System.out.println("Stream Closed.");
47              }
48              catch( IOException e ) {} // do nothing
49          }
50      }
51
52      System.exit(0);
53      }
54 }
```

The ReadURL application in listing 15.1 creates a URL object (line 14) and then retrieves an InputStream object by calling the URL object's *openStream( )* method (line 17). The ReadURL application wraps the InputStream object in a DataInputStream object (line 18) to enable the program to read a line at a time. Finally, the program goes into a loop (lines 24 through 27) in which it reads lines from the input stream and prints each line (line 26) to standard output. The loop continues until a *readLine( )* method returns a null value which indicates the end of the file. Notice that the program catches exception conditions that may result from a bad URL (lines 31 through 34) or I/O errors (lines 35 through 38). The ReadURL application's finally block (lines 39 through 50) is always executed so that the input stream is always closed.

Reading a File

Reading a file is similar to reading a URL except that the FileInputStream class is used instead of a URL object. The constructor for this class takes a file name as a string. If the file cannot be opened, an IOException will be thrown. It may not be possible to open a file, for example, when the specified file is in use or does not exist.

The following code could be used to replace lines 16 and 17 in listing 15.1 to produce an application that reads a file rather than a URL. This illustrates the flexibility of using streams; the only change involves the initial creation of the stream.

```
15
16          System.out.println("Opening File...");
17          in = new FileInputStream("ReadURL.java");
...
```

Buffering the Contents of an Input Stream

Buffering improves performance because it reduces the number of reads that must take place to access data from an InputStream. In the same way the DataInputStream class can be used to wrap an InputStream, you can wrap an InputStream within a BufferedInputStream to buffer its contents. The BufferedInputStream class creates an internal buffer so that a large number of bytes can be read at one time. After the bytes are read, they can be retrieved from the buffer in smaller amounts.

Output Streams

When you use output streams, your program becomes the source of the data. Almost every output stream class has a corresponding input stream class.

As you may have guessed, an output stream is the counterpart of an input stream. These classes provide the functionality required to send data to a destination, such as a file, URL, or monitor.

The *OutputStream* abstract class provided by the java.io package is the parent of all output streams and is derived from the Object class. Output streams provide methods for writing data.

OutputStream-Derived Classes

The following classes are derived directly from the OutputStream class.

➤ *ByteArrayOutputStream*—Useful for transferring bytes in memory.

➤ *FileOutputStream*—Enables the writing of data to a file.

➤ *PipedOutputStream*—Used in combination with a PipedInputStream to facilitate communication between threads. The PipedOutputStream class provides all the functionality required to handle threads and streams.

➤ *FilterOutputStream*—Extends an output stream's functionality by wrapping it within another output stream.

FilterOutputStream-Derived Classes

Just as the FilterInputStream class can be used to nest input streams, the classes derived from FilterOutputStream can be used to nest output streams. This capability is quite useful when you need to take advantage of the functionality provided by the FilterOutputStream-derived classes. You could, for example, nest an output stream in a DataOutputStream object to enable your program to write a line at a time to the stream.

The following classes are derived from FilterOutputStream:

➤ *BufferedOutputStream*—Provides a buffer to hold information from the nested output stream. By buffering the data, the number of writes required to send data to a destination can be reduced.

➤ *DataOutputStream*—Provides methods to write data as primitive types such as boolean or String, instead of in bytes.

➤ *PrintStream*—This class is usually attached to a screen output device, such as standard output. It provides methods to write data as fundamental data types such as boolean or String, instead of in bytes. You can specify whether to autoflush this stream in its class constructor. This causes it to flush its output whenever a new-line character is printed.

Writing to an Output Stream

The *write( )* method writes data to an output stream. This method can be invoked by using the following signatures:

➤ *write(int Data)*—Writes one byte of data to the appropriate stream.

➤ *write(byte[] Data)*—Writes the byte array to the appropriate stream.

➤ *write(byte[] Data, int Offset, int Length)*—Writes part of the byte array, starting at the position specified by *Offset* and ending with the position specified by *Length*. The ending position is calculated as Offset + Length

All OutputStream-derived classes support one or more forms of the *write()* method.

The following line of code writes one byte to the *s* output stream object.

```
s.write(23);
```

The following code writes the entire contents of an array of bytes to the output stream.

```
byte[] data = new byte[512];    // arbitrary array size

// code to fill array with information goes here

s.write(data);
```

The following code writes a subset of an array of bytes, starting at offset 50 and ending at offset 150 (50 + 100) to the output stream.

```
byte[] data = new byte[512];    // arbitrary array size

// code to fill array with information goes here

s.write(data, 50, 100);
```

Just as invoking a *read()* method can cause an entire Java program to wait until all the data has been read, invoking a *write()* method can cause a program to wait until all the data is written. You can avoid this situation by creating a thread for each stream that your Java program writes to.

Closing an Output Stream

The *close()* method provided by the OutputStream class is identical to that of the InputStream class. It closes and cleans up an output stream connection.

Flushing an Output Stream

When a program writes data to an output stream, the data may be buffered in memory before it is actually written. You can use the *flush()* method to ensure that all data is written from the memory buffer to the data's final destination. The final destination could be, for example, a file on a hard drive or another program. Two of Java's output streams classes, BufferedOutputStream and PrintStream, support the *flush()* method.

Processing File Contents

By using streams, you can create Java programs that read data from a source, process the data, and write the results to a destination. The CopyFILE program shown in listing 15.2 reads the contents of a file and writes it to another file.

Listing 15.2   The CopyFILE Application

```
01 import java.io.*;
02
03 public class CopyFILE
04 {
05    public static void main(String args[])
06    {
07        InputStream m_input= null;
08        OutputStream m_output= null;
09
10        try
11        {
12            System.out.println("Opening Files...");
13            m_input = new FileInputStream("CopyFILE.java");
14            m_output = new
➥FileOutputStream("Copyof_CopyFile.txt");
15
16            System.out.println("Copying data...");
17
18            byte data;
19            while( (data = (byte)m_input.read()) != -1 )
20            {
21                m_output.write( data );
22            }
23
24            System.out.println("File Copied.");
25        }
26        catch( IOException e)
27        {
28            System.out.println("IO Error"+e.getMessage());
29        }
30
31        System.exit(0);
32    }
33 }
```

The CopyFILE application shown in listing 15.2 instantiates a FileInputStream object (line 13) that represents a local file called CopyFILE.java (the program's source code file). Next a FileOutputStream object is instantiated (line 14), which creates a local file called Copyof_CopyFile.txt. The CopyFILE application goes into a loop (lines 19 through 22) in which it reads a byte at a time from the input stream and writes each byte to the output stream. The loop ends when the input stream's *read( )* method returns a –1, which indicates the end of the file.

File Handling and Parsing Classes

In addition to the stream classes, Java provides three powerful classes for dealing with files and parsing—File, RandomAccessFile, and StringTokenizer.

The File Class

The File class provides methods for getting the attributes of a file, such as whether or not it is write protected. In addition, you can use File class to rename files, delete files, and create directories.

You can use the File class to create an object that represents a directory or file on the host system. The File class is part of the java.io package.

The RandomAccessFile Class

The RandomAccessFile class provided by the java.io package makes it possible to access data from a file in a nonsequential manner. When a RandomAccessFile object is created, the file object and mode (read or read/write) must be specified.

The StringTokenizer Class

The StringTokenizer class is different from the other classes discussed in this chapter because it is provided by the java.util package as opposed to the java.io or the java.net packages. The

StringTokenizer class comes in handy when dealing with streams because it can parse tokens from a line of data. Therefore, when you use the StringTokenizer class, you must remember to either use the java.util prefix or include an import statement for this class in your program.

If you have experience with the C language, you will find that the StringTokenizer class's functionality is similar to the C language function strtok.

A StringTokenizer object is instantiated by using the following constructor.

```
StringTokenizer(String Data, String Delimiters)
```

The first parameter in the constructor is the line of text to search through. The second parameter is a set of delimiters used to break the line into tokens.

The StringTokenizer class provides the *nextToken()* method that extracts the next token in the String. The *countTokens()* method computes the number of tokens in the String.

The following code shows how the StringTokenizer class extracts the first substring from an input String.

```
StringTokenizer st = new
➥StringTokenizer("item1,item2,item3",",");

String strToken = st.nextToken();

System.out.println( strToken );
```

In the preceding code, the first token, item1, is extracted and written to standard output.

Creating Client/Server Java Programs with Sockets

The Socket and ServerSocket classes can be used to create true client/server applications in Java. These classes are included in the java.io package. The communications between Java client and server programs is made easier because socket objects utilize streams.

Socket programming can be a complex subject. Therefore, this section only covers the fundamentals. You can, however, use the examples provided in this chapter as a starting point for developing more sophisticated client/server Java programs.

The Socket Class

When establishing communications with a server program, you must construct a Socket object by using the name of the host on which your server program resides and the port number to which your server program is listening. The resulting connection can be thought of as direct line of communication between the client and server programs.

The Socket class is described in the Java API documentation as a client socket. Although it is used by a client program to establish a connection to a server, the server application also uses a socket object to communicate with the client.

The following line of code shows how a Socket object can be created.

```
socket = new Socket( "WWW.SOMESERVER.COM", 8888 );
```

The Socket object shown in the preceding line of code indicates that a corresponding server program is running on WWW.SOMESERVER.COm, which is waiting for a client to connect through port number 8888.

Table 15.1 describes the methods provided by the Socket class. For more information regarding these methods, consult the Visual J++ Books Online documentation.

Table 15.1   Socket Class Methods

Socket Class Method	Function
close( )	Closes a socket connection between a client and a server. This method can throw an IOException and does not return any value or object. This method can throw an IOException.
getInetAddress( )	Returns an InetAddress object corresponding to the Internet address to which a socket is connected.
getInputStream( )	Returns the InputStream object to which a socket is connected. This method can throw an IOException.
getLocalPort( )	Returns an int value equal to the port number on the local host to which a socket is connected.
getOutputStream( )	Returns an OutputStream object for a socket. This method can throw an IOException.
getPort( )	Returns an int value equal to the port number on the remote host to which a socket is connected.
setSocketImplFactory( )	Sets the system's client SocketImplFactory interface. This interface is used by the socket class to create socket implementations for various policies. This method can throw an IOException and does not return any value or object. If the factory is already defined, this method can throw a SocketException.
toString()	Converts a Socket object to a String value and returns that String value.

A Sample Socket Client Program

The sample socket client shown in listing 15.3 demonstrates the basics of socket client programming in Java. It establishes a connection to a server, sends data to the server, and waits for a reply. This program can serve as a good starting point for you to create more sophisticated clients that make use of multithreading and graphical user interfaces.

The server program in listing 15.4 must be running on the indicated host for the client program to function properly.

Listing 15.3 A Sample SocketClient

```
01   import java.net.*;
02   import java.io.*;
03
04   public class SocketClient
05   {
06     static public void main(String argv[])
07     {
08       int            Port = 8888;
09       String         host = "";
10       Socket         s;
11       DataInputStream input;
12       String         inmsg = "";
13       String []      outmsg = { "LOGON Request",
14                                 "Server connection
➥established.",
15                                 "Sending meaningful
➥Data...",
16                                 "EXIT"};
17
18       if( argv.length >= 1 ) Port =
➥Integer.parseInt(argv[0]);
19       if( argv.length >= 2 ) host = argv[1];
20
21       System.out.println( "Connecting to "+host+" on port "+
➥Port );
22
23       try
24       {
25         s = new Socket( host, Port);
26
27         BufferedInputStream bufIn;
28         bufIn = new BufferedInputStream( s.getInputStream()
➥);
```

continues

Listing 15.3   Continued

```
29          input = new DataInputStream( bufIn );
30
31          PrintStream printOut =
32              new PrintStream(s.getOutputStream());
33
34          System.out.println( "-----------------------" );
35
36          for( int i = 0; i < outmsg.length; i++ )
37          {
38              System.out.println( " [Client] " + outmsg[i] );
39              printOut.println(outmsg[i]);
40
41              inmsg = input.readLine();
42              System.out.println( "  [Server] " + inmsg );
43
44              try{Thread.sleep(5000);}
➥catch(InterruptedException e){}
45          }
46
47          System.out.println( "-----------------------" );
48
49          s.close();
50          System.out.println( "Socket closed, Session
➥ended." );
51
52      }
53      catch (IOException e)
54      {
55          e.printStackTrace();
56          System.err.println(e.getMessage());
57      }
58  }
59 }
```

The client program initializes the *host* and *Port* variables to " "
and 8888 respectively. These values can be overridden with
command line parameters (lines 18–19). If the host is " ", the
socket will attempt to connect to the local host machine.

Next, a Socket is created to the indicated host and Port (line 25). If the Socket is successfully created, input and output streams are created from the Socket object (lines 27–29).

The main for loop (lines 36–45) sends each message from the outmsg array to the server program and waits for a response. Both messages are printed to the standard output stream. For visual effect, end send is seperated by a delay of five seconds.

After all the messages are sent and acknowledged, the client program closes the Socket and the program terminates (lines 47–52).

Lines 53–57 contain the exception catch processing for all the Socket and input and output stream operations in the try block (lines 23–52).

The ServerSocket Class

The ServerSocket class is used by server applications to listen for client connections and to establish socket connections to the client. A server can handle any number of client connections. To instantiate a ServerSocket object, a port number must be specified. The following line of code, for example, creates a ServerSocket object that listens for client requests on port 8888:

```
serversocket = new ServerSocket( 8888 );
```

The constructor for the ServerSocket class can throw an IOException.

After a ServerSocket object has been instantiated, you can call the *accept()* method (see table 15.2) to listen for a connection and to retrieve a Socket object. After a Socket object has been instantiated, input and output streams can be used for client/server communications.

Table 15.2 describes the methods provided by the ServerSocket class.

Table 15.2   ServerSocket Class Methods

ServerSocket Class Method	Function
accept()	Returns a Socket object that has connected to the port to which the ServerSocket is listening. This method can throw an IOException.
close()	Closes a ServerSocket connection between a client and a server. This method does not return any value or object. This method can throw an IOException.
getInetAddress()	Returns an InetAddress object corresponding to the Internet address to which a ServerSocket is connected.
getLocalPort()	Returns an int value equal to the port number on the local host to which a ServerSocket is listening.
setSocketFactory()	Sets the system's client *SocketImplFactory* interface. This interface is used by the socket class to create socket implementations that implement various policies. This method can throw an IOException and does not return any value or object. If the factory is already defined, this method can also throw a SocketException.
toString()	Converts a ServerSocket object to a String value and returns that String value.

A Sample SocketServer Program

The SocketServer program in listing 15.4 demonstrates the basics of multithreaded socket server programming. It accepts a connection from a client, creates a thread to handle that connection, and returns to wait for the next connection. The thread that handles the connection receives a message from the client and echoes it back to the client. Figure 15.1 illustrates how the SocketServer waits for and handles client requests.

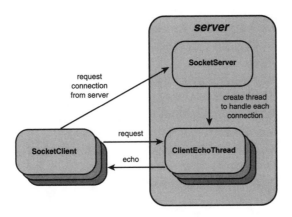

Figure 15.1:
The SocketServer application handles client requests by creating multiple threads.

When the thread that is handling a connection receives an `"EXIT"` message, it closes the socket connection and terminates the thread. Although this program is a fairly simple server example, it can serve as a good starting point for you to create more sophisticated servers.

The server program in listing 15.4 will run continuously unless an exception occurs or a user can cause the server program to terminate by pressing CTRL+C.

This book's CD contains a Visual J++ project called Sockets. This project contains the SocketServer and SocketClient programs. You can execute SocketServer from Visual J++ by specifying the class name in the Debug tab of the Settings dialog box. After you execute SocketServer one time, you should change the Debug settings so that SocketClient is executed. You can then launch multiple execution copies of SocketClient.

Listing 15.4 The SocketServer Application

```
01  import java.net.*;
02  import java.io.*;
03
```

continues

Listing 15.4   Continued

```
04  public class SocketServer
05  {
06      static public void main(String argv[])
07      {
08          Thread thread;
09          int    Port = 8888;
10
11          if( argv.length >= 1 ) Port =
➥Integer.parseInt(argv[0]);
12
13          try
14          {
15              ServerSocket sock = new ServerSocket( Port );
16
17              System.out.println( "Socket connected on port
➥"+Port );
18
19              while (true)
20              {
21                  Socket s = sock.accept();
22
23                  thread = new ClientEchoThread(s);
24                  thread.start();
25
26                  System.out.println( "New Thread created." );
27              }
28          }
29          catch (IOException e)
30          {
31              e.printStackTrace();
32              System.err.println(e.getMessage());
33          }
34
35          System.exit(0);
36      }
37  }
38
39  class ClientEchoThread extends Thread
40  {
```

```
41      private static int ThreadCount = 0;
42
43      private int            ThreadNumber     = 0;
44      private Socket         s;
45      private DataInputStream input;
46      private PrintStream    output;
47      private String         msg;
48
49      public ClientEchoThread( Socket s )
50      {
51         this.s = s;
52
53         try
54         {
55            BufferedInputStream bufIn;
56            bufIn = new BufferedInputStream(
➡s.getInputStream() );
57            input = new DataInputStream( bufIn );
58
59            output = new PrintStream( s.getOutputStream() );
60         }
61         catch (IOException e)
62         {}
63
64         synchronized( getClass() )
65      {
66            ThreadCount++;
67            ThreadNumber = ThreadCount;
68         }
69      }
70
71      public void run()
72      {
73        System.out.println(" "+ThreadNumber+
74           ": Thread listening...");
75
76       while( true )
77       {
78          try
79          {
80             msg = input.readLine();
```

continues

Listing 15.4   Continued

```
81
82          if( msg == null ) break;
83
84          System.out.println(" "+ThreadNumber+":   [Client]
➡"+msg);
85
86          msg = "<ECHO>"+msg;
87
88          System.out.println(" "+ThreadNumber+
89              ":    [Server] "+msg);
90
91          output.println(msg);
92
93          if( msg.equalsIgnoreCase( "<ECHO>EXIT" ) ) break;
94        }
95      catch (IOException e)
96      {
97        break;
98      }
99    }
100
101    try
102    {
103      if( s != null ) s.close();
104    }
105    catch (IOException e)
106    {}
107
108    System.out.println(" "+ThreadNumber+
109                      ": Socket closed, thread
➡terminated.");
110
111    stop();
112  }
113 }
```

The SocketServer program initializes the Port to 8888, matching the client's default. The port number can be overridden with a command line parameter (line 11).

Next, a ServerSocket object is created to listen on the specified port (line 15).

The main while loop (lines 19–27) accepts socket connections from a client program, creates and starts a thread to handle that socket, and returns to waiting for the next connection.

Lines 29–33 provide the exception catch processing for all the ServerSocket operations in the try block (lines 15–28). The program terminates when an exception occurs.

A thread object is declared (line 39) to handle socket communications. The constructor for this class (lines 49–69) creates input/output streams for communicating to the client program and assigns a number to the current thread.

The *run( )* method (lines 71–112) of the thread reads the message from the client, adds the text "<ECHO>" to the start of the message and sends it back to the client program. If the message from the client is "EXIT", the main loop is exited, the socket connection terminates, and the thread's execution stops.

All messages printed from within the thread class include the thread's number. This demonstrates multithreaded processing in action. The following section discusses how you can execute the SocketClient and SocketServer application and see these programs in action.

Running the Client/Server Examples

You can run the client/server example by using more than one machine on a TCP/IP network, or even just one machine as long as it's configured with TCP/IP. When both programs are run on the same machine, no command line parameters are necessary.

The output of the SocketClient program is as follows:

```
C:\>jview SocketClient
Connecting to  on port 8888
---------------------
 [Client] : LOGON Request
  [Server] : <ECHO>LOGON Request
 [Client] : Server connection established.
  [Server] : <ECHO>Server connection established.
 [Client] : Sending meaningful Data...
  [Server] : <ECHO>Sending meaningful Data...
 [Client] : EXIT
  [Server] : <ECHO>EXIT
---------------------
Socket closed, Session ended.

C:\>
```

As you can see from the preceding output, when the SocketClient program sends a request to the server, the server responds by echoing the request back to the client via the socket connection. When the client sends a message to the server with the text "EXIT", the server echoes the message to the client and then closes the socket connection.

The output of the SocketServer program with one client is as follows:

```
C:\>jview SocketServer
Socket connected on port 8888
New Thread created.
 1: Thread listening...
 1:  [Client] LOGON Request
 1:   [Server] <ECHO>LOGON Request
 1:  [Client] Server connection established.
 1:   [Server] <ECHO>Server connection established.
 1:  [Client] Sending meaningful Data...
 1:   [Server] <ECHO>Sending meaningful Data...
 1:  [Client] EXIT
 1:   [Server] <ECHO>EXIT
 1: Socket closed, thread terminated.
```

The preceding output illustrates the server end of the sockets session. You can see that only one socket connection is created because each message is preceded by the same connection number (1:).

The SocketServer program is designed to handle more than one client simultaneously. The following output shows the output from the SocketServer when it is handling requests from two clients at the same time. Notice that the threads alternate between servicing Client 1 and Client 2.

```
C:\>jview SocketServer
Socket connected on port 8888
New Thread created.
 1: Thread listening...
 1:  [Client] LOGON Request
 1:    [Server] <ECHO>LOGON Request
New Thread created.
 2: Thread listening...
 2:  [Client] LOGON Request
 2:    [Server] <ECHO>LOGON Request
 1:  [Client] Server connection established.
 1:    [Server] <ECHO>Server connection established.
 2:  [Client] Server connection established.
 2:    [Server] <ECHO>Server connection established.
 1:  [Client] Sending meaningful Data...
 1:    [Server] <ECHO>Sending meaningful Data...
 2:  [Client] Sending meaningful Data...
 2:    [Server] <ECHO>Sending meaningful Data...
 1:  [Client] EXIT
 1:    [Server] <ECHO>EXIT
 1: Socket closed, thread terminated.
 2:  [Client] EXIT
 2:    [Server] <ECHO>EXIT
 2: Socket closed, thread terminated.
```

As you can see from listing 15.3, more than one SocketClient program can communicate with the SocketServer at the same time. Instead of just one socket now there are two as indicated by the socket numbers, 1: and 2:. This not only demonstrates the power of streams and sockets, but also the capability to implement multithreaded servers in Java.

A Peek at the Future of Distributed Systems

The basic socket programming concepts discussed in this chapter can be used to implement client/server Java applications. Any programmer interested the future of distributed systems, however, should attempt to understand the distributed object models that are competing to become the de facto industry standard. The two most likely candidates are:

CORBA—The Common Object Request Broker Architecture as defined by the Object Management Group (OMG) consortium.

DCOM— Microsoft's Distributed Component Object Model.

With release 4.0 of Windows NT, Microsoft has introduced DCOM as the latest enhancement to its existing Component Object Model (COM). DCOM is a integral part of Microsoft's ActiveX platform (ActiveX is covered in Chapter 17, "Java and the ActiveX Platform"). In fact, because DCOM is built into the operating system, COM objects have now become DCOM objects by default.

The CORBA specification is defined by a consortium of companies and has a significant following of Unix developers and vendors. Although the CORBA market is frequently criticized for being fragmented, the CORBA 2.0 specification has addressed this issue by providing interoperability between the various CORBA implementations.

CORBA and DCOM are robust language-independent platforms for building network-centric software objects. Both architectures provide a series of services that are required to make distributed object-oriented applications a reality. These services address issues such as object persistence, security, and object repositories.

An in-depth discussion of DCOM and CORBA is beyond the scope of this book. If you are interested in a very good discussion of the subject, you should read the book *The Essential Distributed Object Survival Guide* by Orfali, Harkey and Edwards. This book is published by John Wiley & Sons, Inc.

Distributed Java Programming with JavaBeans and RMI

As part of release 1.1 of Java, Sun Microsystems has defined the JavaBeans specification. Many consider JavaBeans to be yet another distributed object standard. Although this may be true in some respects, JavaBeans does, however, bridge the gap between CORBA and DCOM by providing gateways to both environments.

Another way to distribute objects in Java is through Sun's Remote Method Invocation (RMI). Whereas DCOM and CORBA are extremely robust language independent architectures, RMI has been introduced by Sun as a lightweight Java-only mechanism for distributed object-oriented Java networking.

You can download software developer's kits and documentation for RMI and JavaBeans from the JavaSoft web site located at `http://www.javasoft.com`.

Distributed architectures make it possible to implement distributed objects that can be utilized by any program on a network. Instead of passing data between client and server processes by using streams and sockets, for example, programs are able to make method calls directly to network-based objects without having to be concerned about communications protocols, operating systems, and programming languages. Thus, distributed objects are clearly a few rungs higher on the programming evolutionary ladder than the simple networking techniques discussed in this chapter.

Summary

The URL class provides functionality for validating and accessing Internet-based resources such as HTML pages, files, and so on.

Any Java-enabled browser provides an object that implements the AppletContext interface. This object provides functionality that makes it possible for a Java applet to control the web browser within which it is running. The *showDocument()* method can be invoked by an applet, for example, to cause the browser to display a document from a specific URL.

The java.io package contains streams classes that provide useful abstractions for accessing files and data over a network. These classes utilize a standard set of methods that are independent of the source or destination of the data. Streams are divided into classes that handle input and output. The java.io package contains many classes that are derived from the base InputStream and OutputStream classes. These derived classes provide a great deal of additional functionality. Streams can be buffered, for example, to improve performance. Furthermore, the FilterInputStream and FilterOutputStream classes can be used to extend a stream's functionality by nesting, or wrapping, stream objects within other stream objects.

The Java Socket and ServerSocket classes can be used in combination with streams and URLs to create powerful client/server systems. The Socket class is typically used by client programs to open a connection to a server for exchanging data. The SocketServer class can be used by the server to listen for client requests and to instantiate Socket objects on the server. Both the Socket and ServerSocket classes are part of the java.net package.

Stream and Socket objects can throw exceptions. Therefore, when working with streams and sockets, programmers should be careful to include the proper exception handling code in their Java applets and applications.

Only the basics of client/server networking are covered in this chapter. To be ready for the future, developers should pay close attention to emerging standards, such as CORBA, DCOM, JavaBeans, and RMI. In all likelihood, all these architectures will play a role in the distributed object-oriented systems of the future.

Questions

1. What does URL stand for?

2. What is the AppletContext?

3. How can an applet display a message to the user on a web browser's status bar?

4. Stream objects can be nested within other stream objects by using the FilterInputStream and FilterOutputStream classes. What is the maximum number of nested streams that can be created by Java programs?

5. How can a stream be used to access data from a URL?

6. When should streams be based on sockets rather than another source of data?

7. What are the two main socket classes?

8. Is the Socket class only used by the client program?

9. How do buffered streams improve performance?

Answers

1. URL stands for Uniform Resource Locator. It is also sometimes referred to as a Universal Resource Locator.

2. The AppletContext corresponds to the environment within which an applet is running. It can be a Java-enabled web browser or the appletviewer.

3. The *showStatus()* method provided by the AppletContext can be used to display a message on a web browser's status bar.

4. There is no limit. You can use the classes derived from FilterInputStream and FilterOutputStream to wrap a stream as many times as you like. Of course, each level of nesting should add functionality. There may be times, for example, when you will want to buffer an input stream and read from it by using strings. This could be implemented by using the DataInputStream and the BufferedInputStream classes as shown in the following code.

```
try
{
    InputStream in = anURL.openStream();
    BufferedInputStream bufIn = new
➥BufferedInputStream(in);
    DataInputStream bufData = new
➥DataInputStream(in);
}
catch( IOException e)
{
    System.out.println("IO Error: "+e.getMessage());
}
```

5. The *openStream()* method provided by the URL class returns an InputStream object. After the stream object is created, the *read()* method can be used to read bytes from the URL. In addition, the InputStream object can be nested within another stream object to implement the desired functionality.

6. Sockets should be used when two programs need to exchange data. When a client needs to perform an inquiry on a server-based database, for example, it is usually more efficient for the client program to send a query to a server program. The server program can execute the query and only send the results back to the client. In this case, socket-based streams enable the client and server to communicate.

7. The Socket class and the ServerSocket class.

8. The Socket class is used in both the client and the server programs.

9. Buffered streams enable Java programs to read and write larger amounts of data at one time. Performance is likely to improve because the number of time-consuming read and writes are reduced.

Chapter 16

Fun with Sound and Animation

Dancing bologna is a term that is frequently used to describe some of the simple Java animations that can be found on many web pages. Although most of these animations serve a purely cosmetic purpose, it is important for you to understand that Java's animation and audio capabilities can also be used to convey important information to your users. An animation, for example, could simulate the work flow in a bank's mortgage processing department. Another useful animation could be a dynamically updating chart showing projected changes in the value of a bond.

In the future, Java's multimedia capabilities will play an important part in many types of applications. Therefore, by paying close attention to the topics discussed in this chapter, you will learn how to build functionality into your Java programs that can provide users with additional sensory feedback, and thus add real value. Oh, and by the way, you'll also be able to create some really neat dancing bologna.

The following topics are covered in this chapter:

➤ Handling image and audio objects in Java

➤ Using the Visual J++ Applet Wizard to create starter code for an animation

➤ An overview of the Visual J++ Graphics Editor

➤ Creating sound files for use in Java programs

➤ Using off-screen images to create flicker-free animations

The animation applet discussed in the latter part of this chapter is called LogoAnimation. It can be found on the home page of @Work Technologies (`http://www.worktechs.com`). The LogoAnimation applet provides working examples of the topics presented in this chapter and utilizes many of the Java programming techniques discussed in previous chapters.

Working with Images and Sounds in Java

Java Image and AudioClip objects provide a layer of abstraction for manipulating images and sounds within a Java program. In other words, these objects shield the programmer from platform-specific issues when dealing with image and audio files.

As discussed in Chapter 9, "Working with Graphics, Fonts, and Colors," the Java Abstract Windowing Toolkit (AWT) provides functionality for drawing simple shapes and figures. When you want to display more sophisticated graphic images, you will most likely have to work with image files that are created externally from your Java program by an application such as Adobe's PhotoShop.

In release 1.0 of Java, the Image class only supports GIF (Graphics Interchange Format) and JPEG (Joint Photographic Expert Group) format files. The advantages of these file formats are as follows:

➤ GIF and JPEG files can be downloaded quickly over a dial-up link because they are compressed.

➤ They are supported on just about any hardware and operating system platform.

➤ They can be created by using a multitude of graphics drawing packages from many different software vendors.

The AudioClip object supported in Java can be used with AU files. The big advantage of this format is that the files are small when compared with other audio formats. The downside is that the AU format is not generally regarded as suitable for high-fidelity audio.

Applet Class Image Methods

When you work with images in a Java program, you must create an Image object. To create an Image object, you can use the *createImage( )* or *getImage( )* methods provided by the Applet class. You can invoke these methods by using any of the following signatures.

➤ *Image createImage(int width, int height)*—Creates a memory-based or off-screen image.

➤ *Image getImage(URL url)*—Creates an Image object that loads from an image file located at a specified Uniform Resource Locator (URL). The URL must include both the directory and the file name. A URL, for example, could be:

```
http://www.worktechs.com/images/image001.gif.
```

➤ *Image getImage(URL url, String name)*—Creates an Image object from the specified URL and file name. The file name must be specified separately from the URL. This mechanism enables you to use other methods, such as *getCodeBase( )*.

When you invoke the *getImage()* method, an Image object is returned immediately even though the image file hasn't been loaded yet. The image file will only be downloaded when your program attempts to access the Image object. Furthermore, this download occurs asynchronously on a separate thread of execution.

Using the Default Toolkit to Get Images

The applet class's *getImage( )* method requires an applet object. Therefore, when you need to get an image from a class that does not extend the applet class you can use a Toolkit object to create an Image object. To get a Toolkit object, use the static *getDefaultToolkit( )* method provided by the Toolkit class.

The Toolkit class's *getImage( )* method can be invoked specifying a local file name as a parameter as demonstrated by the following line of code:

```
Image image =
➥Toolkit.getDefaultToolkit().getImage("MyImage.gif");
```

Alternatively, you can get an image from a URL as follows:

```
Image image
Toolkit.getDefaultToolkit().getImage("http://
➥www.worktechs.com/MyImage.gif");
```

In Java, the Toolkit provides the actual linkage between the AWT and the native windowing platform, such as Windows, Motif, and so on.

The Image Class

The Image class is an abstract class used to create storage objects for graphical images. This class provides a series of methods that obtain information about an image. Because Image is an abstract class, you cannot directly instantiate an Image object. You can derive your own class from Image, but in most cases you should use the previously discussed *getImage( )* and *createImage( )* methods.

Image Class Methods

The Image class provides the following methods:

➤ *void flush( )*—Flushes all resources and data used by the Image object. The Image object is reset to a state similar to when it was first created. The image data, therefore, has to be recreated or reloaded.

➤ *Graphics getGraphics( )*—Gets a graphics object that can be used to draw on the Image object.

➤ *int getHeight(ImageObserver obs)*—Gets the actual height of the image. If the actual height of the image is not yet known, a value of –1 is returned.

➤ *Object getProperty(String name, ImageObserver obs)*—Gets a property of the image by name. The property names are defined by the various image formats. If a property is not defined for a particular image, this method returns an UndefinedProperty object.

➤ *ImageProducer getSource( )*—Gets the object that produces the pixels for the image.

➤ *int getWidth(ImageObserver observer)*—Gets the actual width of the image. If the width is not yet known, a value of –1 is returned.

An ImageObserver is an object that implements the ImageObserver interface. This interface only defines one method called *imageUpdate()* that receives asynchronous notification of the status of an image that is being constructed. Because the Container class implements ImageObserver, all objects derived from it, such as Applet, are ImageObserver objects. You can, therefore, override *imageUpdate()* within an applet to get information about an image while it is still loading. You can use the *imageUpdate()* method, for example, to find out the size and width of an Image object. Because *imageUpdate()* gets this information before the image file is loaded, you can use it in your program to pre-allocate screen space for the image.

The Graphics Class's *drawImage()* Method

In Java, the Graphics class provides the functionality that enables a program to write to any output device or memory-based image. Therefore, before you can draw to an Image object, you must first associate a Graphics object with it. You can accomplish this by using the *getGraphics( )* method discussed previously.

You can obtain a Graphics object for an applet's display area by calling the Component class's *getGraphics( )* method. This is possible because Applet is derived from Component.

The Graphics object associated with an Image object is typically referred to as the Image object's *graphics context.*

After you have the graphics context of an image, you can draw on the image by using the *drawImage( )* method provided by the Graphics class.

The *drawImage( )* method is invoked by using the following method signatures.

➤ *boolean drawImage(Image image, int x, int y, ImageObserver obs)*—Draws the specified image at the x and y coordinates. The *ImageObserver* parameter can be specified as null if you do not need to make use of the functionality provided by the ImageObserver object's *imageUpdate( )* method. See the section in this chapter entitled "Image Class Methods" for more information on ImageObserver.

➤ *boolean drawImage(Image image, int x, int y, int width, int height, ImageObserver obs)*—Draws the specified image inside a rectangle. The rectangle's upper-left corner is positioned at the specified *x, y* coordinates. The dimensions of the rectangle are defined by *width* and *height.* The image is scaled, if necessary, to fit the rectangle.

➤ *boolean drawImage(Image image, int x, int y, Color bgcolor, ImageObserver obs)*—Draws the specified image at the specified *x, y* coordinates. The image is drawn with a solid background color specified by *bgcolor.*

➤ *boolean drawImage(Image image, int x, int y, int width, int height, Color bgcolor, ImageObserver obs)*—Draws the specified image inside the rectangle defined by *x, y, width* and *height.* The image is scaled, if necessary, to fit the target rectangle. The image is drawn with a solid background color specified by *bgcolor.*

Tracking Image Loading with the MediaTracker Class

As mentioned previously in this chapter, image files are downloaded asynchronously on a separate thread. You may be curious how a Java program ensures that an image is finally loaded and ready to be displayed. Although there are a few techniques for tracking the status of an image download, perhaps the easiest way to accomplish this is to use an AWT utility class called MediaTracker. You can instantiate a MediaTracker object by using the following class constructor:

```
MediaTracker(Component comp)
```

As indicated by the class constructor, when you create a MediaTracker object, you must pass the Component object in which your images will eventually be drawn to the class constructor. In an applet, you should pass the *this* variable which represents the applet itself. After you create a *MediaTracker* object in your program, you can call its *addImage( )* method as shown in the following code:

```
MediaTracker  tracker = new  MediaTracker(this);
➥Image myImage = getImage(getCodeBase(),"images/
➥myimage.gif");

tracker.addImage(myImage,  0);
```

As indicated in the preceding code, the *addImage( )* method has the following signature:

```
addImage(Image image, int id)
```

This adds the specified Image object to the MediaTracker object and gives the image the specified id. The id parameter monitors the status of the image. At a later point in your program, you can use the id to make sure that the image has been loaded before

attempting to draw it to the display area. You can do this by
including the following code in your program:

```
try
{
    tracker.waitForID(0);
}
    catch  (InterruptedException  e)
{
    // Exception handling code goes here
}
```

The *waitForID( )* method shown in the preceding code triggers
the loading process for the image identified by id = 0. This
method causes the program to wait until the image with the
specified id loads.

In addition to the *waitForID( )* method, the MediaTracker class also
provides a *waitForAll( )* method that causes the program to wait until all
tracked images have been loaded.

When you create a sample Java animation by using the Visual J++
Applet Wizard, the code generated by the Wizard utilizes a
MediaTracker object to initiate the image loading process and to
check the status of the image objects. By using the MediaTracker
object, you can ensure that your images are loaded properly
before your program starts an animation.

If there is an error as you are loading or scaling an image, then the image
is considered finished loading. You can check for errors with the
isErrorAny( ) or *isErrorID( )* methods provided by the MediaTracker class.

Creating an AudioClip Object

When you create an animation with a Java program, you can
further enhance the user's sensory experience by combining the
visual effect of the animation with sound. A Java program can
load and play a sound by using an AudioClip object.

AudioClip is an interface as opposed to a proper class. Consequently, you cannot directly instantiate an AudioClip object; however, the Applet class provides a *getAudioClip( )* method that returns an AudioClip object. You can invoke the *getAudioClip( )* method by using the following signatures:

➤ *AudioClip getAudioClip(URL url)*—Gets the audio clip file at the specified URL. The URL must include the file name.

➤ *AudioClip getAudioClip(URL url, String filename)*—Gets the audio clip file at the specified URL and file name. The URL must not include the file name. This version of the *getAudioClip( )* method enables you to load an AudioClip object by combining a base URL with file name. You can, therefore, use methods such as *getDocbase( )* and *getCodebase( )*, which return URL objects, instead of hard coding the URL name into your program.

An object that implements the AudioClip interface can be used as a storage object for audio data.

AudioClip Methods

The following methods are defined by the AudioClip interface:

➤ *void play( )*—Starts playing the audio clip from the beginning. Each time this method is called, the clip restarts from the beginning.

➤ *void loop( )*—Starts playing the audio clip in a perpetual loop.

➤ *void stop( )*—Stops playing the audio clip.

The section in this chapter entitled "Creating Sound Files" describes how to create your own sound files that you can use in your Java programs.

Creating Animations with the Applet Wizard

A good way to start coding an animation in Java is to use the Visual J++ Applet Wizard to create starter code. Chapter 7, "Building Your First Java Applet By Using Visual J++" discusses how to run the Applet Wizard. To generate starter code that includes a sample animation, you can set the appropriate options in Step 3 of the Applet Wizard process, as shown in figure 16.1.

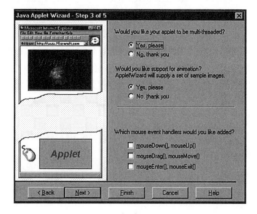

Figure 16.1:

Generating a sample animation with the Applet Wizard.

When you specify the Step 3 options of the Applet Wizard process as shown in figure 16.1, the Applet Wizard produces the applet as shown in listing 16.1.

**Listing 16.1   A Sample Animation Applet Generated
            by the Applet Wizard**

```
import java.applet.*;
import java.awt.*;

public class LogoAnimation extends Applet implements Runnable
{
    Thread        m_LogoAnimation = null;
```

```
    private Graphics    m_Graphics;
    private Image       m_Images[];
    private int         m_nCurrImage;
    private int         m_nImgWidth  = 0;
    private int         m_nImgHeight = 0;
    private boolean     m_fAllLoaded = false;
    private final int   NUM_IMAGES = 18;


    public LogoAnimation()
    {
    }

    public String getAppletInfo()
    {
        return "Name: LogoAnimation\r\n" +
               "Author: @Work Technologies\r\n" +
               "Created with Microsoft Visual J++ Version
➥1.0";
    }


    public void init()
    {
        // If you use a ResourceWizard-generated "control
➥creator" class to
        // arrange controls in your applet, you may want to
➥call its
        // CreateControls() method from within this method.
➥Remove the following
        // call to resize() before adding the call to
➥CreateControls();
        // CreateControls() does its own resizing.
        //-----------------------------------------------------
          resize(320, 240);

    }

    public void destroy()
    {
```

continues

Listing 16.1   Continued

```java
    }

    private void displayImage(Graphics g)
    {
        if (!m_fAllLoaded)
            return;

        g.drawImage(m_Images[m_nCurrImage],
                    (size().width - m_nImgWidth)   / 2,
                    (size().height - m_nImgHeight) / 2,
null);
    }

    public void paint(Graphics g)
    {
        // ANIMATION SUPPORT:
        //            The following code displays a status
message until all the
        // images are loaded. Then it calls displayImage to
display the current
        // image.
        //----------------------------------------------------
        if (m_fAllLoaded)
        {
            Rectangle r = g.getClipRect();

            g.clearRect(r.x, r.y, r.width, r.height);
            displayImage(g);
        }
        else
            g.drawString("Loading images...", 10, 20);

    }

    public void start()
    {
        if (m_LogoAnimation == null)
        {
```

```
                m_LogoAnimation = new Thread(this);
                m_LogoAnimation.start();
        }
    }

    public void stop()
    {
        if (m_LogoAnimation != null)
        {
            m_LogoAnimation.stop();
            m_LogoAnimation = null;
        }
    }

    public void run()
    {
        m_nCurrImage = 0;

        // If re-entering the page, then the images have
➥already been loaded.
        // m_fAllLoaded == TRUE.
        //----------------------------------------------------
        if (!m_fAllLoaded)
        {
            repaint();
            m_Graphics = getGraphics();
            m_Images   = new Image[NUM_IMAGES];

            MediaTracker tracker = new MediaTracker(this);
            String strImage;

            // For each image in the animation, this method
➥first constructs a
            // string containing the path to the image file;
➥then it begins
            // loading the image into the m_Images array.
➥Note that the call to
            // getImage will return before the image is
➥completely loaded.
```

continues

Listing 16.1   Continued

```
                //---------------------------------------------
                for (int i = 1; i <= NUM_IMAGES; i++)
                {
                        strImage = "images/img00" + ((i < 10) ? "0"
: "") + i + ".gif";
                        m_Images[i-1] = getImage(getDocumentBase(),
strImage);

                    tracker.addImage(m_Images[i-1], 0);
                }

                try
                {
                    tracker.waitForAll();
                    m_fAllLoaded = !tracker.isErrorAny();
                }
                catch (InterruptedException e)
                {
                }

                if (!m_fAllLoaded)
                {
                    stop();
                    m_Graphics.drawString("Error loading
images!", 10, 40);
                        return;
                }

                m_nImgWidth  = m_Images[0].getWidth(this);
                m_nImgHeight = m_Images[0].getHeight(this);
        }
            repaint();

            while (true)
            {
                try
                {
                        displayImage(m_Graphics);
                        m_nCurrImage++;
                        if (m_nCurrImage == NUM_IMAGES)
                            m_nCurrImage = 0;
```

```
        Thread.sleep(50);
    }
    catch (InterruptedException e)
    {
        stop();
    }
  }
 }
}
```

In the interest of brevity, the code in listing 16.1 was generated by the Applet Wizard without comments.

In addition to creating sample animation code, the Applet Wizard generates eighteen GIF image files and stores them in a subdirectory called images within the project directory. These images are of the planet Earth shown at varying positions. The sample applet uses these images as frames for its animation.

When the LogoAnimation applet in listing 16.1 is compiled and executed, it creates the animation shown in figure 16.2.

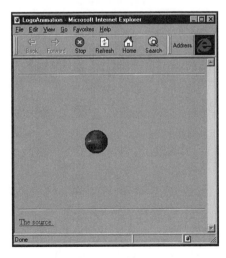

Figure 16.2:
The sample animation generated by the Applet Wizard.

As illustrated in figure 16.2, the sample animation applet draws the wizard-generated images to the display area one after another in a perpetual loop, thus creating an animation effect.

The Wizard-Generated Animation Code

If you look at listing 16.1, you can see that the wizard-generated code utilizes many of the concepts discussed so far in this chapter. The following sections focus on the highlights.

The *run()* Method

As with any multithreaded applet, the main processing in the sample animation applet occurs in the *run( )* method. Figure 16.3 illustrates the flow of this method's processing logic.

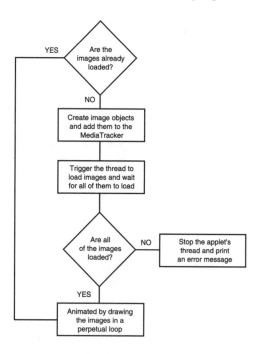

Figure 16.3:

Processing flow of the wizard-generated *run( )* method.

First, the *run( )* method initializes the *m_nCurrentImage* variable, which is used by the animation as a subscript for each image in the m_Images array. Because the *run( )* method may be called more than one time during the life cycle of the applet—the *run( )* method is also called when a user leaves and returns to an applet's web page—the *m_fAllLoaded* Boolean variable must be checked. If the value is *true*, the wizard-generated images have already been loaded. Consequently, the *run( )* method immediately begins the animation. If the value is *false*, the *run( )* method proceeds to load the image files.

Before the images can be loaded, the *run( )* method must obtain the graphics context of the applet's display area and allocate the m_Images array by using the following lines of code in the *run( )* method:

```
m_Graphics = getGraphics();m_Images   = new
Image[NUM_IMAGES];
```

When an applet draws to its display area from the *paint( )* method, the graphics context for the applet's display area is passed as a parameter. Alternatively, when the program draws to the display area outside of the *paint( )* method, as is the case with the wizard-generated applet, the applet's graphics context must be obtained by using the *getGraphics( )* method. By creating the m_Graphics object as shown in the preceding code, any method in the applet can use it to draw to the display area.

The next order of business is to actually load the image files for the animation. This is accomplished with the following lines of code.

```
MediaTracker tracker = new MediaTracker(this);
String strImage;

// For each image in the animation, this method first
➥constructs a
```

```
// string containing the path to the image file; then it
➥begins
// loading the image into the m_Images array.  Note that
➥the call to
// getImage will return before the image is completely
➥loaded.
//-----------------------------------------------------------
for (int i = 1; i <= NUM_IMAGES; i++)
{
    strImage = "images/img00" + ((i < 10) ? "0" : "") +
➥i + ".gif";
    m_Images[i-1] = getImage(getDocumentBase(),
➥strImage);
    tracker.addImage(m_Images[i-1], 0);
}
```

The preceding code loops eighteen times, which is the value to which the *NUM_IMAGES* instance variable is initialized. The Applet class's *getImage()* method is invoked to create Image objects for each of the eighteen wizard-generated image files located in the images directory. All the images will eventually be loaded into the m_Images array. The first parameter used to invoke the *getImage()* method is returned by the *getDocument Base()* method, which returns a URL object representing the location of the applet's web page. Notice that the image file names are conveniently numbered, which makes it relatively simple to construct the *getImage()* method's file name parameter.

After the Image objects have been created, the *addImage( )* method adds each Image object to the *MediaTracker* object (tracker). This makes it possible for the applet to load the image files in the next few lines of the *run( )* method, which are shown in the following code:

```
try
{
    tracker.waitForAll();
    m_fAllLoaded = !tracker.isErrorAny();
```

```
}
catch (InterruptedException e)
{
}
```

The call to the *waitForAll( )* method triggers the thread that loads all the images tracked by the tracker object. In addition, the applet's own execution thread will be suspended until the *waitForAll( )* method completes successfully, fails, or throws an *InterruptedException.* The tracker's *isErrorAny( )* method checks for error conditions and sets the *m_fAllLoaded* variable. If any of the eighteen images fails to load, the *isErrorAny( )* method returns a boolean true value.

In addition to the *isErrorAny( )* method, the MediaTracker class also provides an *isErrorID( )* method that you can use to check the load status of Image object(s) identified by the id you specified as a parameter. The *isErrorID( )* method returns a boolean true value if the specified image has not been loaded properly.

Finally, the *run( )* method creates the animation by using the following lines of code:

```
while (true)
{
    try
    {
        displayImage(m_Graphics);
        m_nCurrImage++;
        if (m_nCurrImage == NUM_IMAGES)
            m_nCurrImage = 0;

        Thread.sleep(50);
    }
    catch (InterruptedException e)
    {
        stop();
    }
}
```

The preceding code perpetually loops through all eighteen images. For each loop, the *m_nCurrImage* variable is either incremented or set to 0. This variable is used by the sample animation applet's *displayImage( )* method that actually draws the image. After calling the *displayImage( )* method, the *run( )* method calls the Thread class's *sleep( )* method to pause the applet's execution for 50 milliseconds.

The *displayImage()* Method

The *displayImage( )* method draws the current image to the applet's display area. The Applet Wizard generates the following code for the *displayImage( )* method:

```
private void displayImage(Graphics g)
{
    if (!m_fAllLoaded)
        return;

    g.drawImage(m_Images[m_nCurrImage],
            (size().width - m_nImgWidth)  / 2,
            (size().height - m_nImgHeight) / 2,
    ➥null);
}
```

Both the *run( )* and *paint( )* methods call the *displayImage( )* method to update the applet's display area. As you can see, this method calls the *drawImage( )* method of the Graphics object that is passed to it as a parameter. In the sample applet, this parameter is always the graphics context of the display area.

The *paint()* Method

The *paint( )* method is a standard Applet class method that draws to an applet's display area. The Applet Wizard generates the following code for the *paint( )* method:

```
public void paint(Graphics g)
{
    // ANIMATION SUPPORT:
    //           The following code displays a status
➥message until all the
    // images are loaded. Then it calls displayImage to
➥display the current
    // image.
    //-----------------------------------------------------
    if (m_fAllLoaded)
    {
        Rectangle r = g.getClipRect();

        g.clearRect(r.x, r.y, r.width, r.height);
        displayImage(g);
    }
    else
        g.drawString("Loading images…", 10, 20);

}
```

When the applet calls the *repaint( )* method, the *paint( )* method
is ultimately invoked. The *paint( )* method is also invoked when a
web browser user changes the size or otherwise obscures the
applet's browser window. If all the images have been loaded
when the *paint( )* method is called, it will clear the screen and call
the *displayImage( )* method by using the graphics context (the *g*
object) of the applet as a parameter.

Remember, the Java environment automatically passes the correct
Graphics object to the *paint()* method.

If the image files have not been loaded when the *paint( )* method
is called, it draws the string "Loading images…" to the applet's
display area. Notice that the *repaint( )* method is called in the
beginning of the *run( )* method. This causes the *paint( )* method
to notify the user that the applet is in the process of loading the
image files.

Reducing Animation Flicker

If you've looked at some of the Java animations available on the World Wide Web, you may have noticed that some produce a significant amount of flicker. One possible cause of this is that to draw the next animation frame in a sequence, the applet clears the previous frame and then draws the various parts of the next frame. Although the frame is drawn very fast, the transition between frames is not smooth. In other words, the animation flickers.

The next few sections describe the cause of animation flicker and how it can be eliminated.

A Flickering Animation Example

The FlickeringSinkingText applet, shown in listing 16.2, creates an animation by repeatedly drawing a black rectangle and a white text string to its display area. Each time the applet draws an animation frame, it increments the text's y coordinate, which results in a sinking effect.

Listing 16.2   The FlickeringSinkingText Applet

```
import java.applet.*;
import java.awt.*;

public class FlickeringSinkingText extends Applet implements
➥Runnable
{
    Thread        FlickeringSinkingTextThread;
    Graphics      ScreenGraphicsContext;

    public void start()
    {
        FlickeringSinkingTextThread = new Thread(this);
        FlickeringSinkingTextThread.start();
    }

    public void run()
```

```
    {
        ScreenGraphicsContext = getGraphics();
        ScreenGraphicsContext.setFont(new Font("Dialog",
➥Font.BOLD, 48));
        for (int y = 0; y < 190; y++)
        {
            drawAnimationFrame("This text is sinking!", y);
        }
    }

    public void drawAnimationFrame(String text, int y)
    {
        ScreenGraphicsContext.setColor(Color.black);
        ScreenGraphicsContext.fillRect(0, 0, 500, 200);
        ScreenGraphicsContext.setColor(Color.white);
        ScreenGraphicsContext.drawString(text, 40, y);
        try
        {
            Thread.sleep(40);
        }
        catch(InterruptedException e) {}
    }
}
```

FlickeringSinkingText applet's *run( )* method gets a Graphics object for the display area by calling the *getGraphics( )* method. Next, the *run( )* method sets the default font to a bold Dialog font with a point size of 48. By using a loop, the *run( )* method calls the *drawAnimationFrame( )* method 190 times. The *run( )* method passes the *drawAnimationFrame( )* method to the text string `"This Text is sinking!"` and the y coordinate at which the text is to be drawn.

The *drawAnimationFrame( )* method draws a black rectangle onto the applet's display area and then sets the default color to white. Consequently, any text subsequently drawn to the display area is shown in white. Next, the *drawAnimationFrame( )* method draws the text parameter passed to it by the *run( )* method at the y coordinate. Because the y coordinate is incremented in the *run( )* method for each invocation of *drawAnimationFrame( )* method, the text appears to sink.

Figure 16.4 shows one of the animation frames produced by the FlickeringSinkingText applet.

Figure 16.4:
Sinking text.

If you execute the FlickeringSinkingText applet, you will see that there is a notable flicker in the animation. This happens because, for each frame, the applet redraws the black rectangle and text string directly to the screen. The result is a minute flicker between animation frames.

Reducing Flicker with an Off-Screen Image

One technique for reducing animation flicker is to use a memory-based, or off-screen, image. By using an off-screen image as a work area, a program can construct a complete frame before moving it to the display area. Because each frame is displayed at the same time, the animation effect is much smoother. The FlickerFreeSinkingText applet, shown in listing 16.3, demonstrates how this technique can be implemented.

Listing 16.3   The FlickerFreeSinkingText Applet

```
import java.applet.*;
import java.awt.*;


public class FlickerFreeSinkingText extends Applet implements
➡Runnable
```

```
{
    Thread        FlickerFreeSinkingTextThread;
    Graphics      ScreenGraphicsContext;
    Graphics      OffScreenGraphicsContext;
    Image         OffScreenImage;

    public void start()
    {
        FlickerFreeSinkingTextThread = new Thread(this);
        FlickerFreeSinkingTextThread.start();

    }

    public void run()
    {
        ScreenGraphicsContext = getGraphics();
        OffScreenImage = createImage(500, 200);
        OffScreenGraphicsContext =
➥OffScreenImage.getGraphics();
        OffScreenGraphicsContext.setFont(new Font("Dialog",
➥Font.BOLD, 48));
        for (int y = 0; y < 190; y++)
        {
            drawAnimationFrame("This text is sinking!", y);
        }
    }

    public void drawAnimationFrame(String text, int y)
    {
        OffScreenGraphicsContext.setColor(Color.black);
        OffScreenGraphicsContext.fillRect(0, 0, 500, 200);
        OffScreenGraphicsContext.setColor(Color.white);
        OffScreenGraphicsContext.drawString(text, 40, y);
        ScreenGraphicsContext.drawImage(OffScreenImage, 0,
➥0, null);
        try
        {
            Thread.sleep(40);
        }
        catch(InterruptedException e) {}
    }

}
```

The FlickeringSinkingText applet in listing 16.2 is similar to the FlickerFreeSinkingText applet in listing 16.3. A few differences, however, are worth noting. In addition to getting the graphics context for the applet's display area, the FlickerFreeSinkingText applet creates a memory-based Image object called OffScreenImage in the *run( )* method. To draw to the OffScreenImage object, the applet creates a Graphics object called OffScreenGraphicsContext.

Instead of drawing an animation frame directly to the display area, the *drawAnimationFrame( )* method draws an entire animation frame in the OffScreenImage object. When a frame is complete the *drawAnimationFrame( )* method draws the entire image to the display area by using the *drawImage( )* method.

The FlickerFreeSinkingText applet eliminates virtually all the flicker in the animation because everything is drawn first to an off-screen Image object (in this case, OffScreenImage). When an entire frame is drawn to the applet's display area at one time, there is no delay between drawing the black rectangle and the white text string.

Although the code generated by the Applet Wizard creates an animation by drawing directly to the display area, many Java applets use the Applet class's *repaint( )* method to update the display area. The *repaint( )* method calls the *update( )* method. Because the standard *update( )* method clears the display area, it creates an even more pronounced flicker. You can address this problem by overriding the *update( )* method so that it only updates the necessary part of the display area. You can accomplish this by using the *clipRect( )* method provided by the Graphics class. The *clipRect( )* method enables you to define a portion of the display area affected by a graphics operation. For more information on the *clipRect( )* method, see the Visual J++ Books Online documentation.

The LogoAnimation Applet

This applet builds an animated logo—our example is the @Work Technologies logo, which uses a coordinated series of animation and audio effects. The LogoAnimation applet was created by using the Applet Wizard's sample animation applet shown in listing 16.1 as starter code. Figure 16.5 shows the final logo rendered by the applet as displayed on the @Work Technologies home page.

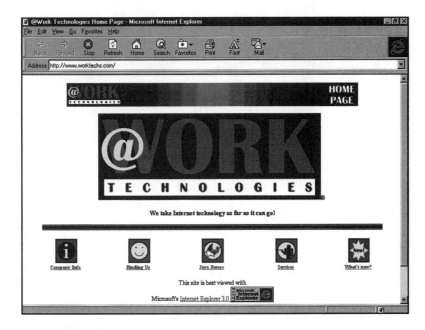

Figure 16.5:

The LogoAnimation applet on the @Work Technologies home page.

When the @Work Technologies home page is accessed by a web browser, the LogoAnimation applet creates the following animation effects.

Animation Step 1

A screen show displays a number of text strings to the user in varying colors, fonts, and positions. The text is drawn on the logo's background, which consists of only a black rectangle and a white rectangle. The screen show serves as a build-up to the more graphical part of the animation and buys the LogoAnimation applet some time so that the image and the audio objects can be loaded (see fig. 16.6).

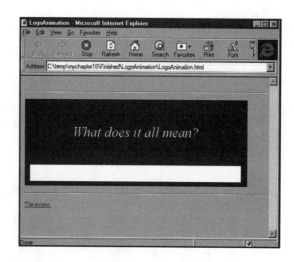

Figure 16.6:
LogoAnimation Step 1—Text show.

Animation Step 2

An "@" (at sign) spins into place from right to left (see fig.16.7). A woosh sound is played twice per revolution to enhance the effect.

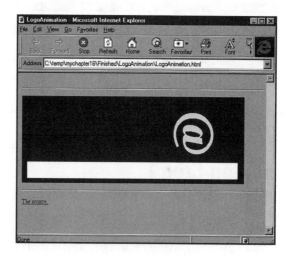

Figure 16.7:
LogoAnimation Step 2—Spinning @ sign.

Animation Step 3

The logo's "WORK" text pops up onto the display area, one letter at a time accompanied by an explosion sound. By combining these audio and visual effects, each letter seems to explode onto the logo (see fig. 16.8).

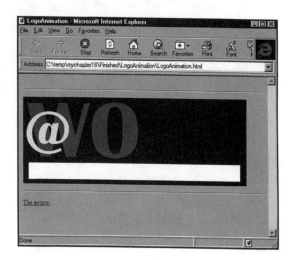

Figure 16.8:

LogoAnimation Step 3—Exploding WORK.

Animation Step 4

The logo's "TECHNOLOGIES" text pops up on the display to create a similar effect to the one produced in Step 3 (see fig. 16.9). The only difference is that the sound played resembles a gun firing. This makes the letters appear to be shot onto the display area.

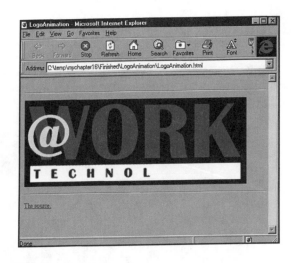

Figure 16.9:

LogoAnimation Step 4—Shooting TECHNOLOGIES.

LogoAnimation Input Files

To create the animation, the LogoAnimation applet loads nine
GIF files. The applet uses the same directory and file names as the
code generated by the Applet Wizard (see listing 16.1). This helps
to minimize the number of changes that have to be made to the
wizard-generated code. Figure 16.10 shows the img001.gif file.

Figure 16.10:

The @Work Logo Image in img001.gif.

The other image files contain the frames used to animate the spinning @ character. The images and file names are shown in figure 16.11.

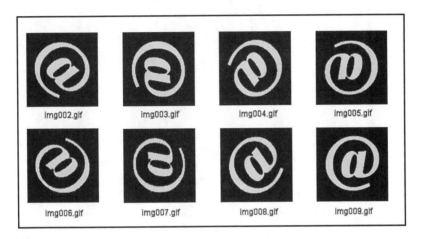

Figure 16.11:
Spinning @ images.

Using the Visual J++ Graphics Editor

The Visual J++ Graphics Editor is a tool that you can use to create or modify GIF, JPEG, BMP, and DIB (device independent bitmap) image files. When the Applet Wizard creates an animation applet, it automatically adds the eighteen image files to the project. You can create an image file by choosing New from the Visual J++ File pull-down menu and then choosing the Bitmap file option in the New dialog box.

You can also add image files to a project manually via the Visual J++ Insert pull-down menu.

You can edit an image file with the Graphics Editor by double-clicking on the file in the FileView pane of the Project Window. Figure 16.12, for example, shows the Graphics Editor after opening the img009.gif file.

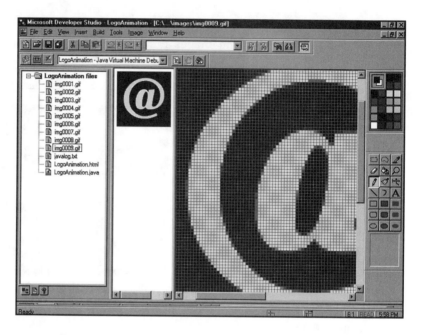

Figure 16.12:
The Graphics Editor.

As shown in figure 16.12, the Graphics Editor is composed of the following components.

➤ *Image Editor Window*—This window shows two views of the image, separated by a moveable *split bar.* The view on the left shows the image displayed at its normal size. The view on the right is enlarged, enabling you to modify individual pixels.

➤ *Graphics Toolbar*—This toolbar provides 21 tools for manipulating images. In addition, when you click on a tool that has options associated with it, the Graphics Toolbar displays an option selector. When you click on the brush tool, for example, the brush width options are displayed.

➤ *Colors Toolbar*—Provides a color palette that can be used to set the colors for drawing on the image. You can set the foreground color of the palette by left-clicking on a color and you can set the background color by right-clicking on a color.

When you have created the image file, you can save it in the desired directory in any of the supported file formats. Because the Graphics Editor supports BMP and DIB in addition to GIF and JPEG, you can use it to convert image files.

Although the Graphics Editor is an extremely useful and easy-to-use tool, when you want to create very high-quality images, you will have to use one of the more high-end specialized graphics applications, such as Adobe's PhotoShop.

Creating Sound Files

Visual J++ does not provide an audio editor for creating AU files; however, there are some packages available that can accomplish this task. One available shareware package, called GoldWave, was developed by Chris Craig and can be downloaded from his web site at:

`http://web.cs.mun.ca/~chris3/goldwave/.`

Figure 16.13 shows the GoldWave user interface.

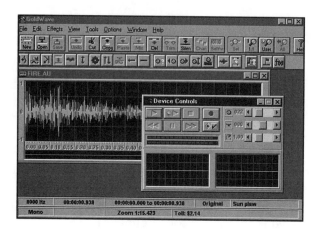

Figure 16.13:

The GoldWave Digital Audio Editor.

Most digital audio editors like GoldWave are user-friendly. In fact, if you can record and play sounds on a simple tape recorder, you should be able to start creating sound files with it right away by using its Device Controls window shown in figure 16.13.

Although tools like GoldWave make it easy to create AU files, you should remember some important things. This is because release 1.0 of the Java environment is particular about its AudioClip objects. If you don't create your AU files correctly, they will not play in a Java program.

First, when you create an AU file, you must specify the following attributes:

➤   Bits = 8

➤   Channels = mono

➤   Sampling Rate = 8000

Figure 16.14 shows how you can set these options in GoldWave.

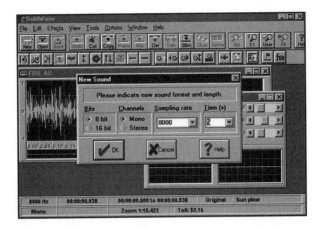

Figure 16.14:

Defining the sound format and length of an AU file in GoldWave.

In addition, when you save an AU file, you must also specify the File Attributes *μlaw, mono* as shown in figure 16.15.

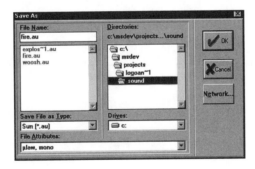

Figure 16.15:

Saving an AU file with the appropriate file attributes.

Design of the LogoAnimation Applet

By using the sample animation generated by the Applet Wizard as starter code, you can create sophisticated customized animations such as the LogoAnimation applet shown in listing 16.4.

Listing 16.4   The Final Version of the LogoAnimation Applet

```java
import java.applet.*;
import java.awt.*;

public class LogoAnimation extends Applet implements Runnable
{

    Thread              m_LogoAnimation = null;
    private TextShow    m_TextShow;
    private Graphics    m_ScreenGC;
    private Graphics    m_OffScreenGC;
    private Image       m_OffScreenImage;
    private Image       m_Images[];
    private boolean     m_fAllLoaded = false;
    private final int   NUM_IMAGES = 9;
    private AudioClip   m_Woosh;
    private AudioClip   m_Explosion;
    private AudioClip   m_GunShot;
    private int         m_nImgWidth  = 458;
    private int         m_nImgHeight = 173;
    private int         m_nBlackRectStart;
    private int         m_nWhiteRectStart;
    private int         m_nBlackRectWidth;
    private int         m_nWhiteRectWidth;

    public void init()
    {
        resize(m_nImgWidth, m_nImgHeight);
    }

    public void paint(Graphics g)
    {
        if ((m_OffScreenImage != null) & (m_ScreenGC !=
➥null))
                drawAnimationFrame(0);
    }

    public void start()
    {
        m_nBlackRectStart  = 0;
```

```
           m_nWhiteRectStart   = 11;
           m_nBlackRectWidth   = 458;
           m_nWhiteRectWidth   = 434;
           Image overlayImage = createImage(m_nImgWidth,
➡m_nImgHeight);
           Graphics overlayGC = overlayImage.getGraphics();
           fillRectangles(overlayGC);
           overlayGC.dispose();

           m_ScreenGC = getGraphics();

           m_OffScreenImage = createImage(m_nImgWidth,
➡m_nImgHeight);
           m_OffScreenGC    = m_OffScreenImage.getGraphics();

           m_TextShow = new TextShow(overlayImage,
➡m_OffScreenImage, m_ScreenGC);
           m_TextShow.start();

           if (m_LogoAnimation == null)
           {
               m_LogoAnimation = new Thread(this);
               m_LogoAnimation.start();
           }
       }

   public void stop()
   {
       if (m_LogoAnimation != null)
       {
           m_LogoAnimation.stop();
           m_LogoAnimation = null;
           m_ScreenGC.dispose();
           m_OffScreenGC.dispose();
       }
   }

   public void run()
   {
      if (!m_fAllLoaded)
       {
           m_Images    = new Image[NUM_IMAGES];
```

continues

Listing 16.4   Continued

```java
            MediaTracker tracker = new MediaTracker(this);
            String strImage;

            for (int i = 1; i <= NUM_IMAGES; i++)
            {
                strImage = "images/img00" + ((i < 10) ? "0"
: "") + i + ".gif";
                m_Images[i-1] = getImage(getCodeBase(),
strImage);

                tracker.addImage(m_Images[i-1], 0);
            }

            tracker.checkAll(true);

            m_GunShot    = getAudioClip(getCodeBase(),
"sound/fire.au");
            m_Explosion = getAudioClip(getCodeBase(),
"sound/explosion.au");
            m_Woosh      = getAudioClip(getCodeBase(),
"sound/woosh.au");

            try
            {
                tracker.waitForAll();
                m_fAllLoaded = !tracker.isErrorAny();
            }
            catch (InterruptedException e)
            {
            }

            if (!m_fAllLoaded)
            {
                stop();
                m_ScreenGC.drawString("Error loading
images!", 10, 40);
                return;
            }

    }
```

```
            while(m_TextShow.isAlive())
            {
                try
                {
                    Thread.sleep(50);
                }
                catch (InterruptedException e){}
            }

            drawSpinningAtSign();
            blowUpBlackRectangle();
            shootUpWhiteRectangle();
        }

    public void fillRectangles(Graphics gC)
    {
        gC.setColor(Color.black);
        gC.fillRect(m_nBlackRectStart, 0, m_nBlackRectWidth,
➥173);
        gC.setColor(Color.white);
        gC.fillRect(m_nWhiteRectStart, 131,
➥m_nWhiteRectWidth, 33);
    }

    public void drawSpinningAtSign()
    {
        int atSignX = 559;
        int j = 0;
        for (int i = 0; i < 7; i++)
        {
            for (int atSignSpinIndex = 1; atSignSpinIndex <
➥9; atSignSpinIndex++)
            {
                j++;
                if (j == 4)
                {
                    m_Woosh.play();
                    j = 0;
                }

                atSignX = atSignX - 10;
```

continues

Listing 16.4   Continued

```
                    fillRectangles(m_OffScreenGC);
                m_OffScreenGC.drawImage(m_Images[atSignSpinIndex],
➥atSignX, 18, null);
                    drawAnimationFrame(35);
                }
        }
        drawAnimationFrame(1000);
    }

    public void blowUpBlackRectangle()
    {
        int sleepTime = 1500;
        m_nBlackRectStart = 136;
        m_Explosion.play();
        m_OffScreenGC.drawImage(m_Images[0], 0, 0, null);
        fillRectangles(m_OffScreenGC);
        drawAnimationFrame(sleepTime);
        sleepTime = 750;
        while (m_nBlackRectStart < 448)
        {
            m_Explosion.play();
            m_nBlackRectStart = m_nBlackRectStart + 106;
            m_nBlackRectWidth = m_nBlackRectWidth - 106;
            m_OffScreenGC.drawImage(m_Images[0], 0, 0,
➥null);
            fillRectangles(m_OffScreenGC);
            drawAnimationFrame(sleepTime);
        }
    }

    public void shootUpWhiteRectangle()
    {
        int sleepTime = 1000;
        for (int i = 0; i < 12; i++)
        {
            m_nWhiteRectStart = m_nWhiteRectStart + 36;
            m_nWhiteRectWidth = m_nWhiteRectWidth - 36;
            m_GunShot.play();
            m_OffScreenGC.drawImage(m_Images[0], 0, 0,
➥null);
```

```
                fillRectangles(m_OffScreenGC);
                drawAnimationFrame(sleepTime);
                sleepTime = 160;
            }
        }

    public void drawAnimationFrame(int sleepTime)
    {
        m_ScreenGC.drawImage(m_OffScreenImage, 0, 0, null);
        try
        {
                Thread.sleep(sleepTime);
        }
        catch(InterruptedException e) {}
    }

}


class TextShow extends Thread
{

    private Image       m_OverlayImage;
    private Graphics    m_ScreenGC;
    private Image       m_OffScreenImage;
    private Graphics    m_OffScreenGC;
    private Font        m_LargeItalicFont = new
➥Font("TimesRoman", Font.ITALIC, 28);
    private Font        m_LargeBoldFont   = new
➥Font("Dialog", Font.BOLD, 24);
    private Font        m_MediumBoldFont  = new
➥Font("Dialog", Font.BOLD, 16);
    private Font        m_MediumPlainFont = new
➥Font("Dialog", Font.PLAIN, 16);

    public TextShow(Image overlayImage, Image offScreenImage,
➥Graphics screenGC)
    {
        m_OverlayImage   = overlayImage;
        m_OffScreenImage = offScreenImage;
        m_ScreenGC       = screenGC;
```

continues

Listing 16.4   Continued

```
    }

    public void run()
    {
        m_OffScreenGC = m_OffScreenImage.getGraphics();

        drawTextFrame("Java",
            100,100, 1000, m_LargeItalicFont, Color.red);

        drawTextFrame("ActiveX",
            350, 50, 1000, m_MediumPlainFont, Color.white);

        drawTextFrame("Firewalls",
            50, 30, 1000, m_MediumPlainFont,
➥Color.yellow);

        drawTextFrame("Digital IDs",
            350, 60, 1000, m_MediumPlainFont, Color.red);

        drawTextFrame("What does it all mean?",
            100, 75, 2000, m_LargeItalicFont,
➥Color.yellow);

        drawTextFrame("Communicate with your customers.",
            90, 40, 2000, m_MediumBoldFont, Color.red);

        drawTextFrame("Share information.",
            150, 60, 2000, m_MediumPlainFont,
➥Color.yellow);

        drawTextFrame("Get it done faster!",
            150, 80, 2500, m_MediumBoldFont, Color.white);

        drawTextFrame("Are you ready to win with new
➥technology?",
            75, 75, 2500, m_MediumPlainFont,
➥Color.yellow);

        drawTextFrame("It's time to activate the Internet!",
            50, 80, 2000, m_LargeBoldFont, Color.red);
```

```
    }

    public void drawTextFrame(String text, int x, int y, int
➥sleepTime,
                                Font textFont, Color
➥textColor)
    {
        m_OffScreenGC.drawImage(m_OverlayImage, 0, 0, null);
        m_OffScreenGC.setColor(textColor);
        m_OffScreenGC.setFont(textFont);
        m_OffScreenGC.drawString(text, x, y);
        m_ScreenGC.drawImage(m_OffScreenImage, 0, 0, null);
        try
        {
            sleep(sleepTime);
        }
        catch(InterruptedException e){} // do nothing
    }
}
```

The diagram shown in figure 16.16 provides a high-level illustration of the design of the LogoAnimation applet.

When the LogoAnimation applet is executed, the following threads are created:

➤ The initial text show thread starts in the applet's *start( )* method. This thread can begin running immediately because the initial text show does not require any external images.

➤ The applet's own execution thread starts in the *start( )* method. This thread uses the external images (see figures 16.10 and 16.11) to create the animation effects that run after the text show. Before this thread runs the animation, it must check to ensure that the images are loaded and the text show thread has completed.

➤ The applet's *run( )* method starts a third thread to load to images when it calls the MediaTracker class's *checkForAll( )* method.

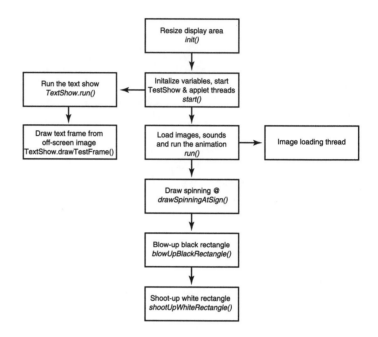

Figure 16.16:

High-level design of the LogoAnimation Applet.

The following sections discuss the techniques utilized in the LogoAnimation applet to create its animation. It may be useful to refer back to listing 16.4 and figure 16.16 as you read the next few sections.

The *init()* Method

This method calls the *resize( )* method to set the applet's display area to the correct size. The size of the display area is also specified in the applet's HTML file, however, the *resize( )* method is called here to ensure that the display area will be the proper dimensions for the animation.

The *start()* Method

This method initializes the applet's instance variables and starts the applet's threads. In addition, the *start( )* method instantiates the TextShow object (m_TextShow) and begins its thread of execution by calling the object's *start( )* method.

The TextShow Thread

The LogoAnimation applet utilizes a helper class called TextShow (see the end of listing 16.4). Because the TextShow class is derived from the Thread class, it can run as a separate task. This is quite useful because it enables the applet to begin the text show part of the animation before the images and sounds load. The TextShow class constructor takes the following three parameters:

➤ *overlayImage*—An Image object drawn by the LogoAnimation applet's *fillRectangles( )* method. The TextShow class uses this image as an overlay upon which it draws the text show frames.

➤ *offScreenImage*—A memory-based Image object that the TextShow class shares with the LogoAnimation applet.

➤ *screenGC*—The graphics context (Graphics object) for the applet's display area. The TextShow object shares this graphics context with the LogoAnimation applet.

The TextShow class's *run( )* method formats the verbiage, color, and position of the text displayed in each frame of the text show. The TextShow class's *drawTextFrame( )* method reduces animation flicker by constructing each text frame in an off-screen image (m_offScreenImage) before drawing it to the applet's display area.

The *run()* Method

The *run( )* method loads the image and sound files required for the animation. If these files are already loaded, the *run( )* method runs the animation immediately.

The *run( )* method uses the same technique as the Applet Wizard's sample animation applet to load image files. The main difference is that the final version of the LogoAnimation applet calls the MediaTracker object's *checkAll( )* method as shown by the following line of code.

```
tracker.checkAll(true);
```

The preceding line of code triggers the thread that downloads all the image files required for the animation. Remember, even though the Image object is created, the actual image file is not loaded until something triggers the download thread. By kicking off the download process first, the *run( )* method can download the sound file (the AudioClip objects) in parallel with the images.

After the *run( )* method calls the tracker object's *waitForAll( )* method to ensure that the images have been loaded, it determines whether the text show has completed by checking the thread object's status using the following code:

```
while(m_TextShow.isAlive())
{
    try
    {
        Thread.sleep(50);
    }
        catch (InterruptedException e){}
}
```

The *Thread* class's *isAlive( )* method returns a boolean true as long as the TextShow object's *run( )* method is executing. Therefore, the preceding code ensures that the text show is finished before the applet continues with the rest of the animation.

Finally, the *run( )* method completes the animation by calling the *drawSpinningAtSign( )*, *blowUpBlackRectangle( )*, and *shootUpWhiteRectangle( )* methods, which are discussed in greater detail in the following sections.

The *drawSpinningAtSign()* Method

This method animates an "@" character spinning into its proper position in the @Work Technologies logo. This is accomplished by drawing the img002.gif through img009.gif images (see fig. 16.11) while reducing the x coordinate of the image for each frame. Therefore, the "@" appears to spin from right to left. The backdrop of the animation is the black and white rectangle areas of the logo. The m_Woosh AudioClip plays twice for every revolution of the "@" character.

The *blowUpBlackRectangle()* Method

This method creates the next phase of the animation. Each letter of the word "WORK" in the logo appears to explode sequentially. This effect is created by first drawing the full logo (img001.gif) and then overlaying the logo with the black and white rectangles drawn by the *fillRectangles( )* method. Because the *fill Rectangles( )* method takes the starting point and width of the black rectangle as parameters, the *blowUpBlackRectangle( )* can create a progressively smaller black rectangle for each frame. In doing so, each frame uncovers another letter of the logo. When the m_Explosion AudioClip object plays simultaneously, each letter of "WORK" appears to blow up.

The *shootUpWhiteRectangle()* Method

The *shootUpWhiteRectangle( )* method uses the same technique employed by the *blowUpBlackRectangle( )* method to create its animation effect. The only difference is that this method specifies a progressively smaller white rectangle and plays the *m_Fire* AudioClip object, which sounds like a gun going off. The result is that the letters of the word "TECHNOLOGIES" appear to be shot onto the screen.

The *drawAnimationFrame()* Method

The *drawSpinningAtSign( )*, *blowUpBlackRectangles( )*, and *shootUpWhiteRectangle( )* methods all call this method after preparing an animation frame in an off-screen Image object (m_OffScreenImage). The *drawAnimationFrame( )* method draws this object onto the applet's display area and sleeps for the number of milliseconds specified by the calling method.

Important Lessons from the LogoAnimation Applet

The LogoAnimation applet example demonstrates how to implement several techniques that can help you create animations in Java. The most important of these techniques are:

➤ Reducing the time that it takes to start the animation by using multiple threads.

➤ Using a MediaTracker object to track the status of loading images.

➤ Eliminating animation flicker by using an off-screen image.

You should refer back to this chapter when you create your own animations in Java. Whether you want to include an animation in a serious application or to dress up a web page, by utilizing the techniques discussed in this chapter, you can make your animations run more efficiently and look more professional.

Summary

The animation and audio capabilities of the Java language enable you to provide the users of your programs with additional sensory feedback. Although the AWT provides functionality for drawing various shapes and colors, if you want to create high-quality animations, you will need to use images generated in a professional graphics package.

You can create an Image object from a file using the *getImage( )* method and create a blank Image using the *createImage( )* method. Both of these methods are provided by the Applet class. When necessary, you can also use the default Toolkit to construct an Image object.

It is important to remember that an image file loads on a separate thread of execution. This thread does not run until the program attempts to access the Image object. MediaTracker is an AWT utility class that can be used to trigger the image loading thread.

The MediaTracker class also provides methods that can be used to check the status of a loading image, such as the *waitForID( )* and *waitForAll( )* methods.

To draw to an Image object, your program must first obtain a graphics context (Graphics object) for the Image. A graphics context can be obtained using the Image class's *getGraphics( )* method. To get a graphics context for an applet's display area, you can call the applet's *getGraphics( )* method.

The AudioClip objects in release 1.0 of Java only support the AU audio file format. If you don't set the file attributes correctly when you create an AU file, it will not play in a Java applet.

You can use off-screen images to reduce animation flicker. This technique involves constructing an entire animation frame in an off-screen Image object and then drawing it all at once onto the display area.

Questions

1. What are the advantages of the GIF and JPEG image file formats?

2. When a program creates an Image object from a file, is the file loaded immediately?

3. In a Java applet, what two methods can be used to create an Image object?

4. What type of object does a program need to get before drawing to an Image object?

5. What AWT utility class can be used to track the status of an Image object while it is being loaded from a file?

6. When you create an AU file, what should the sampling rate be set to?

7. What file attributes should be set when saving an AU file?

8. Explain one technique for reducing animation flicker.

Answers

1. GIF and JPEG image files can be downloaded quickly over a low-speed connection because they are compressed. These file formats are supported on almost any platform and can be created by almost any good graphics software package.

2. No. Image files are loaded asynchronously on a separate thread. This thread does not start until the program attempts to access the image.

3. The Applet class provides a *getImage( )* method that can be used to load an Image object from a file. To create a blank Image object, you can use the Applet class's *createImage( )* method.

4. To draw to an Image object, the program must first get a Graphics object (graphics context) associated with the image.

5. The MediaTracker class can be used to track the status of an Image object while it is being loaded from a file.

6. The sampling rate of an AU file should be set to 8000.

7. When saving an AU file, the file attributes should be set to *μlaw, mono.*

8. Animation flicker can be reduced by constructing each animation frame in an off-screen Image object prior to drawing it onto a display area.

Chapter 17

Java and the ActiveX Platform

Is ActiveX better than Java?

Is a hammer a better tool than a screwdriver?

The same answer can be given to both of these questions—it depends upon what you are trying to do. Just like the hammer and the screwdriver, Java and ActiveX have their place in your toolbox. The most important thing to remember is that the two programs are not mutually exclusive. You can use Java and ActiveX together to accomplish a heck of a lot more than if you used one exclusively.

The computer industry is abundant with individuals who take extreme positions on this issue. Although these people would like you to believe that they are crusaders in some type of technological Holy War, upon closer analysis, it becomes apparent that they're really just trying to further their own economic interest.

Can you really blame them? After all, everyone needs to make a living. At the end of the day, however, it's you the developer that needs to solve real life business problems and produce results.

Is it possible that you would want to be able to integrate a Java applet with an Excel spreadsheet? You bet it is. Would doing this, in all likelihood, make the applet less portable? You bet it would. You don't, however, lose anything by having this capability. The point is that ActiveX provides you with the capability to do more than you can with just Java.

In an effort to transcend the industry rhetoric and focus on what ActiveX can do for Java developers, this chapter covers the following topics:

➤ ActiveX scripting with both VBScript and JavaScript

➤ Creating cabinet files for Java applets and data

➤ Signing Java applets digitally

➤ Integrating ActiveX controls and Java

Although a detailed discussion of the topics covered in this chapter could fill a few books, by the time you're finished, you should have a good idea of the powerful things you can do in Java within the ActiveX framework.

How Java Relates to ActiveX

As discussed in Chapter 1, "Overview of Visual J++ and Java," ActiveX is a name used by Microsoft to refer to a number of technologies and software products. The company hopes that ActiveX will help it maintain its hegemony in a software industry that is rapidly migrating from a desktop-centric model of computing to the more network-centric world of the Internet. The main parts of the ActiveX platform that concern Java developers are as follows:

➤ ActiveX scripting with VBScript and JavaScript

➤ Secure software distribution by using cabinet files and Microsoft's Authenticode technology

➤ ActiveX controls and Java integration

The remainder of this chapter discusses these topics.

It should come as no surprise that Microsoft's Internet Explorer (IE) (version 3.0 or higher) provides the most comprehensive support for ActiveX. Therefore, the discussion in this chapter focuses on IE.

The Netscape Navigator 4.0 (and higher) web browser includes support for ActiveX controls and ActiveX documents. You can also get a number of ActiveX plug-ins for Navigator from a company called NCompass Labs. Their web site can be found at:

`http://www.ncompasslabs.com`

ActiveX Scripting

The ActiveX platform supports HTML scripts written in Netscape's JavaScript language as well as Microsoft's own VBScript. JavaScript has the advantage of being a quite powerful scripting language with many object-oriented features that are built-in.

VBScript's biggest advantage is that, being a subset of Visual Basic for Applications, literally millions of developers are already familiar with its syntax.

Both JavaScript and VBScript are promoted as being safe for use on the public Internet. Scripts, for example, are prevented from performing potentially dangerous functions, such as writing to a local hard drive.

The ActiveX scripting model is designed to support plug-in scripting engines. In other words, if you had the time and re-sources, you could develop your own scripting language, such as the MyScript language. As long as you conformed to the proper Microsoft ActiveX scripting interface requirements, you could use your new scripting language within the ActiveX framework. You can get additional information about the ActiveX scripting model from Microsoft's web site at:

```
http://www.microsoft.com/intdev/sdk/docs/scriptom/
```

At the time that this chapter was written, the majority of users on the public Internet used Netscape Navigator as their primary browser. Therefore, if you want to create a script that most people can use, write it in JavaScript. It is important, however, that you test your JavaScript code in both Netscape and IE because there are minor differences in how each browser interprets scripts.

From a Java developer's point of view, the great thing about scripts are that they can be used to enhance and customize Java programs. You can do this by embedding a script inside an HTML file. HTML-based scripts can call the public methods and change the values of public variables of an applet. Because scripts are easier to learn than programming languages, such as C++ and Java, even relatively nontechnical users can write scripts that add value to your Java applets.

Most web server vendors have, or are in the process of, implementing server-side scripting capabilities. Server-side scripts can be embedded in HTML pages but are executed on the server. It is likely that a whole new market will develop for scriptable server-side ActiveX and Java components.

Overview of the Scripting Examples in This Chapter

The scripting examples presented in this chapter use a modified version of the LogoAnimation applet discussed in Chapter 16, "Fun with Sound and Animation." This applet has been renamed as the ScriptedLogo applet. The following four new methods have been added to the main applet class to facilitate scripting.

```
public void suspendIt()
{
    m_ScriptedLogo.suspend();
    m_TextShow.suspend();
}

public void resumeIt()
{
    m_ScriptedLogo.resume();
    m_TextShow.resume();
}

public void restartIt()
{
    stop();
    start();
}

public void setSpeedFactor(double speedFactor)
{
    m_SpeedFactor = speedFactor;
    m_TextShow.m_SpeedFactor = speedFactor;
}
```

For a script to call a method in a Java program, the method must be declared with the public access modifier.

The methods shown in the preceding code are both called by scripting examples discussed in this chapter. As you can see, these methods can be used to suspend, resume, restart, and change the speed of the applet. The *setSpeedFactor()* method uses a new instance variable called *m_SpeedFactor* created by the following declaration:

```
private double     m_SpeedFactor = 1.0;
```

Both the main applet and the TextShow class declare an *m_SpeedFactor* instance variable. The *m_SpeedFactor* variable determines the speed of execution for the animation. It is used in the ScriptedLogo applet's *drawAnimationFrame()* method and the TextShow helper class's *drawTextFrame()* method. The ScriptedLogo applet's *drawAnimationFrame()* method is coded as follows:

```
public void drawAnimationFrame(int sleepTime)
{
    m_ScreenGC.drawImage(m_OffScreenImage, 0, 0, null);
    try
    {
        Thread.sleep((int)(sleepTime*m_SpeedFactor));
    }
    catch(InterruptedException e) {}
}
```

By setting the value of *m_SpeedFactor* to 0.5, for example, the amount of time that the applet sleeps between frames is reduced by half, meaning that the applet's execution speed would essentially double.

 A Visual J++ project containing the ScriptedLogo applet can be found on this book's CD. The project also includes two HTML files. The `ScriptedLogo.html` file contains the VBScript example and the `ScriptedLogoJS.html` file contains the JavaScript example.

A VBScript Example

By using VBScript, you can write an HTML page that controls a Java applet. The HTML code shown in listing 17.1 contains a VBScript that can be used to script the ScriptedLogo applet from within IE.

Listing 17.1 VBScript Example

```
<html>
<head>
<title>ScriptedLogo</title>
</head>
<script language=VBScript>
<!--
```

```
Dim speedFactor

sub Window_OnLoad
    speedFactor = 1
end sub

' HANDLE A "Faster" BUTTON CLICK
sub Faster_OnClick
    speedFactor = speedFactor - 0.2
    if speedFactor < 0 then
        MsgBox "I am already going too fast", 0, "Speed
➥demon alert"
    else
        document.ScriptedLogo.setSpeedFactor speedFactor
    end if
end sub

' HANDLE A "Normal" BUTTON CLICK
sub Normal_OnClick
    speedFactor = 1
    document.ScriptedLogo.setSpeedFactor speedFactor
end sub

' HANDLE A "Slower" BUTTON CLICK
sub Slower_OnClick
    speedFactor = speedFactor + 0.5
    document.ScriptedLogo.setSpeedFactor speedFactor
end sub

-->
</script>
<center>
<body>
<hr>
<applet
    code=ScriptedLogo.class
    id=ScriptedLogo
    width=458
    height=173 >
<param name="cabbase" value="scriptedlogocab.cab">
</applet>
```

continues

Listing 17.1   Continued

```
<hr>
<form>
<input type=button name=Suspend value="Suspend"
onclick="document.ScriptedLogo.suspendIt">
<input type=button name=Resume  value="Resume"
onclick="document.ScriptedLogo.resumeIt">
<input type=button name=Restart value="Restart"
onclick="document.ScriptedLogo.restartIt">
<input type=button name=Faster  value="Faster">
<input type=button name=Normal  value="Normal">
<input type=button name=Slower  value="Slower">
</form>
<br>
</center>
</body>
</html>
```

When IE encounters the `<script language=VBScript>` tag shown in listing 17.1, the browser knows that a Visual Basic script follows. The HTML comment delimiters, `<!--` and `-->`, are included so that browsers that cannot interpret VBScript will treat the script as a comment and, therefore, will not display the script as text on the web page.

Consider the folowing line of HTML code:

```
<input type=button name=Resume  value="Resume"
➥onclick="document.ScriptedLogo.resumeIt">
```

Because of this line, when a user clicks on the Resume button, the ScriptedLogo applet's *resumeIt( )* method is called. How does the script know that ScriptedLogo is the applet? This is because of the id attribute that is set within the `<applet>` tag. You may recall from Chapter 7, "Building Your First Java Applet By Using Visual J++," that the Java Applet Wizard automatically includes an id attribute when it creates an HTML file. The event handling built into the form does not have to invoke VBScript. The power of VBScript is its capability to run subroutines and functions, such as the case when the user clicks on the Faster, Normal, or Slower buttons.

VBScript Subroutines

VBScript subroutines are declared by using the Sub keyword and delimited by the End Sub statement. The following subroutine, for example

```
sub Faster_OnClick
    speedFactor = speedFactor - 0.2
    if speedFactor < 0 then
        MsgBox "I am already going too fast!", 0,
➥"Speed demon alert"
    else
        document.ScriptedLogo.setSpeedFactor
➥speedFactor
    end if
end sub
```

is invoked in response to an event generated when the user clicks the button with the name Faster. This subroutine subtracts 0.2 from the VBScript *speedFactor* variable; however, if *speedFactor* is less than 0, an informational message displays to the user. Otherwise, the *speedFactor* variable is reduced by 0.2 and is passed as a parameter to the ScriptedLogo applet by invoking the *setSpeedFactor( )* method. As discussed previously in this chapter, the *setSpeedFactor( )* method sets the value of the *m_SpeedFactor* instance variables in the main applet class as well as in the TextShow helper class. Take a look at the subroutines that handle the click events for the Slower and Normal buttons and you will see that these buttons also set the *speedFactor* variable and call the *setSpeedFactor( )* method.

Adding Value to Java Applets with Scripts

The main point of the VBScript example is to show that a Java applet can be enhanced and customized by using a scripting language. What this means for the developer is that if you design your programs to be highly scriptable, then even relatively nontechnical individuals will be able to easily build on your work—making your applets more valuable to them and to you!

You can put VBScript code anywhere you want within an HTML page; however, you may want to put all of the code together so that it is easier to read and to follow.

Executing the VBScript Example

When the ScriptedLogo applet is executed by IE, using the HTML file in listing 17.1, it appears as shown in figure 17.1. Notice the warning message displayed by VBScript when a user clicks on the Faster button too many times.

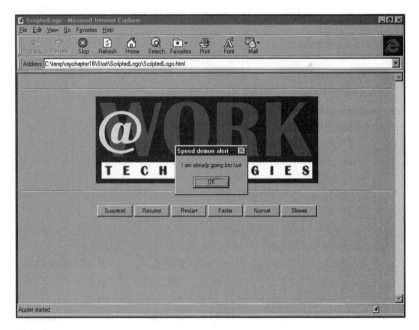

Figure 17.1:

The ScriptedLogo applet displayed by IE.

The ScriptedLogo VBScript sample only touches on a fraction of the functionality available with VBScript. For more information, see Microsoft's VBScript page at:

http://www.microsoft.com/vbscript/

A JavaScript Example

In addition to VBScript, the ActiveX scripting model supports JavaScript. To script the ScriptedLogo applet by using JavaScript, you could run it in the HTML page shown in listing 17.2.

Listing 17.2   A JavaScript Example

```html
<html>
<head>
<title>ScriptedLogo</title>
</head>
<script language="JAVASCRIPT">

var speedFactor = 1

// HANDLE A "Faster" BUTTON CLICK
function makeItFaster()
{
    speedFactor = speedFactor - 0.2
    if (speedFactor < 0.2)
        alert("I am already going too fast!")
    else
        document.ScriptedLogo.setSpeedFactor(speedFactor)
}

// HANDLE A "Normal" BUTTON CLICK
function makeItNormal()
{
    speedFactor = 1
    document.ScriptedLogo.setSpeedFactor(speedFactor)
}

// HANDLE A "Slower" BUTTON CLICK
function makeItSlower()
{
    speedFactor = speedFactor + 0.5
    document.ScriptedLogo.setSpeedFactor(speedFactor)
}

</script>
<center>
```

continues

Listing 17.2   Continued

```
<body>
<hr>
<applet
    code=ScriptedLogo.class
    name=ScriptedLogo
    width=458
    height=173 >
</applet>
<hr>
<form>
<input type=button name=Suspend value="Suspend"
onclick="document.ScriptedLogo.suspendIt()">
<input type=button name=Resume  value="Resume"
onclick="document.ScriptedLogo.resumeIt()">
<input type=button name=Restart value="Restart"
onclick="document.ScriptedLogo.restartIt()">
<input type=button name=Faster  value="Faster"
➥onclick="makeItFaster()">
<input type=button name=Normal  value="Normal"
➥onclick="makeItNormal()">
<input type=button name=Slower  value="Slower"
➥onclick="makeItSlower()">
</form>
<br>
</center>
</body>
</html>
```

You can run the JavaScript example shown in listing 17.2 in either Netscape Navigator or IE.

As you can see from listing 17.2, the syntax of JavaScript is somewhat different from that of VBScript. Notice that instead of the id attribute, JavaScript locates the applet via the name attribute in the `<applet>` tag.

JavaScript Functions

Although the event handling for the Suspend, Resume, and Restart buttons is identical to the VBScript example, the HTML code used to create the form in listing 17.2 invokes JavaScript functions whenever a user clicks on the Faster, Normal, or Slower buttons. These functions perform the same tasks as their VBScript subroutine counterparts in listing 17.1.

Like VBScript, JavaScript is capable of a lot more than what is shown here. For more information, see the Netscape home page at:

`http//www.netscape.com/`

Distributing Your Java Classes in Cabinet Files

As a developer, you may have noticed one of the drawbacks to using Java applets is that they are typically downloaded to your web browser for each and every execution. Consequently, when you try to access a sophisticated applet, such as an applet composed of many large `.class` files, it takes so long that you start wondering if you'll ever see the applet in this lifetime!

Another aspect of traditional Java applets that can be particularly frustrating to a developer is the so-called sandbox security model. Run-of-the-mill Java applets can't have read or write access to a local hard drive and can't communicate, via opening a socket session, for example, with any host other than the one from which it was downloaded. Although the Java sandbox was implemented for extremely good reasons—it prevents a rogue programmer from writing an applet that erases your hard drive—it is nonetheless limiting for some of the more robust network-centric applets that you might want to develop.

To address these issues, Microsoft has implemented a security framework called Authenticode, which enables you to create Java applets, and store them in a cabinet, or cab, files. Because cab files are compressed by using a standard Lempel-Ziv algorithm, they reduce the time it takes to download an applet. Furthermore, IE caches cab files so that you don't have to download them every time you execute an applet.

Lempel-Ziv is a standard text compression algorithm. It is widely used in various compression utilities such as PKZIP and the Greenbar computer output to laser disk (COLD) system originally developed by Bill Clarke.

Another neat thing about cab files is that they can be digitally signed. Suppose a person named *Jim Flynn*, for example, signs a cab file. When a user's IE web browser accesses the cab file, it attempts to validate the signature. When the signature is valid, two things are known with relative certainty:

➤ Jim Flynn was the creator of the cab file

➤ The cab file has not been altered—nobody has inserted a virus into it—since Jim Flynn signed it.

If Jim Flynn is considered trusted by the user (we should hope so!), then the applet is permitted to run on the user's system, outside of the restrictions imposed by the sandbox. As Microsoft's logic goes, when an applet is signed, it's as safe as if you went into your local software retailer and purchased a shrink-wrapped copy of the program. In other words, you know the source. Before a signed applet executes, IE displays the digital certificate to the user. If, when you verified the cab file's digital signature, you found that it was signed by "Two Kids in Garage Inc.," and not by some party that you know to be reputable, such as Jim Flynn, you have the option of not letting it run on your workstation.

Although almost all vendors involved with Java have endorsed code signing as a means to enable Java applets out of the sandbox, Microsoft was the first to actually implement it with the introduction of IE3. To the company's credit, Microsoft has pledged that it will also support any other code signing mechanism ultimately adopted as the industry standard.

The next few sections describe how cab files can be created and run within IE. In addition, you will learn how Authenticode technology is used to create a signed cab file for a Java applet so that it can run outside of the sandbox.

Creating a Cab File

At the time that this chapter was written, the process of creating cab files was still a bit cryptic. After you understand how it's done, however, you should be able to create your own cab files with relative ease.

The Cab Developer's Kit is included with Visual J++. You can also check for the latest version on Microsoft's web site at:

`http://www.microsoft.com/workshop/java/cab-f.htm`

Before reading through the example in this chapter, it may be a good idea for you to install the Cab Developer's Kit on your workstation so that you can follow along.

The ScriptedLogo applet discussed in this chapter is composed of two class files, nine images, and three sound files. As you may be aware, downloading all these files over a dial-up modem link can take a bit of time. This example shows how you can create a compressed cab file that contains the ScriptedLogo applet's class, images, and sound files.

The easiest way to create a cab file is to use the cabarc utility included in the Cab Developer's Kit. To create a cab file for the ScriptedLogo applet with this utility, you should take the following steps:

1. Create a directory, such as *ScriptedLogoCab*, that contains nothing but the class, image, and sound files used by the ScriptedLogo applet in their respective directories.

2. Go to the MS-DOS prompt and change the current directory to `c:\ScriptedLogoCab`.

3. Enter the following instruction from the MS-DOS command
    line:

    ```
    c:\cabkit\cabarc -r -p n ScriptedLogo.cab *.*
    ```

When you follow these steps, a cab file called ScriptedLogo.cab
should be created in the current directory.

If you installed the Cab Developer's Kit in a directory other than
c:\cabkit, you must substitute that directory for the one shown in the
preceding command line instruction.

Figure 17.2 shows the output produced by a successful execution
of the cabarc utility.

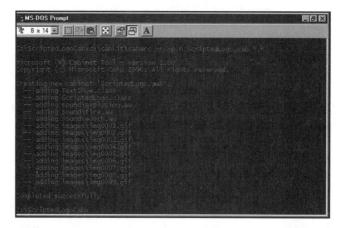

Figure 17.2:

Running the cabarc utility.

When you run the cabarc utility as shown in figure 17.2, it will add all the
files found in the current directory as well as any subdirectories to the
cab file. You should make sure that you only add the appropriate files
(class, image, and sound) when you create cab files. If you add extrane-
ous files, the resulting cab file will be larger than it needs to be, and even
worse, you may not be able to execute the applet that is stored in it.

After creating a cab file, you can copy it to a web server. The following section discusses the HTML that enables IE users to access programs and data stored in a cab file.

If you have trouble creating a cab file with the cabarc utility, you can try creating one by defining a *Diamond Directive File* (DDF) and running the Diamond compression utility that is also included in the Cab Developer's Kit. See the kit's documentation for more information.

Accessing Your Cab File from an HTML Page

To actually use your cab file, you must include a `<param>` HTML tag that specifies the cabbase parameter. This tag must be placed between the `<applet>` and `</applet>` tags as shown in the following HTML code:

```
<applet
    code=ScriptedLogo.class
    id=ScriptedLogo
    width=458
    height=173 >
<param name="cabbase" value="ScriptedLogo.cab">
</applet>
```

When the preceding code is run in IE, the browser extracts all the applet files out of the `ScriptedLogo.cab` file. It is also important to note that if a codebase attribute had been specified, IE would locate the `ScriptedLogo.cab` file in the directory specified by the codebase attribute.

The cabbase parameter will not interfere with the execution of the applet in a browser that does not recognize cab files, such as Netscape Navigator 3.0. You should remember, however, that browsers that are not cab-enabled will look for the applet's original class, image, and sound files. Therefore, for non-IE users to be able to access your applet, you must still store the original files on the web server.

When to Use Cab Files

If you run the ScriptedLogo applet from a cab file stored on a web server, you may notice that it can actually take longer for the applet to start running. This is because the browser must download the entire contents of the cab file before it can begin executing the applet. If you remember how the ScriptedLogo applet is designed, you know that the TextShow thread is started before all of the GIF images and AU audio files are loaded.

The fact that the entire cab file must be downloaded before the applet executes is only a problem the first time you access the cab file. This is because IE saves the cab file in a local cache directory. Consequently, the next time you access the applet, it will load directly from the cache area.

The moral of this story is that you should be careful about how you use cab files. In the real world, you probably wouldn't want to store the ScriptedLogo applet in a cab file because, after the first time, most users don't have much of a need to run it again. For workhorse type applets that may be used frequently, the cab format is a great mechanism for Java software distribution over a network.

Although Microsoft has already implemented the capability to extract class files from a cab file in IE, Sun Microsystems has begun to promote its own JAR (Java archive) file format. The neat thing about the JAR file specification is that it supports a feature called streaming. In other words, when your applet is stored in a JAR file, it can begin executing before the entire file is downloaded. You can get more information about JAR files from the JavaSoft web site at:

`http://www.javasoft.com`

Another situation where you'll need to use cab files is when you want to distribute applets that can execute without being subject to restrictions of the Java sandbox. This topic is discussed in the next section.

Signing Java Applets

When running in IE, trusted applets can perform all the same functions as Java applications or even binary executables that may have been developed in languages such as C++. When IE encounters a signed applet, it verifies the digital signature. If the signature is valid and the user trusts the signer, the applet will be permitted to run outside of the sandbox.

When you run an applet from Visual J++, it is considered to be trusted, even if it isn't signed. Microsoft did this to make it more convenient for programmers to develop and test programs; however, to distribute trusted applets to your users, you will need to digitally sign them.

To sign applets, you'll have to generate two encryption keys; one is called a *public key*, which is made available to anyone and the other is called a *private key*, which you keep secret. These keys are asymmetric, meaning what you encrypt with one, you can only de-encrypt with the other. Furthermore, it is virtually impossible to recalculate one key from the other.

When you sign a piece of code, you will use your private key to create a digest, which is a one-way hash, or fingerprint of the code. When someone wants to verify the signature, they must de-encrypt the digest by using your public key. Then they recalculate their own digest. If the recalculated digest doesn't match the de-encrypted one, then the signature is not valid. In other words, somebody could be trying to distribute a virus or Trojan horse under your name! As long as you keep your private key secret, it is virtually impossible for someone to create a valid encrypted digest that can be used to impersonate you. This is how the asymmetric nature of the public/private key pair guards against someone being able to forge your digital signature.

The Software Publisher Certificate

The greatest weakness of the public/private key pair is that public key is vulnerable to attack. If Betty were able to substitute her public key for John's, for example, she could sign an applet and make a user think that the program came from John. If the user doesn't know for sure what John's public key is, there is no way to verify the signature beyond a reasonable doubt. Fortunately, a solution does exist. John could go to a certificate authority (CA) to get what is known as a Software Publisher Certificate (SPC).

A *Software Publisher Certificate* (SPC) identifies the unique public key of either an individual software developer (such as Bill Clarke), or a software publishing organization (such as @Work Technologies).

A *Certificate Authority* (CA), such as Verisign Inc., is an organization that issues Software Publisher Certificates and other cryptographic products.

Among other things, an SPC contains the public key of the software publisher. The CA signs the SPC with their private key. Consequently, users can verify the authenticity of the SPC by using the CA's well-known public key.

The public keys of the major CAs are well-known because they are built into many browsers, such as Netscape Navigator, and even some operating systems, such as NT 4.0.

Getting a Software Publisher Certificate

You can obtain an SPC from any number of CAs. You can purchase an SPC, for example, directly from Verisign's web site at:

```
http://www.versign.com
```

Verisign makes the whole process very easy. When you sign-up for an ID through their web site, IE automatically generates your public and private keys. Verisign sends you back an electronic mail message containing a private identification number (PIN). You can use this PIN to download your SPC from the Verisign web site.

Signing an Applet with the Code Signing Developer's Kit

After you obtain a valid SPC and IE3 generates your public/private key pair, you can use the Code Signing Developer's Kit, which is included with Visual J++, to create a signed Java applet.

The WordProcessor applet shown in listing 17.3 demonstrates how code signing can lift the sandbox security restrictions. This applet is probably a little different from most applets that you have seen before because when it's trusted, it can actually read from and write to a local hard drive!

Listing 17.3   The Word Processing Applet

```
import java.applet.*;
import java.awt.*;
import java.io.*;

public class WordProcessor extends Applet
{

    private TextArea    m_TextArea;
    private Label       m_Label;
    private Button      m_ButtonOpen;
    private Button      m_ButtonSave;
    private Button      m_ButtonClear;

    public void init()
    {
        setLayout(new BorderLayout());
        m_Label = new Label("Enter your word processing text
➡below.");
        add("North", m_Label);
        m_TextArea = new TextArea(20, 60);
        Panel ButtonPanel = new Panel();
        add("Center", m_TextArea);
        m_ButtonOpen = new Button("Open");
        ButtonPanel.add(m_ButtonOpen);
        m_ButtonSave = new Button("Save");
        ButtonPanel.add(m_ButtonSave);
```

continues

Listing 17.3   Continued

```
        m_ButtonClear = new Button("Clear");
        ButtonPanel.add(m_ButtonClear);
        add("South", ButtonPanel);
    }

    public boolean action(Event evt, Object arg)
    {
        if (evt.target instanceof Button)
        {
            String label = (String)arg;
            if (label.equals("Open"))
                    openFile();
                if (label.equals("Save"))
                saveFile();
                if (label.equals("Clear"))
                m_TextArea.setText("");
            return true;
        }
        else return false;
    }

    private void openFile()
    {
        Frame f = (Frame)getParent();
        FileDialog fd;
        fd = new FileDialog(f, "Open Word Processing File",
➡FileDialog.LOAD);
        fd.show();
        String fileName = fd.getFile();
        if (fileName != null)
        {
            DataInputStream input;
            try
            {
                input = new DataInputStream( new
➡FileInputStream( fileName ) );
            }
            catch(FileNotFoundException e)
            {
                System.out.println("Error encountered on
```

```
➥opening file:" + fileName);
                    return;
            }
            String inputString;
            String inputText = "";
            while (true)
            {
                try
                {
                    inputString = input.readLine();
                }
                catch(IOException e)
                {
                    System.out.println("Error encountered
➥on reading file:" + fileName);
                    return;
                }
                if (inputString == null) break;
                inputText = inputText + inputString +
➥"\n";
            }
            m_TextArea.setText(inputText);
            try
            {
                input.close();
            }
            catch(IOException e)
            {
                System.out.println("Error encountered on
➥closing file:" + fileName);
                return;
            }
        }
    }

    private void saveFile()
    {
        Frame f = new Frame();
        FileDialog fd = new FileDialog(f, "Save Word
➥Processing File", FileDialog.SAVE);
        fd.show();
```

continues

```
Listing 17.3   Continued
            String fileName = fd.getFile();
            if (fileName != null)
            {
                PrintStream output;
                try
                {
                    output = new PrintStream( new
➡FileOutputStream(fileName));
                    output.print(m_TextArea.getText());
                    output.close();
                }
                catch(IOException e)
                {
                    System.out.println("Error encountered on
➡saving file:" + fileName);
                    return;
                }
            }
        }
}
```

In the *init()* method, the WordProcessor applet adds a number of UI components to the applet's display area. A TextArea component called m_TextArea displays the contents of a text file for editing. The *init()* method creates three button objects— m_ButtonOpen, m_ButtonSave, and m_ButtonClear, so that a user can open a text file, save a text file, and clear the contents of the m_TextArea component, respectively. The *action()* method responds appropriately when a user clicks on any of these buttons.

The *openFile()* and *closeFile()* methods perform the necessary file operations. Notice that both methods utilize streams for file access and both create a FileDialog object to enable the user to specify the file name to open or save. In Windows 95, for example, when the WordProcessor applet displays a FileDialog object, the standard Windows 95 open\save dialog displays.

When WordProcessor is run as a normal Java applet, it is not permitted to open or save local files; however, if you digitally sign it, you can open, edit, or save a text file just like in many other applications. Figure 17.3 shows the WordProcessor applet after opening up the local autoexec.bat file.

Figure 17.3:

The WordProcessor applet.

As mentioned earlier in this chapter, applets launched from Visual J++ are considered to be trusted by IE. Therefore, even though the WordProcessor applet violates Java's sandbox security restrictions, it can be tested without code signing.

Creating a Signable Cab File

To create a cab file that can be digitally signed, you must allocate space for the digital signature. For the WordProcessor applet, this can be accomplished by executing the cabarc utility with the following MS-DOS command:

```
C:\SignedWordProcessor>c:\cabkit\cabarc -s 6144 -p n
➥SignedWordProcessor.cab *.class
```

The argument –s 6144 tells the cabarc utility to set aside 6K in the cab file for a digital signature. Also, because no image or sound files are associated with the WordProcessor applet, the argument *.class is used in the preceding MS-DOS command to add all the .class files in the directory. Please note that the current directory must contain the applet's class file for the previous command to work properly.

Running the signcode Utility

The signcode utility uses Microsoft's Authenticode technology to create a digital signature that can be verified by IE. After you've gone through the process of getting a public and private key, you can use the signcode utility included in the Code Signing Developer's Kit to create a signed Java applet. You can execute signcode from the MS-DOS command line. The utility launches the Code Signing Wizard as shown in figure 17.4. Notice that figure 17.4 shows the MS-DOS command that invokes the signcode utility.

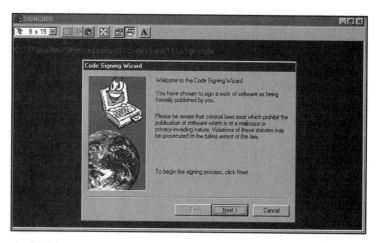

Figure 17.4:

Running the signcode utility.

Step One: Specifying Program Information

The Code Signing Wizard is composed of two steps. In the first step, a dialog box displays. This dialog box requests that you specify the following:

➤ *Which program would you like to sign?* You must specify the name of the cab file that contains the applet's class files. Although the Code Signing Wizard enables you to sign the original class files, IE only recognizes signed cab files.

➤ *What would you like to call this program?* This name appears on the certificate displayed when the user accesses the applet.

➤ *Where can people find more information about it?* Typically, your home page should be specified here.

Figure 17.5 shows the options specified for the WordProcessor applet.

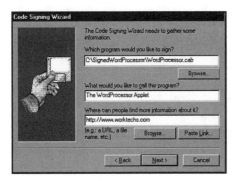

Figure 17.5:
In step one of the Code Signing Wizard, you must specify information about the program.

Step Two: Specifying the Publisher's SPC and Private Key

In step two of the Code Signing Wizard process, you specify the files that contain your SPC and private key.

When you purchase an SPC from the Verisign web site, a private key will be generated by IE and you will be prompted for a file name. It is best to keep your private key on a floppy disk that is locked away from potentially mischievous hands. Otherwise, somebody can use it to impersonate you!

Figure 17.6 shows the SPC and private key file specified for William D. Clarke in step two of the Code Signing Wizard.

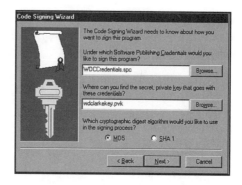

Figure 17.6:

In step two of the Code Signing Wizard, you must specify your SPC and private key files.

After you've specified your SPC and private key files, the rest of the Wizard gives you a chance to verify your settings and then signs your cab file. If you've done everything correctly, when a user attempts to access the applet, it displays a certificate as shown in figure 17.7.

Figure 17.7:

The WordProcessor applet's Digital Certificate.

Verisign provides two types of SPCs. The one used in this example is an individual SPC, which costs $20 annually. You can also get an SPC for your organization for $400 annually. If you work for a company that is distributing commercial software, you should purchase an SPC for your organization

After you create a signed cab file, you can copy the cab file to your web site. At the user's discretion, the applets stored in a signed cab file can be let out of the Java sandbox.

Notice that all the data members and most of the methods declared in the WordProcessor applet are declared as private. It is important that you remember to always make your declarations private unless you have a good reason not to, especially for applets that you put your digital signature on—you wouldn't want someone to take one of your signed Java applets and use a script to make it do something harmful. You might even get blamed for it!

Integrating Java and ActiveX Controls

When Microsoft licensed Java from JavaSoft, one of the enhancements they made to the environment is that they added features that enable developers to integrate their Java programs with the thousands of existing ActiveX controls. These controls are similar to Java applets because they are relatively small, self-contained software objects.

ActiveX controls are different from Java objects in that they can be written in almost any programming language—even Java. In most cases, however, ActiveX controls are binary executables developed in languages such as C++ or Visual Basic. With the functionality provided by Visual J++ and Microsoft's implementation of the Java Virtual Machine (JVM), you can integrate nonvisual ActiveX controls (that is, OLE automation servers) directly into your Java programs. You can do this by using the control's Component Object Model (COM) interface. Through COM, an ActiveX control exposes its functionality. In other words, the controls that you will integrate with your Java programs can also be referred to as COM objects.

COM is the technical foundation of the ActiveX platform. In addition to enabling ActiveX controls to interact on a single workstation, Distributed COM, or DCOM, enables software components to interact over a network. COM and DCOM are discussed in Chapter 1, "Overview of Visual J++ and Java" and at the end of Chapter 15, "Working with IO Streams and Sockets."

Using COM Objects in Java

When you use a COM object in a Java program, you must use an import statement, just like you would with a standard Java class. First, you must do two things to prepare your system:

1. Ensure that the COM object you use is registered on your system. If it's not, you can register it by using the Regsvr32 utility.

2. Create a Java interface for the COM object by using the Visual J++ Type Library Wizard.

Registering a COM Component

Under Windows95, the Registry is a system database that contains configuration information and provides the necessary bindings between COM component identifiers and the implementation of those components.

Most commercial software components are added to the system Registry as part of the installation process.

The regsvr32 utility can be used to register server Dynamic Link Libraries (DLLs) that include self-registration information. Under Windows 95, you could register a COM object called Beeper (`Beeper.dll`) by using the following command:

```
%windir%\system\regsvr32 Beeper.dll
```

The `Beeper.dll` file can be found on the Visual J++ CD in the following directory:

```
msdev\samples\microsoft\cabandsign
```

The preceding command executes the `regsvr32.exe` utility stored in the System directory under the Windows directory.

Under Windows NT 4.0, you can execute the regsvr32 utility to register `Beeper.dll` by entering the following command:

```
regsvr32 Beeper.dll
```

Running the Java Type Library Wizard

After you have successfully registered a COM object, you can create a Java wrapper class for it by using the Visual J++ Java Type Library Wizard. As the name implies, the Java Type Library Wizard reads the type library for a COM object and creates a Java interface.

You can execute the Type Library Wizard from the Visual J++ Tools pull-down menu. The Type Library Wizard displays a dialog box (see fig. 17.8) that lists all the registered COM objects for which you can create a Java interface.

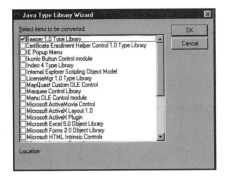

Figure 17.8:
The Java Type Library Wizard.

You can choose one or more COM components in the Java Type Library Wizard dialog box. The Wizard then displays the following information in the Visual J++ output window.

➤ The import statement that you can use in a Java program to import the correct class file for a COM component.

➤ The name of a text file (summary.txt) that contains summary information about the Java class file just created by the Wizard. You can view this information by double-clicking on the file name in the output window as shown in figure 17.9.

The summary.txt file shown in figure 17.9 lists the interfaces and classes in the Java description of the Beeper COM object's type library.

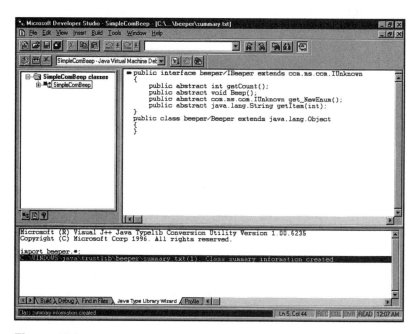

Figure 17.9:

Output of the Java Type Library Wizard.

You can use the summary.txt file to find out the types of return values and parameters required by the COM object's methods. Notice that no method implementations are listed in summary.txt because when you access a COM object from Java, you must use the interface file.

Accessing the Beeper COM Object from a Java Program

After you run the Java Type Library Wizard for `Beeper.dll`, you can import this COM object into a Java program just like a Java class. Listing 17.4 shows an applet called SimpleComBeep that accesses the Beeper COM object.

Listing 17.4 The SimpleComBeeper Applet

```
import java.applet.*;
import java.awt.*;

import beeper.*;

public class SimpleComBeep extends Applet
{

    IBeeper m_Beeper=null;

    public boolean mouseDown(Event evt, int x, int y)
    {
        Graphics ScreenGraphics = getGraphics();

        String BeeperString = new String();

        if(m_Beeper == null)
            m_Beeper = (IBeeper) new Beeper();

        try
        {
            m_Beeper.Beep();
        }
        catch(com.ms.com.ComException e)
        {
            m_Beeper=null;
            m_Beeper = (IBeeper) new Beeper();
            m_Beeper.Beep();
            ScreenGraphics.setColor(Color.red);
            ScreenGraphics.drawString("ComException
➡thrown", x, y);
```

continues

Listing 17.4   Continued

```
            ScreenGraphics.setColor(Color.black);
            return true;
        }

        for(int i=1; i<=m_Beeper.getCount(); i++)
        {
            BeeperString += m_Beeper.getItem(i)+" ";
        }

        ScreenGraphics.drawString(BeeperString, x, y);

        return true;
    }
}
```

SimpleComBeep utilizes the method calls for the Beeper COM object listed in the summary.txt file. Notice that when a Beeper object is instantiated, it must be cast as an IBeeper object. This is because the Beeper class has no methods. You may remember that this is indicated in the summary.txt file. The applet overrides the *mouseDown( )* method so that when the user clicks anywhere in the applet's display area, an m_Beeper object is created. The applet then calls m_Beeper's *Beep( )* method (or function) causing an audible beep to play. In addition, the m_Beeper object's *getItem( )* method is called to construct the string "Hello World From Beeper", that is then drawn to the applet's display area.

This applet also demonstrates the exception mapping that Microsoft has made possible by creating a ComException object. The Beeper COM object's *Beep( )* method is designed to throw an exception every fifth time it's called. The applet catches this exception and draws an informational message to the display area.

It is not required to catch a ComException because it is derived from RuntimeException.

When run from Visual J++ in IE, the SimpleComBeep applet generates the output shown in figure 17.10.

When you're not executing an applet from Visual J++, it must be trusted to access a COM object.

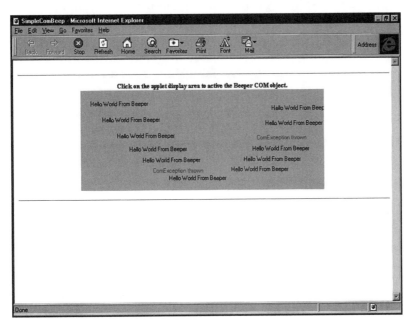

Figure 17.10:
The SimpleComBeep applet.

Summary

Many individuals have made the argument that Microsoft's ActiveX platform and Java are competing technologies. Although this may be true in some cases, ActiveX still has a great deal to offer Java developers. The first web browser to support ActiveX was Microsoft's Internet Explorer 3.0; however, Netscape's Navigator 4.0 (and higher) supports some ActiveX standards and technologies.

It is possible to control a Java applet directly from an HTML page using scripts. This opens the possibility for even nontechnical individuals to customize and enhance Java executables without having to learn how to actually program in Java. The ActiveX scripting model supports VBScript and JavaScript. In addition, ActiveX scripting can support plug-in scripting engines.

Because sophisticated Java applets can be composed of many files, they typically take a long time to download from a web server, especially over a dial-up link. You can help solve this problem by storing all your applet's class, image, and sound files in a compressed cabinet, or cab file. IE will attempt to access an applet's files from a cab file when it is specified as a parameter in the applet's HTML file. In addition, IE saves a copy of the cab file in cache, which makes it unnecessary to download the applet for each execution.

For an applet to access COM objects or run outside of the Java sandbox, it must be stored in a signed cab file. Before you can sign a cab file, you must generate a public/private key pair and obtain a software publisher certificate (SPC) from a certificate authority (CA). Verisign is one CA that enables you to purchase SPC directly from their web site at `http://www.verisign.com`. In addition, IE automatically generates a public/private key pair when you request your SPC. When you sign a cab file by using your SPC and private key, IE verifies that you signed the cab file and it has not been tampered with. Signed applets can be trusted by IE and, therefore, are enabled to execute without being restricted by the Java sandbox.

Microsoft has enhanced the Java environment so that it is possible to access COM objects in the same manner as Java classes. To use a COM object in a Java program, it must be registered under Windows and you must create a Java interface for it. You can do this by using the Visual J++ Java Type Library Wizard.

Questions

1. How can ActiveX scripting make your applets more useful?

2. What are the relative advantages and disadvantages of VBScript and JavaScript?

3. Where can you go to find out more about VBScript and JavaScript?

4. What are cab files used for?

5. For IE to locate a cab file, what do you need to include in the applet's HTML file?

6. What do you need to sign a cab file?

7. How is a digitally signed cab file essentially the same as shrink-wrapped software that you might buy from a retail store?

8. What do you need to do to access a COM object from a Java applet?

9. How can a COM object notify a calling Java program that an error condition has occurred?

Answers

1. ActiveX scripting makes it possible for relatively nontechnical individuals to enhance and customize Java applets without having to learn how to program in Java.

2. JavaScript is a powerful scripting language that can run in either Netscape Navigator or IE. VBScript can only be run natively by IE. Because VBScript is based on Visual Basic for Applications, however, literally millions of VB programmers are already familiar with its syntax.

3. You can get the most up-to-date information on JavaScript from the Netscape web site at `http://www.netscape.com/`. Extensive VBScript information is available from the Microsoft site at `http://www.microsoft.com/vbscript/`.

4. You can store the class, sound, and image files required by Java applets in cab files. Because cab files are compressed, they download faster from a web server. IE can access applets from cab files and also save cab files in a cache area so they don't have to be downloaded for every execution. Finally, to create a trusted applet, you must store it in a digitally signed cab file.

5. For IE to find a cab file, you must specify a cabbase parameter using the HTML `<param>` tag.

6. To sign a cab file, you need to generate a public/private key pair and obtain a software publisher certificate (SPC). You can then use the signcode utility included in the Code Signing Developer's Kit to create a signed cab file.

7. When a cab file is digitally signed, you can verify both the signer's identity and that the file has not been changed since it was signed. This is essentially the same as purchasing a shrink-wrapped software package.

8. To access a COM object from a Java applet, you must make sure that the COM object is registered with Windows. You can then use the Visual J++ Template Wizard to generate a Java interface for the COM object.

9. Microsoft has created a new exception called ComException, which is derived from the RuntimeException class. A COM object can throw a ComException that can be caught by your Java program when an error condition occurs.

Part IV

Appendices

Appendix A

java.lang

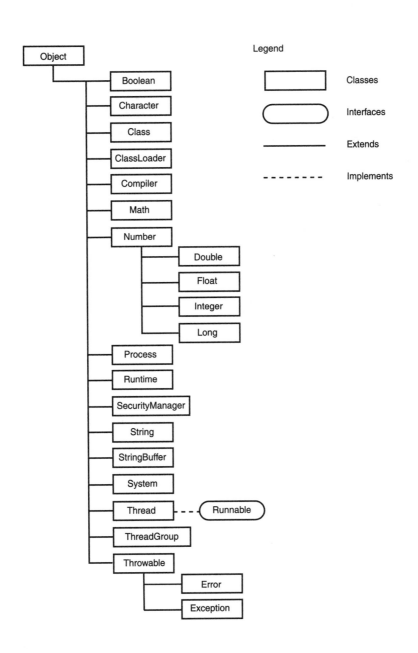

Errors and Exceptions

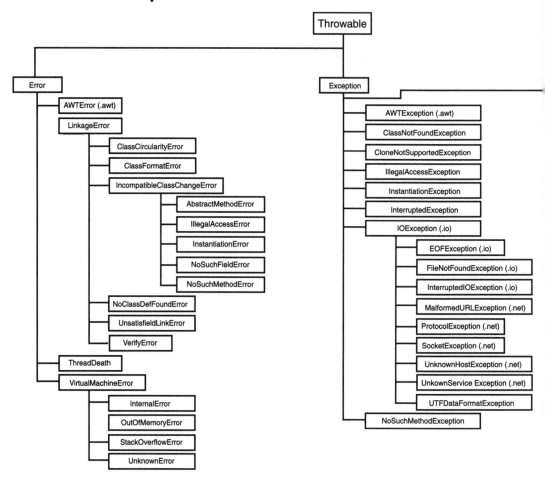

Legend

Classes

Interfaces

Extends

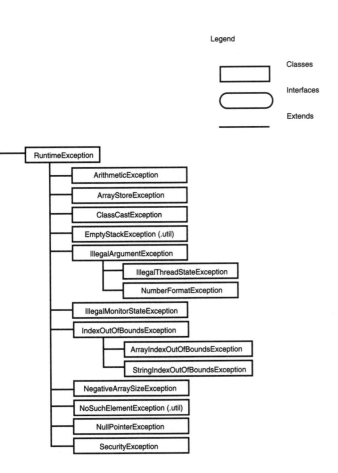

java. util

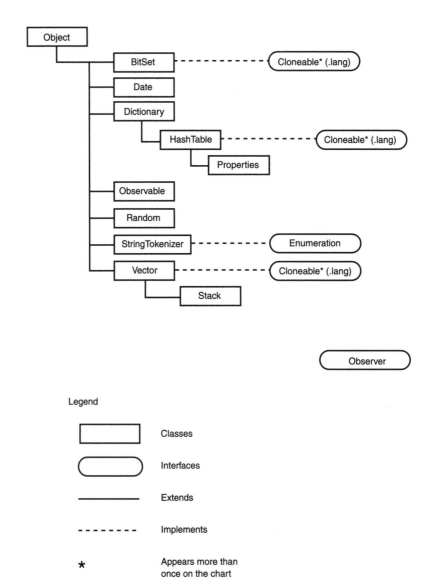

Legend

☐ Classes

⬭ Interfaces

─────── Extends

- - - - - - - Implements

* Appears more than
once on the chart

java.io

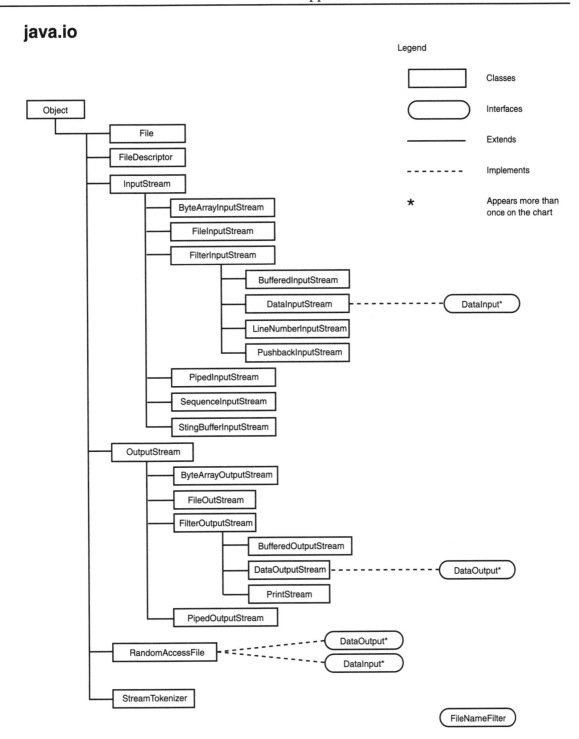

java.net

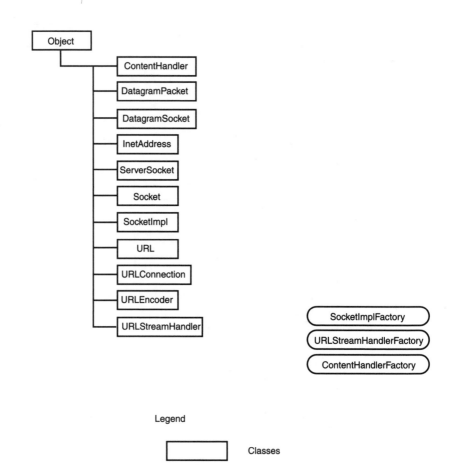

Legend

Classes

Interfaces

———— Extends

java.awt.image

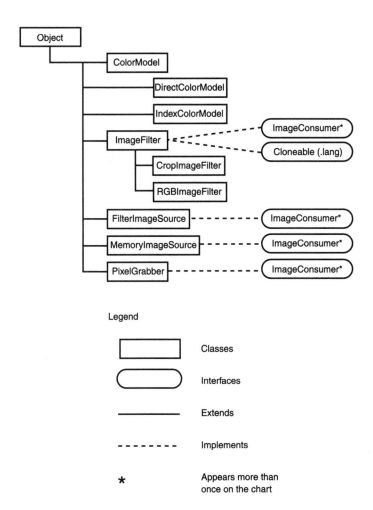

Legend

Classes

Interfaces

——————— Extends

- - - - - - - Implements

*   Appears more than
once on the chart

java.awt

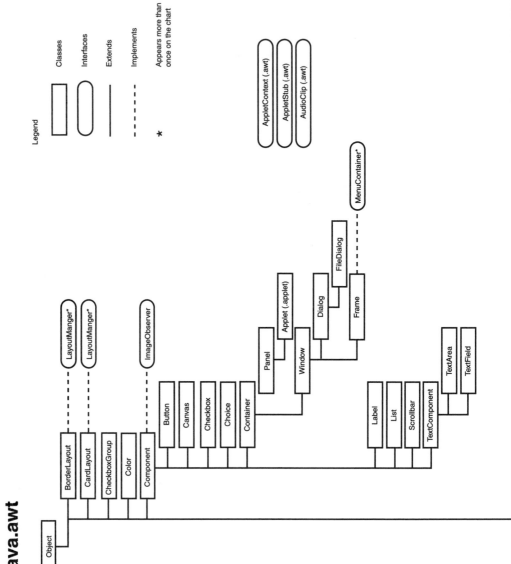

Legend

Classes

Interfaces

Extends

Implements

* Appears more than once on the chart

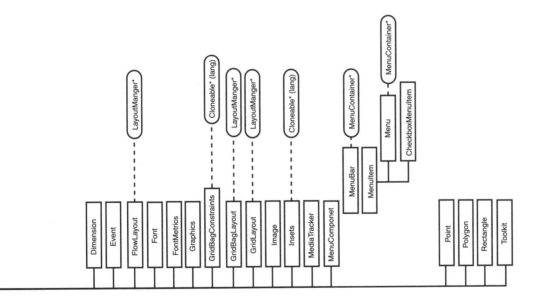

java.awt.peer

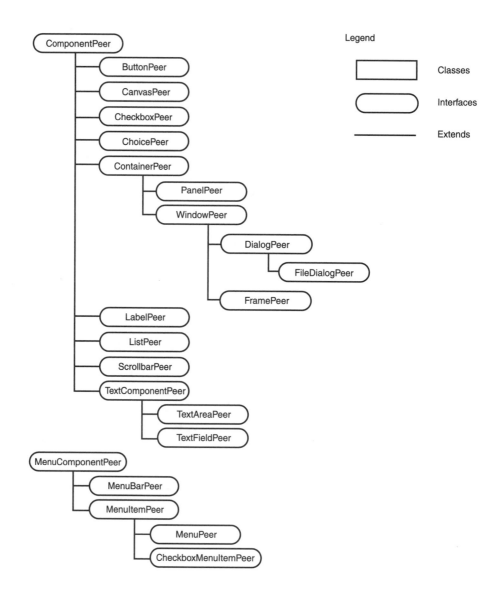

Appendix B

Glossary

Programming with Visual J++ has its challenges and pitfalls. As with any new software product targeted for use by professional programmers and web developers, J++ (and the myriad of related technologies and protocols) will spring new terms on you.

This glossary has been compiled from text in the book as well as relative terms, definitions, and standards from the worlds of C++, ActiveX, and HTML programming.

<applet>   An HTML tag used to define an embedded Java applet. The <applet> tag's attributes can be used to specify applet characteristics, such as the location of the applet's executable files and the size and position of the applet's display area.

abstract class   A class that is declared abstract can have abstract methods and cannot be directly instantiated. An attempt to create an instance of an abstract class would generate a compiler error in Java, as it would in C++. It is illegal to define abstract methods in any class not defined as abstract.

Abstract Windowing Toolkit (AWT)   A collection of classes used to build a user interface with J++. The AWT provides UI components, containers for GUI components, an event delivery system, and layout managers for controlling the placement of UI components within containers.

abstraction layer   Unifying methodology that negates many underlying differences between operating systems or objects.

ActiveX controls   Small, self-contained executables that can be integrated with desktop applications, or delivered over a network.

ActiveX scripting   Programs that can be used to customize and add functionality to HTML pages, Java applets, and ActiveX controls.

ActiveX   A collection of technologies created by Microsoft that includes ActiveX scripting, ActiveX controls, document objects, and database access. ActiveX technologies are based on Microsoft's Component Object Model (COM), a standard that enables software components to interact with one another in a networked environment—regardless of the language in which they were created.

alias   A name, usually a domain name or e-mail address, intended to represent a more complicated or undesirable name.

angle   Degree of tilt of a character's vertical lines.

Application Programming Interface (API)   A set of interface functions available to applications.

Applet Wizard   A graphical tool provided by Visual J++ that enables developers to quickly develop starter Java and HTML code for a project.

applet   A self-contained executable that can be dynamically distributed over a network and run in a web browser.

application   Software that can be used to perform a specific type of work, such as word processing.

architecture   The overall design of a program.

array   A matrix of elements that are instantiated.

ascent   The portion of the letters that extends above the baseline is known as the ascent of the font. The font's height is the sum of the ascent and the descent.

attributes   In HTML, additional information that further defines a tag.

Authenticode   A security technology developed by Microsoft that enables developers to digitally sign code. A valid signature proves the identity of the signer and that the code has not been altered since it was signed.

bandwidth   The maximum volume of data that can be sent over a network, most often referred to in thousands of bytes-per-second.

baseline   All fonts extend upward from a reference point called a baseline.

Bézier   A mathematically constructed curve, such as that used in drawing programs.

binary executable   A program that has been compiled into a binary form that will only execute on a specific hardware platform.

binary file   Any file that contains characters other than text.

Boolean   Java provides a boolean data type. Variables that are declared as boolean can have a value that is either *true* or *false*. A boolean variable in Java is not a representation of an integer as in C and C++.

break statement   A break statement causes program flow to break out of the current loop.

breakpoints   User-specified points in program code that direct a debugger to automatically stop. Used for testing purposes. When you set a breakpoint, a red dot is displayed to the left of the line of code.

browser   *See web browser.*

bytecode   A Java compiler translates Java source code into a format known as bytecode. Bytecode is close to machine code, but still platform-independent, it can be efficiently translated into the native instructions of any Java-enabled platform at runtime.

Cab Developer's Kit   A set of utilities that comes with J++, which helps you to create cab files.

cabinet files (cab files)   A way of storing Java classes and packages on disk. A cabinet or cab file is an archive file that contains other files. Cab files are compressed by using the standard Lempel-Ziv algorithm.

casting   An object or primitive type is cast when it is converted to a new type or object.

Certificate Authority or CA (Verisign Inc.)   An organization that issues Software Publisher Certificates and other cryptographic products.

character literal   A character literal is represented by a single character, or an escape sequence, enclosed in single quotation marks (''). The character may be any character from the Unicode character set and is stored as a 16-bit unsigned integer.

character string   A sequence of characters enclosed in double quotation marks. In Java, a string literal is implemented as a String object, not as an array of characters, as in C and C++. An occurrence of a string literal causes the creation of an instance of a String object.

class library   A set of classes that can be created or provided by a vendor.

class   A blueprint or definition of an object.

Code Signing Developer's Kit   A utility provided with J++ that enables the programmer to digitally sign a cab file.

code signing   The process of adding a digital signature to a program file.

collaborative computing   Similar to workgroup computing, but designed to function across both local and wide area networks.

collection classes   Collection classes are used to manage collections of other objects. Some good candidates for collection classes are, for example, a hash table class and a sortable list class.

comments   Java supports three types of comments: single-line, multiline, and program documentation. Single-line and multiline comments have identical implementations in C++.

Component Object Model (COM)   Microsoft's binary object model that facilitates the interaction of software objects.

component   A visual item, such as a button or a list box, that can be used to create a user interface.

concurrency   Two processes or threads executing at the same time.

constructors   Constructors are methods that perform the required initializations for each new instance of a class. When you declare a class in Java, you can also declare one or more constructors for that class.

container   A Java container is a display area (applets, panels, windows, frames, and dialogs) into which UI components are placed. A container can also contain other containers.

continue statement   A continue statement (without a label) causes program flow to resume at the top of the current loop.

control flow   The path of processing through the various routines in a program.

cyberspace   A term that refers to any location for information accessible via the Internet.

daemon   A program that performs a service, or services, for the operating system.

database   A file or group of related files that are designed to hold recurring data types as though the files were lists.

deadlock   A condition where a locked object is never unlocked, causing a thread waiting to put a lock on it to wait indefinitely. This condition occurs when two or more threads are permanently frozen because each is waiting for a lock that is already held by the other.

debug   The act of proactively searching and testing an applet or applications with the goal of finding errors.

delimiter   Denotes the beginning or the end of a comment or code.

dialog resource   Defines the layout and size of the elements (such as display area, push-buttons, static text, and so on) that make up a user interface. A dialog resource should not be confused with the Java Dialog class, which is just one of the classes that can be used to create a container for UI components.

dial-up   A connection that utilizes a modem and a phone line to connect to other computers and to the Internet.

digital signature   A verifiable, almost incontrovertible, fingerprint that proves the signer's identity and that the file has not been altered since it was signed.

Distributed COM, or DCOM   A COM object that can interact across a network. *See also Component Object Model (COM).*

distributed processing   The distribution of programming tasks across multiple computer processors on a network.

document objects   Compound documents that derive their behavior and functionality from one or more software objects.

domain   The name of an entity on the Internet. Outside of the U.S., domain names are suffixed with the two digit code that indicates nationality. In America, domain names can be suffixed to indicate that the entity is of the government, a company, and so on.

download   Transfer a file from a remote computer to your own local computer.

End User License Agreement (EULA)   The terms that the user must abide by to use a software product.

escape sequence   A nonprintable character, such as a line feed. In Java, escape sequences are preceded by a backslash (\).

events   Events are typically generated by user actions. When a user moves the mouse or presses a key, events are generated and delivered to the Java program. Therefore, event handling enables your program to react to the user's commands.

exception handling   The mechanism used to trap an exception and the propagation of the exception up through the call stack. A Java program can trap an exception and deal with it accordingly, or pass it on to the calling method.

executable   A program that is ready to be run by the operating system or the Java Virtual Machine.

finally clause   A statement that is used to identify the last code block in a code segment. The code in this block will be executed regardless of whether an exception is thrown or not.

firewalls A software/hardware device array that provides isolation and security.

floating-point literals A base-10 integer part, a decimal point, and a fractional part.

font A collection of similarly styled characters and digits intended for display.

FORTRAN PowerStation A FORTRAN development environment that provides the same features and user interfaces as Visual C++ and Visual J++.

File Transfer Protocol (FTP) A method of transferring information over the Internet.

garbage Programming objects that are no longer utilized in the scope of its original intent.

hacking Hacking is usually used in the context of doing damage over the Internet.

Hypertext Transport Protocol (HTTP) One of the communications protocols used to transfer data over the Internet.

Hypertext Markup Language (HTML) A text-based standard for defining the layout and content of documents on the World Wide Web.

hypertext An online document that has words or graphics containing links to other documents. Usually, choosing the link area on-screen when a mouse or keyboard command activates these links.

Integrated Development Environment (IDE) An application that organizes programming tools into a single user interface.

inheritance A class can inherit attributes and behavior from its parent or super class. The *extends* keyword is used to establish an inheritance relationship between a subclass and a super class.

initialize Giving a starting value to a variable or object. In Java all variables and objects are initialized.

input arguments To pass command line arguments to a Java application, you must code your program's *main()* method so that it can accept arguments.

input streams Input streams provide methods for reading data from a source.

instance variables Declared within the class definition, outside of the body of any method. They can be of any type and may be initialized in their declaration.

instantiate The act of a program, creating an object from a class.

integers Numbers in the decimal, octal (base 8), or hexadecimal (base 16) formats.

interface In Java, it is possible to formally declare a set of public methods and constants as an interface. A Java interface is similar to an abstract class in that it cannot be directly instantiated.

Internet Explorer A web browser program offered by Microsoft.

Java exceptions An occurrence, which is typically an unexpected error. When an exception occurs, an Exception object is created either implicitly by the Java environment, or explicitly by the Java program.

Java Security Model A set of rules imposed upon Java applets that are downloaded over a network, which prevent the applets from performing potentially dangerous functions, such as reading from or writing to the local hard drive. *See also sandbox.*

Java Virtual Machine (JVM) Provides a standard Java execution environment regardless of the underlying platform. This makes it possible to run any standard Java program on any computer platform that supports a JVM.

Java A programming language developed by Sun's JavaSoft division. It is specifically designed to run over wide area networks, such as the public Internet.

JavaBeans A distributed object architecture for Java that enables you to integrate your Java programs with both DCOM and CORBA.

JavaScript A powerful scripting language that can run in either Netscape Navigator or IE.

kerning pairs Pairs of characters in a font that are kerned automatically when they occur together in a line.

kerning Adjusting the spacing between characters on a line; can be automatic (application-controlled) or manual (user-selected).

keyword Predefined variables that are assigned by Java.

labeled break A labeled break is used to cause the program flow to break out of any number of enclosing loops and resume at the label.

layout managers Java classes that control the placement and dimensions of UI components within a container.

life cycle The period of time from the point where an applet is initialized, starts, displays, and stops.

local variables Local variables are variables declared within the body of a method. It is illegal for a parameter that is passed to the method to have the same name as one of the method's local variables. Before a local variable can be used, it must be initialized. The initialization of local variables is checked at compile time.

lock When an object is locked, any thread that attempts to obtain a lock on the object must wait until the object is unlocked. Java has one lock associated with every object.

memory leak   A condition that occurs when unused memory is not properly released by a program.

method   A characteristic or activity of an object.

mission-critical   An applet or application that is essential to the core responsibilities of a user or group of users.

modifier keys   Modifier keys, such as Alt, Shift, and Ctrl, for example, that change the behavior of other keys.

moniker   A named resource, such as a file.

multiline comments   All text between /* and */ is treated as multiline comments by the compiler. The beginning and end of the comment can be on the same line or can span any number of lines.

multiple document interface   The GUI of an applet or application that will enable the concurrent display of multiple documents.

multiple inheritance   The capability to inherit characteristics from more than one parent class.

multithreading   When multiple procedures are executed by a program at the same time.

native method   Native methods are typically platform-specific binary executables that are written in C or C++.

network-centric   An applet, application, or resource that is tailored for use on a network.

null value   A default state for an object before its appropriate value has been assigned.

object-oriented   A programming methodology that encapsulates all functionality of a program within a class.

object   An instance of a class.

OLE Control   Now called an ActiveX control, a program object that exposes its functionality as a component object model interface.

operation   A fundamental programming task.

operator overloading   The capability of a programmer to define operators. This function cannot be used in Java.

output streams   When you use output streams, your program becomes the source of the data. Almost every output stream class has a corresponding input stream class.

package   In Java, classes are grouped into packages. Java packages are similar to C++ class libraries.

platform-independent   A program that will run on any hardware platform.

platform   A specific hardware or software operating environment.

platform-specific   A program that was created to run on a specific platform.

pointer   An address that relates to a location in physical memory.

pseudo code   Programming syntax only given for example purposes.

release mode   An executable program that is optimized for performance and ready for distribution.

Remote Method Invocation (RMI)   A distributed object platform, RMI has been introduced by Sun as a lightweight Java-only mechanism for distributed object-oriented Java networking.

request   An action taken by a program that gates an operation by another program.

reserved words   Words that have been predefined to have special meaning within a programming environment.

return types   The object or fundamental data type returned from a method call.

sandbox   A euphemism for the security restrictions imposed by Java.

server   On a network, the server is the computer that supports the client or user computers who need its file storage and other services.

signed code   An executable file that has been digitally signed. *See also Authenticode.*

single-line comments   All text to the right of double-slash characters is treated as a comment.

socket object   Establishes communication between the client and server programs. When establishing communications with a server program, you must construct a Socket object by using the name of the host on which your server program resides and the port to which your server program is listening. *See also socket.*

socket   A communications path between two programs either locally or remotely.

Software Publisher Certificate (SPC)   Identifies the unique public key of either an individual software developer or software publishing company.

source code   The actual programming code used to create a program.

static code block   Implements code that is only executed once for the entire class.

static methods   A method associated with a class.

stepping   The process of incrementing through the execution of an applet or project to debug.

streams   A stream is a communications path between a source of information and a destination. A stream can be used by Java programs to access resources over a network. The Java stream classes can be used by a Java program to read from a source and write to a destination.

super class   Also called a parent class, is the class from which another class is derived. A class will typically inherit its basic attributes and behavior from a super class.

suspend   A state where an applet or application stops execution, but does not terminate.

synchronized statement   A synchronized statement can be used to lock an object while a block of code is executing. In this way, the lock does not remain in effect for the entire execution of the method and the program is likely to be more efficient.

target machine   The computer where a program is executed.

thin client   A client workstation configuration that requires minimal hardware resources because most of the application software is located on a server or dynamically downloaded at runtime.

thread deadlock   A condition that occurs when two threads are forced into a perpetual wait state because both threads are waiting to obtain a lock on a resource that is currently locked by the other thread.

thread priority   The Java Virtual Machine assigns priorities to thread objects. In Java, the priority of a thread is expressed as an integer value between 1 and 10.

thread scheduling   Threads are scheduled by the operating system. Every multithreaded operating system has a thread scheduler. In Windows 95 and NT, each process has a priority class that is shared by all threads created from that process.

threads   By using threads, a program can perform more than one task at a time.

trusted applets   Applets that can perform all the same functions as Java applications or binary executables that may have been developed in languages such as C++.

Unicode   A character set that includes ASCII characters and thousands of characters used in many languages.

unpack   To unzip, or uncompress, the contents of a single file in multiple files.

Uniform Resource Locator (URL)   Also referred to as a Universal Resource Locator, URL represents a unique identifier for a resource on either the public Internet or a private intranet.

value   The content of a variable or an object.

variable   A segment of memory that is assigned unique information useful to an application or applet.

Visual C++   An integrated development environment that enables programmers to rapidly code, test, and debug C++ programs.

Visual J++   A world-class Java development environment that is integrated with Microsoft's Developer Studio.

Visual SourceSafe   A source code control system that can be used with Developer Studio projects. This application's features include source code archiving and version control.

Visual Test   A tool that automates software testing. This product was originally developed by Microsoft; however, it is now owned by a company called Rational Software.

web browser   An application designed to enable the user to view files via the HTTP protocol and others on a network, such as the Internet or a local intranet.

web page   A document displayed by a web browser.

wizard   A utility that is designed to perform a single but often complex task, with limited input from the user.

Index

REGISTRATION CARD

Visual J++ Java Programming

Name _____ Title _____

Company_____ Type of business _____

Address _____

City/State/ZIP _____

Have you used these types of books before?   ☐ yes   ☐ no

If yes, which ones? _____

_____

How many computer books do you purchase each year?   ☐ 1–5   ☐ 6 or more

How did you learn about this book? _____

Where did you purchase this book? _____

Which applications do you currently use? _____

_____

Which computer magazines do you subscribe to? _____

_____

What trade shows do you attend? _____

_____

Comments: _____

_____

_____

Would you like to be placed on our preferred mailing list?   ☐ yes   ☐ no

☐ **I would like to see my name in print!** You may use my name and quote me in future New Riders products and promotions. My daytime phone number is: _____

New Riders Publishing   201 West 103rd Street ◆ Indianapolis, Indiana 46290 USA

Fax to 317-581-4670

Fold Here

- -

‖‖‖‖

BUSINESS REPLY MAIL
FIRST-CLASS MAIL PERMIT NO. 9918 INDIANAPOLIS IN

POSTAGE WILL BE PAID BY THE ADDRESSEE

**NEW RIDERS PUBLISHING
201 W 103RD ST
INDIANAPOLIS IN 46290-9058**

Check Us Out Online!

New Riders has emerged as a premier publisher of computer books for the professional computer user. Focusing on CAD/graphics/multimedia, communications/internetworking, and networking/operating systems, New Riders continues to provide expert advice on high-end topics and software.

Check out the online version of *New Riders' Official World Wide Web Yellow Pages, 1996 Edition* for the most engaging, entertaining, and informative sites on the Web! You can even add your own site!

Brave our site for the finest collection of CAD and 3D imagery produced today. Professionals from all over the world contribute to our gallery, which features new designs every month.

From Novell to Microsoft, New Riders publishes the training guides you need to attain your certification. Visit our site and try your hand at the CNE Endeavor, a test engine created by VFX Technologies, Inc. that enables you to measure what you know—and what you don't!

New Riders

http://www.mcp.com/newriders

Getting Started with the CD-ROM

This page provides instructions for installing software from the CD-ROM.

Windows 95/NT 4 Installation

Insert the disc into your CD-ROM drive. If autoplay is enabled on your machine, the CD-ROM setup program starts automatically the first time you insert the disc.

If setup does not run automatically, perform these steps:

1. From the Start menu, choose Programs, Windows Explorer.

2. Select your CD-ROM drive under My Computer.

3. Double-click SETUP.EXE in the contents list.

4. Follow the on-screen instructions that appear.

5. Setup adds an icon named CD-ROM Contents to a program group for this book. To explore the CD-ROM, double-click on the CD-ROM Contents icon.

How to Contact New Riders Publishing

If you have a question or comment about this product, there are several ways to contact New Riders Publishing. You can write us at the following address:

New Riders Publishing
Attn: Publishing Manager
201 W. 103rd Street
Indianapolis, IN 46290

If you prefer, you can fax New Riders Publishing at 1-317-817-7448.

To send Internet electronic mail to New Riders, address it to support@mcp.com.

You can also contact us through the Macmillan Computer Publishing CompuServe forum at GO NEWRIDERS. Our World Wide Web address is http://www.mcp.com/newriders.